D1616953

Honored by the
Glory of Islam

Honored by the Glory of Islam

*Conversion and Conquest
in Ottoman Europe*

MARC DAVID BAER

OXFORD
UNIVERSITY PRESS

2008

OXFORD
UNIVERSITY PRESS

Oxford University Press, Inc., publishes works that further
Oxford University's objective of excellence
in research, scholarship, and education.

Oxford   New York
Auckland   Cape Town   Dar es Salaam   Hong Kong   Karachi
Kuala Lumpur   Madrid   Melbourne   Mexico City   Nairobi
New Delhi   Shanghai   Taipei   Toronto

With offices in
Argentina   Austria   Brazil   Chile   Czech Republic   France   Greece
Guatemala   Hungary   Italy   Japan   Poland   Portugal   Singapore
South Korea   Switzerland   Thailand   Turkey   Ukraine   Vietnam

Published by Oxford University Press, Inc.
198 Madison Avenue, New York, New York 10016

www.oup.com

Oxford is a registered trademark of Oxford University Press

Library of Congress Cataloging-in-Publication Data
Baer, Marc David, 1970–
Honored by the glory of Islam : conversion and conquest in Ottoman Europe /
Marc David Baer.
   p. cm.
Includes bibliographical references and index.
ISBN 978-0-19-533175-2
1. Muslim converts from Christianity—Europe—History.
2. Mehmed IV, Sultan of the Turks, 1642–1693. 3. Turkey—History—
Mehmed IV, 1648–1687. 4. Turkey—History—
Ottoman Empire, 1288–1918. I. Title.
BP170.5.B34 2007
297.5'74094—dc22   2007014740

9 8 7 6 5 4 3 2 1

Printed in the United States of America
on acid-free paper

In memory of my grandparents,
Max Braun, Bernice Wolf Braun,
  and Phyllis Manassee Baer,
and to my grandfather,
Harvey Baer

Acknowledgments

I have benefited from the assistance of many individuals who have taken an interest in my work. With the risk of inadvertently leaving someone out, I thank those who have allowed me to conduct research and those who educated and supported me, discussed my work and read it critically. I am especially grateful to those who inspired me. I am indebted to Filiz Çağman, İlber Ortaylı, Zeyneb Çelik, and Ülkü Altındağ and their staffs at the Topkapı Palace Museum Library and Archive for allowing me to conduct research in such an awesome setting. I am also indebted to the directors of other Istanbul libraries, such as Nevzat Kaya at the Suleimaniye Library, for allowing me full access to their rich manuscript collections and for assisting me. I have been permitted to work in the Prime Ministry's Ottoman Archive; the Office of the Istanbul Mufti, Islamic Law Court Records Archive; and the Islamic Research Center. In Berlin I was granted access to the collection of the State Museum of Berlin, Art Library, and in Vienna was given permission to work in the Austrian National Library, Manuscript Collection, and Portrait Collection, Picture Archive and Library, which allowed me to examine Ottoman miniatures.

My interpretation of the texts I read in Istanbul, Berlin, and Vienna reflects the diverse influence of training by many scholars. Chief among them are Carl Petry at Northwestern University, whose stimulating lectures introduced me to the richness of Islamic history and who inspired me to pursue graduate studies in the subject. At the University of Michigan, Fatma Müge Göçek first guided me with patience and humor through the intricacies of Ottoman history and paleography, with James Redhouse on my left, an estate register from an eighteenth-century Armenian grocer of Galata before me, and Professor Göçek on my right. Ron Suny encouraged me to engage with theory and see the big picture, becoming a great mentor first at Michigan and then at the University of Chicago. Michael Bonner, who first introduced me to Islamic chronicles and fatwa collections, and Juan Cole, who alerted me to the political nature of historical narratives, furthered my education in medieval and modern Islamic history, respectively. Todd Endelman introduced me to the topic of religious conversion. John Woods and Rashid Khalidi eased the transition to the University of Chicago. Fred Donner and John Woods provided excellent models of how best to critically approach Islamic history. Cornell Fleischer taught me how to think historically, paying attention to the nuances of Ottoman narratives, and compelled me to excel. Robert Dankoff patiently taught me Ottoman Turkish, attempting to instill in me *Sprachgefühl*, and carefully corrected every inaccurate transliteration and translation that I insisted he read. Joel Kraemer showed me the interrelated aspects of Jewish and Muslim history. It is my hope that each of these scholars can see in this book a reflection of his or her own best work.

Access to collections and linguistic and historical training mean little without a supportive work environment, financial assistance, and time for contemplation. I am thankful to the History Department and School of Humanities at the University of California, Irvine, for providing a setting that allows me to pursue research and focus on my writing. The School of Humanities supported summer research travel to Istanbul. Fulbright, Social Sciences Research Council, and American Research Institute in Turkey fellowships enabled me to conduct the research for this book in Istanbul, and the Institute of Turkish Studies gave support to its initial writing. A Humboldt Fellowship in Germany allowed me time to complete the narrative. I thank my colleagues and friends Maurus Reinkowski at the Albert-Ludwigs University in Freiburg and Gudrun Krämer at the Free University in Berlin, who served as my hosts during my stay in Germany.

One does not write a book alone. Discussions with many colleagues enabled me to better articulate its themes. The fellows of the SIAS Institute, "Hierarchy, Marginality, and Ethnicity in Muslim Societies," convened by Mark Cohen and Gudrun Krämer at the Wissenschaftskolleg zu Berlin and Princeton University; the fellows at the Dartmouth College Humanities Center's seminar on conversion, convened by Kevin Reinhart and Dennis Washburn; the fellows in the University of California Humanities Research Institute, "Gender and Sexual

Dissidence in Muslim Communities," at the University of California, Irvine, convened by Nayan Shah; and the questions and comments of audiences at Tulane University, the University of Washington, the American Research Institute in Turkey, the Orient-Institut der Deutschen Morgenländischen Gesellschaft and Bilgi University in Istanbul, the University of Thessaly in Volos, Greece, and the Free University in Berlin gave crucial feedback as the argument of the book was developing. Gottfried Hagen, Selim Deringil, Tony Greenwood, Heath Lowry, Victor Ostapchuk, George Bernstein, James Boyden, Jane Hathaway, and Rıfat Bali commented on versions of the argument. Robert Dankoff and Sara Yıldız provided indispensable aid deciphering key passages of Ottoman texts. James Given (Latin), Richard Wittman (German), and Michelle Campos (Arabic) generously provided their linguistic knowledge. Çiçek Öztek prepared several of the miniatures, and Johann Büssow facilitated archival matters in Berlin. I am very thankful to Michelle Molina, Anne Walthall, Caroline Finkel, and Esra Özyürek, plus the two anonymous readers at Oxford University Press for critically engaging with the text and giving substantial suggestions for revision. Their crucial intervention shaped the book immeasurably. I appreciate the labor of my enthusiastic and responsive editor at Oxford University Press, Cynthia Read, and my friend and colleague Eliza Kent for recommending her to me and vice versa.

I would never have had the desire to be a historian nor had curiosity about religion had it not been for my parents, Barry and Sue Baer, who instilled in me a sense of curiosity about other cultures, languages, and places, gave me the greatest gift of raising me in diverse environments in far-flung corners of the globe, and made studious role models. My brother, Steve, taught me not to take myself too seriously. The generous assistance of my grandmother Bernice Wolf Braun enabled me to begin my pursuit of graduate studies. Earlier, her keen interest in my youthful observations of European society, in the form of letters I wrote her from Germany, encouraged my initial interest in history and history writing. My grandfather Harvey Baer respected me enough to argue with me about the interpretation of history. Sünter and Mustafa Özyürek took me into their family, removed every obstacle in my path in Istanbul, and shared in my excitement in learning Turkish and uncovering the most surprising aspects of the Ottoman past.

What an amazing journey it has been. From graduate school in Ann Arbor and Chicago, to research in Istanbul, from teaching in California, to launching the latest research projects in Berlin, for over a dozen years my partner, Esra Özyürek, and I have pursued knowledge together. She has always pushed me to stretch beyond my expected limits, to never be satisfied with conventions or conventional wisdom. She is as ever one step ahead of me, always inspiring, always challenging. This book is as much hers as mine, and whatever grace and intelligence it possesses is due to her. For her partnership I am deeply grateful.

The official modern Turkish orthography has been used in transcribing Ottoman and Turkish words in the Latin script. Readers unacquainted with Turkish should note the following: c = j as in John, ç = ch as in church, ğ = soft g lengthens the preceding vowel, ı = similar to the u in radium, ö = French eu as in deux, ü = French u as in durée, and ş = sh as in ship. Diacritical marks have been minimized. For some terms, such as sheikh and pasha, modern anglicized versions have been used.

Portions of chapter 4 previously appeared in "The Great Fire of 1660 and the Islamization of Christian and Jewish Space in Istanbul," *International Journal of Middle East Studies* 36, no. 2 (May 2004): 159–81. Portions of chapter 6 appeared in "17. Yüzyılda Yahudilerin Osmanlı İmparatorluğu'ndaki Nüfuz ve Mevkilerini Yitirmeleri," *Toplum ve Bilim* 83 (Kış 1999–2000): 202–22; and "Messiah King or Rebel? Jewish and Ottoman Reactions to Sabbatai Sevi's Arrival in Istanbul," *Kabbalah: Journal for the Study of Jewish Mystical Texts* 9 (2003): 153–74.

Contents

Honored by the Glory of Islam

Introduction

Conversion of Self, Others, and Sacred Space

The compound of the leading Muslim religious authority (*mufti*)
of Istanbul lies in the shadow of the magnificent sixteenth-century
mosque of Sulieman in one of the most religious neighborhoods of
the city. One building of the complex houses the Ottoman Islamic Law
Court (*Shariah*) Archive. Its small reading room lined with wooden
bookshelves built by nineteenth-century sultan Abdülhamid II has
just enough room for a long table seating several researchers and the
director of the archive. A pious Muslim from Erzurum, the director
favored faded green suits and a brown, knitted skullcap, and fielded
calls from the "Hello Islamic Legal Opinion" (Alo Fetva) telephone
line. The head of the archive, who has committed the Qur'an to
memory, insisted that I inform him of every conversion I located in
the yellowed pages of the court registers. He wanted me to interrupt
his phone calls or proofreading of Qur'ans or sipping of bracing tea in
tiny tulip-shaped glasses. He and the assistant director, whose main
function was to serve tea, and several other Turkish researchers would
gather behind me and look over my shoulder as I read aloud to them
the brief texts written in Ottoman Turkish and Arabic. Inevitably, the
head of the archive would put his hand on my shoulder and, inexplica-
bly addressing me by the Muslim name Ahmed, state, "Three hundred years ago that Armenian boy or that Jewish man or that Orthodox
Christian woman understood the truth and was rightly guided into
Islam. Why aren't you?" This continued for the two and a half years
I worked there and on subsequent visits as well.

The director and some of the Turkish researchers used a number of different methods to try to convert me to Islam. The first was social pressure. Two or three times during the day, upon hearing the call to prayer from the Suleimaniye Mosque, the director would put slippers at my feet and a towel on my shoulder and say, "Come, Ahmed, let's go do our ablutions before praying in the mosque. We're locking the archive; you might as well come with us." Another method was more intellectual or theological. The head of the archive would often explain that Christianity, Judaism, and Islam all are branches of one original monotheist religion, but that Islam—being the last revelation, the final call, and the one whose message had never been corrupted—was its truest form. To convert from Christianity or Judaism to Islam, therefore, was to turn back to the authentic and original form of the erroneous religious practices in which I may have currently been engaged. One day the director, not a young man, sprang from his chair and said, "Ahmed, look at me. I am Ibrahim [Abraham]. My left arm is Ishak [Isaac]; my right is Ismail [Ishmael]. They both spring from the same body. They are branches connected to the same trunk. Why don't you start using your right side?" At this moment, not being able to humor the well-meaning man any longer and intent on finishing a transliteration of a text in the waning afternoon light from the single window before the archive closed, I rudely said, "Look at that Japanese researcher. He is a polytheist. He is not even aware that there is only one, true God. Wouldn't it be more impressive to bring such an unbeliever to the true path?" Undeterred, the head of the archive responded, "But he is hopeless. You are much closer. You are already a monotheist. Convert," he added, turning to an aesthetic appeal, "and you could pray with all the other Muslim brothers in the glorious Suleimaniye Mosque beneath its impressive, lofty dome."

While conducting my research concerning the change of religion of several hundred Christians and Jews to Islam in late seventeenth-century Istanbul, I became the unwilling target of fervent proselytization. As I have slowly realized, I gained better understanding of conversion from my daily encounters with devout Muslims in the archive than from the brief, frustratingly incomplete narratives of conversion in Ottoman archival records. The director's exhortations made me realize that one of my original aims, to discover the motivation of the convert, was misguided. I had sought to answer why Christians and Jews became Muslims in the early modern Ottoman Empire only to discover that this was a question that I could not answer by reading the available documentary material, as it does not inform us of the conditions of conversion.

As I began reading seventeenth- and eighteenth-century Ottoman chronicles, I realized that in Ottoman Europe (Rumili, Rumelia, "the land of the

Romans"), an area stretching from Istanbul to near Vienna in central Europe, Crete in the Mediterranean, and Podolia in Ukraine, when Christians and Jews converted to Islam before the grand vizier, sultan, or other Ottoman official such as a magistrate, his or her change of religion was invariably referred to in Ottoman archival and literary sources as "being honored by the glory of Islam," which I have chosen as the book's title. No matter the diverse circumstances in which people left their former religion and entered Islam, whether on the battlefield in the face of certain death or compelled by the sultan, his mother (the valide sultan), or the grand vizier, whether in a conversion ceremony before the ruler or at a meeting of an Istanbul Shariah court, and whether written in gold ink in a presentation copy of a literary masterpiece to the sultan or jotted down in black ink in the inside cover of a Shariah court register, Ottoman writers and bureaucrats labeled it in this manner. They were not concerned with the motivations of the convert and rarely recorded any of his or her intentions in changing religion, let alone the former religion or name.

Subjected to constant proselytization efforts and increasingly familiar with the nature of Ottoman sources, I reversed my research questions. I began to wonder what drove the head of the archive and other convert makers rather than what compels people to change religion. Now my questions were these: Why do people attempt to bring others of the same religion to their understanding of that religion, or try to ensure that people of completely different religions join their tradition? What is the connection between personal piety and proselytization? Who mediates conversion? Because every day I was invited to convert and then pray at the imposing sixteenth-century Suleimaniye Mosque, I also began to think about the effects of conversion on the urban environment: How does conversion affect the religious geography and sacred space of a city? The fact that Constantinople was conquered with much bloodshed in a war conceived on both sides as a struggle against the infidel caused me to also finally ask, What role do war, violence, and changing power relations play in the motivations of proselytizers in converting people and places? These are important questions worthy of investigation because their answers offer broad implications for the way scholars approach and conceptualize religious conversion, while presenting an original reading of Ottoman European history seen through the prism of religious transformation. Answering these questions for the seventeenth-century Ottoman Empire provides new insight into the reign of a forgotten sultan, an understudied era in Ottoman history, the changing nature of Islam and understanding and practice of jihad, relations between Muslims, Christians, and Jews in Europe, and the history of Istanbul.

Mehmed IV, Conversion, and War on the Path of God

This book is a study of the religious transformation of people and places in early modern Ottoman Europe. It is based on the argument that the intersection of three interdependent modalities of conversion resulted in Islamization: a turn to piety or conversion of the self, the conversion of others, and the transformation of sacred space. These three constitute intricately related concentric rings of change set in motion by conversion to a reformist interpretation of Islam of the most important members of the dynasty and ruling elite (queen mother, grand vizier, sultan). Linked to this argument is a second one: that conversion is best understood in the context of war, conquest, and changing power relations. This book is concerned with conversion during the unique historical epoch of Ottoman Sultan Mehmed IV (reigned 1648–87), when Islamization occurred according to this pattern. I first describe the intensification of faith of the sultan's inner circle, including his preacher, grand vizier, and mother, and the sultan, leading to their efforts to bring other Muslims to the same understanding of Islam and the conversion of Christians and Jews and their holy space, especially in Istanbul. Then I examine how the same conviction compelled Mehmed IV and his court to wage war against the Habsburgs, Romanovs, and Venetians, seeking to bring foreign Christians to Islam and transform the sacred geography of Europe into a sanctified Muslim landscape accompanying the greatest territorial expansion and extension of the boundaries of the Ottoman Empire.

I posit a link between Islamic piety and conversion in the seventeenth century. I argue that piety can lead to both conversion within Islam and conversion to Islam. A turn to piety is considered a transformation in a person's beliefs and practices. Fazıl Ahmed Pasha ("pasha" is a title for a military commander, or statesman, particularly the grand vizier), Hatice Turhan Sultan (male and female members of the Ottoman dynasty were referred to as "sultan"), and Sultan Mehmed IV experienced a revival of their faith, an intensification of religious fervor. When the grand vizier, queen mother, and sultan adopted the Kadızadeli tenets preached by Vani Mehmed Efendi ("efendi" is a title for a member of the religious class) and turned belief in a purified, reformed Islam into political policy, attempting to transform the way Muslims practiced their religion, they spurred the conversion of other Muslims to their interpretation of Islam, just as the preaching of Kadızadeli preachers in Istanbul's mosques led to the similar conversion of other Muslims (as well as resistance to that interpretation). Some Christians and Jews may have been swayed by Islamic piety to abandon their own religion, a sentiment that sometimes makes its way into Shariah court records. More germane to my argument, which concerns the mentality of the convert makers, the piety of Muslims was connected in contemporary writers' minds not only to conversion within Islam, but to conversion of Christians and Jews to Islam. Vani Mehmed Efendi made the connection between the Turks' conversion to Islam and the subsequent conquest and conversion of much of Eurasia by their pious descendants. Many contemporary Ottoman historical narratives claim that just as the piety of Hatice Turhan both compelled her to "conquer" Jewish space in Istanbul in order to convert the imperial capital's sacred geography and to compel Jews to become Muslim, Mehmed IV and Grand Vizier Fazıl Ahmed Pasha were incited by their piety to wage both the jihad of personal moral transformation and the jihad of military campaign that would result in the conversion of the religious geography and people from the Mediterranean to Poland and Ukraine.

The first conversion I explore is conversion of the self facilitated by mediators. Complicating the usual depiction of top-down conversions, whereby the king converts, followed by his kingdom, I relate a chain of conversion whereby the sultan was the fourth link following his preacher, grand vizier, and mother. Before exploring conversion, I lay out the context of crisis and political instability in which it occurred. Chapter 1 explores Mehmed IV's turbulent accession to the sultanate at the tender age of seven following the dethronement (and subsequent execution) of his father, Ibrahim. Chapter 2 analyzes a decade of economic, military, and political crisis during his minority which led to perceptions of a cultural crisis whose resolution was sought in conversion to a purified Islam as advocated by pietist preachers. Chapters 3 to 6 follow Mehmed IV's coming of age and his turn to piety, as well as that of his former regent and queen mother, the valide sultan Hatice Turhan Sultan, a converted former Christian slave named after the first convert in Islamic history, Muhammad's wife, Khadija, under the influence of the Kadızadeli movement. Their conversion was mediated by the preacher Vani Mehmed Efendi. The preacher was brought to the attention of Mehmed IV and Hatice Turhan by Grand Vizier Fazıl Ahmed Pasha, who had encountered the preacher on a provincial posting and was the first one swayed by his charismatic advocacy of revivalist pietism. Chapter 3 provides the historical background of the Kadızadeli movement through the 1650s. Chapter 5 discusses the Kadızadeli movement led by Vani Mehmed Efendi beginning in the 1660s, which linked "rigorous self-discipline" (enjoining good) and "strident social activism" (forbidding wrong).[1] These Muslims encouraged the interiorization of religion, undergoing a spiritual conversion, a revitalized commitment to the faith. They also promoted rationality in religion, stripping the ecstatic Islam practiced in Istanbul of innovations that they believed ran counter to the practices of the first Muslim community. This included Sufi rituals such as repeating God's name or dancing to music as a form of prayer and visiting the tombs of Sufis to ask for intercession. Purification requires an opposing practice or person that is to be purified.[2] The wrath of the Kadızadelis particularly targeted Bektashi, Halveti, and Mevlevi Sufis, members of orders previously instrumental in facilitating conversion. Kadızadeli-inspired conversion of the self is connected to the conversion of other Muslims in Mehmed IV's immediate inner circle.

The next ring of conversion encompasses people and places nearest this inner circle. The sultan, usually depicted in the secondary literature, like his predecessors, as an aloof figure unconcerned about the beliefs and practices of his subjects, became an interventionist ruler and convert maker. Chapter 4 examines the Islamization of Istanbul in the aftermath of the 1660 fire. It narrates how places nearest the residence of key palace figures, considered an extension of the sultan's personal space, were transformed into Muslim space, including the predominantly Jewish neighborhoods closest to Topkapı Palace in Istanbul. Just as the hearts of the pietists had turned, so did they turn the heart of Istanbul into Muslim sacred space. Mehmed IV's reign witnessed the transformation of the religious geography of Istanbul in the wake of the most devastating fire ever to have befallen the city, a connection of conflagration and conversion. The sultan expelled Jews from the city's main port area and prohibited their return to a wide swath of the peninsula, especially those areas nearest the palace and the monumental imperial mosque, the Valide Sultan Mosque (New Mosque), built by Mehmed IV's mother. Those who constructed the mosque compared the exile of Jews from Eminönü to Hasköy with Muhammad's exile of the Jewish tribe of Banu Nadir from Medina. This act exposes the historical consciousness of this sultan and his mother. They linked their actions to those of the final prophet and considered their actions to be justified because they represented the conquest of infidel places in the present and were associated with future conquests abroad when lamps lit between the minarets of the new mosque illuminated the name of Christian citadels taken by the Ottomans. Christian areas of Galata, the district across the Golden Horn from Istanbul proper, were also Islamized by means of converting church properties to mosques and prohibiting Christians from residing in their vicinity. At the same time, many formerly Christian- and Jewish-inhabited areas of the city saw mosques replace churches and synagogues in the aftermath of the fire, as officials limited the districts that Christians and Jews could inhabit. As Armenians, Orthodox Christians, and Jews began to live in formerly predominantly Muslim neighborhoods, Muslim commoners asked for official interference to expel the encroachers.

The conversion of places nearest the sultan's inner circle paralleled the conversion of Christians and Jews allowed within that elite group. Chapter 6 presents the story of the conversion of Jewish palace physicians converted by the valide sultan Hatice Turhan. She was praised for her piety, which included both constructing the imperial mosque complex in Istanbul and not permitting a renowned Jewish physician named Moses son of Raphael Abravanel to continue in his post as privy physician unless he became a Muslim. He had to dress as a Muslim and figuratively be clothed in the teaching of Islam and renamed Hayatizade Mustafa Fevzi Efendi. He was transformed internally and externally. Only after cleansing himself of his former religion could he touch the sultan, examine his body to determine what ailed him, and restore his health. Subsequently, other Jewish palace physicians converted, so that where once Jews had outnumbered members of any other group in this position, after the conversion of Hayatizade there were more convert physicians than Jews.

The imperial capital also witnessed the conversion of other Muslims to the inner circle's form of piety, which linked elite and commoner in the Kadızadeli pietistic movement. New forms of belief such as the prohibition of what were considered harmful innovations, the implementation of new laws and regulations such as the banning of alcohol, and the punishment of those who would not change their behavior served as manifestations of the piety that passed through the palace. Chapter 5 explores more deeply Mehmed IV's newfound piety mediated by the Kadızadeli preacher Vani Mehmed Efendi and links the sultan's coming of age with the abandonment of Topkapı Palace for the palace at Edirne and the composition of chronicles that emphasize his pious persona. A campaign against Sufis and the illicit behavior of Muslims quickly followed.

Following these conversions of self, inner circle, places, and people contiguous to the inner circle and those of the same religion were conversions of hundreds of Christians and Jews encountered by the pious within the domains of the empire, whose conversions signaled the sultan's Islamic virtues. Chapter 6 describes how the sultan's conversion of others led to converts bringing additional Christians and Jews to Islam. Rabbi Shabbatai Tzevi became a Muslim rather than prove his prophetic pluck in the presence of the sultan, to whom the rabbi appeared as another antinomian, ecstatic dervish. Engaged in a crackdown on Sufis and Sufi practices, Mehmed IV could not tolerate the rabbi's advocacy of conversion to millenarianism, which challenged the sultan's mediating others' change to *his* interpretation of the best means of fulfilling God's will. Once Shabbatai Tzevi was converted by the sultan, he in turn became a convert maker, translating the phrase "Enjoin good and forbid wrong" into Hebrew and compelling his wife and many of his followers to change religion. The rabbi, who was instructed in the tenets of Islam by Vani Mehmed Efendi, was given a ceremonial gatekeeper position in the palace after conversion, serving as a daily, visible reminder that confirmed the superiority of the sultan's beliefs.

Chapters 9 and 11 reexamine Mehmed IV's devotion to hunting and the link between hunting and conversion, calling into question the critical interpretations of hunting advanced by later Ottoman and modern historians of his reign. These chapters demonstrate that Christian peasants who drove the game for the sultan when he held massive hunting parties, and others encountered by him on his frequent, large, and lengthy chases or on the military campaign trail, and those appearing before him and the grand vizier also converted. After their change of religion, converts engaged in ritual ceremonies affirming internal and external transformation, where they publicly proclaimed leaving the false religion and joining the true faith and affirmed the unity of God. Christian men were circumcised on the spot. Converts were re-dressed from head to toe and given Muslim names and purses of Ottoman coins (silver asper, *akçe*) minted for the occasion, which had more symbolic than real value. Because hierarchies of dress were intended to distinguish members of different religions, changing the body by dressing it in new clothing was fundamental to transforming Christians and Jews into Muslims. This practice linked Mehmed IV to his prophetic namesake, who had given his cloak to a convert, and to a millennium of Muslim leaders while ensuring his control over the distribution of signs that marked society's hierarchies.

The broadest circle of conversion reached deep into central Europe and the Mediterranean, accompanying the greatest extension of Ottoman boundaries. Chapters 7, 8, and 10 follow Mehmed IV out of Edirne into the battlefields, where he made his mark in the middle years of his reign after his impotent minority and before the defeat at Vienna. I discuss how the pious sultan and those closest to him, including his preacher, Vani Mehmed Efendi, are depicted as desiring the conquest and conversion of foreign territories and their inhabitants and places of worship and often being able to fulfill this wish. The preacher accompanied the sultan and grand vizier on military campaigns, brandishing Muhammad's black wool banner, which the Ottomans had used in imperial campaigns since Selim I conquered Egypt, and motivated by the example of the Arabian prophet, inciting the besieging troops in the trenches to fight on the path of God against infidels. He believed that the Ottomans had inherited the mantle of warfare from the Arabs in the struggle against the infidels, which ended in their conversion. Chapters 7 and 8 discuss how, accordingly, Mehmed IV began the well-known jihad for Candia (Iraklion), Crete (1666–69), which, along with conquests in central and eastern Europe (Uyvar/Nové Zámky and Yanık/Raab/Győr in Hungary, Kamaniça/Kamenets-Podol'skiy in Poland, and Çehrin/Chyhyryn in Ukraine) several years later signified the greatest extent of Ottoman expansion. Chapter 10 explains how he also launched the siege of the Habsburg capital of Vienna (1683), where the defenders were offered the chance to convert to Islam and the besieging armies were depicted as being on a mission to propagate the word of God. The failed siege actually ended Ottoman conquest in Europe and marked the beginning of withdrawal. Chapters 10 and 11 trace Mehmed IV's sudden reversal of fortune during and after the siege of Vienna, narrating his dethronement and death and revealing the sources of the negative image of the sultan advanced in subsequent historiography.

The wave of religiously inspired warfare resulted in the successful conversion of many Christians and much Christian sacred geography into sanctified Muslim space and the purification and rededication of Muslim sacred space previously lost to Christian armies such as at Bozca (Tenedos) Island. Mehmed IV's efforts ensured that the Muslim call to prayer was chanted from church bell towers. The silencing of the pealing of bells demonstrated the truth of Islam, as it was the aural and visible sign of victory.

Along with being depicted during his reign as pious and God-fearing, a ruler who spread the faith within and without his domains, Mehmed IV was also described as a warrior for the faith against the infidels. Contrary to earlier periods, the terms "mujahid" and "jihad" were commonly used by authors during Mehmed IV's reign interchangeably with "ghazi" and "ghaza" to designate warriors and warfare against Christian powers, whether the Habsburgs, Romanovs, or Venice. Mehmed IV was depicted as a ghazi, the one who "spreads a clamor to the East and West, a cry of horror and lament to all lands of the infidel and all peoples," and vanquishes the enemy with prophetic zeal.[3] Mehmed IV's move to the former capital of Edirne, an "abode of glory, power, and victory," is described in the context of a noble intent to personally wage perennial war against the infidels.[4] The sultan "incited all to ghaza and jihad."[5] One writer narrates how Ottoman soldiers "exerted and endeavored to obtain the rewards of ghaza and jihad."[6]

To the chronicle writers of Mehmed IV's era, he was a warrior fighting ghaza and jihad against the infidel. The sultan's official chronicler, Abdi Pasha, promotes the view that he was a throwback to an earlier era, for Mehmed IV acted to inculcate the position with greater symbolic and real power. He wished both to return to an age when sultans were mobile, active military leaders and warriors, bringing war to the heart of the Christian enemy, and to instill it with new meaning—breaking out of the cage in the palace of Istanbul and spending most of his reign in Edirne and Rumelia, the heartland of the empire, having contact with commoners, intervening in their lives, and, motivated by his religious zeal and working with his pious mother, grand vizier, and spiritual advisor, engaging in policies of religious patronage that Islamized people and places, promoting the image of a worthy, virile Islamic sovereign. Mehmed

Halife served the sultan in one of the wards of the palace and wrote in the mid-1660s, when Mehmed IV first established himself as a warrior king. In a section of his history entitled "The Praiseworthy Moral Qualities of Our Felicitous Sultan," he claimed that Mehmed IV "acted in accordance with [Qur'an 22:78] 'Wage jihad for the cause of God, with the devotion due to God,' and followed the path of his great ancestors and illustrious forefathers, may God bless their souls, waging ghaza and jihad and proclaiming the true religion to unbelievers night and day."[7] Ahmed Dede, writing in Arabic toward the end of his reign, labels Mehmed IV "the mujahid, ghazi king, deliverer of conquest and ghazi."[8]

This book offers a unique lens through which to view seventeenth-century Ottoman Europe. It is neither a comprehensive historical survey nor a biography, but a reinterpretation centered on recognizing the link between conversion and conquest in this period of history. Mehmed IV's turn to piety, along with that of his mother, grand vizier, and royal preacher, converted him to a more rigorous and severe interpretation of Islam. This in turn compelled him to at least facilitate by means of group ceremonies and at times compel the conversion of others—Christian, Jewish, and Muslim, following face-to-face encounters—to his path of Islam. Related to this conversion in both senses, a revival of faith for those already members and a change of religion for those not yet believers, Mehmed IV waged war throughout central and eastern Europe and the Mediterranean, reviving ghaza, and sent his military forces to conquer many citadels, hundreds of cities, and thousands of villages, leading campaigns in person as well. In this way, the sultan, enthroned while a child, became a brave warrior praised for his manliness. He also proved himself as sultan. While his mother handled ceremonial matters that gave his reign further dynastic and Islamic legitimacy and, more important, cover, Mehmed IV was free to move his court to Edirne, which would serve as his capital for two decades. There he appointed a court historian and even named the work. This spatial and symbolic move away from Istanbul and his mother confirmed the coming into being of the sultan as man and ruler. He was conscious of the momentousness of the relocation that would mark his reign and thereafter wanted a sultan-centered narrative to record what he experienced. In Edirne he became a good rider and mobile ghazi, leading jihad and the hunt, residing most often in a tent, rarely setting foot in Topkapı Palace or Istanbul. Contemporary writers linked the sultan's hunting to waging war, pious behavior, and Islamic zeal. Conversion of self, others, and sacred space and war on the path of God referred to as both ghaza and jihad are intersecting themes that marked Mehmed IV's reign.

Theorizing Religious Conversion: Connecting Conversion of Self, Others, and Sacred Space

Although this book is based on a detailed investigation of the reign of one Ottoman sultan, I also adopt an interpretive stance worth considering for the study of religious conversion in other times and places. I take an integrated approach to conversion, linking conversion of self, others, and space, and include the dimension of power and the context of war and conquest. This is one of the few works that examines the intricacies of religious change in its individual (personal) and social and political (public) aspects and places it in historical context. I argue that conversion is a decision or experience followed by a gradually unfolding, dynamic process through which an individual embarks on religious transformation.[9] This can entail an intensification of belief and practice of one's own religion, moving from one level of observation to another, or exchanging the beliefs and practices in which one was raised for those of another religious tradition. In both cases, a person becomes someone else because his or her internal mind-set and/or external actions are transformed. In the case of intensification, where one formally did not give other than cursory thought or attention to the theology of one's faith or engage in or keep wholeheartedly to its requirements, one devotes one's mind and body fully to understanding and embracing the religion. Whereas some scholars still posit an artificial distinction between "exterior" and "interior" conversion, I argue that conversion has an internal component entailing belief and an external component involving behavior, leading to the creation of a new self-identity and new way of life. In Sunni Islamic law, faith has three elements: internal conviction, verbal affirmation, and the performance of works; the first is the internal component of conversion, the latter two the external elements.[10]

The internal component includes a change in worldview, a turning toward a new axis or set of ideals that motivate converts to transform themselves and their environment. Converts reject or denounce their past and former beliefs and practices, or indifference in the case of revivalists, labeling them wrong when compared with a different future on the path of the new, conceived as being right.[11] The convert accepts a new reference point for his or her identity, a new foundation of salvific power, and commits to a new moral authority.[12]

Whereas the internal component demands a change in consciousness, the external requires commitments to another salvific community, devotion to piety or the new religion, which entails changing the way the individual behaves and the adoption of a new social identity. The external sign of transformation is important for the individual, the religious community he or she abandons, and the one he or she joins. Conversion here is begun by rituals of rejection and bridge burning, which hinder return to the original way and allow the convert to demonstrate commitment to the new religiosity or religion, to transition into it, and to be incorporated by the members of the group he or she is joining.[13] Converts change their daily private and public routine; learn another sacred tongue; dress differently; act and move according to a different choreography of ritual and prayer; consume certain food and drink and no longer consume others; surround themselves with a new group of people and separate from others, even family members, including spouses who do not follow the new piety or faith; and face the consequences of their decision, which may lead to newfound popularity with some members of society and a cutting of ties with others. Conversion leads to social mobility offered by a change in status and communal affiliation. The convert engages in rituals of deconstruction, which demonstrate a severing of former beliefs and behaviors, and in symbolic acts of reconstruction.

Part of demonstrating that one is a new person may entail public testimony praising the new piety or religion, promoting one's commitment to it to prove oneself in the eyes of one's new coreligionists, and condemning those left behind.[14] Converts continually engage in rituals that symbolize the change, allow them to perform piety, embody the new religious identity, and play a role in society that satisfies expectations and consolidates their new place and involvement with the group.[15] Yet there are instances when a convert to another religion cannot or does not wish to completely reject or break away from former beliefs and practices, but instead continues to engage in some of them despite privately and publicly changing religion. There may be an adaptation or modification of the former and new ways of life, potentially encouraged by the converter or mediator as a temporary means of ensuring religious transformation.[16]

Most scholars writing about religious conversion today have moved away from the school of thought associated with the eminent William James, based on an uncritical reading of converts' narratives that emphasizes the (Protestant) individual's psychological experience of conversion. Historical sources, especially Ottoman material, seldom provide insight into the converted, so the psychological approach developed first by James is limited in its utility. Instead of such an interiorist approach, which focuses on an individual in isolation, scholars emphasize the social and historical context and aspects of conversion, arguing that conversion is motivated by social relationships and interpersonal bonds. Arguing against James, they maintain that conversion, which entails internal and external transformation, whether revivalist or transition to another tradition, does not occur in a vacuum, is not merely the result of an individual's studied reflection of his or her relation to the divine or the transformation of an individual living in solitude.[17] Nor does conversion concern only an autonomous quest for spiritual meaning, the isolated interior path of self-realization, or a moment in a single individual's private personal destiny.[18] It is not only the life of the mind that matters, but also the life of the social being, for conversion is not only deeply private, but also deeply social.[19]

Avoiding the pitfalls of studies that focus on the social to the exclusion of the spiritual, I unite a study of the piety and religious conviction of converts with the social effects of their religious change. In so doing I advance scholarly discussions of the social aspects of conversion by focusing on motivations of the converter, insofar as these can be gleaned from their historical context, and concentric rings of conversion set into motion as the most powerful people in the dynasty and administration are convinced to change their religious outlook. Conversion is influenced by contextual situations and personal relations. An important element in the process of conversion is an encounter with an advocate, mediator, or external agent who exposes the individual to the new way of being and, through dynamic interplay and dialogic encounter with the convert, brings him or her to the advocated manner of piety or faith.[20] In Islamic societies, Sufis or magistrates frequently served as mediators in conversion.[21] Here I focus on the mediating role of preachers and the sultan. Interaction with the mediator, especially when followed by the establishment of affective, interpersonal bonds and a relationship, leads to change and commitment by the convert.[22] The way the instigator communicates the message, whether through propaganda, proselytization, teachings, or the examples of pious individuals, brings others to piety or a new religion.[23] Conversion can have its rewards when the converter offers the convert gifts of money and other financial and social incentives such as tax breaks, pardon for crimes, and clothing.[24] The giving of clothes, especially robes of honor, signals both a change in social status of the convert and his or her introduction into an ongoing relationship with the agent of conversion: "The hand of the giver left its 'essence' on the robe."[25] The object serves to embody the recognition of the conversion, serving as a reminder of the transformation. Converts display the effect of the adoption of a new moral system on the body, such as when Muhammad offered his mantle to his former opponent, Ka'b ibn Zuhayr, who recorded the occasion in his poem, the "Mantle Ode," symbolizing the acceptance of the convert into the community.[26]

Intellectual or religious, political, and social contexts and constraints, situated within events that are not always of the convert's choosing, lead to potentially radical social results and ramifications, whether the convert is the ruler, whose conversion compels him to launch military conquests, or his subject. Whether involving a single person or the masses, religious change can be one of the most unsettling and destabilizing political events in the life of a society, affecting members of the pietistic movement and those who come into contact with them, not to mention the religion abandoned and the one joined.[27]

Focusing on the converter, I argue that having undergone an intensification of faith or changing to another religion, converts tend to articulate their enthusiasm for the religion in private practices and public actions. If they are revivalists, they may attempt to bring members of the original faith to their new understanding of its significance for everyday life, and then convince members of other religions to join the newly discovered old religion. Converts to piety are especially zealous in compelling through their words and actions less observant members of their own religion to become awakened and heed the religion's tenets, which they have reformed, devoting themselves to what they consider a purified version of the faith.[28] After all, "religious revivals grow by the conversion of new adherents."[29] When a ruler's aims and those of pietists converge, it establishes the most conducive environment for the conversion of members of the sovereign's religion and his subjects committed to other religions. As in Christendom, where "the missionary and the warrior traveled and worked together in the process of extending both Christ's kingdom and that of the king," pacifying foes and expanding the kingdom, the proselytizer in Islamic societies received "protection, endowments (often on a very grand scale) . . . the status that came with association with a king, the infectious example of a royal conversion," and "access to royal powers of coercion," all of which would spread the religion in areas of recent conquest and intensify it among subjects at home.[30] Perhaps adopting the methods, strategies, style, techniques, and mode of encounter of the individual that first compelled him or her to change religion, the convert serves as a mediator in converting outsiders. This confirms the validity of his or her newly chosen path, for there is nothing more self-validating than having others undergo the same transformation he or she experiences and in having associates in the new lifestyle.

The conversion of peoples is incomplete without the conversion of space, place, and the landscape.[31] Few scholars, however, have linked conversion of self and others to a major impact on the built environment, or the spatial dimensions of religious change. If the ruler (usually male) of a society converts, whether to piety or a different religion altogether, he converts holy spaces of other religions to his own, including the most grand and significant structures located in the capital and major cities of his state, or constructs new edifices celebrating and announcing his personal decision. Female members of the royal family and male members of his retinue may do likewise. When the masses change religion, this occurs on a much wider scale, as all those new believers and those compelling their conversion demand spaces where their newfound faith can be articulated and demonstrated. Either way, we witness the ultimate transformation of sacred space as cityscapes reflect the revival movement or demographic change, and the sacred geography of the countryside is likewise transformed. Throughout lands conquered, colonized, and ruled by Muslims, the conversion of sacred space and the establishment of Muslim institutions led to the conversion of the population, just as the conversion of the population led to the transformation of holy sites.[32] Over time, churches, synagogues, and fire temples were destroyed or appropriated and converted into regular and congregational mosques, shrines, and Sufi complexes to serve the needs of and accommodate a population undergoing a radical change in religious demography.[33]

The layered history of transformed buildings and glorious new masterpieces in turn become tools of proselytization, "theaters of conversion" that set the stage for religious change.[34] The changed landscapes are readable to all passersby as didactic instruments promoting conversion and communicating its reward: divine favor. When a religious sanctuary or house of worship of one religion is modified to conform to the new religion of the convert, the preserving of the sanctity yet adaptive use of the same sacred space by the victorious religion sends a message to those who formerly worshipped there: the sanctification of the same site means holy space serves another belief system. If those who venerate the familiar spot and have memories of praying there want to continue revering older sacralities, they ostensibly have to do so in another form. To facilitate conversion of others, the converters of a place may use "expedient selection," choosing to emphasize, accommodate, and even repackage those elements of belief and practices of their religion most resembling those of the possessors of the former house of worship who offered rituals there.[35] Visitors may engage in similar rituals in the same place, but the converters' aim is for their hearts to eventually be changed.[36] This allows those whose buildings were taken over to comprehend the new religion within the framework of their own religion. The converters may expect some former accretions to continue for a while, believing that after old locales and rituals are given new meaning the new practices will eventually lead to the new beliefs wiping away the old. Syncretism, the reconciling or fusing of diverse beliefs and practices, is not an exchange between equals. It is usually a temporary phenomenon, for in the end the religion with the most power behind it tends to subsume the other and completely take over the sacred space.[37] To not claim already sanctioned sites for the conquering religion is to allow echoes of the previous religion to remain unmarked, its power unappropriated.[38]

Conversion has intellectual and social contexts, and the transformation of holy space by conquerors, rulers, and pietists causes us to also pay attention to the fact that it does not occur in a vacuum free of political framework or power relations. Religious conversion efforts come in waves that are historically contingent. Peaks of such movements arise out of specific historical circumstances conditioned by economic, political, and social factors seen by people who convert as a period of crisis that serves as the catalyst of religious change.[39] Each wave has its own characteristics, whether conversion to Islam in seventeenth-century Ottoman Europe, or conversion to Christianity in colonial Africa and Latin America. Conversion takes place in the context of political events, including the breaking down of societies in the wake of foreign invasion, conquest, and occupation.[40] The aims of the converters may be considered to form their politics of conversion. When conquerors obtain power over the political, they also acquire the power to frame meaning, including values, ways of being and perceiving the universe, and the activities of the everyday, such as architecture, dress, social structure, and language.[41]

Language is crucial, because conversion can be synonymous with translation. Proselytizers translate the doctrine of their religion into the language of those they are attempting to convert, finding parallels, equivalences, and antecedents in their mode of expression and belief system while the convert translates and assimilates ideas into his or her own language and idiom.[42] The convert to Islam may speak Arabic, the language of the Qur'an, for the first time and adopt an Arabic name harkening back to the beginnings of the Muslim era. Converts declared that they left the false religion and entered the true religion. This signifies the communal basis of religious identity and the religious base of communal identity.[43] Entering the religion is equivalent to joining the community. Conquest transforms the religious geography, as temporal power creates a new environment that allows previously unimaginable religious possibilities to be realized.[44] Institutions of the conquering religion replace those of the defeated religion, and a new political authority permits the colonization of the territory by coreligionists.[45] At the same time, conquest, translation strategies, and capturing of sacred spaces compel indigenous accommodation to or transformation and subversion of the new forms of belief and practice.[46]

Historiography: Mehmed IV, Conquest, and Conversion in Ottoman History

While speaking to scholarship on religious conversion, this book also intervenes in a number of historiographical debates concerning Ottoman history. I offer a reinterpretation of the history of the second half of the seventeenth century in Ottoman Europe, a relatively understudied although crucial period, entering fundamental debates concerning the reputation of Mehmed IV, the understanding and implementation of ghaza and jihad, and religious conversion. This book is distinct in three main ways. First, it presents Mehmed IV in a new light. For generations of modern scholars, the chaotic state of affairs at the beginning and end of Mehmed IV's reign, the former the period of his minority between 1648 and 1656, the latter the debacle between the failed siege of Vienna in 1683 and Mehmed IV's dethronement in 1687, have constituted all that was deemed worthy of knowing about this sultan's epoch. In contrast to contemporary accounts about Mehmed IV, many of which have not been published or utilized by modern scholars, later chronicles have depicted him as weak, ineffectual, and a spendthrift. This sultan has been either overlooked or treated harshly by moderns, who, when they have written about his reign, have been overly critical or dismissive, as they mainly rely on the published eighteenth-century chronicles of Naima and Silahdar, arguing, for example, that "although he reigned in a very important period of Ottoman history, he was not a very important figure."[47] Because Mehmed IV apparently had neither agency nor significance, there has not been a single study in any language devoted to him for thirty years. Modern scholars who have written about Mehmed IV display disapproval of religious piety and an inability to take religious faith seriously, neither accepting that religious zeal could be anything other than a destructive force intimately tied to ignorance, nor even allowing that the sultan's religious feelings could have been sincere. The failure of the siege of Vienna turned Mehmed IV and the Kadızadeli movement into a historical dead end, another reason he is denigrated and little studied. Rescuing that dead end is an important historical task, for it is important to understand not only what happened in the past, but what might have been. Readers familiar with Mehmed IV's poor reputation as a hapless fool, manipulated by the ignorant zealots around him, who wasted his reign hunting and satisfying his pleasures in his harem while the empire crumbled, will be surprised to meet the pious Mehmed IV who here rides to war converting Christians and churches in his wake. This book explains this shift in historical memory by focusing on his achievements and putting them in the context of what was considered to be important to rulers at the time.[48]

The Mehmed IV described in this book also stands in contrast to his depiction in the secondary literature, which rarely extends analysis of changes in the institution of the sultanate to the second half of the seventeenth century.[49] Studies do not extend beyond the point at which Mehmed IV is still a minor, or skip over the second half of the seventeenth century altogether.[50] It is unfortunate that scholars have been so reluctant to reconsider conventional wisdom, since, contrary to most other sultans after Mehmed III (reigned 1595–1603),

Mehmed IV's life is evidence that sultans could still matter and not be hidden in the palace like a pearl in an oyster, aloof, secluded, and sublime, hermetically sealed from the world, confined and condemned to a wilted life in the harem.

The second way this study is different lies in how it enters the longest-running debate among scholars of Ottoman history through its analysis of ghaza and jihad. Until recently, the prevailing argument concerning ghaza was that it was an ideology of "holy war" by which Ottoman sultans "both fostered and were themselves impelled by the ghazi urge to conquer the infidel lands for Islam," since "the Holy War or *ghazā* was the foundation stone of the Ottoman state."[51] According to this view, still emphasized in Turkish historiography, the principal factor and dominant idea, the very reason and will to exist of the early Ottoman enterprise and cause of its success was struggle against Christians.[52] More recently, scholars have cast doubt on this thesis, arguing that the terms "ghaza" and "ghazi" were deployed merely as literary devices, serving to legitimate early Ottoman expansion against Muslim as well as Christian enemies, and that the term "ghaza" or "jihad" was an ideological gloss given to the earlier term for raid and plundering (*akın*) deployed before the Turks became Muslims.[53] The most influential recent history of the rise of the Ottomans argues that ghaza consisted of predatory raids against the ever-shifting current enemy, fighting not for a set of beliefs, but for one's own side in military campaigns undertaken for honor and booty, and that individuals frequently changed sides and identities, establishing alliances, falling in love, marrying, and converting.[54] Another study goes so far in zealously divorcing the material and spiritual realms that it declines to take seriously the religious motivation for ghaza. It expunges it of any religious meaning and implies that zeal for plunder and zeal for religiously motivated war are two opposite and distinguishable motivations.[55] This approach fails to recognize that ghaza emphasizes the plundering of the infidel enemy's land and wealth. It is intimately tied to religion since it can only be undertaken against those labeled infidels; warring against the infidel enemy, seen as an incumbent duty whether labeled ghaza or jihad, can occur only in conditions defined by the religion.[56]

In this study I argue that the second half of the seventeenth century, a period that has not been considered in the debate because scholars have been most concerned with the relation between ghaza and the achievements of the early Ottomans, was an era in which the terms "ghaza" and "ghazi" were put to considerable use promoting the pious image of the sultan. Ottoman authors depicted Mehmed IV as a ghazi waging ghaza in the sense of ghaza that Paul Wittek claimed for the early Ottomans: as the sword of God purifying the earth of the filth of polytheism, a champion of Islam devoted to the struggle with Christians.[57] The terms "jihad" and "mujahid," the one who engages in jihad,

were also commonly used to designate the soldiers who battled them for spiritual and material rewards. Jihad was understood as a combination of moral
self-discipline and enjoining good and forbidding evil within the community,
and public action to reassert Islam in society, a reform movement targeting
Muslims as well as war against the infidel abroad.

The discussion of ghaza and jihad is relevant to explaining the ways this
study also contributes to the history of conversion to Islam in the Ottoman Empire, the third way this book departs from previous historiography. It is important to recognize that modes of conversion changed, and these changes were
historically significant. Previous scholars have discussed how the Ottomans
were able to facilitate the near total conversion of Anatolia and urban southeastern Europe by rising to power through conquest and jihad, establishing a
unified Islamic state with Muslim institutions, including dervish lodges, encouraging Sufis to preach and propagate Islam to Turkish nomads, Christians,
and Jews, and recruiting Christian boys to serve the sultan.[58] Dervishes acted
as an avant-garde to colonize and proselytize, and institutions and incorpora-
tion followed the trailblazing path of Sufis uncontrolled by political power.[59]
Sufis who had a close relationship with the sultan played a role in conversion,
including the Halveti dervishes, who boasted of sultans among their ranks;
the Mevlevi dervishes, who girded the Ottoman sultans with a sword as part of
their enthronement ceremonies at the tomb of Muhammad's flag-bearer Abu
Ayyub al-Ansari in Istanbul; and the Bektashis, named after thirteenth-century
Sufi Hajji Bektash, who served as the patron saint of the elite infantry corps of
converted Christian recruits known as the Janissaries, who were members of
the order.[60] From the sixteenth century a Bektashi was assigned to the corps as
spiritual guide. The Bektashi-Janissary link points to how, along with promoting Sufi proselytization, sultans also based their administration and military
on the continuous recruitment, conversion, and training of Christians.[61] Until
the end of the seventeenth century, the dynasty used the *devshirme*, the levy of
Christian boys who were converted and trained to be the administrative and
military elite.[62] According to the Ottoman historian Sa'deddin, by the end of the
sixteenth century two hundred thousand Christians had become Muslim by
this process.[63] Ottoman expansion, the proselytization of Sufis, and the creation
of the Ottoman elite led to the conversion of the lived environment from central Europe to Yemen. One of the first acts of the Ottomans upon conquering
Christian cities was to convert cathedral churches into Friday mosques in the
captured citadels and urban areas. The city that underwent the greatest transformation of its sacred geography was the former Byzantine capital of Constantinople, which was remade to suit an Islamic dynasty, the process launched by
the conversion of Hagia Sophia, the religious and political center of Orthodox

Christianity, into the main royal mosque of the city, and the construction of many sultanic and grand vizieral mosque complexes.[64] Ottomans linked the construction of mosques, replete with mementos of victory that served as triumphant memorials within the imperial domains, to victorious ghaza and jihad from Bulgaria to Baghdad.[65] In celebration of successes abroad, sultans also ordered churches in the imperial capital to be converted into mosques.[66] The transformation of sacred spaces continued to be an important element in the process of conversion.

In contrast to the first three centuries of Ottoman rule, when propagation of Islam by dervishes and the recruitment of servants of the sultan, facilitated by war and conquest, were probably equally significant forces of religious change, the seventeenth century, this book argues, was a turning point in the history of conversion in the Ottoman Empire. Gone are encouragement of Sufi proselytization, no longer promoted by the sultan and the leading men and women of the dynasty, and the devshirme, which was phased out. While the abandonment of the devshirme was the outcome of demographic change, since the Muslim population had greatly expanded to become the majority and there was no longer a need to rely on converted Christians to fuel the empire's expansion, turning away from affiliating with and supporting Sufi groups who had once been an essential element in the conversion of the population of Anatolia and southeastern Europe was directly related to the conversion to reformist piety-mindedness by the sultan and his court, which took an active role in Islamizing people and places in Istanbul and elsewhere in Ottoman Europe.

Although conversion has come under renewed scrutiny by scholars able to read Ottoman archival sources, the most recent published studies present only half of the picture because they do not utilize literary sources such as chronicles, do not contextualize their studies within imperial politics or developments in Islam, and, most surprisingly, do not engage the scholarly literature on religious conversion.[67] Offering detailed accounts of archival documentation of conversion in Bursa, Trabzon, and southeastern Europe, their largely ahistorical accounts attempt to provide the reader with insights into the mentality, personality, psychology, mind-set, attitude, and motivation of converts and not on those who converted them.[68] In studying the process of conversion, it is important to juxtapose different types of historical record because none gives a complete picture. The problem with earlier arguments is that they rely too much on archival sources, which are so formulaic as to say nothing that a critical historian could claim speak to the actual motivations of the convert. The only way to build on previous scholarship and understand such archival sources as petitions to the sultan is to put them in the context of other documentation, especially chronicles.

What makes this book different is that it does not seek to answer why Christians and Jews became Muslim, which is an unproductive question based on the source material. Modern studies of conversion have noted that converts may not be able to pinpoint the reasons or know why they converted, change their explanations over time, or narrate their religious transformation according to a set prototype. Facing the extant documentary record, which views conversion from the standpoint of the converters, a historian can best hope to accomplish an understanding of the worldview of Islamic rulers who were active agents in the conversion of Christians and Jews. The aim is to bring the sultan back into the process, based on the most significant Ottoman chronicles written during the reign of Mehmed IV and after, as well as legal sources, archival and other literary sources generated at the sultan's court, epigraphic and visual sources.[69] This material provides the historian insight into how elite men and women at that time shaped, formed, and articulated their understanding of the moment in which they lived and the cultural value of conversion in that era.

The unraveling of Mehmed IV's legacy began at the end of his reign and continued after his death precisely because he was so successful earlier on. His achievements in expanding the empire, converting people and places to Islam, and reestablishing the image of the active ruler ended in catastrophe. But he also left a standard for sultanic behavior that subsequent sultans and the advisors and chronicle writers who tried to contain it wanted to forget. The last thing the bureaucracy and grand viziers wanted was an activist sultan. Although Mehmed IV expanded the empire, he also ruled during the beginning of its territorial decline, which modern historians imbued with nationalism have not been able to avoid highlighting. In this book I analyze what came before the siege of Vienna and ultimately led to it. Mehmed IV's participation in a pietistic Islamic reform movement—with its concomitant thrust toward conversion of Muslims, Christians, and Jews that led to the Ottoman Empire's greatest expansion—has to be evaluated in terms of its impact on what later became divided into European and Ottoman history. In particular, I put that siege in a new light. This perspective also reminds us that the Ottoman Empire was very much a European Islamic empire, controlling up to one-third of what is today considered Europe, and that not only interaction but intricate interrelations between the Ottoman Empire and central and eastern Europe—and among Muslims, Christians, and Jews—were long term and had many dimensions.[70] Between the sixteenth and the eighteenth century, the Ottoman Empire was "a full and active member" of the European states; by the end of Mehmed IV's reign in the seventeenth century, it "was as integrated into Europe as it ever would be."[71] Western European denigration of the empire—and by extension its head, the sultan—at the end of the nineteenth century as "the sick man of Europe" conceals a background of Ottoman European history when the empire and sultan were anything but.

I have traveled a long path from my original archival research. Many others are sharing that journey now. Today researchers no longer have the thrill of touching the original Istanbul Shariah court records in the intimate and dusty reading room where they are kept, the fear of spilling tea on historical documents, or the gentle but not so subtle proselytization efforts of the director, who has since retired. Saved from the proselytization efforts of the gentle memorizer of the Qur'an, researchers today may be exposed to the earnest efforts of university-age reward seekers, for all of the court records have been microfilmed and sent to the new Islamic Research Centre located on the Asian side of the city in a nondescript suburb. Although this effort has ensured the survival of the records (and that tea will no longer be spilled by nervous PhD candidates on their yellowed pages), it also guarantees that today's researcher, sitting at a microfilm reader in an air-conditioned library and staring at a screen, viewing texts whose important writing in the margins has been cut off in the copying process and whose original gold or red ink is illegible, will not have access to the insights I gained starting a decade ago, when the subject of my research and the subject of my life intersected. I did not become the Muslim the head of the archive would have desired. But in the end his earnest proselytizing efforts compelled me to write a book explaining the conversion to piety of Muslims and the circumstances that motivated them to convert Christians and Jews and their churches and synagogues in seventeenth-century Ottoman Europe.

I

Inauspicious Enthronement

The Uprising against Sultan Ibrahim and
Enthronement of Mehmed IV

In the summer of 1648, the men of the sword (the elite infantry
Janissaries and the cavalry known as *sipahis*) united with men of the
turban (the *sheikhulislam*—leading Muslim religious authority in the
empire—and magistrates of the city) to demand the dethronement of
Sultan Ibrahim on account of his abandoning Islamic law, the domination of women in the affairs of state, the suffering of commoners,
the loss of numerous citadels on the frontiers, the threat to Istanbul
of foreign navies, and the inattention of the sultan, who allegedly
spent all his time with his concubines.[1] To complete their act and
fulfill their political wishes, the rebels knew that the most important
person in the dynasty was not the sultan, but his mother.

   An anonymous miniature album circa 1650 contains a portrait of
Kösem Sultan, the valide sultan (figure 1.1). She is depicted sitting on
a golden throne, her hands palm down on her thighs, wearing a gold
head covering and fur-lined, gold-pinstriped light blue cloak over a
pink garment and gold sash.[2] All the symbols of royal power—gold,
fur, and throne—illustrate her might. Yet knowing the reign of her
son Ibrahim was effectively over, she attempted to control the process of transition to ensure her continued relevance. The valide sultan
refused to send Ibrahim's oldest son, Mehmed, to Ahmed I's mosque
(popularly known as the Blue Mosque) on the Hippodrome to receive

FIGURE 1.1. Mehmed IV's first regent, Kösem Sultan. Anonymous, "Valide Sultan/la Maore Regina," Staatliche Museen zu Berlin, Preußischer Kulturbesitz, Kunstbibliothek, Lipperheide OZ 52, 68. Reproduced with permission.

the Janissaries' and sipahis' oath of allegiance, demanding that they come to the palace for the enthronement.[3]

The rebellious men proceeded past Hagia Sophia to the gates of Topkapı Palace. They entered the Imperial Gate and passed through the usually crowded first courtyard, to which all subjects had access. They passed a hospital, a depot for firewood, the imperial armory, the mint, a bakery, the sixth-century Byzantine church Hagia Irene, a pavilion for collecting petitions to the sultan for the redress of grievances, and the spot where the heads of decapitated rebels were displayed. Unstopped by guards, they continued through the second gate, the Gate of Greeting, or Middle Gate, usually accessible only to officials, palace pages, foreign ambassadors, or those with legitimate business at the palace. They rushed past a parade ground for elite military units, the imperial treasury, and the Divan (Imperial Council Hall), with its imposing Tower of Justice, where an assembly of officials, including the grand vizier, controllers of finance, chief secretary, chief justices of Anatolia and Rumelia, and chancellor, met. Finally, they stopped before the third gate, the Gate of Felicity, before which occurred enthronements of sultans, presenting the oath of allegiance to the sultan, funerals, and the raising of Muhammad's banner before campaigns. Only pages and royal family members usually had access to the Throne Room, the Chamber of Petitions and Audience Hall, and the private quarters of the sultan and his household (the harem) located beyond the gate. Fully cognizant of Ottoman tradition, they stood before the place reserved for the loosening and fastening of the reigns of power and demanded the enthronement of Prince Mehmed. It was Judgment Day for Ibrahim.[4]

At this critical juncture, Ibrahim's sole support was his mother. At the anteroom to the third gate, the valide sultan rebuked the men before her for their hypocrisy for consenting to whatever her son Ibrahim desired, neither admonishing nor hindering him: "Now you want to replace him with a small child. What an evil plan this is. This crime of sedition is your doing."[5] She asked how it was possible to enthrone a seven-year-old. They responded that legal opinions (*fatwa*) had been issued that it was impermissible for a fool to rule; when an unreasonable man is on the throne, he cannot be reasoned with and causes much harm, whereas when a child is on the throne viziers carry out governance.[6] They disputed for a couple of hours, and she met with the sheikhulislam and grand vizier. It may have seemed that there was nothing to quarrel about. After all, an elderly woman facing a mob of armed men allied with magistrates and pillars of state would appear to have little power. But she was the representative of the dynasty, the power broker for the leading Islamic empire in the world. As Leslie Peirce notes, the valide sultan provided "sanction for the rejection of the *individual* sultan, thus allowing *dynastic* legitimacy to be preserved."[7] More important, she controlled access to the present and future sultans. Her body stood in the way of the fulfilling of their demands. Until the end she resisted, even though she understood that in order to quell the uprising, she had to put the young prince on the throne.[8] As Sheikhulislam Karaçelebizade notes in his history, written just under a decade later, additional soldiers had arrived, and "little time remained before the tide would rise drowning all in the great flood of calamity." The valide sultan asked whether they could disperse the rebels saying they would "renounce those acts which go against the dignity of the sultanate and will have benefited from counsel."[9] According to Karaçelebizade's contemporary, the financial clerk and author of over twenty books on history, geography, and bibliography, Katip Çelebi ("çelebi" is a title given to litterateurs), the rebels threatened "If you do not give us the prince we will enter the palace and use force to take him."[10] Having given permission to take out the emerald throne and set it before the Gate of Felicity according to custom, "she tucked up her skirts in fury" and went inside to get the prince.[11]

According to the Ottoman historian Mehmed Hemdani Solakzade, like Karaçelebizade and Katip Çelebi writing just under a decade after the events he describes and a main source for the oft-quoted eighteenth-century official historian Naima, the assembled, "looking with the eye of hope," were "waiting expectantly for the rising of the world-illuminating sun of the noble hearted prince." For this reason, the author relates the chronogram for his enthronement as "the sun rising to a favorable position in the sky."[12] Immediately, the valide sultan, who feared becoming the discarded former mother of the sultan once her son was no longer the ruler, "displayed the light of the eye of mankind" and said, "Is this what you want? Here is the prince," with "apparent distress and hatred in her face." While the prince "gazed all around," Karaçelebizade took the little boy by the right arm as another took his left and set him upon the throne. Karaçelebizade compares his gaze to the sun: "Like the glowing sun, rays were scattered" throughout the courtyard. Mehmed IV's sultanate begins when his eyes fix upon his servants, who, waiting to catch the "felicitous gaze of the beautiful eye of the happy sovereign," greet him with "May God's assistance be upon you" and commence the enthronement ceremony.[13] Karaçelebizade thus introduces the boy king as an omniscient leader.

The chronogram composed for this moment by Cevri Çelebi, a well-known poet and dervish of the Mevlevi order, stated optimistically, "The enthronement of Mehmed Khan made the world tranquil."[14] The poet's words were ironic because Mehmed IV's enthronement was greeted with bloodshed. "The Battle of the Hippodrome" raged in the main plaza of the city, whose gates and markets had been closed while terrified inhabitants hid indoors. Janissaries, responsible in the end for deposing Ibrahim, and sipahis, their archrivals for power and the supporters of Ibrahim, battled each other on the Hippodrome, a site of ritualized violence for over a thousand years, beginning with the chariot races between the blues and greens in Byzantine times. The sipahis had rebelled to avenge the dethroning of Ibrahim; after a fatwa was issued sanctioning the spilling of their blood, Janissaries were sent after them to fight them "like battling polytheists and enemies of the religion."[15] They were told, "The one killed is a martyr, the one who kills is a ghazi."[16] The outcome was predictable. Mid-seventeenth-century miniatures depict sipahis with body armor and shields but only swords and arrows for weapons; Janissaries have long rifles.[17] Because the sipahis would not disband, the Janissaries marched on those gathered in the Hippodrome, who fired on them with arrows and withdrew. The Janissaries charged with swords and used muskets to fire on those inside the mosque. The heads of hundreds of bearded men and beardless youth filled the Hippodrome. They turned the bloody ground into the place where the resurrected are said to assemble on the Day of Judgment.[18] The surviving sipahis withdrew into the Ahmed I Mosque or fled to board boats heading toward Üsküdar; one of these sank because it was overfilled with terrified cavalrymen. The Janissaries showed no mercy. They attacked the sipahis taking refuge in the mosque sanctuary and minarets, massacring them before the pulpit and prayer niche, riddling the delicately beautiful decorated doors and windows with bullets, which "rained down on them."[19] Contrary to Sunni Islamic custom, prayers were not said over the dead sipahis and their corpses were dumped into the sea.[20]

As battle raged, "weak and thin" seven-year-old Mehmed became the sultan of the Ottoman dynasty.[21] The little boy, who had not yet even been circumcised, was seated on the throne set up before the Gate of Felicity for the oath-swearing ceremony and kissing of the sultan's skirt. As was customary, all the ministers took their oaths of allegiance before him. The sheikhulislam wore a white fur. The grand vizier was dressed in a white satin coat covered in sable fur and wore a thirty-five-centimeter turban composed of a cylinder-shaped base around which he wrapped a white muslin cloth ornamented by a red cloth at the tip.[22] All other ministers were cloaked in a sable fur covered in silver brocade, with the same turban as the grand vizier.[23] But so little Mehmed would not be scared or frightened, hundreds of others, such as the Janissaries with their oversized handlebar mustaches and high caps, were hindered from taking the oath lest he be overwhelmed by the crowd.[24] Their customary shout, "Let us meet at the Golden Apple," or the capital of the Christian world, which at that time referred to Vienna, was silenced.[25] After the subdued ceremony, the sun king then took a nap in the royal ward guarded by harem eunuchs.[26]

One could imagine a prodigal son being entertained by court jesters, fools, and midgets, living a quiet life of luxury and ease, as in a contemporary Ottoman miniature portrait circa 1650 by an anonymous Ottoman painter. It depicts a tiny, chubby child with a thick neck wearing a pink, fur-lined cloak over an orange garment clutching the arms of the throne as he half sits, half

FIGURE 1.2. Mehmed IV as child sultan. Anonymous, "Sultan Mechemet Imp. de'Turchi," Staatliche Museen zu Berlin, Preußischer Kulturbesitz, Kunstbibliothek, Lipperheide OZ 52, 1. Reproduced with permission.

leans on a cushion while two colorfully dressed midgets clap and cheer and distract him.[27] Little Mehmed looks not at his brightly dressed entertainers, both of whom are smaller than he is, one of whom is bearded and the other wearing a purple cap covered in golden stars, but off to the distance.

The seven-year-old became sultan, if not making the world tranquil then at least quelling rebellion; his father, with the consent of his valide sultan, was placed under house arrest in a room in the palace. When they came for him, Ibrahim said, "'Hey! Traitors! What are you doing? Am I not the sultan?' Karaçelebizade responded 'No, you are not the sultan. You destroyed the world by neglecting the matters of Islamic law and religion, skipped over the five daily prayers, spent your time amusing yourself heedless of the affairs of state, filled the world with bribery, corruption and tyranny, and squandered the treasury. You are not suitable for the throne.'" Ibrahim was incredulous that they would put a tiny boy who barely came up to his waist on the throne in his place.[28]

A Ceremonial Visit to Eyüp and the Execution of Ibrahim

Nearly a week after Ibrahim was dethroned and put under house arrest and his son and future hope of the dynasty, Prince Mehmed, became Sultan Mehmed IV, the royal family boarded a skiff at the imperial boathouse down the hill from Topkapı Palace and took a short journey up the Golden Horn to make a pilgrimage to the district of Eyüp, a fundamental part of an Ottoman sultan's enthronement.[29] The purpose of the boy's first trip beyond the palace walls was for him to visit the city's most sacred cemetery, gird the sword of the sultanate in its most holy mosque, acquire both the charisma of a man who fought for Muhammad and that of his sultanic predecessors, ride on horseback through the city mimicking Mehmed II's triumphant path after the conquest, and, finally, to display his munificence to his subjects, who would be able to see him for the first time.[30] On the return journey overland, with great ceremony he entered Edirne Gate and visited the tombs of previous sultans. His hazel eyes were tinged with kohl. On top of an embroidered gold inner garment he wore a spotted violet and gold embroidered cloak. On his head he wore a sixty-five-centimeter cylinder wrapped in fine white cloth, with two aigrettes; in the upper one was a green emerald the size of half an egg. On his return to Topkapı Palace he showed his face to the people by dispersing coins to the poor and passing through the city markets.[31] People who paid careful attention to his face noticed "his radiant, noble beauty."[32] And when they saw him they cried, "May God help him."

Each neighborhood and district of Istanbul that the sultan passed through had a particular character. Although many neighborhoods were marked by the predominance of one group, no neighborhoods were exclusive to members of only one religious group. Christians, Jews, and Muslims interacted on a daily basis, in the market, in the tavern, on the street, during public festivals and imperial celebrations, in the Shariah court and other institutions. By the end of the seventeenth century the city had an estimated population of between six hundred thousand and three quarters of a million, including an estimated 350,000 to 450,000 Muslims, Sunni, including those who were members of diverse Sufi orders, and Alevi (members of a heterodox offshoot of Shi'ism) of all ethnic backgrounds, from southeastern European to central Asian; 200,000 to 250,000 Christians, Armenian, Assyrian, Catholic, and Orthodox; and 50,000 to 60,000 Jews, Ashkenazi (central European), Karaite (those who do not recognize the "oral law" of other Jews), Romaniot (Greek-speaking, rooted in the Byzantine era), and Sephardi (Spanish and Portuguese).[33] As the royal family boarded the vessel their gaze would be directed up the European side of the Bosporus, where they would see Beşiktaş, a town located on the straits within sight of Topkapı Palace, which had a mixed population and was known for the octagonal tomb of the sixteenth-century admiral of the Ottoman navy and conqueror of much of northern Africa, Barbaros Hayrettin Pasha, built by the famous Ottoman architect Sinan on the coast upon a foundation of ruins of the Byzantine columns located in the same area; the seaside mansions, gardens, and vineyards of Ottoman men and women of state and royalty; and the Mevlevi dervish lodge on the coast overlooking the Bosporus, a Sufi center known for its rituals, which incorporated prayer with dance and music.[34] Beşiktaş was also the staging ground where ships built at the imperial dockyards would dock to board soldiers for campaign in the Mediterranean. Further along the Bosporus were the villages of Ortaköy, "chock full of infidels and Jews," which boasted hundreds of taverns, along with gardens and vineyards, and wealthy Jews who were seaside mansion owners; Kuruçeşme, also noted for its seaside residences of notables, numerous gardens and vineyards, and Jewish inhabitants; Arnavutköy, all of whose inhabitants were Orthodox Christians from the Black Sea (renowned for their hard biscuits) or Jews (famous for being soft, pleasure lovers and musicians); İstinye, site of a well-known harbor with an ample bounty of fruits and vegetables from the many gardens and fish from the Bosporus, a predominantly Orthodox Christian village chosen by Sheikhulislam Yahya Efendi for his waterside mansion; and Yeniköy, known for pastrami made from elk and roe meat captured by Janissary hunters and cured for the sultan, biscuits made in over a hundred stores, taverns such as Little Priest and Son of the Priest, its "fabulously rich" Orthodox Christian merchants from Trabzon and anti-Jewish Laz who made sure Jews never set foot there.[35]

Gazing across from where they embarked, the royal family would have observed Galata, the district directly across the Golden Horn from the peninsula of Istanbul. It was also the main city view from the royal vantage point in the outermost Baghdad Kiosk built by Murad IV in the fourth courtyard of the palace. Galata's most imposing landmark remains a thirteenth-century Genoese tower, although in the seventeenth century it was without the mosque-like cap added centuries later. In this district Catholics and western Europeans, especially French and Italians, lived paradoxically along with Moriscos, Muslims who had ostensibly converted to Catholicism, who had fled from Catholic persecution in Spain, and smaller numbers of Orthodox Christians, Armenians, Muslims, and Jews. Galata had been a Genoese commercial colony in Byzantine Constantinople and remained an important entrepôt, with large warehouses and workshops another defining feature.[36] Following surrender to Ottoman forces in 1453, most Galata Catholics became poll-tax-paying subjects of the sultan, while some merchants became resident foreigners. Some of their churches were converted to mosques immediately following the district's surrender to Sultan Mehmed II, including Saints Paul and Dominic, which became the Mosque of the Arabs; the bell tower became a minaret. Other churches, such as San Michele, were converted during the following century. Yet in 1648, Galata presented a Christian landscape to the gaze: the predominant buildings that made up Galata's skyline remained the Genoese tower and imposing Catholic churches.

As the skiff made its way up the Golden Horn, the royal family would have had a chance to look back on the tip of the peninsula of Istanbul and up the hill, first to Topkapı Palace and then to the immense structure formerly known as Hagia Sophia, the grandest cathedral in Christendom, the Church of Divine Wisdom, which had been converted by Sultan Mehmed II into the most imposing mosque in the Islamic world. On the other side of Hagia Sophia stood Sultan Ahmed I's six-minaret mosque, its massive dome completed in 1617, built on the ruins of the last Byzantine palace adjacent to the Hippodrome. The two imposing imperial structures of the Sultan Ahmed Mosque and Topkapı Palace, established by Sultan Mehmed II, flanked Hagia Sophia.

The royal family could then redirect their gaze to the port district of Eminönü in the well-situated and safe harbor on the Golden Horn opposite Galata, a kaleidoscope of goods and people. Eminönü was the embarkation and disembarkation point for the goods of international trade, such as timber, cloth, iron, lead, tin, dye, leather, cotton, and precious stones, taxed by the head controller of customs. The goods were then either stored in the great warehouses lining the coast, such as the huge bins of wheat and barley that fed the large city, or handled in the major trading houses inland at Tahtakale and uphill stretching all the way to the old and new markets, including the covered bazaar established by Sultan Mehmed II.[37] According to the Ottoman Armenian writer Eremya Çelebi, the fish sold in the market nearby were apparently so colorful that a person walking past the fishmongers might think he or she was walking through a flower garden in spring.[38] Merchants from Yemen unloaded coffee, traders from India brought valuable cloth, Crimean slave-traders disgorged their human cargo of Circassians and Georgians to be sold as slaves, a central pillar of the Ottoman economy, and hundreds of porters carried their immense burdens on poles.[39] Eminönü Square bustled with crowds coming and going. Skiffs for hire constantly dropped off and carried people to and fro along the Golden Horn and up the Bosporus. Noticeable about the district was its Jewish neighborhood, stretching along the coast to the walls of the palace. The Eminönü region, or the area bordered by Jews' Gate/Fish Gate and Garden Gate, was almost entirely made up of Istanbul's Jewish residents, two-thirds of whom lived in this district.[40] Istanbul Jews lived and worked primarily in the economic center of the city on the Golden Horn. Eminönü appeared as a partially Islamized landscape. It was also the site of the hulking foundation of an incomplete sixteenth-century imperial mosque constructed as high as the arches or grilles above the first windows half a century before, yet "like an orphan son its arches did not reach the prime of manhood, instead remaining deficient and incomplete. According to its foregoing condition it became abandoned."[41]

Even with its shadow of a mosque at its heart, Eminönü sat beneath the largest and most imposing mosque in the city built by the Ottomans, that of Sultan Suleiman I. It contains four huge ancient porphyry marble pillars, two of which are Byzantine pillars found in Istanbul. Completed in 1557, it allowed thousands of Muslims to pray simultaneously beneath its lofty dome and in its immense courtyard.[42] The mosque also articulates Muslim confidence in placing a stunning mosque on a dominant hill in the city.

Further along the Golden Horn en route to Eyüp the skiff passed the imperial dockyards near Galata, which were busy preparing vessels for the ongoing costly battles with Venice; the ships would pass Topkapı Palace, take on troops at Beşiktaş, and then sail on to Gallipoli, Chios, and finally Crete. The skiff passed visible Armenian and Orthodox Christian settlements on the coast of the peninsula of Istanbul, including Fener, where the Orthodox Patriarchate has been located since 1601. Finally, as the skiff neared its destination, the royal family could observe Hasköy across the water. It was the only district the majority of whose inhabitants were Jewish, and it was renowned for sacred springs, the Jewish cemetery up the hill, and an estimated one hundred taverns, where, according to the records of Shariah courts, which had to arbitrate brawls that arose between drunken men, Christians, Jews, and Muslims rubbed shoulders. The same was true of the bars along the Bosporus and in Galata. The taverns in Hasköy served, among other drinks an Earring-Wearing Jew's liquor made from musky apple juice and a muscatel grape wine made from the grapes he grew. The gardens and vineyards of Hasköy were famous for their lemons and Seville oranges, peaches, and pomegranates.

After the royal family disembarked at the royal pier in Eyüp, its members soon arrived at the Grand Mosque. Located in the most holy Muslim district of the city, it was a pilgrimage site. It was commonly believed that when Ottoman forces took Constantinople in 1453, Sultan Mehmed II's spiritual advisor, the dervish Akşemseddin, had located the tomb of Abu Ayyub, Muhammad's companion, who had been among the Arab Muslim armies attempting to conquer Byzantine Constantinople. This discovery gave the Ottomans further legitimacy in the Islamic world. In this holy space of Muslim inspiration, a most uninspiring little boy weighted down by large rubies and emeralds was girded with the mighty sword, which was about as long as Mehmed was tall. Believed to have been used by Muhammad, it was taken from Cairo in 1517, when the Ottomans conquered the Mamluk Empire, previous possessors of the sacred precincts of Mecca and Medina.

The leading members of the administration and dynasty took this journey up the Golden Horn through their diverse city to complete the ceremonies replacing Ibrahim with an undistinguished candidate, his young son, at that time overshadowed by two women who competed for power. Nearby hovered Mehmed's elderly grandmother, Kösem Sultan, who considered herself Mehmed's guardian. She was a well-known figure in the palace, having long been a significant player in dynastic politics. She was the favorite concubine of Sultan Ahmed I (reigned 1603–17), mother and regent of Sultan Murad IV (reigned 1623–40), who was twelve years old when he became sultan, and Ibrahim (reigned 1640–48), who was at the time the only surviving male member of the dynasty. During all of these reigns Kösem Sultan played a role in conducting the administration and had much experience ruling in place of mad or child sultans.[43] She was a religious woman, inclined to support Sufis of the Mevlevi order, which had long been associated with the Ottoman urban elite. The Mevlevi Mehmed Pasha presided over Mehmed IV's sword-girding ceremony at the Grand Mosque.[44] Also present was the sultan's twentysomething mother, Hatice Turhan Sultan, a Russian taken captive when a girl by the Ottoman ally, the Crimean Khan, brought to the Ottoman palace, and given as a gift to the valide sultan Kösem Sultan. Later she would have her patron strangled. Meanwhile, she would have to bide her time before becoming as influential as the boy's grandmother. Even after her son became sultan, Hatice Turhan was young, not yet worldly wise, unable to handle affairs of state. For this reason, Kösem Sultan could not be banished so easily to the Old Palace in Fatih at the middle of the peninsula of Istanbul, as was customary for the mothers of former sultans. This septuagenarian who had played a key role in Ottoman affairs for half a century as favorite, mother, and grandmother of sultans remained as regent and the most important member of the dynasty.[45]

Even if the sultan was only a boy, the water-borne procession to the holy Muslim tomb and return to the palace overland in a great military procession offered the dynasty an opportunity to display to the public its link with Muhammad, its historical continuity, and its latest leader.[46] The sentiment of a court poet, that the enthronement of the boy sultan made the world serene, however, could not have been further from the truth. The question facing the dynasty at this point was who would actually run the empire. One of the first imperial decrees issued in Mehmed IV's name concerned the challenge that his father posed. It states that Ibrahim was stirring insurrection with the help of his loyal followers, making it necessary to "remove this injurious thorn from the skirt of the realm and Muslim people."[47] Some within the palace desired to spring the former sultan from prison and reinthrone him.[48] He had numerous supporters among the harem eunuchs and palace guards, and there was a "gathering storm of opposition" to the little sultan.[49] Some began to claim that "because he had not reached puberty, he is not ready or prepared to take measures for the order of the kingdom. It is necessary to again enthrone his father."[50] Knowing that so long as the deposed sultan was alive the threat of rebellion was real, and wishing to protect their class interests, men of the bureaucracy and military asked for a legal opinion to execute Ibrahim.[51] The sheikhulislam gave an affirmative answer. Thus leaders of all three branches of state sought the sultan's execution because they reasoned that to prevent rebellion it was necessary to kill him. The former valide sultan apparently wept while praying before the mantle of Muhammad, agreeing to spare Ibrahim the indignity of imprisonment in favor of journeying to the afterlife. Still, she asked, "Who gave this man the evil eye?" In the end, she allowed him to be killed, just as she gave permission for him to be deposed. She articulated the fact that only she could make the final decision concerning who sat on the throne and whether the sultan lived or died: "They said my son Ibrahim was not suitable for the sultanate. I said 'depose him.' They said his presence is harmful, I said 'let him be removed.' I said 'let him be executed.' If anyone is under my protection, it is my son."[52]

When the grand vizier and the sheikhulislam entered Ibrahim's chamber with the executioners, he was wearing a rose-colored satin robe, red breeches ornamented with gold, and a skullcap on his head, and held a Qur'an in his hand. Wailing, he asked, "Why will you kill me? This is God's book, you tyrants, what authority permits you to murder me?"[53] Three weeks after he was deposed, and soon after Mehmed IV made his journey to Eyüp, the merciless hand of the executioner Kara Ali executed the thirty-five-year-old former ruler with an oiled lasso.[54] A miniature painting from the period depicts a stern-looking executioner, without a cloak or overcoat, sleeves rolled up, the coil of oiled rope in his right hand, the tip of the rope in his left, an oversized executioner's sword tucked into his sash as he moves off the page, presumably toward his victim.[55]

2

A Decade of Crisis

Ottoman chroniclers writing during Mehmed IV's minority gave
Ibrahim's murder meaning by composing didactic works that fit into
the genre of advice literature (advice to kings, or mirror for princes,
Nasihatname) in which elite authors, aggravated by their own loss of
status and privilege and the unraveling of a legal order that served
their interests, articulated their grievances in the framework of
declining moral values that threatened the empire and dynasty. Their
works mainly consisted of writing that consciously aims to warn the
ruler to heed the mistakes of his predecessor and not repeat them.
They depict most of the decade of the 1650s as a period of startling
insecurity for subject and ruler alike, blaming the situation on the
weakness of the sultan and the power of female royals. The solution
to the crisis offered by the writers of the advice literature was for a
strong sultan to reclaim power from the valide sultan, take charge,
and clean up the mess, making sure men were on top.

This chapter provides the crucial context of disorder and turmoil
perceived as crises within which conversion to piety among the leading members of the administration and dynasty are situated. Many
scholars writing about conversion agree that conversion is often
preceded by crisis, whether at the societal or personal level. Because
context is the "total environment in which conversion transpires,"
a context of crisis sets the stage for religious change to occur. When
that crisis is severe, prolonged, extensive, and external, offering a
startling contrast with what came before, a discrepancy between the

ideal and reality, people may be compelled to look inward and try to understand how their religious beliefs and practices triggered such a troubled situation.[1]

Before Mehmed IV underwent his own conversion and subsequently embarked on a journey of bringing others to his interpretation of Islam and waging war, he had to first mature and weather the crises triggered during his father and predecessor Ibrahim's reign that the empire and dynasty faced. Mehmed IV's chaotic enthronement, following an uprising and the dethronement of Ibrahim in 1648, set the unfortunate tone for the first decade of his rule. This chapter surveys the interrelated administrative, economic and financial, and military crises that beset the empire during Mehmed IV's minority. These crises included a sorry parade of grand viziers and power struggles between the leading women of the dynasty, financial quandaries, war with Venice, and continual rebellion. These issues are presented to provide the background against which can be understood the emergence of the convert maker Mehmed IV in the 1660s, as depicted by contemporary chroniclers.

Making Sense of Ibrahim's Execution and a Turbulent Decade

We cannot reach the past other than by viewing it mediated through the artifacts that survive in stone or script. Historical narratives and archival documents are the textual remnants of that lost world used to grasp the past. Texts allow no more than a glimpse of a no longer present material reality and of how people in the past perceived or imagined that reality. Ottoman chronicles are merely accounts or stories about what happened; they are not complete portraits of what happened, they do not represent the totality of what occurred.[2]

Historians attempt to narrate a history or give an account of what appeared to have happened in an era. They also try to understand how the period about which they write was depicted at the time, how that epoch was understood by the writers who lived through it. Historians have a duty to attempt to draw a picture of a period of time and describe changes over time while acknowledging that access to the worldviews of the past emerge primarily from literary sources shaped by men who not only imagined the world from a distinct standpoint, but who also wrote about it with an eye toward past models and future posterity.

As Gabrielle Spiegel argues, "What is the past but a once material existence now silenced, extant only as sign and as sign drawing to itself chains of conflicting interpretations that hover over its absent presence and compete for possession of the relics, seeking to invest traces of significance upon the bodies of the dead?" Spiegel offers a "theory of the middle ground," which encourages historians to view historical documents as sources embedded in a knowable social world that allow us to assume the material reality and lived experience of the past, while at the same time perceiving historical documents as texts that display a certain linguistic construction or literary consciousness of that world.[3] She argues that we can accept that language reflects that world because it is mimetic, documenting and describing the past to which it refers, describing a perceived reality, and constitutive of that world or performative and generative, being a self-reflective, literary discourse.

Spiegel's approach can be used to read the chronicles of the seventeenth-century Ottoman Empire. As in earlier periods of Islamic history, their authors were court officials who often witnessed events as they unfolded, had close relations with the leading members of the administration and the dynasty, and incorporated official documents, which they may have composed, into their works. They were "members of a class who shared a common educational background, certain stylistic approaches to literary composition and specific political concerns; their writings therefore exhibit many common assumptions as to the purposes and the proper content of history, as well as how it should be written."[4]

Ottoman chronicles of the seventeenth century often display a unity of form and content.[5] The meaning of Ibrahim's deposition and murder was determined after the fact and revealed in the future by authors who used it to articulate their understandings of the era.[6] Many of them were concerned with writing "ethical-rhetorical" history, using rhetorical styles to express ethical concerns in order to articulate a usable past for the present audience.[7] Their works provide insight into the imaginal world of late seventeenth-century writers. By the time Mehmed IV turned sixteeen in 1657, Karaçelebizade, Katip Çelebi, and Solakzade had completed their works of history addressed to the sovereign. They begin their narratives with tumult, noise, anger, uprising, confusion, and disorder, making for good drama. The finest example is *The Gardens of Fruit*, written by Sheikhulislam Karaçelebizade after his tumultuous period in office (1651–52), composed in the guise of a memoir while he was in exile in Bursa and reflecting back on the first ten years of Mehmed IV's reign. In the critical view of Karaçelebizade, Ottoman society faced insurmountable woes. Even if we bear in mind that Karaçelebizade was a disgruntled, dismissed official writing after being banished from the court, labeled full of wrath, excessively critical, and even slanderous by a contemporary writer, we cannot miss how members of the Ottoman elite such as this former sheikhulislam articulated what they saw as the woes of their era and what needed to be done to remedy them, namely, the restoration of the idealized system with a morally virtuous male ruler at its head.[8]

Summing up the state of the empire in the 1650s, Karaçelebizade turns to the "circle of justice" concept, a favorite theme of Ottoman writers of advice literature. The production of an Ottoman service class created a group self-conscious of its identity, privileged place, and history, whose members saw themselves as the bearers and articulators of the Ottoman way.[9] This led to the birth of the literary genre of the advice to kings. The political and social commentary assumed that life was golden during the time of Mehmed the Conqueror and Suleiman I, between 1451 and 1566, when there was an equitable system of taxation and distribution of positions, a rational organization of the administration and military, and order in the empire. It posited that the empire was ruled with justice, war was effective, and the spoils of war went to the production of magnificent mosques benefiting the public. Writers complained that statutes were no longer followed, that long-standing custom was violated.

Karaçelebizade continued the line of critique begun by earlier writers, such as Mustafa Ali and Karaçelebizade's contemporary Katip Çelebi.[10] In toto, these were the violations of the Ottoman system that they witnessed: infiltration of elite orders, military inefficiency, and corruption, especially of the *timar* system of military land grants, since they were no longer always given to actual sipahi, but to others who passed them on to their sons, and the auctioning of positions, which had ethical as well as financial implications. People on the imperial payroll were given offices higher than their deserved status. The sultan could no longer meet his obligations to all these people on the rolls. Changing the relation between the sultan and those in the provinces disrupted the elite structured society. The military class was infiltrated by commoners and foreigners, allegedly bad and unworthy folk who swelled its ranks: the size of the elite Janissary corps and of the sipahi group each quadrupled.[11] Claim to their share in imperial largesse led to the elites' believing there was an erosion of justice, military inefficiency, and corruption.

Mustafa Ali began his *Counsel for Sultans* by arguing that it is essential that servitors who proved their worth gradually increase in rank and positions. In his notion of fairness, the palace-educated, Istanbul-appointed servitors would be rewarded, not disloyal Kurds and Turks on the fringes with independent sources of power, who would acquire more power when given higher status. Mustafa Ali and others complained that the established path of ascension to the top regulated relations with peers and maintained a smoothly operating administration, but it could not be relied on when people wanted to enter the military class just to gain power. He posited that in the past there were clearer relations between people. But new entry paths to power emerged; there were new ways to be "in." When Anatolian Muslim commoners shared in the privileges of the sultan's servants, shattering the

social and political foundations of military administration, it caused a rending of the social contract.

The Ottomans were in part to blame for their own turn away from the norm.
At the end of the sixteenth century, they had begun to use mercenary units
equipped with firearms that more often than not acted on their own as armed
bands using handguns.[12] The government used them because it needed a larger
infantry with firepower to face constant warfare with the Habsburgs and Safavids, and they seemed to be an inexpensive and effective solution to financial
and military problems. In turn, they drew peasants away from agriculture and
into military pursuits, whether legitimate as mercenaries, or illegitimate, ran-
sacking and rebelling, as after demobilization they often kept their weapons
and turned to banditry or became mercenaries for governors and local military
leaders, further hurting the economy as rebels devastated Anatolia, especially
between 1596 and 1607 but then throughout the seventeenth century.[13] At the
same time, the Ottoman monetary system collapsed, leading to inflation and
devaluation and impoverishing the elite military class. Rebels controlled parts
of Anatolia, and even threatened Istanbul. This led to decentralization as military commanders and pashas built up independent strength. Because the central government could not maintain order in the provinces, provincial people
turned to the upstart military men for self-defense. The government tried to
disarm and disband the mercenaries, but without success. Sipahis were inef-
fective against them. The only solution was to incorporate them into the military and to reward rebels, which further undermined elite morale.

The problem, undetected by Mustafa Ali and others in the elite, was that
the political economy of the Eurasian empires had changed.[14] A decline in
military prebends (timars), commercialization, and the growth of large estate
holders led to the development of ever more complex societies and the rise of
provincial notables. Topkapı Palace had formerly been the authority that legiti-
mated power, trained an elite, and sent it out to control the empire. It had created the force for maintaining social stability, by keeping people in their correct
social class, and economic stability, by controlling prices through price fixing
and directing trade, especially the sending of goods to Istanbul. The administration was supposed to regulate the market while ensuring the flow of supply and
keeping the currency sound. Yet it failed. Price controls were central to keeping
goods flowing at fair prices, yet controlled to prevent shortages, and to uphold-
ing the economy that upheld the power structure and social structure. With free
prices, others benefited. Officials tried to halt the flow of wealth to commoners,
to merchants, to foreigners. They wanted the economy to be subsumed to the
political and power structure, capital to be consumed by the upper strata alone,
to hinder the distribution of wealth and power. They understood all too well

what was happening. The guiding economic idea was that the peasants, not merchants, should produce the wealth and that the sultan would distribute the surplus. But this was no longer possible by the seventeenth century, when market forces became so prevalent and a nouveau riche class came into being. New cities such as Izmir on the Mediterranean coast emerged illegally and began to direct trade away from Istanbul as the empire was flooded with western European coins, which began to be used as the currency of exchange.[15] Elite writers were not ready to let go of the primacy of politics in the economy, not ready for market forces and nonelites to displace them, and not able to recognize or accept how increased monetization (paying mercenaries) meant that pay and not patronage was most important. What had become of the Ottoman way?

Karaçelebizade's plea for a return to the "circle of justice" thus becomes understandable in this context. He urged the men of state to heed the advice of this proverb:

> You cannot have a king without subjects.
> If you do not have subjects you do not have an army.
> You cannot have an army if you do not have wealth.
> You cannot have wealth unless you have a territory.
> There is no territory without subjects.
> There are no subjects if there is no justice.

Returning to a Suleimanic model, the author relates the tale of how one day Suleiman I asked, "Who is the protector of the good fortune of the world?" All those around him responded in unison: "You are!" But Suleiman I said, "No. It is the commoners because they cultivate and plow the earth without rest, feeding us."[16]

In the critical view of Karaçelebizade, Ottoman society faced insurmountable woes in the 1650s. Concerning the military, the navy was headed by cowards "who rather than acquiring praise on the path of ghaza, their gallbladders burst from fear and they tremble with the terror of anxiety."[17] The fleet was incapable in battle; the Janissaries were out of control and constantly rebelling. As for the administration, most officeholders were corrupt, caring only about personal profit at the expense of those below them; it was a free-for-all, as selfish men who did not care about the good of the empire took all they could from it; decent officials were dismissed based on slander. The royal household was little better: there was division among power factions in the palace; the sultan was nonexistent, hardly a presence as his mother and grandmother were battling it out; and no one was thinking about the good of the dynasty. One may be tempted to dismiss these complaints, including the one that religious scholars (including the author) were mistreated and disrespected, as little more than the idealization by a disaffected member of the elite of a golden age of justice and military success that never was, nor was ever conceived as such.[18] But Karaçelebizade put his finger on real problems of the age.

A Sorry Parade of Grand Viziers and Power
Struggles between Royal Women

Larger causes of such unrest were administrative, economic and financial, and military. Some authors emphasize the weaknesses of the leading administrators in the empire: a string of twelve incapable, feeble, and often senile grand viziers served terms of one to twelve months in office between 1648 and 1656. Other writers emphasize larger structural reasons greater than the frailities of any one man. Katip Çelebi points out that these grand viziers were appointed or dismissed not due to their weaknesses, for some were actually courageous, but because "the Janissary commanders predominated, the administration of state was in their hands, and appointments were made according to their approval."[19] This sentiment was echoed by contemporary western Europeans as well. Sir Thomas Roe wrote, "The Turkish emperor is now but the Janizaries treasurer."[20] It is not accidental that when Kurdish Preacher Mustafa, employed as one of the sultan's imams beginning in 1664, writes in the mid-1670s of the grand viziers who served between 1648 and 1656, he spills more ink describing their deaths than their lives.

Ottoman chroniclers focus on the succession of grand viziers who held office during the first eight years of Mehmed IV's reign, whose names become a blur before the reader. Representative was Melek (Angel) Ahmed Pasha (1650–51), who became grand vizier on condition that the Janissary commanders would not meddle in the affairs of state.[21] But Melek Ahmed Pasha had his hands tied since the grand vizier had no influence whatsoever. Symbolic of the affairs of state at the time, Melek Ahmed Pasha desired to build an immense sailing galleon for himself. It was constructed near Garden Gate, the most crowded and visible public square in the city. People gathered in awe to watch the enormous hulk of the ship rise above the harbor and proclaimed that "such a galleon had never been built before."[22] When it was ready to be set afloat, a great crowd gathered to view the launch of the magnificent galleon, presided over by the leading men of state. After the ropes were loosened the ship was let down on runners into the Golden Horn. When the ship entered the sea, it immediately began to take on water. It capsized, and then "the grand vizier's boat sank in the sea with a sigh."[23] The grand vizier cried "and the immense crowd was speechless from shock."[24] Crews of other boats could not pull the galleon out of the water and it was lost, along with scores of men who had been letting the ship into the water. Two years later Evliya Çelebi, Katip Çelebi's younger contemporary, a travel writer who wrote a self-promoting work that aimed to entertain, educate, and criticize society, dreamed about the boat. Melek Ahmed Pasha interpreted the dream to mean that the boat was his body. The top-heavy bow symbolized that he had been "too concerned with worldly pomp" and had a swelled head, which caused his downfall.[25] Melek Ahmed Pasha's half-submerged ship symbolized the state of the empire in the 1650s as depicted in the narrative sources of the era. The captains of the ship of state were not capable of bringing it to safety.

In 1651, following an uprising of merchants during Melek Ahmed Pasha's vizierate, which actually caused his dismissal, Janissaries intended to dethrone the sultan and even marched to the gates of Topkapı Palace. All of the sultan's servants within its gates were compelled to take arms to repulse the rebels.[26] This brought to a swift end the rivalry between the factions allied with the former valide sultan and the current one. Immediately after Mehmed IV's enthronement, the parties of the two leading Ottoman women, Kösem Sultan and Hatice Turhan Sultan, had competed to be the boy's regent. According to Solakzade, the harem eunuchs and inner pages connected to their patron, Hatice Turhan, were not able to intervene in the affairs of state and could no longer endure the former valide's dominion in alliance with the Janissary commanders.[27] At first they made plans only to drive her away from the palace, then they claimed that the former valide was plotting to murder Mehmed IV and his mother and allying with the Janissary commanders to enthrone Prince Suleiman. The treason demanded that she be permanently removed from palace politics. The group in the harem who supported the valide sultan Hatice Turhan was determined to kill Kösem Sultan.[28] It was a matter of factional politics in the palace; a powerful person makes enemies. Acting on the pretext that the former valide was attempting to reclaim the throne, they had her and the head of the palace guards killed.[29] The Janissaries who sided with Hatice Turhan had to fight their way to the suite of Kösem Sultan. She hid in a secret compartment inside, but they found and killed the seventy-year-old woman; the giant palace guard Tiny Mehmed strangled her.[30] Evliya Çelebi puts it crudely, claiming that she was killed when he "twisted her braids around her neck."[31] The brutal murder of Kösem Sultan in 1651 barely three years after her own son had been killed caused tumult and rioting in Istanbul and resulted in the execution of hundreds of men.

The death of Kösem Sultan contributed to a dampening of the power of the Janissary commanders and a rise in the authority of the young valide sultan and her supporters, particularly the chief eunuch of the harem. Following the

murder of Kösem Sultan, and after a fatwa was delivered justifying the killing of Janissaries, the banner of Muhammad was taken out and placed before
the outermost or Imperial Gate. This flag was usually taken out at the start of
imperial campaigns against Christian or Shi'i powers. To implement a general
levy of all able-bodied men for public defense, criers ran through the streets
of Istanbul shouting, "Whoever is a Muslim, let him rally around the banner
of the religion. Those who do not come are rendered infidels and they are di-
vorced from their [Muslim] wives."[32] Within an hour, more than one hundred
thousand heavily armed men gathered. Fortunately for the Janissaries, a bloody
battle was avoided. Some of the ringleaders were given new positions, and others were killed. For fifty years Kösem Sultan had been on the stage of Ottoman
politics and she and her men were loath to exit. They feared their young com-
petitor, who was terrified of them. Many leading Janissaries were executed or
imprisoned; the sheikhulislam was exiled for being their ally.

Bloodshed and rebellion accompanied the period in office of another typical
grand vizier, the governor-general of Aleppo İpşir Mustafa Pasha, who served
from 1654 to 1655. Just when one might have thought a worse person could
not have been found for the most important administrative position in the empire, the court selected this pasha, who had rebelled against the sultan and
was the relative of Abaza Mehmed Pasha, a governor-general turned rebel who
had sought to avenge the 1622 murder of Sultan Osman II, Young Osman.[33]
Similar to the mature Mehmed IV, İpşir Mustafa Pasha excelled in horseman-
ship, javelin, swordplay, and hunting.[34] He also was known as a religious, if not
obedient, short man who stood up for no one, respecting neither ceremony nor
rank.[35] People were amazed that a person with a reputation for injustice who
had sided with the sipahis would be made grand vizier; they believed the position was offered with the intention of bringing him under control.[36] Ordered
to depart Aleppo and make haste to the capital, this rebel, fearing the court
offered him the position as a pretext to destroy the power he had accrued and
as a means to keep an eye on him in the capital, was in no hurry. He met with
dismissed military officials, gathered a militia, and took four months to reach
Istanbul.[37] When he arrived with tens of thousands of armed men, Istanbul
was filled with sedition: "The city of Constantinople was like the Day of Judgement, the heavens full of battles."[38] The Hippodrome was filled with "sipahis,
Janissaries, the rabble, armorers, artillerymen and gunners, other soldiers,
scoundrels, and bandits" who opposed the grand vizier and his army and the
sheikhulislam.[39] Soon after his arrival, the Janissaries pressed their demand
that this grand vizier, who not only represented the sipahis but also dared cancel their payments owed in arrears, be killed. According to Mehmed Halife,
they assembled in the biggest protest in history.[40] Because there was no way to

quiet down the Janissaries this time, in the end, "they had İpşir's head cut off and caused the bird of his soul to fly to the plains of the hereafter."[41] The head was sent to the crowd gathered in the Hippodrome, who stuck it on the end of a javelin and paraded it around the plaza.[42]

The last forsaken grand vizier of the period was the octogenarian Damascus governor Boynueğri Mehmed Pasha, who was appointed in 1656. The most interesting debate about him concerned the manliness of his name: was he *boynueğri* (bowed neck), or *boynuyaralı* (wounded neck)? During his brief period in office, which lasted but a couple of crucial months, the Ottoman navy suffered the worst rout in nearly a century, and the treasury was utterly depleted. While the sultan was taking pleasure in the company of his boon companions and listening to poetry recitations, news arrived of the rout of the navy. This caused many people in Istanbul to proclaim, "Our sultan must certainly return to Islambol [full of Islam]. This is no time for riding and promenading about, or amusing himself in parks and gardens. The infidels will arrive in Islambol tomorrow or the next day. The straits have been closed. There will be scarcity and famine in Islambol. What is he doing in Üsküdar?" Learning of this outcry, the sultan immediately crossed the Bosporus. His mother ordered a military campaign. But Boynueğri Mehmed Pasha said, "If 20,000 purses can be procured from the treasury, fantastic, I can launch a campaign. Otherwise, no way."[43] Without guns and treasure, how could the Ottomans launch a war?[44] Although he was correct in his judgment, the grand vizier was imprisoned in Yedikule on the Marmara Sea coast, where foreign ambassadors whiled away their lives etching the number of days of their captivity into the walls.[45]

Financial Quandaries

The twelve grand viziers who served between 1648 and 1656 were unsuccessful in their attempts to fill the depleted imperial treasury, regulate the coinage, and enable prosperity to return. False and worthless coins floated freely in circulation, and merchants and Janissaries clashed over the value of the coinage. Janissary commanders, seeking a great profit, forced Istanbul merchants to accept their debased aspers, including coins made of scrap metal, and exchange them at a great loss for gold coins, which they compelled money changers to accept in return for more valuable silver.[46] When the merchants went to the grand vizier Melek Ahmed Pasha and told him it was difficult to pay their store rents and that they could not pay new taxes, the grand vizier scolded them. According to Karaçelebizade, the grand vizier, "anxious about the dearth" of coins in the treasury, "made many abominable choices and distressed the merchants;

while one wound had not healed he opened another, harming those unfortu-nate ones further."⁴⁷ But he was obstinate: "When they petitioned that he annul the decision to decrease the weight of coins, he refused; meanwhile, since it was unsafe to send salaries of the fort commanders of Azov [Crimea] by sea [due to Cossack patrols], they had to send [devalued coins] by land," causing the value of the weak asper to fall even further. They had sent messengers to Istanbul to collect their salaries, but since Cossacks controlled the sea, it was not possible to send their pay directly. Corrupt officials, including the treasurer, exchanged the promised pay for clipped coins and gave them to the tradesmen, who were supposed to exchange them for gold that would be sent to the troops in Azov.⁴⁸ They revolted instead.

Merchants had become conscious that, like the Janissaries and sipahis, they too had a shared interest. And when that interest was threatened it was time to act. In 1650 they closed their stores, took to the streets, and rose in rebellion, demanding the dismissal of the grand vizier and execution of Janissary com-manders. A great crowd of fifteen thousand artisans and merchants marched to the home of Sheikhulislam Karaçelebizade. They wept, rending their clothes, crying that their complaints fell on deaf ears, that they suffered from harm-ful innovations, such as monthly extraordinary taxation, and feared debtor's prison.⁴⁹ The sheikhulislam was sympathetic to their laments and wished to send word to the sultan to "cancel evil innovations," but they surrounded him and compelled him to go with them to the palace. They placed the unwilling sheikhulislam on horseback in the lead to give them legitimacy.⁵⁰ At the Hippo-drome the crowd swelled to twenty thousand men. They entered the compound of Hagia Sophia hoping for an audience with the sultan in the ancient house of worship, but then were permitted to enter the palace. Passing through its grounds they marched as far as the Gate of Felicity to press their grievances.⁵¹ Kösem Sultan arrived in an uproar, angrily asking, "Why did you not turn back these people, instead bringing them to the palace?" The sheikhulislam claimed, "We did not bring them, they brought us."⁵²

Hearing the shouts of the merchants, the sultan asked what caused the clamor. When the sheikhulislam brought their grievances to him, Mehmed IV told them to return the next day, but they responded, "We will not take a step backward until we receive what we deserve." Moreover, "in Istanbul there are five sultans. We cannot take their oppression."⁵³ After this the sultan wanted to see his grand vizier, but Melek Ahmed Pasha preferred to return his seal of office rather then appear before him, wisely reasoning that "it is generally a great mistake and dangerous to go inside [when beckoned by the sultan dur-ing a crisis]." He cited the Qur'anic verse, "And do not with your own hands cast yourselves into destruction" as he repeated, "I will not cast myself into destruction."[54] Kösem Sultan said that the room where they were meeting was claustrophobic, and she went outside to the great pool, where she decided to give the seal of office to another.[55]

The square filled with soldiers and the smell of gunpowder, and the city was put under curfew. Armed Janissaries, set up at entrances to roads, seized and killed those who dared venture outside. Accordingly, commoners gave up explaining their problems to the sultan, for they saw that the Janissaries were intent not to let them gather and approach the palace again.[56] Karaçelebizade did not remain long in office, either. He claimed that Kösem Sultan, the harem eunuchs, and Janissaries were against him, especially after he was seen at the head of a rebellion.[57]

Mehmed IV asked another grand vizier why it was that "during my father's reign, the treasury was sufficient for Janissary salaries and other expenditures. Why is this not the case now?" He ordered him to calculate the state's revenues and expenses. The latter mainly consisted of the military payroll and outstripped income.[58] This deficit angered the sultan and he dismissed and executed the grand vizier. Katip Çelebi attended the meeting at the palace of the treasurer to discuss the reasons the treasury was empty.[59] He recorded pessimistically that even if they said they had recited his treatise *The Guide for the Rectification of Defects* "to the eye of the sultan," which argued that only a decisive, powerful leader who did not wilt in the face of opposition could resolve the financial and military problems, he knew "that the necessary action would not be taken" because too many people had vested interests in continuing corrupt practices that benefited individuals to the detriment of the empire.[60] Karaçelebizade concurred. The problem was simple: because "income was decreasing day after day, and expenses were increasing moment by moment," the treasury was not able to pay salaries.[61] And no one was willing to give up their stipends. Naima confirms that no one listened to Katip Çelebi's rescript for change, as the easiest thing to do was *not* do anything.[62]

When describing the events of 1654–56, Karaçelebizade rants against what he sees as corrupt new financial practices that led inevitably to problems of sultanic legitimacy, abuse of commoners, loss of prosperity in the countryside, and weakening of the borders of the empire. He begins by summarizing the main economic problem, namely, the excess of expenses and paucity of income. Corruption and bribery led to oppression, "the likes of which has not been seen in a century." The men of state invented what he terms "seditious innovations," the worst being the literal buying and selling of Ottoman state offices "like commercial goods." Like the farming of revenue, official positions were sold at auction every six months at the office of the treasurer. New salary holders, "while taking a loan from the treasury upon receiving a position, cause the difficult state of the treasury to worsen at the same time as the state does not receive in return service that is worthy of the dynasty and religion." Supporters of the grand vizier and treasurer also took their cut, and then the remainder went to the treasury. He disapproved of how "without shame they are then recorded in the register of financial transactions," thus legalizing illegal practices.[63] And the sultan made no effort to stem illegal profit.

We need to take seriously how members of the Ottoman elite such as this former sheikhulislam articulated what they saw as the woes of their era and what needed to be done to remedy them. But to Karaçelebizade, it was as if it was almost too late. He compares the treasury to a human body needing appropriate medicine—it had a barely readable pulse, hardly a spark of life remained, and the patient was in need of immediate intensive care But how could the patient rebound when the physicians (the viziers) would take two to three years of the sultan's wealth in advance payment and, when salaries were about to be paid, would borrow weak akçe from "opportunist Jews" and "other traitors to the dynasty and religion," and because of similar unwise and illegal profits that wealth would not return to the treasury? Day by day the treasury became less sound as "dishonest viziers take incorrect and harmful measures." Especially galling for the author was bribery. He quotes a saying of Muhammad (Hadith) cursing those who give or take bribes. This legitimizing of corruption led to a problem of legitimacy for the sultan, as "tyrants, acquiring office this way, God forbid, engage in various types of oppression on behalf of the sultan," who theoretically delegated his authority to them to carry out their office. They were supposed to serve as his eyes in the provinces, but because of their actions, the symbolic eye of justice was robbed blind. As a result, many commoners faced injustice as fearless men without scruples, who lived to enjoy the moment at others' expense and not worry about the future state of health of the empire, lording it over them. When commoners came to the capital seeking redress to their grievances, rather than "being spoiled by kind treatment" if they complained at the meeting of the imperial council, "they would be subject to a violent blow or extended imprisonment from which they would emerge utterly crushed."[64]

Karaçelebizade sums it up by writing, "From the evil of bribery and oppressive innovations" arise only the "moan, groan, and wailing of the poor and commoners."[65] He may have exaggerated some of the conditions of state. Yet archival documents attest to the root causes of his lamentation. The people of Anatolia complained that they suffered from an excessive number of men being called up to military duty, that their towns and villages had been destroyed, and that they were overtaxed.[66] Tiring of exploitation, having lost their wealth and sense of peace, commoners set fire to their land and homes, "which became the abodes of owls and crows": weeping, they fled their natal regions and moved to the city.[67] This caused "the formerly prosperous towns and cities [of Anatolia] to be destroyed and in ruins." The ruin of Anatolia was coupled with citadels on the frontier being "usurped by the aggressive hand of the enemy and day by day the territorial possessions and wealth of the empire decreased."[68]

Another indicator of Ottoman financial crisis in the period includes the instability and eventual abandonment of Ottoman coinage. In the mid- to late seventeenth century the Ottoman mint output declined, Ottoman coinage disappeared from local markets, and western European coinage replaced it.[69] The Ottoman silver asper became merely a unit of account, while the elite and commoners alike made actual payments in stable foreign coins such as the Dutch thaler and Spanish reales de la ocho. Mint output virtually ceased, the shortage of coins intensified, and counterfeit and debased western European coinage flooded the market. In this period the Ottomans lost control of their own currency and were unable to regulate their own economy.[70] The ability to mint coins was a primary concern of empires; giving up this right meant forfeiting an opportunity to instill public confidence in the dynasty and empire.

As commoners stopped using Ottoman coinage in everyday transactions, displaying a profound lack of confidence in the financial health of the empire, and merchants and Janissaries rebelled in Istanbul over debased coinage, rebellions in the countryside led to economic crisis there as well. Peasant mercenaries armed by the administration, as well as rogue Janissaries, sipahis, and governors, exacerbated highway robbery and violent crime committed by rootless peasants. Conditions became so bad that pillaging and looting even led to famine in some areas.[71] This upheaval attended the shift from "a military conquest state to a bureaucratic, revenue-collecting state" characterized by the "localization of the empire's servants in the provinces," who became "entrenched local interest groups."[72] All these revolts led to a renewal of the disastrous conditions of the late sixteenth and early seventeenth centuries: economic disruption, flight and hardship in the countryside, and an urban crime wave that knew no religious bounds, following migration to urban centers of marginal, young, armed, single landless men attracted by the opportunities of the city.[73] Dozens of violent crimes, including armed robbery, assault, sexual assault, and murder, were recorded in the mid- to late seventeenth-century Shariah records of five representative districts of Istanbul (Beşiktaş, Galata, Hasköy, Istanbul, and Yeniköy). Jews are depicted assaulting and killing Muslim men and women; Muslims also appear as murderers; Christians threaten Christians with death and murder Jews. Crime knew no religious bounds as the populace of Istanbul complained of assaults night and day, on the streets and even on the waterways that skirted the metropolis. Even foreign brigands assaulted the city. Cossacks attacked Ottoman boats in the Black Sea, and because they were virtually unopposed, came up the Bosporus as far as Trabya on the European coast. British consul and longtime resident in Izmir Sir Paul Rycaut observed that this caused much fear throughout the city.[74]

War Abroad and Rebellion at Home

That Cossack flotillas could mercilessly assault the imperial capital testifies to the state of the Ottoman military. The important question was: How did Ottoman forces fight? The Ottomans had not defeated the Venetian enemy at sea for over a decade, the soldiers were a burden on each other, unable to fight together, and during battle Janissaries caused the defeat of other forces when they landed ships head rather than rear first. Morever, they were accused of "knowing nothing of ghaza, or Islam, or piety," nor why desertion was a sin.[75] Formerly feared in western and central Europe for its strict discipline and absolute obedience to commanders and the sultan, the Ottoman military faced defeat and stalemate. Karaçelebizade complains about a peace treaty with the Habsburgs, for it signaled that the Ottomans had wasted blood and treasure "on the inauspicious, unblessed Hungarian campaign. How many Muslims became captives in the hands of polytheists? How many countless masjids and mosques became the monasteries of infidels?"[76] The armed forces also faced the nightmare of the interminable siege of Candia, Crete, launched by Ibrahim in 1645, "which caused pain and distress," making Muslims "weak of heart and full of anxiety."[77]

The biggest failure continued to be the siege of Candia, the last Venetian citadel on Crete. So long as it controlled the island of Crete, Venice would be the master of the eastern Mediterranean and thus control the trade transiting from eastern Asia and southern Asia to western Europe. The Ottomans had to wrest this power from their hands. Yet to do so necessitated spending a great amount of Ottoman treasure. Part of the reason for the military failure was financial, as the soldiers besieging Candia did not receive their pay on time and thus suffered low morale. The war for Candia was extremely expensive, and the price of conquering the island seemed disproportionate to the goal.[78] Katip Çelebi writes at length about the reasons for the difficulty of successfully conquering all of Crete. The Ottomans faced insurgency on land and by sea in the coastal areas they seized. They could barely keep watch over the territories they conquered, let alone imagine conquering Candia. When Ottoman forces initially landed before the citadel of Candia, "there was no time to construct trenches, so they alighted before the citadel and waited for munitions to arrive." They repeatedly battled the Venetians, losing their commanders. Unfortunately for the Ottoman military, the Venetians had reinforced Candia for years, "making it a fortress inspiring the greatest level of confidence," adding mines and tunnels, thousands of cannons, and tens of thousands of soldiers. Men sent to take the fortress complained they could not draw the besieged out of the fortress to fight. The leaders of the military petitioned the sultan for assistance, claiming that they needed long-range artillery pieces because they lacked suitable firepower for attacking the massive citadel.[79]

Ottoman forces were able to take complete possession of the land side of the well-fortified citadel, but because necessary men and matériel did not arrive, they waited to enter the trenches until the navy arrived with more provisions, more miners, and more artillerymen. Yet the desperate soldiers waited in vain. The Ottoman navy would not arrive because it could not leave the blockaded Dardanelles. According to Katip Çelebi, not even a rowboat could pass.[80] Several times their commanders promised falsely that the navy was on the way, and the men entered the trenches only to soon find out the truth. At the same time, the frustrated soldiers not only had to demand aid to fight, but had to fight for their grain, provisions, clothing, and pay, which also did not arrive. The depressed troops turned to collecting plants, roots, grass, and herbs to eat.[81] Accordingly, they sent the Janissary commander to Istanbul to demand men, matériel, and money, but he had no luck. The Janissary commanders in Istanbul did not want to send their men to the island.

The dejected Ottoman army and navy were in mourning. Already early in the Candia campaign, Janissaries in Crete, unable to bear the constant siege and battle, suffering constant pain and carnage, unable to endure the lack of men, matériel, and provisions any longer, started an uprising on Crete and attacked the commander's palace in a pitched battle; numerous Janissaries and sipahis were killed. The palace was looted, the slave boys and slave girls found within were sexually assaulted and abducted, and the palace was burned to the ground. As Naima notes, "The honor of the dynasty [and by extension the sultan], and not only that of the commander, was violated."[82]

Their commanders complained that the men of state neglected the effort, did not consider it important, and that no one strove with heart and soul.[83] The Ottoman ships containing grain, provisions, troops, or ammunition found when they arrived at the Dardanelles that the galleons of their enemy "were anchored there and formed a wall at the passage" and also blockaded the citadel of Candia. Even if its ships did manage to break out of the Dardanelles, the navy could not discharge its load at Candia, but had to do so at the other coastal areas already conquered, from which the supplies would be sent by land.[84] As a result, written in the mournful tone of Naima, the Muslim soldiers became disgusted by the war, grew cold to battle, had no strength to take the citadel, were tired of living on false hopes, recognized their powerlessness, and faced a seemingly countless enemy without salary, reinforcements, or provisions. Withering under a constant barrage of enemy fire, their earthworks filled with winter rain, they lost all will to fight with the latest arrival of enemy reinforcements.[85] When Ottoman forces arrived to drop off supplies, seeing the enemy ships nearby they would panic and quickly set sail again, fleeing so quickly that they would not deposit all the soldiers. The disgorged soldiers did not have time to take their provisions, rain gear, or weapons, and soldiers already on the island would curse the cowards.[86] Contrary to statute, Karaçelebizade states that the Janissaries "who had been on that unfortunate island" for years without relief were known to take the fleet and return to Istanbul. By 1652, Karaçelebizade could describe the campaign as "not blessed," because the Ottoman forces could do nothing to stop the Venetians. While "the sultanic treasury was forsaken of seeing the countenance of a silver or gold coin, the soldiers of Islam were hungry and desolate, stuck on that island for years, crying for help, lost in the calamity of exile, pain, anxiety, grief and homesickness." This caused "the honor of the manifest religion [Islam] to be broken."[87]

While the grand viziers that held office during Mehmed IV's first eight years in power were overwhelmed trying to solve financial deficiencies, put down rebellion, and bring about order in the imperial dominions, Venetian naval victories and occupation of islands crucial to the defense of the imperial capital became the clearest indicators of Ottoman military crisis. Naval battles between ships that caused "the vault of heaven to fill with the clamerous sound of cannonfire" usually did not go the Ottoman way. Ottoman admirals were accused of being cowards when facing the enemy (but being happy to oppress and pillage Ottoman commoners), of having poor battle plans and no backup plans, which caused the sinking of many ships and the loss of many commanders.[88] War with Venice dragged on and constant news of routs filled the population of Istanbul with sorrow and stress and placed them at direct risk.

To Karaçelebizade, it became an issue of male honor. Facing the humiliation of being routed by the infidels, it was crucial to raise "a proud navy" that would not "flee in the direction of the wind, be impotent with crushed honor," or be led by commanders who would "hand over their ships to save their own necks."[89] It is not surprising that there were eighteen admirals of the navy from the start of the Crete campaign in 1645 through the end of 1656.[90] Karaçelebizade complained that the "overpowering whip of the sultanate" and capital punishment were not used to sternly punish these commanders and make them public examples; instead, despite the terrible situation, their actions were not even frowned upon.[91]

In these circumstances it is also not surprising that Venetian warships defeated the Ottoman navy in twelve of thirteen campaigns between 1645 and
1656, in part due to the Ottoman use of large, clumsy, slower, oar-driven galleys
rather than smaller, speedy galleons with sails used by the Venetians.[92] A rout
of the Ottoman navy in 1655 was considered the greatest Ottoman naval defeat
since Lepanto nearly a century earlier: "Until today Muslims had never been
routed like this and the accursed infidels had never celebrated such victory and
acquired so much plunder," causing the evil eye to strike.[93] To Naima, when
people heard the news, "eyes which saw suffering cried blood."[94] Muslims were
heartbroken; the soldiers were stripped of their bravery.[95]

Ten years' effort on Crete and still the island had not been completely subjected; Ottoman forces had been besieging Candia to no effect. Soldiers suffered
without supplies; without supplies they could not be an effective fighting force;
not being an effective fighting force they could not protect the citadels they had
conquered up to that point, let alone conquer new ones. Not even receiving their
pay, or their pay being deficient or in weak akçes, they sent representatives to Istanbul. In Istanbul the treasurer was in difficult straits, paying in debased coins,
giving additional income with falsified receipts from a treasury whose expenses
had already been doled out.[96]

Janissaries, later joined by sipahis, again revolted in 1656, mainly complaining that they sacrificed their lives for the empire in ghaza and jihad but that
they were rewarded by being paid in weak coins that the merchants would not
accept.[97] They also demanded that the sultan order an imperial land campaign,
as only naval campaigns had been launched in the recent past. A throng thousands strong marched on the palace and told the sultan that he had matured into
a young brave and had the power to take independent control of state affairs, a
statement freighted with irony given that the throng controlled the power. The
sultan offered to exile those who cheated them in this way, but they demanded
the corpses of numerous officials, subsequently delivered to them. The revolt
was named after the plane tree in the Hippodrome from which the treasurer
of the imperial harem, customs administrator, and many others were hanged
upside down. As Karaçelebizade wrote, "Go and see the tree which the gardener
of vengeance planted in the Hippodrome."[98] For the treasonous crime of paying
in weak akçes, the former treasurer was also executed; his corpse hung for three
days covered in dust before Yedikule prison. The mob tied ropes to the feet of
corpses and dragged them from the palace to the Hippodrome, exposing their
genitals along the way as a form of humiliation. Mehmed Halife, whose aim was
to relate "the strange and wondrous events" that occurred during the era, then
claims that the Janissaries took the ritualized shaming of their enemies a step
further by distributing the fat and flesh of those whose corpses were thrown to

them, or those they killed outside the palace, to onlookers who were tricked into believing that consuming them would provide remedies for various ills.[99] The author also heard that Janissaries cut off the flesh of these corpses and had it cooked in taverns. It may sound incredible that Janissaries turned to cannibalism. What is important is that during this chaotic time their reputation was so poor that tales of flesh eating were believable.

Military rebellion at home and failure abroad made the imperial capital vulnerable. Janissary and sipahi rebellion in Istanbul cast doubt on the Ottoman ability to bring the Candian campaign to a successful close. Ottoman territory was besieged because there were no Muslim braves who would battle the enemy.[100] Subsequently, by 1656 Venice occupied the crucial islands of Bozca, Limni (Limnos), and Semadirek (Samothraki) that form an arc around the entrance to the Dardanelles. The loss of these islands was too great to bear. They had been part of the empire since the era of Istanbul's conquest. To Karaçelebizade, Bozca was "the shelter of the army of faith," its citadel filled "with the clamor of Muslim martial music." The loss of Limni was couched in gendered terms that evinced a feeling of male vulnerability and humiliation. The island, "formerly a well-protected castle with lights of the signs of Islam resembling an adorned bridal chamber, ornamented with mosques where people recited the names of God and God's unity," was violated and made into "a place of cross and churchbell, a place of Muslim lamentation."[101] The Muslims who surrendered the island went out to the shore with only enough clothing to cover their genitals.[102]

The three islands were at the entrance to the straits controlling the shipping lanes to Istanbul. Bozca was the linchpin to the straits of Istanbul.[103] Able to cut Istanbul's sea link to the Mediterranean, Venetians blockaded the city and metaphorically had a hand on the throat of empire, able to both starve the capital, which was the Ottomans' worst fear, and prevent the Ottoman navy from reaching Crete. Ironically, the siege of Candia had in part been launched to hinder the Venetians from cutting off their supply routes in the Mediterranean. The Venetians had previously tried to close the Dardanelles during the beginning of the campaign for Crete, but the Ottoman navy had stopped them.[104] Finally, grain ships destined for Istanbul could not pass and the city was cut off from provisions.[105]

The inhabitants of Istanbul experienced unprecedented famine. In the words of Kurdish Preacher Mustafa, "In the gardens, other than the smoke of sighs, no smoke arose, and in the homes, the only flame seen was the flame of hunger. If the price for a sprig of mint was giving one's life, the masses, knowing the obligation to life, would give it." Famine "scorched Muslims with the flame of misery and filled them with sorrow as the afflicted eye flooded with the tears of grief."[106] The Venetians had blocked Istanbul's sea route to Egypt. Rice, coffee, and other products could not be sent to the capital.[107] The sultan fled to the Asian side of Istanbul. He was not the only resident of the city to panic. Fearing imminent foreign occupation, thousands of Istanbul residents also crossed to the Anatolian side of the city. When, as a defensive measure, soldiers began to demolish homes built on the city walls, terror struck the hearts of people and caused them to uproot and seek a safe region of the city. Even the rich suffered greatly as they too lost their means of livelihood and life-sustaining rations.[108] The grand vizier Boynueğri was ordered to "start a victorious campaign against the enemies of religion and with the soldiers of Islam get rid of the enemies by means of religious zeal and expel the wretched infidels from the straits."[109] But, as has been seen, he stated that he could not take that duty upon himself and was dismissed.

Sipahis rebelled in Anatolia and Istanbul. Sipahi Gürcü Nebi, brother of Grand Vizier Gürcü Mehmed Pasha, revolted to take revenge for the deposing and executing of Ibrahim, the killing of his cavalry brethren at the Hippodrome and in Ahmed I's mosque, and the dumping of their corpses in the sea soon after Mehmed IV's enthronement.[110] With "Satan whispering in his ear tempting him to sin," he joined ranks with other sipahis and irregular militias who had a reputation for looting and raping their way across Anatolia.[111] He asked a notorious highway robber to join him, a man who had previously killed the governor-general of Anatolia, and began marching toward the imperial capital. The threat was real: Janissaries crossed the Bosporus to Üsküdar to dig trenches and set up cannons and artillery to defend Istanbul. Fifty thousand soldiers gathered to battle a rebel force twice that number.[112]

The rebel demands were typical for that era. They wanted tradition to be maintained and for a role in institutions, to be included in military administration, not to set up a counter one. These were not revolutionaries. Irked that prayers had not been said over their fallen comrades in Istanbul, they demanded the dismissal of the sheikhulislam. They desired provincial administrative-military positions to be bestowed on them.[113] Although at first the pasha sent to suppress the revolt acted in an unhurried and nonconfrontational manner because he was an old friend of the rebel leader, by the time the rebels actually arrived in Istanbul, loyal forces battled them and defeated them in the vicinity of Üsküdar. It was a massive battle, and up to a thousand Janissaries were killed. Religious conversion helped the rebels' second in command achieve his desires. He became a pious Muslim, or "found the way of God" and "repented of his evil ways." Petitioning the sultan, he asked that his religious turn and newfound devotion to God be recognized, and he was granted a provincial position with landholding. Karaçelebizade complains that "the bandit who traversed all of Anatolia committing highway robbery, by merely seeking favor, became a state official."[114]

Many rebellious governors alternated between working for the administration and fighting against it with unsettling shows of force during this period. Repeatedly, men in state service, competing over positions and tax and property revenue, desiring to gain more power and income, saw that the best path to accomplish their desires was rebellion to draw attention to themselves. They calculated that at worst they would be imprisoned and their wealth confiscated, but then they would be reappointed elsewhere. Outlaws who aimed to legalize their grabs for power and wealth desired to be part of the system. In the end, many highway robbers were in fact given positions and representation in the capital, and those who possessed positions were given better ones.[115]

Karaçelebizade argued that the remedies used to cure the illnesses of corruption and rebellion caused the situation to worsen: by giving a state position "to one with bribes several times more than he can provide, are you not giving permission to him to loot the wealth of the commoners?" Oppression exists when people given positions are told to hurry up and recoup their losses, when officials are compelled to make up the money they used as bribes to acquire the position in the first place. Why would a vizier who was corrupt be exiled to Anatolia? "Wasn't that saying to him, be a rebel?" Once there he would certainly gather bandits so as not to be deprived of wealth. Furthermore, "If the law of God and sultan demanded his execution, why did you slacken the reins while you have him? And if not, is it permissible to compel an innocent person [by sending him to the lawless countryside] to profit from wicked corruption?" The sheikhulislam's objections were met with derision at the court by people who claimed, "Let a rebellious vizier go wherever he goes, let him gather as many bandits as he wishes, for he will not amount to anything, but will instead dissolve like dust, and disappear in the massive empire." But the religious authority objected, claiming, "These measures never worked, how often were the people in Anatolia ruined by the succession of authorities?"[116]

Converting the Patriarch and Putting Women in Their Place

As if all of these problems were not enough, the normally quiescent Christian population of Istanbul, and the Orthodox Christian patriarch in particular, apparently showed signs of treason and rebellion as well. Later historians narrate how Orthodox Patriarch Parthenios III was executed in 1657 for his alleged crime of inciting Christians in southeastern Europe and Istanbul to rebel against the authority of the sultan.[117] According to Nihadi, "The filthy one who is the polytheists' patriarch" was hanged at Parmak Gate for attempting to undermine the Ottomans while they were at their weakest, a time when treason was most dangerous. Immediately after describing the campaign of the Ottoman ally the Crimean khan against Muscovy, in which he claims hundreds of thousands of enemy were killed and tens of thousands taken captive, which "made Muslims joyous and Christians hard-hearted in their resistance to God," Nihadi launched into a tirade against "the accursed one who is the patriarch of the Greek infidels residing in Istanbul." He accuses the patriarch of secretly corresponding with Venice and the Habsburgs, urging them to attack Istanbul while the Ottoman military was in a precarious state. If the foreign Christians would attack from without and the Ottoman Christians attack from within, the patriarch hoped that they could "completely do away with the Muslims."[118] When these letters, which had the patriarch's seals on them, were seized, the grand vizier ordered the religious figure to appear before him. After ascertaining that these were official patriarchal correspondence, a translator read their contents. The grand vizier flew into a fit of rage and asked how this accursed one could dare engage in the sin of backstabbing. Instead of denying his activities, the patriarch defended them, claiming that he desired calamity for the Muslims and that he was willing to sacrifice his life on the path of his religion. At this point the grand vizier tried another strategy: conversion. "Come," he said, "became a Muslim and this offense will be pardoned." But the patriarch insistently defended his actions, so the grand vizier immediately had him hanged.[119]

Instead of rebellious Christians, for some Muslims the problems of the empire and dynasty all boiled down to not policing gender roles. A sheikh named Mahmud came to Istanbul from Diyarbekir and withdrew to a dervish cell for forty days of prayer. When he emerged, he told the head representative of the descendants of Muhammad that the reason Muslims were afflicted with crises was because the Shariah had been abandoned and men and women had switched roles. The valide sultan was a special concern. The sheikh argued that it was necessary to marry her off to get her out of the palace; a husband would presumably control her. The sheikh was admonished and sent to the insane asylum that is part of Suleiman I's mosque complex. There he continued to tell his many visitors that if only the valide sultan were married, all problems would be resolved. He was finally sent back to Diyarbekir. Naima, who frequently employs misogynist rhetoric in his history, here defends the valide sultan by claiming that the sheikh misunderstood the interests of state, the role the valide sultan played in palace and public ceremonies, why she was linked to the honor of the dynasty, and how changes to her key role would be even more damaging.[120] The valide sultan, the most important person in the palace in the 1650s, was indispensable.

In the eye of writers during the first decade of Mehmed IV's reign, the ruler wilted into the background, overshadowed by his powerful mother. She always stood by his side, if behind a curtain, present when the sultan met with the grand vizier and other advisors, asking questions or responding to her son's questions, and stopped at nothing to ensure she lead the dynasty.[121] There is much evidence that this female regent ran the empire in place of her son. From 1651 until 1656, writs of the grand viziers concerning administration, war, and the state of imperial finances, which customarily were addressed to the sultan, were actually addressed instead to Hatice Turhan, attesting to who was the real decision maker and de facto head of the dynasty.[122] The body of the documents consisted of the petition of the grand vizier, and the top of the document contained the command of the valide sultan, covered in gold. In one such document the valide sultan refers to her son in the diminutive, as "my lion."[123] By 1653, when the sultan was twelve, he was still referred to by his tutor as "a lion who has not yet hunted," "an inexperienced white hawk without knowledge of the world," and "a blindfolded falcon."[124] A falcon can hover above the earth, staying motionlessly aloft in one spot while riding the currents, like a ruler who rises above palace factions to claim sovereign power alone. The solution offered by the writers of the advice literature was just such a strong sultan who would take charge. The answer to their critiques was couched in the language of conversion and conquest.

3

Enjoining Good and Forbidding Wrong

Unique to the mid- to late seventeenth century was how a religious response amid crisis became the prevailing mode for ameliorating the woes that beset Muslims. Reformist preachers served as mediators in the conversion of other Muslims to their understanding of Islam, which in turn set in motion the concentric rings of conversion about which this book is concerned. The preaching of Muhammad called on believers to reform themselves and their society, to command right and forbid wrong. This serves both to distinguish Muslims from other peoples and to unite the believers.[1] Within each society in each and every era there arise individuals who try to put Muslims back on the path of the Muslim ideal, to strive to revive the faith when believers have slipped from it. In some periods pietists have allowed the ruler to "play the main role" in forbidding wrong, while in others they have used Qur'anic prescriptions to legitimize their opposition to rulers and authorities considered unethical, or to oppose the practices of their neighbors, particularly concerning wine, women, and song.[2] Religious trends cannot always dependably be mapped onto sociopolitical trends. Many of the ideas promoted by the Kadızadelis in the seventeenth century were first articulated in the previous century. What is crucial, however, are those periods where religious movements became linked with political power. The late seventeenth-century Ottoman Empire witnessed an alliance of political power and religious zeal as the sultan and like-minded pietists actively transformed Muslim behavior and trained their collective eye on Christians and Jews, resulting in an unprecedented emphasis on public piety whose outcome was conversion of Muslims, Christians, and Jews.

This chapter addresses the book's themes concerning why people attempt to bring others of the same religion to their understanding of that religion (the motivation of the Kadızadelis), the link between piety and proselytization, and the central role played by those who mediate conversion. Scholars formerly were content to focus exclusively on the internal spiritual journey of the convert, but now many more also examine the interaction between the advocate or mediator of religious change and the potential convert.[3] They investigate the methods of the advocate and their understanding of what signifies conversion. I chart the rise to prominence of the Kadızadeli religious movement in the 1650s, explaining the movement's origins in the 1620s and 1630s with Kadızade Mehmed Efendi, who propagated the interpretations of Islam of the sixteenth-century pietist Birgili Mehmed Efendi. I discuss their main conversionary method of preaching reform to other Muslims from the pulpits of Istanbul's imperial mosques. Charismatic preachers convinced the public to change their ways through didactic interpretations of the Qur'an and Hadith; interpersonal bonds also enabled the movement to spread at the Ottoman court. The central tenets of Kadızadeli piety were commanding good and forbidding wrong. In their view, to convert to Islam as it was meant to be lived required public commitment to a religion freed from accretions assimilated into Muslim practice after the death of Muhammad. Their theory of conversion necessitated the complete rejection of the practices of several Sufi orders, and they were outspoken opponents of any form of religious syncretism. Accordingly, also using coercion and violence as conversionary strategies, they attacked the innovative practices of several Sufi orders, their dervish lodges, and even the Sufis themselves.

I also describe relations between Kadızadelis and sultans, the larger societal response to their incitations to abolish many common religious practices as well as forms of entertainment, and debates among Muslims about the proper way to be Muslim. I conclude with a discussion of conversion of religious geography and sacred space during the grand vizierate of Köprülü Mehmed Pasha (1656–61), who conventional wisdom claims ended the movement. A discussion of his policies also points to the ever waxing strength of the grand vizierate and waning of the sultanate's power, crucial for understanding Mehmed IV's interest in conversion and conquest once he obtained his majority.

Kadızade Mehmed Efendi and the Origins of the Kadızadelis

The most influential seventeenth-century Islamic movement in the Ottoman Empire began when a preacher converted from one interpretation of piety to another.[4] Kadızade Mehmed Efendi began his spiritual life as a Sufi. Born in Balıkesir, the son of a magistrate, he became a preacher who was inclined toward Sufism with the encouragement of a Halveti sheikh.[5] But later he turned against the Sufi way. He based his arguments against innovative practices on the works of the preacher Birgili Mehmed Efendi (d. 1573), particularly his Arabic-language *The Way of Muhammad* and *The Treatise of Birgili Mehmed*, which, among other principles, opposed payment for religious services and foundations endowed with moveable goods such as cash since the practice appeared to condone usury.[6] Kadızade contended that the true Islam of the first Muslim community had been corrupted by such contemporary practices or innovations as Sufi dance and song, pilgrimage to tombs of saints, the use of coffee, tobacco, and opium, and even adding more than one minaret to a mosque. The newly completed Sultan Ahmed I Mosque, where his rival Sivasi Efendi (d. 1639) preached, has six minarets.

Kadızade arrived in Istanbul to preach against Sufi innovation and in favor of returning to the principles and practices that guided the first believers in Medina. Famous for "the beauty of his expressions and gracefulness of his delivery," he was appointed preacher in turn at the mosques of Selim, Bayezid, and Suleiman I before finally becoming the main preacher at Hagia Sophia in 1631, putting him spatially close to the palace.[7] From this pulpit he argued that all errors stemmed from not following Muslim law and tradition. Like Ahmad ibn Hanbal (d. 855), Kadızade was able to link personal asceticism and the public forbidding of wrong to inspire like-minded pious Muslims to social action.[8] Following the example of Birgili Mehmed Efendi, who wrote, "It is incumbent on me to defend the people with my pen and with my tongue from what God has prohibited, and it is a sin for me to be silent," Kadızade declared that true Muslims and their rulers had a duty to promote the Qur'anic command of "enjoining what is proper or good and forbidding what is reprehensible or evil."[9] The phrase refers both to preaching Islam to people belonging to other religions and to imploring other Muslims to live ethical lives in accordance with practices found in the Qur'an, Hadith, and Shariah.

Prior to this, "forbidding wrong," or compelling other Muslims to behave piously, had not been a defining feature of Ottoman Sunnism.[10] Earlier influential Muslim scholars, such as Taşköprüzade (d. 1561), had toned down views on the acceptable use of violence by ordinary Muslims engaged in the practice. He was opposed to commoners taking up arms to censure their sinning neighbors and had declared, "God preserve us from those who show fanaticism in religion."[11] Birgili Mehmed Efendi had written a popular book in Turkish concerning the obligations of a believer, which included forbidding wrong, and in a more learned treatise promoted martyrdom in the name of the act. This radical approach was contrary to the prevailing accommodationist stance to the diversity of Sunni practices.[12] For Kadızade and the preachers who followed him, however, forbidding wrong was their main obligation. Muslims had diverged from the way of Muhammad, Kadızade argued. He urged those who engaged in innovative practices to renew their faith and return to the straight path.[13]

In every sermon Kadızade and his followers renewed old allegations and objections against the "vile" dancing, whirling, and music playing of Halveti and Mevlevi Sufis, becoming their vociferous adversaries. Kadızadelis even labeled those who visited Halveti lodges infidels.[14] They also publicly criticized learned scholars by calling them unbelievers, heretics, and infidels. More disturbing to many Muslims was their condemnation of and labeling infidel common Muslim practices not denounced in the Qur'an or Shariah. These included blessing another by saying "God be pleased with him"; embellishing the reading of the Qur'an; chanting the call to prayer with a musical tone; invoking blessing on Muhammad by offering the benediction "May God shower benedictions upon him and bless him," a phrase that Solakzade purposely deploys while mentioning Kadızadeli detestation of the phrase; and supererogatory services of worship performed on the night of the first Friday of the month of Rajab and the night of the twelfth of the same month, the anniversary of the conception of Muhammad, and on the Night of Power, the twenty-seventh night of Ramadan, when Muslims mark Muhammad's reception of the first revelations of the Qur'an.[15]

Kadızade's first target was the consumption of tobacco; he advocated the execution of those who engaged in the habit.[16] In 1633, after he had become affiliated with the palace, and following a massive fire in Istanbul, he convinced Sultan Murad IV to raze all the coffeehouses and ban the consumption of tobacco, prohibitions maintained by his successor, Ibrahim.[17] Kadızade preached "every Friday from the pulpit of this very Hagia Sophia, and wasn't that the reason the coffeehouses were closed and public gatherings were forbidden?"[18] Coffee sellers were known for dealing opium. According to Mehmed Halife, there were so many illegal activities engaged in at the coffeehouses and taverns and by their customers elsewhere that city life turned into utter chaos. Janissaries, fueled by coffee or wine, "were so disobedient that they abducted naked women wearing only waistcloths from the bathhouses in broad daylight." The

Janissaries also consumed tobacco in Fatih Mosque, molested Muslims, and "hastily yet openly engaged in fornication and sodomy" on street corners, in addition to spilling blood and raiding palaces and homes throughout the city. Some blamed such widespread immorality and vice for a great conflagration that burned perhaps one-fifth of the city; the prohibition of coffee and tobacco and the razing of the places where they were consumed was issued soon after the fire since coffee, tobacco, and wine appeared to incite men to commit abominable acts and sexual violence and engage in debauchery. Countless humble coffee drinkers and tobacco smokers were executed in Istanbul and wherever Murad IV traveled. Such an atmosphere of terror was created that everyone's intentions were considered suspect; innocent people, even young sons of imams who stayed too late at mosque, were executed for not going about at night with a lantern.[19] While en route to the Baghdad campaign, Murad IV had fourteen people executed for using tobacco, including the head of the gatekeepers and Janissaries.[20] Until he died in 1640, tobacco was not openly consumed in Istanbul. Soon after the ban on coffee and tobacco was decreed, wine and opium consumption were also prohibited.

Muslims Resist Converting to Piety

Not all Muslims desired to turn to the straight path envisioned by the Kadızadelis. For Solakzade, writing soon after outburst of violent intra-Muslim discord in 1656, the Kadızadelis' pronouncing some common Muslim practices as erroneous shook the foundations of the world.[21] Katip Çelebi, a harsh critic of the preacher, acknowledged that Kadızade was "famous for his knowledge and virtue" and "eloquent of speech," a preacher who taught Shariah four days a week and preached three, educating many people and rescuing them "from the lowest depths of ignorance."[22] On the other hand, the author, who attended Kadızadeli lessons numerous times, considered their preaching to be simple and misleading, as they criticized perfectly permissable acts and became the cause of much turmoil among Muslims. He asked how they could hinder people from engaging in beliefs and practices that were so popular and well-established. Silahdar, whose history was a continuation of Katip Çelebi's, also takes a harsh stance against them, labeling their preaching clamorous sophistry.[23]

Many Muslims opposed the suppression of pleasure-bringing habits. Solakzade records the views of those who objected to the Kadızadelis by saying that if the people are hindered from smoking tobacco, the preacher would neither gain nor lose anything, so there was no point to the reprimand. Furthermore, they ridiculed Kadızade: unless a little smoke would cause the end of the world, why raise a ruckus?[24] The Kadızadelis responded by saying that those who did not voluntarily drop the habit deserved to be killed. Mustafa Altıoklar's 1996 film *Istanbul beneath My Wings (İstanbul Kanatlarımın Altında)* makes an interesting attempt to convey the mood of the period. The director places much of the blame for the severity of the era incorrectly on the sheikhulislam. In fact, the sheikhulislam actually opposed the Kadızadelis, a group that does not appear in the film. Nevertheless, Altıoklar accurately depicts raids on underground coffee and wine shops and mass hangings of their patrons, so that when the inhabitants of Istanbul awoke in the morning, they would behold corpses hanging from trees and be terrorized enough to forgo enjoying themselves again. Whether the director realized it or not, this depiction reflects Solakzade's complaint that because of Kadızadeli incitement, thousands of innocent people faced the sultan's wrath and were executed.[25]

Kadızadelis and Sultans

The crucial issue for the historian is the relation of the movement's leaders with the sovereign and whether he fully supported encouraging or compelling Muslims to create a more pious society. As Roy Mottahedeh notes concerning an earlier period in Islamic history, "Kings sometimes accepted the intercession of such men, and they did so not only because they admired men of outstanding piety, but also because such men had a certain following."[26] Murad IV was not a Kadızadeli. He maintained personal connections with Sufis condemned by the movement, including the disciples of Sivasi Efendi, whom he honored, and was often their benefactor, supporting Sufi orders throughout the empire.[27] He was a patron of Mevlevis and Halvetis. Thus Halvetis and their enemies the Kadızadelis both benefited from their relation with this sultan. Murad IV implemented only those Kadızadeli ideas, such as closing coffeehouses, that befitted his authoritarian rule. There was economic and political support for the suppression of the coffee trade. When the members of the Istanbul butchers' guild complained of being placed behind the Egyptian merchants in a procession, they criticized goods from Egypt, including coffee, which "is an innovation; it prevents sleep; it dulls the generative powers; and coffee houses are dens of sedition."[28] Rycaut also considered coffeehouses abodes of insurrection, "melancholy places where Seditions were vented, where reflections were made on all occurrences of State, & discontents published and aggravated."[29]

Along with banning allegedly morally harmful and politically dangerous products such as tobacco and coffee, the Kadızadeli preacher urged Murad IV to fulfill his duty as head of an Islamic empire to struggle against widespread erroneous beliefs and to condemn and punish those who held them. What this led to, however, was "dispute and fighting," in the words of Katip Çelebi. In place of reasoned critiques of superstitious practices, "stupid men" imitated Kadızade and joined the faction of "bigoted zealots, having a passion for quarreling and brawling." "Bigoted antagonism" reached such a level that, in the view of the Kadızadelis, "massacre became canonically lawful." The levelheaded writer Katip Çelebi called on the sultan to not let people go too far and upset the order of society, to prevent "men of folly" from brandishing their weapons, not to allow any group of fanatics to appear victorious, but to "subdue, punish, and chastise these false bigots because much sedition emerges from the strife of bigotry," whether it is caused by Sufis (Halvetis) or revivalists (Kadızadelis).[30]

Kadızade remained close to Murad IV. Anticipating the future exploits of the Kadızadeli preacher Vani Mehmed Efendi, Kadızade initially accompanied the sultan on the Armenian campaign. But after becoming ill, he turned back at Konya, where he passed away in 1635.[31] After Kadızade's death his followers maintained influence in the palace among the halberdiers, palace guards, sweet makers, gatekeepers, servants of the inner palace, harem eunuchs, and artisans, and in the market among merchants. Members of these well-connected groups served as mediators, proselytizing the Kadızadeli path to piety. Child Sultan Mehmed IV's mother, Hatice Turhan, and the commanders of the palace supported the movement against a palace faction consisting of Mehmed IV's grandmother Kösem Sultan and the commanders of the military who supported such Sufi orders as the Halvetis and Bektashis.[32] The murder of Kösem Sultan in 1651 cleared the path for greater Kadızadeli influence.

At first the young Sultan Mehmed IV and those around him showed no inclination to act any differently from their predecessors in matters of religion. Mehmed IV received religious instruction from some of the leading Sufi dervishes of the day. Mevlevi dervishes in particular played an important role early in his reign. Not only did the Mevlevi Mehmed Pasha participate in the girding of Mehmed IV at Eyüp in 1648, but the following year Sari Abdullah Efendi (d. 1661) presented to the young sultan *Advice to Kings Encouraging a Good Career* in an effort to teach him to keep on the straight path and avoid the errors made by men of state.[33] Sari Abdullah Efendi was also the author of a commentary on the first volume of the *Mesnevi*, the thirteenth-century mystic Jalaluddin Rumi's six-volume work of rhymed couplets explaining the Sufi path of love. The Sufi Minkari Ali Halife Efendi presented the sultan with *The Spiritual Healing of the Believer* in 1653.[34] The second chapter in the second book includes sections entitled "The Virtues of Dhikr," repeatedly invoking God's ninety-nine names as a form of prayer, and "The Etiquette of Dhikr." All of these works were presented to the young sultan and deposited in the royal treasury with other valuable books. Finally, as a child Mehmed IV studied with the imam Sami Hüseyin Efendi (d. 1658), a man of great learning referred to in contemporary narrative sources by the Sufi phrase "luminous spiritual teacher."[35]

In addition to a Mevlevi Sufi interpretation of Sunni Islam, the presence of Kadızade's successor, Arab Üstüvani Mehmed Efendi of Damascus (d. 1661), illustrates the presence of the Kadızadeli religious trend at Mehmed IV's court. Because of Üstüvani Mehmed Efendi's close connections with palace servants and his intimate relationship with the sultan's teacher, he even entered the royal ward in 1651 and began to preach there contrary to statute, which hints at his charisma. According to Naima, this man mediating conversion to piety became the sultan's sheikh and gained quite a following as he cursed dervishes and labeled them infidels.[36]

Muslims such as Üstüvani Mehmed Efendi underwent a spiritual conversion, a revitalized commitment to the faith, and spurred other Muslims to join their religious revival. In a period in which rebels acted not only as mercenaries, but as quasi-Sufi brotherhoods complete with a hierarchy of sheikhs and disciples and secret rituals, an Islamic reform movement came to the fore in the midst of crisis, upheaval, and change.[37] The leaders of this movement, such as Üstüvani Mehmed Efendi, championed restrictions on the practices of Muslims they labeled innovations, which had not been sanctioned by Muhammad. The Kadızadelis sought to replace the Islam practiced in Istanbul with a religion purified of such innovations. This religious movement blamed the empire's military defeat abroad and economic difficulties at home on the affiliation and patronage of members of the Ottoman religious and administrative establishment with Sufi orders and the moral corruption of the religious class.[38]

Enjoining the good and forbidding the wrong entails transforming oneself and then cleaning up society. Yet how could society be returned to the right path when the head of the religious establishment engaged in corrupt practices? Two-time sheikhulislam Baha'i Efendi spent his time "chatting with friends and using narcotics." He was so immersed in them that "he gave the reins of his decisions to the hand of narcotics."[39] Since the "shameless pleasure-seeking" sheikhulislam was so incapacitated from hemp or opium syrup, "giving the pen of fatwa to him abrogated time-honored law and even violated the honor of the Shariah." Within a couple of years, "by continually swallowing at one gulp the deadly poison of pure soluble opium syrup and opium acquired from postman Ahmed and coffee seller Mehmed, he was thrown into the agony of death putting dust into his mouth with his own hand trying to satisfy his pleasure."[40] Üstüvani Mehmed Efendi's followers had been the enemy of opium-eating Baha'i Efendi, who gave a fatwa permitting tobacco.

Other examples of corruption included Sheikhulislam Sunizade's downfall for bribery and lenient treatment of heretical scholars. In 1653 the mosque
lecturer Kurdish Mehmed Efendi, based at the madrasa affiliated with Suleiman I's mosque, was released with a mere renewal of his vows of faith and was
not executed "although his heresy was well known."[41] At the same time there
were disputes in the ranks over who should rise to become the leading Muslim religious authority in the land, also illustrating chaos in administration.[42]
Üstüvani Mehmed Efendi even went so far as to call the sheikhulislam Yahya
Efendi an infidel for the poetry he had written. The sheikhulislam responded
boldly by writing, "In the mosque let hypocrites have their hypocrisy. Come to
the tavern where neither pretense nor pretender be."[43] Rising in influence in
part due to a reaction to early and mid-seventeenth-century corruption among
religious scholars, and the economic and political failures of the Ottoman pol-
ity, the Kadızadelis offered steps to restore Muslim society to greatness.

Üstüvani Mehmed Efendi promoted coercion and violence as means of
converting Muslims to his vision of piety. He gained considerable influence
over members of the dynasty in the 1650s, which caused a crackdown on
Sufis, questioned dynastic links with Sufis, and caused unrest among Muslims
throughout the imperial capital. Üstüvani Mehmed Efendi convinced Grand
Vizier Melek Ahmed Pasha to raid the Halveti lodge at Demirkapı in 1651 and
storm other lodges in this manner. Janissary disciples of a Sufi sheikh managed to save a Halveti lodge of Sivasi Efendi's cousin and disciple, a preacher
at Suleiman I's mosque. The grand vizier ordered that Sufi rituals not be disturbed, but the Kadızadelis intended to purify the city of Sufi practices and
Sufis. They especially targeted Sivasi's Sufi brotherhood because of its dancing
and whirling. Intending to prevent any interpretation of Islam other than their
own understanding, the Kadızadelis told them they would raid their lodge,
kill them, dig out the foundations of their building, and dump them into the
sea.[44] In addition, the Kadızadelis also trashed the tombs or refuges for Sufis
that served as popular pleasure gardens, such as one in Çamlıca in Üsküdar
that Mehmed IV enjoyed frequenting and in which he had constructed a place
for repose that Kadızadelis broke apart in 1655. They wanted a landscape de-
nuded of such ornaments of pleasure. At that time Üstüvani Mehmed Efendi
preached at Fatih Mosque. When the Venetians captured the islands of Bozca
and Limni, the Kadızadelis blamed the loss of the islands on the fact that Grand
Vizier Boynueğri Mehmed Pasha was a Sufi. Around the same time, Kadızadeli
preachers attached to the privy garden incited the head of the palace guards to
shut down dervish lodges in Üsküdar and to raid another lodge in Kasımpaşa
and seize its Sufis.[45] In Eyüp Kadızadelis also put pressure on a sheikh and his
disciples to desist from engaging in whirling, which they considered an act of

polytheism, but the sheikh refused to change his ritual unless there was a decree from the sultan ordering him to abandon the practice. At that time, before Mehmed IV's majority, one was not forthcoming.

Further Opposition to the Kadızadelis and Strife among Muslims

The growth in the movement's influence did not follow a linear trajectory. There were setbacks when administration interest in law and order hindered both Kadızadelis and their opponents the Halvetis. Following the actions of the head of the palace guards, the sultan returned to Istanbul, dismissed him from office, and sent him into exile.[46] In the 1653 battle of the books, zealous Halvetis, including a Kurdish scholar named Molla Mehmed, wrote treatises defending their whirling devotions and criticizing and satirizing the foundational treatise of the Kadızadelis, Birgili Mehmed Efendi's *Way of Muhammad*, a book read by most Kadızadelis and used as their propaganda tool.[47] Üstüvani and his followers argued that the Halvetis articulated ideas contrary to Sunni Islam and deserved to be executed as heretics. Instead, *their* books were banned and the sheikhs were exiled. According to Katip Çelebi, "no one benefited."[48] A book was at the center of another dispute involving a follower of Kadızade in eastern Anatolia two years later. Evliya Çelebi criticized humorless fanatics because they hindered conversion, gave Islam a bad name, and caused strife because they told other Muslims what it means to be a Muslim. He satirized a Kadızadeli follower as "a person claiming to belong to the hypocritical, fanatical and pederastic sect of the followers of Kadızade, a cowardly and slanderous usurer, a catamite and mischief-maker, despised even by the ignorant, an obscure and nasty individual, mothered in sin, belonging to the tribe of the deniers." This particular Kadızadeli destroyed the fifty miniatures in a Persian *Book of Kings*, which he had pledged to purchase at auction, because he believed painting was forbidden. When asked why he had ruined the book, he responded, "Is that a book? I thought it was a priest's writing. I 'forbade evil.' I did well to destroy it." The pasha responded, "You are not charged to 'forbid evil.' But I am charged to practice government."[49] In this case, a struggle between enforcing communal morality and following the laws of the land and protecting the sultan's property was decided in favor of the latter.

Opposition to the Kadızadelis continued to be voiced in intellectual circles. Sheikhulislams, who were head of the official religious hierarchy, and magistrates in Istanbul, responsible for applying Shariah, frequently opposed them for challenging their religious authority, violating the law, not observing their citations, and inciting rebellion, in addition to attacking Sufi orders to which they were affiliated or at least sympathetic.[50] Katip Çelebi wrote *The Balance of Truth* arguing the futility of forcing people to abandon long-held customs and beliefs.[51] Concerning the prohibitions of the age, he argued that dancing or whirling, if it was intended for God, was acceptable; that the consumption of tobacco should be allowed because its use was widespread and unstoppable; that coffee could not be perpetually banned; that it was foolish to interfere with drug addicts; and that people could not be deterred from visiting tombs to seek favors. He further argued that it was folly to hope to contain innovation, for once a custom has taken root it becomes legitimate and cannot simply be wiped out. Rebuking the Kadızadelis, he wrote that "enjoining right and forbidding wrong" was an acceptable practice, but there should be no prying. He warned that those who sought to police morals and labeled others as heretics were arrogant and unkind. They stirred up fanaticism, leading to bloodshed.

Katip Çelebi's admonitions proved accurate. The intrareligious dispute incited by the Kadızadelis caused Muslims to split into factions and take every opportunity to dispute with each other on every street corner, at every public gathering, and in every mosque, each side attempting to expose the other to public scorn.[52] By the mid-1650s, the disputes had turned violent. Friday prayers at imperial mosques devolved into shouting matches and brawls. On one Friday in August 1656, when the muezzins at the Fatih Mosque began to chant a laudatory melody to Muhammad, a group of Kadızadelis, to silence the song, raised a ruckus and began to insolently revile the muezzins in an obscene manner.[53] When their opponents tried to stop them, "it nearly caused them to slaughter each other." After this the Kadızadelis decided to raid and raze all the Halveti lodges. They planned to gather at Fatih Mosque with weapons to do away with those who would hinder them from attacking members of that order and their lodges. Most of the religious class expressed its opinion to the sultan that "in accordance with the Shariah it was necessary that those who caused the spread of sedition and disorder be killed."[54] In the minds of religious scholars, the Kadızadelis were both ignoramuses who preached unreasonable things, ideas that not coincidentally went against what the elite and most of the religious class supported, and a popular group with a wide following. They had to be repelled. The sultan agreed with them, as he had not yet converted to Kadızadeli piety, yet the grand vizier intervened and exiled their leaders instead.

Some of the harshest criticism of the group, unsurprisingly, comes from the sultan's astrologer, the Salonican-born Mevlevi Sufi Ahmed Dede, son of Lutfullah. He referred to the Kadızadeli affair as an uprising or rebellion and offered dire warnings about their real motives. He called them a "ragged group of bigots" and ignoramuses, led by "ignorant, banal preachers." They aimed to murder not only Sufis, but also "monotheists" (Muslims) who opposed them and plotted to use violence to intimidate and exercise power or dominate the sultan "just as the wicked and rebels have done since ancient times."[55] Threatened by their rise in influence, the urbane astrologer looked down on them as country bumpkins who dared attack his interpretation of Islam.

Modern scholars have often adapted similar anti-Kadızadeli viewpoints, which has hindered exploration of the prevailing interpretation of Islam in the late seventeenth century so crucial for understanding conversion and conquest in that era. Normally sober scholars become intemperate when writing about the Kadızadelis. In a chapter entitled "The Triumph of Fanaticism" in his history of the Ottoman Empire, Halil Inalcik seems positively relieved when the grand vizier exiles "the inflammatory fakîs from Istanbul," which prevents civil war since the "faki demagogues," who appealed to "popular religious fanaticism," intended "a general massacre."[56] Ahmed Yaşar Ocak denigrates the intelligence of the Kadızadelis and their followers, considering their movement to have been based on "a very superficial, simple minded" set of ideas "without any serious intellectual content"; they were "quite superficial" and "rather crude" and took advantage of "the ignorance and naivete of the public."[57]

Ocak is correct to point out that it is fruitful to consider the struggle among Muslims over the correct interpretation of Islam to also be social strife "articulated in a religious idiom."[58] Militant Kadızadeli activism had socioeconomic, class, and ideological motivations and pointed to underlying ethnic tensions. Similar to concerns voiced by writers of advice literature anxious about what they perceived to be the corruption of societal organization, opposition to the Kadızadelis was in part based on the usurping of elite positions by outsiders. Kadızadelis were usually not Ottomans in the limited sense of the word, trained in the imperial schools of the capital, but often of provincial origin, and received their initial training in the provinces. Once in Istanbul they struggled for positions within the religious hierarchy. As mosque preachers they held positions that paid less and carried less prestige than the judgeships and professorial positions held by the well-established jurists they attacked. Their primary targets were members of the establishment-supported Sufi orders such as the Halvetis and Mevlevis, who, not coincidentally, were their main competitors for posts as preachers in Istanbul's imperial mosques.[59] In the seventeenth century, many rebels originated in the Caucasus (Abkhazia and Georgia), while their opponents were from southeastern Europe (Albania, Bosnia), pointing to ethnic tensions among the ranks of Muslims serving the state.[60] The dispute between the Kadızadelis and the Halvetis displays similar dynamics of ethnic antagonism, as the former were mainly migrants from the Anatolian provinces, including Turks from central Anatolia and Kurds from eastern Anatolia, or Arabs from Syria, while their opponents were from Istanbul and southeastern Europe.

Like rebels in the countryside who desired not autonomy but to be recognized with imperial positions and made part of the elite of the military hierarchy, Kadızadelis sought recognition from the top and an elevated place in the religious hierarchy. Perhaps wisely, the Kadızadelis did not target Sufi orders affiliated with the military to achieve this purpose. They did not attack the Bektashis, intimately associated with the Janissaries, who continued to play an important social and even military role during this period.[61] Because members of the official religious hierarchy were also members of Sufi orders, this was less a conflict between orthodoxy and Sufism than a clash between the proponents of an imagined pristine Islam and their Ottoman rivals who supported certain Sufi practices, personalities, and orders while attacking others. As mosque preachers the Kadızadelis were in a position to stir up the populace and upset intra- and interreligious relations in society. As preachers to the sultan, they would be able to promote the implementation of unprecedented practices concerning conversion of people and places.

Kadızadelis and Grand Viziers

Üstüvani Mehmed Efendi's popularity in the palace among some of the sultan's servants ended when the movement he headed appeared uncontrollably violent and Kadızadeli preachers were blamed for inciting rebellion. Following the loss of Bozca and Limni islands, the sultan's court, agreeing implicitly with some Kadızadeli critiques, decided to offer the post of grand vizier to the septuagenarian Köprülü Mehmed Pasha, a person known for having good moral qualities.[62] It was forgotten how Köprülü Mehmed Pasha had once sided with the rebel turned grand vizier İpşir Mustafa Pasha. Karaçelebizade, echoed by other contemporary writers, compares the new grand vizier to King Solomon's vizier, Asaf, the prototype in Islamic history writing of the perfect administrator.[63] He hoped the appointment of this official could serve as the answer to all the complaints the author makes in the preceding several hundred pages of his book, as if he is the one person (since the sultan is almost entirely absent from the narrative following his enthronement, other than as the audience of his sustained critique of society) who can make things right in the empire.[64] Köprülü Mehmed Pasha, who sided with the religious establishment and not the upstart preachers, immediately exiled Üstüvani Mehmed Efendi and two other leaders of the movement, Seyyid Mustafa Efendi and Turkish Ahmed Efendi, to Cyprus in hopes of restoring order to the city; they had gone beyond the pale in their sermons, inciting riot, inspiring bloodshed, using weapons to promote good and prohibit evil, and gathering men and weapons at Fatih mosque, preparing for a general assault on Halveti Sufis.[65]

Chronicle writers concluded that the Kadızadelis faced an insurmountable foe in the person of Grand Vizier Köprülu Mehmed Pasha. Solakzade noted that since the three leaders of the group were exiled, "the names were forgotten like the renown of liars."[66] The Kadızade affair of 1656 serves as one of the last events narrated in Solakzade's history. This placement at the end of his text leaves the reader curious about whether the movement was stamped out so easily.

Köprülü Mehmed Pasha's actions against the Kadızadeli preachers and religious scholars illustrate some of the successful policies he implemented, which have earned him fame for ushering in a period of relative stability in the empire. Sultan Mehmed IV appointed the Albanian Köprülü Mehmed Pasha, who had risen from a cook serving Murad IV to a vizier in Ibrahim's Divan, to be grand vizier by agreeing to the latter's condition that he receive unlimited freedom to enact even unpopular and draconian policies, that he would make all appointments, and that no one could challenge his independence.[67] Evliya Çelebi accurately refers to him as an "independent grand vizier."[68] Köprülü Mehmed Pasha's policies soon put an end to the serious troubles afflicting the empire, in part through spilling blood in purges and mass executions of alleged troublemakers, including rebels, viziers, governors general, provincial officials, and religious scholars, which allowed him to achieve remarkable political control within a short period of time. According to Ahmed Dede, his bloodbath "terrorized and frightened everyone"; as Silahdar notes, "He restored health to the constitution of the state with the elixir of the sword."[69] In his first year in office, the grand vizier apparently killed as many as ten thousand rebels and outlaws and had the severed heads of the ringleaders sent to the capital.[70] He is credited for wiping out bandits and banditry, rebels and rebellion in Anatolia, and even the families of outlaws, and seizing their wealth. He collected nearly one hundred thousand muskets of commoners and sent them all to the armory in Istanbul, pacifying the countryside. Because he had total authority concerning the administration of state, opponents were silenced, and when executed their wealth accrued to the treasury. He wiped out all opposition, beginning with Janissaries who had immediately gathered at the Hippodrome when he became grand vizier, sipahis settled in Istanbul, and any other rebels in the empire that he could find.[71]

Mehmed Halife argues that the new grand vizier had to brandish his sword and strike terror into the heart of the Janissaries because between the execution of Ibrahim in 1648 and 1656 they had rebelled nine times. The Janissaries had unjustly killed countless people, looted the wealth and property of the viziers, attacked Topkapı Palace, and even allegedly ate the flesh of their enemies; yet against foreign soldiers they failed to fight well, and, because their salaries could not be paid, caused officials to oppress people to collect the money. Muslim, Christian, and Jewish commoners then took the dire step of fleeing to Iran or western Europe, which harmed the empire further. Accordingly, Köprülü Mehmed Pasha, a wise old man who knew of their treachery firsthand, had to wipe the Janissaries out: "He killed so many sipahis and Janissaries in Edirne that the Tunca River was filled with corpses."[72] These actions allowed him to take credit for putting the empire in order and making the state sound.[73] Playing on the name of the grand vizier, Kurdish Preacher Mustafa notes that he became renowned for building "a strong and sound, fortified bridge [köprü] across the waters of the kingdom."[74] Köprülü Mehmed Pasha was successful in recapturing the seas, retaking the islands, reconquering outlying provinces, and ridding the countryside of rebels. Forced loans, improved tax collection, the raising of new levies, limiting expenses, and increasing the tribute of provinces enabled him to refill the treasury and balance the budget.[75] One problem he did not solve, however, was Crete.

Köprülü Mehmed Pasha, Conquest, and Conversion

With Köprülü Mehmed Pasha as grand vizier, we witness a brief period of conquest and conversion of sacred space abroad. This became significant when Ottoman writers during Mehmed IV's majority connected these prior conquests to the conversion of the religious geography of the imperial capital during the 1660s. The Ottoman navy defeated the Venetian navy and reconquered the islands of Bozca and Limni in 1657. Karaçelebizade notes that this caused "unbounded joy for the warriors of the religion," but "grief and sorrow to the damned and disappointed." He adds that the entire Muslim world had been desperate to hear cheerful news, especially word of conquest and victory, so when it arrived, their joyous celebration in Istanbul "lit up the dark night like a spring day."[76] The victory also caused relief because it opened the straits to Ottoman ships, ending the threat of starvation in the capital. The Ottoman soldiers who took the island found that the Venetians had expended great effort building a deep trench, a great wall, a well-fortified tower, and numerous bastions. If the formidable defense network had been completed, it would have ensured that the island would be all but unconquerable. Istanbul would truly have been cut off because provisions would not be able to reach it from the Mediterranean via the Dardanelles. With the imperial capital's only accessible water being the Black Sea, its inhabitants would have been robbed of peace.

But that did not happen. Instead, mosque prayer niches and minarets transformed by crosses and church bells were rededicated to Muslim worship as the landscape of the island was converted. Friday prayers were rendered in spaces purified and cleansed by rose water and perfumed with aloe wood and ambergris. The island again became a Muslim space, "luminous with the lights of the marks of Islam."[77] Kurdish Preacher Mustafa also describes the battle for Bozca Island and subsequent rededication of Muslim sacred space in religious language: "The zeal of religion overflowed in [Köprülü Mehmed Pasha's] breast and with a large, undulating army, he commanded a campaign, whose fruit is victory, against the miserable infidels." When the naval forces of Admiral Topal (Lame) Mehmed Pasha reached the navy of the enemy, "the ships of the enemies of religion were scattered, routed, ruined, and sunk; with divine aid the navy of the miserable infidels was cut in pieces like their unlucky hearts. And on that victorious day, the Qur'anic verse 'those of the party of God are successful and prosperous' (Al-Mujadilah, the Disputation, 58:22) was manifest. The Muslim soldiers and true monotheists raised the battle call and prayer of conquest," and the Ottoman forces "surrounded the island like an ocean and the heavens reverberated with the echo of cannon and musket, and the jaw-rattling sound of the kettledrum and horn of the ghazis."[78] A miniature from that era shows a drummer from the military band banging away on a pair of very large drums half his height; another miniature illustrates a man playing the shrill double reed pipe that, when accompanying the drum, must have caused a chill to run down the enemy's spine.[79] According to Kurdish Preacher Mustafa, conquest and victory were facilitated by God. To thank God and symbolize their conquest of the island over the enemies of religion, Ottoman soldiers "chanted the call to prayer and prayers in the masjids and mosques. The call to prayer obstructed [stuffed straw into] the bells of the churches, the candle of Islam illuminated every corner of the churches, and the Qur'anic verse beginning with 'revenge over the infidels' was manifest."[80] This fulfilled Kara-çelebizade's wish that "the sultan will cleanse the islands of church bells and raise again minarets so Muslims can pronounce the call to prayer."[81]

The Weak Sultanate

Ottoman chroniclers praised the grand vizier for re-Islamizing islands in the Aegean. Köprülü Mehmed Pasha is conventionally praised in modern historiography for his dictatorial policies that brought order to the realm. His era is referred to as a return to the status quo, in which the empire was soundly administered, orderly, and militarily and financially successful: the tenure of

Köprülü "gave to the Ottoman Empire a further, though brief interval of glittering, but illusive splendour."[82] Most modern histories of the second half of the seventeenth century, which mention Mehmed IV only in passing, wax eloquently on the "Köprülü Era."[83] It is claimed that "Ottoman history of the second half of the seventeenth century is dominated by the name of Köprülü."[84] What is meant is that modern history writing is dominated by attention to the Köprülü viziers, since contemporary history writers did not pay them as much attention as the moderns. This bears some explaining. Some accounts of his vizierate cause the reader to wonder why, in light of the knowledge of the horrors of authoritarianism and militarism, scholars are so enthusiastic about praising "a régime of terror" by a man Silahdar labeled "an opinionated, selfish, merciless, cruel tyrant who unjustly killed people and shed blood."[85] He was also accused of ultimately weakening the empire over the long term because he broke the back of the administration and military, placing in office unknown people and giving them no power. It is curious that modern scholars seem so desperate for a strong man to appear on the seventeenth-century Ottoman scene. Perhaps it is a desire to see the Ottomans stave off their post-Vienna territorial decline and ultimate ruin in the ashes of war and the humiliation of colonial occupation in the early twentieth century. An undertone of "if onlys" can be read into such accounts, such as "If only there had been more grand viziers like Köprülü the empire could have rebounded and taken Vienna."

What is confused in such accounts is the question of what the vizier was trying to restore: Was it the empire, or the dynasty? Or was he trying to establish his own Köprülü household at the expense of the Ottoman household, seizing the opportunity afforded by Hatice Turhan Sultan, who had tried to use his elite household to control all others?[86] At least one opposition figure, a sheikhulislam who was dismissed from office and exiled, claimed that Köprülü Mehmed Pasha was not serving the dynasty and religion, but his office.[87] Sultans such as Mehmed IV then had to reassert their own household in politics. Scholars often do not distinguish between the empire and the dynasty, which were intricately related, each acquiring legitimacy from the other, but the grand vizier was more concerned with the empire than the royal household, whose effective power had been slipping for at least half a century. By demanding almost absolute powers that even the sultan could not oppose, he aimed to improve imperial finances, strengthen the military, and end religious and military threats to the empire's authority and even survival. By working to strengthen the office of the grand vizier at the expense of the sultanate, the grand vizier hastened the process that decreased the relevance of the sultan. During his short reign in office it was clear that the grand vizier was the effective head of state. And in fact, the empire received some respite from its troubles after he was appointed grand vizier. But the Ottoman royal household still lacked the powerful symbols that would signify its renewed strength and for nearly five years was overshadowed in every respect by an iron-fisted elderly statesman whom it had agreed to place in office. How could the dynasty assert its relevance following years of crisis and upheaval and upstaging by ministers?

Colin Imber's wide-ranging book devoted to the Ottoman Empire from its origins to 1650, which actually ends before the reign of Mehmed IV, argues that when sultans could no longer serve as heroic figures propelling the empire to success after success, the empire depended on the scribal service on the one hand, and the Shariah courts and legal system on the other, to maintain popular confidence and ensure its empire's survival.[88] The writer of this study seems to be closed to the possibility that sultans could indeed again become mobile ghazis, pious models of behavior. This raises the question of whether sultans were ever again heroic or again aimed to be depicted that way. What was necessary to guarantee the survival of the dynasty? Would any sultan ever echo Mehmed II, who had declared, "The ghaza is our basic duty, as it was in the case of our fathers"?[89]

To see how the leading members of the dynasty responded in the 1660s to crisis, calls to turn to piety, and subordination to the grand vizier, one has to return to Mehmed IV, no longer a boy, by this point a young man of nineteen or twenty. As Naima notes, at the same time that Köprülü Mehmed Pasha was taking back Bozca Island, Mehmed IV, by being attentive to the needs of his subjects, was demonstrating his mature behavior, intelligence, and vigilance necessary for being sultan.[90] One has to look also at the actions of valide sultan Hatice Turhan, who was primarily responsible for shaping the public image of the Ottoman dynasty. The two worked hand in hand to strengthen the dynasty and sultanate.

4

Islamizing Istanbul

At the beginning of Mehmed IV's majority, cataclysmic natural disaster served as a watershed in conversion. Fire that devastated most of Istanbul provided an opportunity for the valide sultan to manifest her conversion to piety by engaging in unprecedented policies, converting a Jewish landscape into a Muslim landscape, including building an imperial mosque complex in the heart of the city's main Jewish neighborhood. The Ottoman narratives of the construction of the mosque in Eminönü demonstrate how the creation of an Islamic sacred geography in Istanbul occurred alongside and in place of Jewish structures, an act considered by chroniclers as conversion and conquest of infidel space, mirroring the same processes on Bozca Island. In an era where ghaza was emphasized, it was natural to compare the conversion of the sacred geography of Istanbul to jihad. The most visible and symbolic manifestation of the conversion of the landscape in Ottoman territories in the wake of conquest had always been the transformation of churches and synagogues into mosques and the construction of grand royal mosques to mark the hegemony of the new rulers. Imperial mosques marked spaces and delimited boundaries, expressed power, supported political and hegemonic interests, and conveyed meaning both to those who entered them and those who passed by outside.[1] Major changes to urban space redefine the dominant features of a city, how people perceive and experience their environment, and influence world outlooks.[2] For Muslims,

Islamization offered a visible sign of the successes of the dynasty and religion emerging phoenixlike out of the ashes of despair.

Köprülü Mehmed Pasha's successor, his son Fazıl Ahmed Pasha, marked his turn to a more rigorous interpretation of Islam with the promotion of the Islamization of Christian space in the capital in the wake of the same cataclysmic event. Chroniclers linked Fazıl Ahmed Pasha's Islamization policies in Istanbul with his waging war against Christians in central Europe and converting their churches to mosques. Thus writers surveyed the terrain from Hungary to Istanbul and considered the raising of minarets in place of church bells and the construction of prayer niches facing Mecca rather than Jerusalem to be part of the same manifestation of piety.

This chapter mainly addresses one of the book's central themes: how conversion affects religious geography and sacred space. I discuss the great fire of the summer of 1660 and the meaning given to it by contemporary writers, Hatice Turhan's converting of Jewish places in the wake of the fire, the construction and dedication of the Valide Sultan Mosque in the heart of the former main Jewish neighborhood, Fazıl Ahmed Pasha's Islamization of Christian places, and how Muslim commoners followed the rulers' example in articulating the call to enjoin good and forbid wrong by removing perceived obstacles to Muslim piety. These processes transformed the religious geography of the imperial capital, shaping a more Islamic landscape.

The Great Fire of 1660 and the Meaning
Given to It by Contemporary Writers

On a hot summer day in July 1660, a great conflagration broke out in Istanbul and incinerated most of the city. Throughout its history, many fires had burned half the city.[3] Although fire was a frequent occurrence in seventeenth-century Istanbul, this was the most devastating the city had ever experienced.[4] It gave meaning to the Turkish proverb, "May God protect Istanbul from fire and Anatolia from plague (or invasion)." Just when "Islambol" was prosperous and flourishing, a city of palaces, great size, population, and wealth, the pride of the Ottomans and Islamic world, it was ruined by fire.[5]

Writing only five years later, Mehmed Halife blames the fire on the immoral behavior of Istanbul's inhabitants. He claims they became conceited because of their prosperity and success and then deviated from the path of God. He spares no class of society in his critique. Commoners cheated each other and did not respect the religious class. The religious class did not act according to the Shariah. Ignoring the Shariah, the merchants, most of whom were liars and hypocrites, engaged in wiles and tricks and did not give alms to the poor. The sultan's servants were excessively disobedient and on the verge of rebellion. Worse still, all classes apparently could think of nothing other than engaging in adultery, fornication, sodomy, and pederasty. In short, Mehmed Halife argues that all Muslims were heedless of the Hadith, which states, "If a city is desecrated and defiled by adultery and fornication, or usury, or rebellion and sin, and there is no one who is faithful, God will purify it by means of four things: fire, famine, epidemic, or by the sword."[6] According to this logic, fire was sent from the other world.

Set off by a young man's tobacco smoking, the fire began in the afternoon either in a store that sold straw products outside of the appropriately named Firewood Gate west of Eminönü, or in one of the stores in the ramparts outside the Gate of the Holy Spring, spreading quickly to the timber stores in the area. It devastated densely crowded neighborhoods consisting of nearly adjoining timbered homes situated on narrow streets bordered by apartment houses several stories tall. It especially affected the lower classes of society, as the well-to-do lived in stone houses surrounded by open spaces. The strong winds of Istanbul caused the fire to spread violently in all directions despite the efforts of the deputy grand vizier and others who attempted the impossible task of holding it back with hooks, axes, and water carriers. Patrols were dispersed in all directions to battle the blaze, but they were bewildered by the quickly moving flames and were unable to hinder the conflagration.[7] Sultan Mehmed IV's chronicler, Abdi Pasha, notes that the fire marched across the city like an invading army: the flames "split into divisions, and every single division, by the decree of God, spread to a different district."[8] The fire spread north, west, and to Unkapanı. According to Mehmed Halife, the spires of the four minarets of the great mosque of Suleiman burned like candles.[9] By evening, the districts of Suleimaniye, Şehzade, and Bayezid had turned to ash. Overnight, the flames did not spare the top of the Hippodrome in the east, nor Mahmud Pasha and the markets at the center of the peninsula, nor Tahtakale and the Jewish neighborhoods of Eminönü, nor areas bordering Topkapı Palace such as Ahırkapı, nor even the Janissary barracks. By the time the fire reached Molla Gurani hardly any structures were still standing. The second day the blaze moved south and west to Davud Pasha, Kumkapı, and even as far west as Samatya. In short, "in a twinkling of an eye, the most sumptuous homes and palaces were turned into wood ashes."[10]

Commentators had a field day. According to Mehmed Halife, "It was as if the flames of Hell had taken over the world, destroyed its people, and drove their souls to the palace of assembly for the Last Judgement."[11] An Ottoman writer in the valide sultan's employ writing only a couple of years after the fire conveys the horror of the event: "Thousands of homes and households burned with fire. And in accordance with God's eternal will, God changed the distinguishing marks of night and day by making the very dark night luminous with flames bearing sparks, and darkening the light-filled day with black smoke and soot."[12] People were terrified and thought it was the end of time. Losing hope that their homes would save them, men, women, and children had sought shelter and refuge for their lives and belongings in the inner courtyards of the large royal mosques, especially Suleimaniye and Bayezid, or other buildings considered safe, but the flames did not spare them there either: "Wherever people sought refuge saying 'we will be saved,' the opposite occurred."[13] People burned along with their possessions as the wind made the flames rain upon them like hail. This fire spared neither a single grain nor a copper coin.

Contemporary writers frequently referred to burning candles when describing the fire. Relying on a Sufi motif, Nihadi writes that hundreds of people, "renouncing all things save love for God," burned like moths that eagerly fly round and round a candle until they ultimately burn.[14] The merciless flames burned countless people along with their goods, and the survivors, "naked and weeping, barefoot and bareheaded, were driven and brought to the Hippodrome" and the inner courtyards of Hagia Sophia and Sultan Ahmed I's mosque. More than one hundred thousand men and women, Muslim, Christian, and Jewish, came to the Hippodrome out of fear of the violent flames of the fire; the throng grew into such a great crowd that people could barely move or breathe.[15] Feeling the fervent flames, the heat of a swelteringly humid July day, and the crush of the pressing crowd made the people fear they would drown in sweat.

Miraculously, the fire died down on the third afternoon, which brought inexpressible relief to the suffering people.[16] Two-thirds of Istanbul was destroyed in the conflagration and as many as forty thousand people lost their lives. Writing soon after the inferno, Vecihi Hasan Çelebi claimed that in only forty-eight hours, "that graceful city that was like paradise the sublime was turned upside down, destroyed and leveled and reduced to ash by the violent fire, and not a trace of the inhabited, prosperous city remained."[17] Writing a generation later, an anonymous chronicler claims that even the thought of the storm of wind-driven violent flames was enough to cause terror.[18]

Without food or water for days, many people were on the verge of death. Thousands died in the famine and plague in Thrace that followed the fire, which Mehmed Halife related were perceived as either signs of the end or caused by people's sins.[19] Only rats that feasted on unburied corpses were satiated. Officials were executed for being negligent in extinguishing the fire.[20] Because three months prior to this fire a conflagration had broken out in the heart of the district of Galata, much of the city lay in ruins in the summer of 1660.

Hatice Turhan's Converting of Jewish Space in the Wake of Fire

The fire served as an opportunity for Valide Sultan Hatice Turhan to conceive of the urban landscape in a new way and to promote Islamization, the conversion of Jewish space into Muslim space. Evliya Çelebi notes that Hatice Turhan traveled around Istanbul in the days after much of it burned, while it was still nothing but an ash heap, to survey the damage.[21] Referring to Köprülü Mehmed Pasha, who had restored a burned mosque, she also desired "to obtain a magnificent reward from God for a pious act." She said, "If there were a mosque in need, I should also repair it." The grand vizier, "knowing the valide sultan's lofty zeal," encouraged the valide sultan to repair" the unfinished imperial mosque complex in Eminönü.[22] Kurdish Preacher Mustafa concludes that the valide sultan "was pleased with the suggestion and that day sent 40,000 gold coins to her steward ordering him to immediately commence work on that noble mosque."[23]

For the valide sultan, not only did constructing her own imperial mosque complex in Eminönü demonstrate the piety and legitimacy of the dynasty she represented, but linking the fire to Jews further legitimized the mosque's construction. While rebuilding the city, unprecedented policies were enacted concerning Jewish houses of worship. Contrary to previous periods in which synagogues were usually allowed to be built or rebuilt, in this period Islamic laws prohibiting reconstruction were strictly applied. Jews had to abandon properties, could not restore their homes or synagogues, and were even expelled from the district where most had resided prior to the fire. In the end, the visual presence of a prominent mosque in Eminönü symbolized the Islamization of the heart of Istanbul.[24]

Hatice Turhan engaged in frequent royal trips that displayed the dynasty's magnificence, munificence, and piety. Although thrilling to the populace when they occurred, Hatice Turhan's showy marches and gifts to the poor left no permanent mark on the skin of an Ottoman city. Because of her sex and age, she could engage in impressive public outings but had no means of articulating a martial message like her son. Instead, she did the next best thing by demonstrating her concern for safeguarding the domains of Islam. Writers celebrated Hatice Turhan for being cognizant of the military situation and building or repairing fortresses guarding the Bosporus, the Black Sea, and especially the Dardanelles (Kilidbahir/Seddülbahir [Lock of the Sea/Dam of the Sea] on the

Rumelian side and Kale-i Sultaniye [Sultanic Citadel] on the Anatolian shore).[25] According to Karaçelebizade, "Noticing infidel ships anchored where the cannons of [Ottoman fortresses] could not reach, which hindered the imperial navy from passing, she exerted herself with manly zeal and endeavored to build two large citadels near where the strait empties into the sea."[26]

Constructing fortresses was important, but it was natural disaster that afforded Hatice Turhan the opportunity to have a physical impact on Istanbul by building a mosque complex in Eminönü, the most meaningful of her monumental public works and a lasting sign of her and her son's Islamic virtue. Her response to cataclysmic fire in 1660 served as the first opportunity to observe Mehmed IV's court in action at the beginning of the crucial part of his reign—his majority—when the dynasty began to assert itself.

In selecting the area in which to erect her mosque and choosing which groups would be moved from the area Hatice Turhan acted on dynastic precedent. The mosque was to be built in a prominent area at the port and near the palace. When a previous valide sultan, Safiye Sultan, like Hatice Turhan a Christian convert raised in the palace, commanded the head of the imperial architects, Davud Agha, to begin the foundation for a mosque in Eminönü in late summer 1597, she had taken advantage of the anger voiced by both Muslim and Venetian traders against Jewish merchants and tax farmers.[27] They claimed that Jews monopolized the textile and other trades and set untenable conditions on foreign traders and Muslims who wished to enter the market. Muslims petitioned the sultan, claiming that Jewish collectors of customs taxes behaved in an unbecoming manner toward Muslims. They requested that Jews be prohibited from collecting the tax, and their wish was granted. Safiye Sultan then expropriated property from Jewish merchants and residents and began to construct the mosque. Following the loss of their property, the Jews of Eminönü began migrating to other parts of the city.

Although the architects had completed its massive foundations, a number of factors stood in the way of the structure's completion. These included criticism of the project in some palace circles, the death of Davud Agha in 1598, the difficulty of placing a large building at that location, and the death in 1603 of both Sultan Mehmed III and his mother, Safiye Sultan.[28] The unfinished mosque was nicknamed "Oppression" (*Zulmiyye*) since many complained about the great expense of an imperial building that the Ottomans were unable to complete.[29] *Zulm* originally meant in Arabic "acting in whatsoever way one pleases in the disposing of the property of another."[30] There was thus criticism that it had not been financed in a proper manner. Shortly thereafter, Jews began to resettle in Eminönü and quickly made it again their primary residence and commercial zone, what Evliya Çelebi called a "weird" situation.[31] The mosque remained in a ruined state until the massive fire of 1660. The fire excavated the foundations of the mosque by clearing all the surrounding buildings that had obscured them.

Hatice Turhan took the opportunity afforded by the fire to clear the neighborhood of Jews and complete the mosque with her own wealth—the second time a valide sultan had expelled the Jews of Eminönü. Although Jews offered a bribe to nullify the decision of the valide sultan, an offer that may have been as great as one-third the total cost of construction for the entire mosque complex, it was refused; in addition, according to Silahdar, Jews were threatened with death if they did not sell their property.[32] Although Jews probably attempted to have the order rescinded in other ways, whether by influencing a key figure at court to intervene on their behalf or through petitioning the imperial council, no other evidence of Jewish attempts to hinder the imperial order has been uncovered. Just under one year after the fire was extinguished, Hatice Turhan, using a portion of her own wealth, began construction of the mosque and complex, which had not been a royal concern for over half a century.[33]

Kurdish Preacher Mustafa's treatise narrating events during the reign of Mehmed IV "is embellished with praise of her Excellency, the valide sultan" Hatice Turhan, and "adorned with her good moral qualities and virtues." As he relates panegyrically, "There is no end to the pious works of her excellency, the valide sultan. Just as her laudable moral qualities are many, so, too, are her works. Among them is the noble mosque whose match has not been seen and whose peer has not been heard, which she constructed in the place known as Eminönü in the well-protected city of Istanbul." The writer makes obvious exaggerations. After all, it was a great stretch to compare this mosque with Hagia Sophia, as he does when he writes, "Intelligent people know that the mosque's foundation and edifice are more sound and lasting than Hagia Sophia," or more solid than the mosques of Ahmed I or Suleiman I which tower over the city.[34] Nevertheless, the emphasis on the Islamic virtue of Hatice Turhan is evident.

This Islamic virtue, which added favorably to the dynasty's good name, came at the expense of Jews, who were viewed at this stage as being less valuable and more vulnerable than Christians, including Orthodox Christians, the largest Christian group in the city, who had a patriarch and increasing financial strength, or Catholics, who had the political, military, and economic weight of western European powers as well as the French ambassador at Istanbul behind them. The French were not on very good terms with the court since they, along with the pope, had sent dozens of galleons to Crete to help Venice beat back the Ottoman siege; still, they could convey Catholic interests at court, whereas no European ambassador stood up for the interests of Jews. The Orthodox Christians in particular were gaining stature in the opinion of key members of the

Ottoman dynasty and administration. Jews were losing their struggle with Orthodox Christian competitors. The Kadızadeli struggle for positions within the religious hierarchy mirrored the competition between Jews and Orthodox Christians for palace favor. In the early 1660s, Kadızadelis and Orthodox Christians were in the ascendancy. Without a patriarch or European support or even the economic wherewithal of the Orthodox Christian elite to counter any move against them, Jews were easy to deport without facing backlash.

Of an estimated forty synagogues in the city, the Shariah court records of Istanbul reveal that at least seven burned in the great fire, representing diverse groups of Jews who had originated in central and southeastern Europe, the Crimea, Anatolia, and Iberia.[35] These synagogues included that of the German congregation of Ashkenazi Jews who had voluntarily migrated to the city in the fifteenth century; the synagogues of the Antalya and Borlu, Dimetoka, Borlu, and Zeitouni/İzdin congregations of Anatolian and Rumelian Romaniot Jews deported to the city by Sultan Mehmed II; the synagogue of the Istanbul congregation of Karaites deported from Kaffa in the Crimea; and the synagogue of the Aragon congregation of Jews who voluntarily migrated to the city following their expulsion from Spain in the fifteenth century.[36] The plots of land on which the synagogues were located and the properties the congregations possessed accrued to the state treasury and became state-owned land, and Muslim foundations purchased them at auction.

Once the synagogue lands were purchased, Jews were also expelled from the area so that they would not rebuild their homes, houses of worship, and shops. Uriel Heyd notes that the Jewish communities of ten neighborhoods in Istanbul, including Zeyrek, Balkapanı, and Hoja Pasha, which had appeared in a population register early in the seventeenth century, were not recorded in a register of 1691–92. He concludes that the Jews must have abandoned these areas since fires had destroyed their neighborhoods.[37] Fire alone, however, did not chase them away. Soon after the blaze an imperial decree copied into the Shariah court record ordered "that after the fire Jews not reside in Istanbul from Hoja Pasha [bordering the walls of Topkapı Palace in the east] to Zeyrek [or Saraçhane in the west]." Another commanded that "the households in which Jews resided located in Istanbul in the neighborhoods of Hoja Pasha and its vicinity that burned in the great fire of the sixteenth of Dhu al-Qa'da 1070 [July 24, 1660] that are private property are to be sold to Muslims, and those that are owned by endowments are to be entrusted to Muslims."[38] Silahdar confirms that the area from Tahtakale (near the Rüstem Pasha Mosque) to Hoja Pasha had been filled with apartment buildings rented out to Jews, which, after burning in the fire, were prohibited by imperial decree from being rebuilt.[39] Authorities also expelled Jews from rented rooms in apartments owned by Muslims in these districts. For example, the members of a Spanish congregation—Gedalya son of Menahem, Musa son of Avraham, and Mena-hem son of Avraham—who rented rooms near Balkapanı had to turn over the property to a Muslim trustee. Likewise, the Portuguese Jew Yasef son of Yako had to relinquish the rented land on which stood a Jewish apartment, and another Portuguese Jew, Ishak son of Avraham, who also resided in a Jewish apartment, had to abandon any claim to the rooms in which he lived.[40]

Most Jews found themselves banished from the peninsula of Istanbul and sent across the Golden Horn to Hasköy after they first lost their homes and synagogues to fire, and then had to evacuate their property so that the valide sultan's mosque could be built. Hasköy's Jewish population nearly doubled, from eleven to over twenty neighborhoods. There were so many Jews in Hasköy—an estimated eleven thousand following the banishment of the Jews of Eminönü—that Evliya Çelebi wrote, "Hasköy is as brimful of Jews as are the cities of Salonica and Safed."[41] These displacements completely transformed Istanbul Jewry. Romaniot and Karaite Jews from displaced independent Anatolian and Rumelian congregations settled along the Golden Horn and Bosporus and were absorbed by congregations of Jews who had migrated from Iberia.[42] These events would help predispose Istanbul Jewry to await a savior who would relieve them of their suffering.

Ottoman narratives concerning the construction of the valide sultan's imperial mosque complex illustrate her concern with Jews. Ottoman historians, writers, and palace preachers cursed Jews for residing around the foundations of the mosque and viewed the destruction of Jewish homes as divine punishment. Referring to the foundations of the original, though incomplete, mosque, Silahdar explained, "It was not suitable for the religion and kingdom of the emperor for the mosque to lie destroyed in a dunghill in the midst of numerous Jewish neighborhoods."[43] Kurdish Preacher Mustafa explains:

> That abandoned and ruined mosque remained amidst the Jews. Just as the darkness of infidelity cloaks their religion, so, too, did they hide the aforementioned mosque's base and foundations with sticks and straws to such a degree that no one knew that it was a foundation of a mosque. By chance one day in the year seventy-one [AH 1071], by divine wisdom an immense fire and burning flame appeared around the aforementioned mosque's foundations and burned most places in the well-protected city of Istanbul. Some Friday mosques and small mosques also became burned and demolished.[44]

Evliya Çelebi, who had a predisposition against Jews, whom he considered fanatical in their adherence to their own customs and their refusal to mingle with other groups, gloated, "By the command of God, all Jewish homes were incinerated and all Jews were banished from that area," and "when there was a great incineration in Islambol the filthy homes of Jews residing within Jews' Gate were destroyed and burned in the flames."[45]

The endowment deed for the mosque uses harsh language to narrate events. More significant is the appearance of the document itself: Sultan Mehmed IV's gilded imperial monogram adorns the first page. The history of the mosque, written for the approval of the sultan and valide sultan, describes the fire in the following fashion:

> By the decree of God the exalted, the fire of divine wrath turned
> all the neighborhoods of the Jews upside down. The effect of the
> flames of the wrath of God made the homes and abodes belonging
> to that straying community resemble ashes. Every one of the Jew-
> ish households was turned into a fire temple full of sparks. Since
> the residences and dwellings of Jews, who are the enemy of Islam,
> resembled the deepest part of Hell, the secret of the verse which
> is incontrovertible, "those that do evil shall be cast into the fire"
> (Qur'an 32:20), became clear, and in order to promise and threaten
> those who deny Islam with frightening things, the verse, "woe to
> the unbelievers because of a violent punishment" (Qur'an 14:2), also
> became manifest.[46]

Qur'an 32:20 is an appropriate verse, for it states, "Those who have faith and do good works shall be received in the gardens of Paradise, as a reward for that which they have done. But those who do evil shall be cast into the Fire. Whenever they try to get out of Hell they shall be driven back, and a voice will say to them: 'Taste the torment of Hell-fire, which you have persistently denied.'"

Scribes in the main Shariah court of Istanbul also gave meaning to the Islamization of Jewish neighborhoods. Some sprinkled gold dust on the phrase "the appropriation of the land of synagogues" in the margin of the Shariah records.[47] These few flakes of gold jump out at the modern researcher whose eyes become dulled by thousands of dusty register pages of monotonous faded black ink. The presence of the glittering metal reflects approval of the dynasty's action, marking it so that it stands out from the other cases of buying and selling of property and other mundane transactions that the scribe recorded.

New dynastic and elite perceptions of Jews, visibly manifest in the striking gold letters of the endowment deed of the Valide Sultan Mosque and Shariah court records describing the appropriation of Jewish properties, indicate how much attitudes had changed since the reign of the conqueror of Constantinople, Mehmed II. That sultan had welcomed Jews expelled from central Europe and brought Anatolian and Rumelian Jews to repopulate Istanbul after it was conquered. Bayezid II allowed Iberian Jews to settle in the city following their expulsion from Spain and Portugal. But Mehmed IV's court confiscated the synagogue properties of the descendants of these Jews and expelled their congregants from the heart of the city to a predominantly Jewish-inhabited village on the Golden Horn.

Completing the Mosque

No expense was spared for the mosque's decoration. The valide sultan's new mosque boasts stunning tile work, some of the finest ever made by Ottoman artisans. The Sovereignty (*Al-Mulk*) chapter of the Qur'an is legible on glazed tiles above all the windows. The shutters of the windows and doors were covered from top to bottom in mother-of-pearl, the floors covered in beautiful Persian and Egyptian carpets. The calligraphy was stunning. It was also an illuminated mosque reflecting the ascribed luminous qualities of the sultan. Evliya Çelebi was struck by its lighting, claiming that the mosque's chandeliers are unlike any other in Istanbul, and perhaps anywhere in the Islamic world, and that it is a well-lit mosque due to its rock crystal and cut glass windows and numerous places for burning candles.[48] He was seconded by the French scientist Joseph Pitton de Tournefort, visiting in 1700, who also noted, "The lamps, chandeliers, spheres of ivory and crystal globes embellish the mosque greatly when lit."[49] As was written near the marker of the direction to Mecca in gilded calligraphy, after the valide sultan found the mosque of (a previous) valide sultan and completed it, "it truly became a Ka'aba for the pious."[50]

In late autumn 1665, Muslims held their first Friday prayers in the valide sultan's new mosque, following an elaborate ceremony attended by the royal family, administration, religious class, military, mosque personnel, and the retinues of the grand vizier and valide sultan.[51] The sultan, "the refuge of religion," the valide sultan, the sultan's favorite concubine, and the "brave prince" arrived at the mosque to perform prayers and then "bestow so many gifts and favors that it boggles the mind and is beyond comprehension."[52] The valide sultan presented to her son a stunning jewel-covered dagger with a handle made from a single solid emerald, on display today in the Treasury Exhibit of Topkapı Palace. She also gave him a diamond-studded sash and ghazi aigrette, also adorned with a pure diamond and ten sumptuously adorned pure Arabian horses.[53] The sultan bestowed forty sable fur cloaks and 150 cloaks upon the leading men of state, including Grand Vizier Fazıl Ahmed Pasha; the sheikhulislam who is "the mufti of mankind"; Sheikh Vani Mehmed Efendi, considered "the famous felicity of religion," for whom the valide sultan had built a lodge in the complex as well; the representative of the descendants of Muhammad; the preacher and imam of the mosque; and the chief eunuch.[54]

The mosque that had once been nicknamed "Oppression" became known as "Justice" (Adliye) since, when she decided to build the mosque, the valide sultan had said, "Let the task be undertaken with justice."[55] "Justice" refers to the just expenditure of the dynasty's wealth. In the sixteenth century Mustafa Ali explained that charitable establishments such as imperial complexes, including Suleiman I's mosque complex, were to be financed by the spoils of war since using funds from the public treasury squandered wealth.[56] By linking the building of the mosque to the conquest of an infidel (Jewish) place, by framing it in an older ghazi language of appropriation, legitimizing the building program by considering it the Islamization of infidel space, and by contributing a great deal of the dynasty's wealth (her own) to the complex's construction, Hatice Turhan sought to promote the view that it was financed appropriately.

A key aspect of the mosque complex is its economic significance. The strategic location of the mosque was chosen in part because of "the commercial advantage of the waterfront site."[57] A central element of the mosque complex was the Egyptian Market, a major center of commerce both within the T-shaped, red brick, domed structure and in the plazas and streets that radiate from it. The dynasty's treasury, like the empire's, had been depleted, and this market consisting of numerous stores enriched both. The opening of the market and the eye-dazzling glitter of its copper-covered spires signaled that the city of Istanbul would continue to be a major international center for trade even after devastating natural disaster.[58] The dynasty's clearing out a space at the city's center and endowing a building whose benefits would accrue to it was a smart financial move, especially as all incoming traders would be pulled into its vortex by the flow of people from the harbor. The hundreds of fruit-bearing trees ornamenting an outer courtyard of the mosque symbolized the spiritual gain to be made from the construction of the mosque and the financial gain from its affiliated markets. As it is today, the Egyptian Market was an unavoidable first stop in the city; then it was a financial plus for the royal family, and a morale booster for those traders who would benefit from it.

Constructing such an important mosque that, although possessing an exterior wall, seems to mingle among the subjects, not tower over them, points to one of the outstanding features of Mehmed IV's reign: a symbolic and often actual return to the personal presence of the sovereign. It was built not on a promontory, as were Topkapı Palace and Suleiman I's mosque, but practically at sea level. Mehmed IV was not like his father, Ibrahim, who did not want commoners to hinder his excursions with their annoying complaints.[59]

Mehmed IV was depicted as relishing being among his subjects. Like his contemporary Charles II of England, who despite a trend of decreasing access to monarchs throughout western Europe, such as at the court of Louis XIV of France, was more approachable than his predecessors, Mehmed IV was also more open and accessible than previous seventeenth-century sultans.[60]

The Valide Sultan Mosque was built in a highly visible place on the seafront in the main harbor of Istanbul, viewable by a maximum number of passersby, Christian, Jewish, and Muslim. As the French commentator de Tournefort noted, "The site of the mosque, which is entirely within the gaze of the palace and in the most visited and crowded spot in the city, makes it the preferred spot during public festivities."[61] Evliya Çelebi also noted its unique situation, for the mosque was literally elevated, requiring marble steps leading to the gates on its four sides.[62] Although it was among the people, it still rose above them. Because of its hilltop location, the Mosque of Suleiman I towered over the city, yet the Mosque of the Valide Sultan held an even more commanding position, for it served as the first imperial edifice that greeted a person arriving at the main port. The valide sultan ordered a royal pavilion to be built adjoining the mosque to serve as an occasional residence for her and other members of the dynasty.[63] The sultan also had an elevated pavilion built on a tower outside the garden in front of the prayer niche.[64] Thus the mosque complex was both among and above the commoners who milled about it, offering the royal household an opportunity to be connected with its subjects. Located beside the city's teeming harbor, this abode placed the royal family downhill from Topkapı Palace and in a more intimate setting near commoners in the most active and lively part of the city.

Conversion as Conquest

The narrative of the Islamization of Eminönü sought to explain the unprecedented policies toward Jews by linking them to fire and utilizing current notions of the conquest of infidel space. It is striking that the leading men and women of the empire viewed the banishment of the Jews and construction of the mosque as a conquest of formerly infidel-occupied land, stages in the construction of an Islamic cityscape.

Those who constructed the mosque displayed considerable historical consciousness. They compared the banishment of Jews from Eminönü to Hasköy with Muhammad's banishment of the Jewish tribe of Banu Nadir from Medina since they chose the Qur'anic chapter "Exile" (or "Banishment," al-Hashr, 59) to adorn the gallery level near the royal lodge.[65] "Exile" narrates how God cast unbelieving Jews out of the city of believers, Medina. And, in what could be understood in late seventeenth-century Istanbul as a reference to recent events, the chapter warns that in the world to come those Jews will also be punished in hellfire.

The mosque and its inscriptions served as public texts which conveyed several meanings to the intended audience of Christians and Jews. Although few knew the meaning of the inscriptions, Christians and Jews recognized that they were Qur'anic texts written in Arabic. They did not need to understand Arabic to realize the radical transformation of the neighborhood and to recognize what the building was.[66] They had to be aware that the ruler had converted the place into a space restricted to Muslims, which they could not enter unless they converted to Islam. Thus the three doors on the gates in the mosque's main courtyard included the shahadah or profession of faith, "There is no God save God and Muhammad is God's messenger," which converts recite when becoming Muslim. This major change to the urban environment altered Christians' and Jews' daily pattern of behavior, causing them to change the way they traveled through and experienced the city, and may have transformed their worldview, leading to belief in prophecies of deliverance, or conversion to Islam.[67]

For many Muslims, the existence of the great mosque on the waterfront facing largely Christian Galata declared the conquest of Jewish space and its enclosure by sacred, Muslim space. In this view the scourge of God manifested in fiery form erased the onerous presence of the Jews. The forlorn neighborhood at the heart of the city, which had been overrun by Jews and represented by the ruined hulk of an incomplete mosque, a symbol of indecisiveness and failure, had been replaced by a proud mosque in a prominent position on the seafront at the center of the city.

While the expulsion order of 1660 was not as severe as Austro-Hungarian Emperor Leopold I's expelling Jews from his imperial capital of Vienna a decade after the Jews were sent from Eminönü, these transformations had a great impact on the face of the city. Istanbul's main port and commercial district of Eminönü had been home to most of the city's Jewish population. Synagogues flourished throughout the peninsula; a synagogue of a Romaniot Jewish community even stood near the Rüstem Pasha mosque on the waterfront. Approximately a year after the 1660 great fire in Istanbul, when Hatice Turhan began construction of the Valide Sultan Mosque in Eminönü, Jews were ordered to leave a wide area; they were expelled from rented rooms, made to sell their property, and compelled to turn over endowments to Muslims. The beginning of a massive public works project radically affected the Jewish population by redistributing them throughout the city.[68] With Hatice Turhan making decisions at court in 1660, attitudes toward Jews contributed to a major geographic and cultural transformation of Istanbul Jewry.

The policy stood in stark contrast to centuries of practice concerning Ottoman treatment of Jews. In accordance with a fatwa issued for the unusual situation, "old" synagogues and their properties destroyed in the fire were appropriated by the state treasury. This policy contradicted earlier Islamic and Ottoman practice; prior to this time only "new" churches or synagogues were razed or appropriated. In some circumstances Jews had been given preferential treatment regarding the construction of new houses of worship in Istanbul.[69] In this case Eminönü, the first area to be Islamized, contained the foundations of an abandoned imperial mosque. Jews who lived there were not able to offer resistance because their economic and political clout was waning, and the valide sultan did not want Jews residing in proximity to her and other members of the dynasty. The imperial complex, which included a Friday mosque, royal mausoleum, fountain, water conduits and channels, school, and the complex of stores that make up the Egyptian Market, was built at the center of the neighborhood. A turn-of-the-eighteenth-century writer adds that the valide sultan not only converted the neighborhood by building a mosque, but also surrounded the new house of prayer with homes for Muslims. She turned a former Jewish apartment into a palatial home in which the preachers and teachers from the mosque complex Hadith school could reside, providing another example of how this dynasty converted Jewish space into Muslim space.[70]

Islamizing the urban landscape in Istanbul was linked to the sultan's military zeal and conquest and conversion of territories abroad. During public celebrations, oil lamps tied to ropes strung between the minarets of the Valide Sultan Mosque in Eminönü were lit, and sometimes colored water added a multihued effect, illuminating the name and seal of the sultan and also the names of cities and principal victories that were the reason for the festival.[71] Thus the mosque was both a place that the sultan and valide sultan could view from the palace, in the throbbing heartbeat of the city, and at the same time a monument from which the sultan could be viewed representationally in the form of his illuminated name and seal, which soared high over the heads of the milling crowds, and visiting dignitaries, viewable throughout the peninsula of Istanbul and across the Golden Horn in Galata, and connected to his successful military conquests. Previously, Istanbul and other major cities in the empire were illuminated and decorated for seven days and seven nights to share the joy of glad tidings, whether the birth of a prince or a military conquest.[72] This was accomplished by lighting the minarets of all mosques and shooting fireworks from boats in the Golden Horn decked out in lights, in addition to exploding models of citadels and cannons made of gunpowder. By illuminating the mosque, the royal household finally had a central location for making the news known. The conquest of one urban space was then used as a billboard posting the name of other conquests in faraway places in central and eastern Europe and the Mediterranean. Putting the sultan's name up in lights was a means of making him present when he was not. Another connection to foreign military conquests was visible every day inside the mosque: one of the columns was brought by a pasha who conquered territory in Crete.[73]

Fazıl Ahmed Pasha and the Islamization of Christian Space

Hatice Turhan transformed a predominantly Jewish neighborhood and commercial district into an area that housed Muslim holy space and international trade. These acts benefited the dynasty's image and financial strength. Yet not all in the targeted audience of Muslims were pleased. After all, owners of Muslim endowments had also lost many properties to the confiscations. As the Shariah court records narrate, they demanded compensation for losses incurred when the valide sultan seized the property (such as stores and Jewish apartments) that they had owned in Eminönü.[74] For example, Ali Çelebi had possessed a Jewish apartment in Eminönü that burned in the fire, but because the land was located near the site of the valide sultan's proposed "Mosque of Justice," he lost possession of it.[75] Mehmed Cemal Efendi son of Mahmud was the trustee of an endowment in Istanbul who had owned stores near the new mosque but had to relinquish the properties to make way for the mosque complex.[76] These are but two examples. Who would stand up for the interests of Muslims similar to these men? Alienating Muslim men of means was no way to boost confidence in the sultan, his mother, or the dynasty.

A second phase of Islamization in the city, this time of Christian places, owed more to the new grand vizier, Fazıl Ahmed Pasha, than to the valide sultan. The new grand vizier was receptive to the complaints of Muslims who had lost property. He discovered that policy toward Christians was markedly different from that concerning Jews. One year and several months after the fire, Grand Vizier Köprülü Mehmed Pasha passed away.[77] He was succeeded in office by his black-bearded, shortsighted, and overweight son, a former governor who was considered a generation after his death to have been "excessively conceited and ill-tempered," yet not "bloodthirsty" like his father.[78] He was one who fought the infidel on the path of Islam (writers use the terms "ghazi" and "mujahid" to describe him), a pious man and former madrasa professor who had studied under former sheikhulislam Karaçelebizade. He was originally educated in the Islamic languages and sciences, including jurisprudence, as a member of the religious class. As evidence of his devotion to learning, Fazıl Ahmed Pasha established a library in Istanbul where the best version of Abdi Pasha's history would eventually be deposited. He may have been young, probably in his mid-twenties, just a few years older than the sultan, but he was intelligent and shrewd and, according to the astrologer Ahmed Dede, "one whose good luck is assured."[79] Once in office, he turned his attention to the situation of Christian churches in Istanbul.

Beginning a year after the fire, while Hatice Turhan was the most important person at court, Armenian, Catholic, and Orthodox Christians in Galata and Istanbul and French and Italian foreign residents in Galata purchased the land where their burned churches stood. According to information culled from the Shariah court records, of an estimated fifty to sixty churches in Galata and Istanbul that existed before the fire in 1660 (thirty to forty Orthodox, ten Armenian, and ten Catholic), at least twenty-five had burned to the ground.[80] Christians who purchased former church land constructed homes there, since the authorities insisted that if they built churches they would lose their property. They were warned not to use their new homes as houses of prayer. In late summer and fall 1661 and winter 1662, Christians reclaimed eighteen church properties in this manner. By permitting Christians to initially reclaim their properties and rebuild their buildings, the valide sultan expressed her dynasty's magnanimity toward them, yet at the same time articulated its sovereignty by limiting what type of structures Christians could erect. At all times Hatice Turhan maintained control over the process that would preserve, or even diminish, but not increase the Christian presence in the city. But this magnanimity would be temporary.

The Catholics' situation was urgent because they were allowed to maintain churches only in Galata, and six of seven churches in use in Galata had burned in 1660.[81] The properties of five ruined Catholic churches were initially purchased at auction.[82] A year after the fire, the Orthodox Christian dragoman Georgi son of Lazari purchased the land of Saints Peter and Paul, located in the Bereketzade quarter. Georgi, who owned a garden bordering the church property, proclaimed his intent to build a home in which to reside. The Muslim magistrate made him record this promise: "If by some means I build a church, let the state treasury again seize the property and take it out of my possession."[83] On that day, Constantine son of Andrea also purchased church properties in the same quarter and made an identical pledge. The foreign Christian resident Riboni son of Martin followed suit and at the same auction purchased the property of the burned Saint George Church, located in the same quarter. Giving the same promise as the others, a group of seven men with Italian names pur-chased the land of the thirteenth-century Italian Franciscan church of Saint Francis, called by Muslims the "ornamented church," and the main church of the Catholics of Galata, along with the property of neighboring Saint Anne Church and a bell tower.[84]

But many of these properties would face the same fate as Jewish proper-ties. According to Rycaut, "And as it happened in the great and notable Fires of Galata first, and then of Constantinople, in the year 1660, that many of the Christian Churches and Chappels were brought to Ashes; and afterwards by the Piety and Zeal of Christians scarce reedified, before by publick order they were thrown down again into their former heaps, being judged contrary to the Turkish Law, to permit Churches again to be restored, of which no more remained than the meer foundation."[85]

This western European perspective is verified and explained by an im-perial decree of 1662, copied into the register of the main Shariah court of Istanbul:

> After some churches of the infidels, polytheists, and those who go
> astray burned in the abode of the exalted caliph, the protected city
> of Constantinople, during the great conflagration of Saturday, Dhu
> al-Qa'da 16, 1070 [July 24, 1660] the state treasury seized them since
> according to canonical law they were not to be restored [to their prior
> condition]. Subsequently, when some [churches] among them were
> purchased for the known price in order not to establish them [again
> as churches], in truth they built and constructed every single church
> in order to be registered. When it became evident that they engaged
> in infidelity, polytheism, and error as before within every single one
> of them, an exalted decree was issued that in accordance with noble
> canonical law, every one of them was to be razed and destroyed and
> the land and walls that were ordered to be demolished be surveyed,
> then investigated and recorded. In compliance with the decree, the
> glory of his peers, Mustafa Çavuş, and magistrate Mustafa Efendi,
> who follows the true path of canonical law, were appointed to the
> aforementioned matter and sent [to investigate it] by the most excel-
> lent of honored men, the treasurer of the European provinces [no
> name provided] pasha, may all sultanic goodness never cease in
> perpetuity with divine providence. He, together with Master Ahmed
> Halife and Frenk Ali Halife of the privy architects, investigated every
> single burned church. The following is a copy of the register that
> he recorded and wrote down after they made their investigations

and survey. It was narrated and recorded on the twentieth day of the
blessed month of Ramadan in the year one thousand seventy two
[May 9, 1662].[86]

One of the privy architects, Frenk Ali, was likely a western European convert
to Islam who oversaw the conversion of Christian places in his adopted city. In
May and June 1662, authorities seized twelve of these eighteen church properties. The imperial decree states the not surprising fact that Christians had rebuilt their churches in the guise of residences and warehouses and used them
to celebrate Christian rites.[87]

While the significance of undertaking such an action during Ramadan
cannot be overlooked, a larger political context may also have contributed to the
apparent about-face concerning Christian houses of worship. In the fall of 1661
an imperial decree caused all present to cry with joy when it was announced
that Fazıl Ahmed Pasha would lead a ghaza to Hungary. The aim was to take
revenge on the Habsburgs, who had seized Ottoman citadels, converted masjids to churches, and taken Muslims captive; the effort was considered "battling
infidels on behalf of the community of Muhammad" by the author who wrote
to preserve for posterity Fazıl Ahmed Pasha's military exploits. Several weeks
prior to the imperial decree concerning the razing of churches in the imperial
capital, the black banner of Muhammad was taken out and the grand vizier led
the army of Islam against the "infidels who have no religion."[88] On the battlefield the soldiers of Islam faced mud up to their knees in the pouring rain,
yet an Ottoman historian wrote, "The mud of jihad on the path of God is the
musk of paradise." After the citadel was conquered, two large churches inside
it were made into mosques for the sovereign, "purified of idols" and "marks of
infidelity," and Friday prayers were rendered.[89] Fazıl Ahmed Pasha's panegyrist
made the connection between making Christians, whether in central Europe
or "Islambol," obey the law and previous agreements, and the conversion of
sacred spaces.[90]

Scribes at the Shariah court expressed what they considered divine approval for the Islamization of Christian places. One wrote a Hadith in Arabic
in the margin of an entry recording the appropriation of Christian property:
"God builds a home in Paradise for the one who builds a mosque for God on
earth."

Religious authorities also gave backing to these decisions. Legal opinions of Sheikhulislam Yahya Efendi Minkarizade (sheikhulislam 1662–73;
d. 1677) reason that a new church or synagogue should be demolished if it had
been built within a municipality whose inhabitants included Muslims who
possessed a mosque. If a church already existed, it could be repaired so long

as it was not enlarged. New buildings or structures were not to be added to preexisting church buildings. If an old church, monastery, or religious school fell into disrepair or even a state of near ruin, its owners could still repair and rebuild it so long as they added nothing to it and built on its original foundation.[91] According to these opinions, not only would Christians and Jews be allowed to rebuild their churches and synagogues if they adhered to these conditions, but there would be no reason to grant permission to one group to build new structures and not to another. An imperial decree claims that, according to canonical law, burned churches were not to be restored. One would infer that, since in 1660 nothing at all remained of the burned churches and synagogues, the state treasury was justified in appropriating the property.

Another legal opinion, a copy of which appears in the Istanbul Shariah court records, reveals why synagogues were not rebuilt. In the extraordinary period following the great fire, a fatwa stated that the lands of *old* synagogues that had burned in the conflagration were to be taken over by the state treasury. Another court record refers to a fatwa that justifies the actions of the state treasury in appropriating the lands of burned churches in Galata.[92] In both cases, the state treasury was able to acquire the land because, according to canonical law, "there is no owner of the land of the burned old church (or synagogue)," or the "builder of the old church (or synagogue) is not known." In addition, Ottoman authorities justified razing the buildings because they had decided that Christians had broken their pledge not to rebuild churches but only homes and, by extension, not to use those homes as churches. One is left wondering, however, whether the Ottoman authorities believed the Catholics of Galata would not rebuild their churches.

Two years after the fire, Christians held on to six properties on which once stood churches that had been destroyed in the conflagration. Two Catholic churches, Saints Peter and Paul and Saint George, are used today.[93] The second phase of Islamization of the built environment had the result that Christians, while managing to hold on to approximately one-fifth of their properties containing burned churches, still lost nineteen.[94] In exchange for the property that Ali Çelebi lost in Eminönü, he became the owner of property that had formerly been connected to a church and a Jewish apartment in Galata. Mehmed Cemal Efendi son of Mahmud, who had lost properties to the valide sultan in Istanbul, took over properties in exchange formerly belonging to Saint Mary (Santa Maria Draperis) in Galata, a Franciscan Catholic church located near Saint Francis Church (which was among the disappearing churches). The parish relocated to Pera, where inside one can view a five-hundred-year-old icon of Mary that, despite being silver, which burns at a relatively low temperature, miraculously survived the fire of 1660.

Rabia Gülnuş Emetullah Sultan, Sultan Mehmed IV's favorite and mother of Sultan Mustafa II and Sultan Ahmed III, transformed the Saint Francis Church into the Valide Sultan Mosque in 1696–97.[95] An early eighteenth-century Ottoman historian gave credit to her pious deed of being "firmly resolved" to build a royal mosque in Istanbul upon the ruins of an important Catholic church and permitting only Muslims to reside in the formerly Christian neighborhood.[96] Another wrote, "Originally, there was a church on the site of this mosque. Later, when it burned, legal permission for its reconstruction was not given and a vacant plot of land remained. Subsequently, this mosque was built. [This is] a chronogram for its completion: 'May the place of worship of the valide sultan be an abode of pious acts!' 1109 [1697–98]."[97] From the mosque in Galata one could see its namesake in Eminönü.[98] Thus two successive mothers of the sultan built mosques that mirrored each other's magnificence by locating them across from each other on the Golden Horn.

Islamization policies reflected the intersection of religion and politics in a specific historic context. Restrictions on church and synagogue building depended on contemporary interests and religious piety. Rulers could carry out these restrictions when they desired to be viewed as pious, to gain political strength, or to distract the population from internal social pressures, hard times, calamities, or foreign debacles. Without considering the intentions of the leading political actors and the historical circumstances in which they found themselves, one could not predict the behavior of Ottoman authorities or the outcome of reconstruction plans following the 1660 fire. Islamization in Eminönü and Galata was neither preordained nor based on interpretations of Islam alone. There were other alternatives. The valide sultan could have built or repaired a mosque elsewhere, as Fazıl Ahmed Pasha's predecessor suggested, and Jews could have again thrived in Eminönü and Catholics in the heart of Galata. Yet in a period of crisis, Islamization of areas inhabited by Christians and Jews in Istanbul served as a visible sign of the authority of the dynasty and religion that Hatice Turhan represented.

To demonstrate the uniqueness of this period, it is crucial to point out that during the reign of Ibrahim, officials acted very differently concerning new churches. Christians built new churches in the first Ottoman capital of Bursa in 1642.[99] The magistrates of the city were indifferent, despite the open flouting of Islamic law. However, a new magistrate, Hojazade Mesud Efendi, later the sheikhulislam, rejected the laissez-faire attitude of his predecessors and, after providing evidence that it was indeed newly built, locked a church on his own initiative. But because he did so without the grand vizier's authorization, he was punished and dismissed from office. A Muslim mob, angered by his dismissal, destroyed that church and three others. Numerous people who torched the churches were brought before the grand vizier, reprimanded, and treated harshly. The grand vizier then rendered the new churches permanent, allowing these illegal structures to be rebuilt, a very different outcome from that which followed the fire in 1660.

Commoners Follow the Rulers' Example

The fire of 1660 served to exacerbate tensions between members of different religious groups and compel Muslims to enjoin the good and forbid the wrong. Everyone suffered from the fire and plague, and interreligious tensions in the city ran high following the great dislocations. While many of the Jews forced to leave their former quarters settled in Jewish neighborhoods in Balat, Hasköy, and Ortaköy, others tried to move into Muslim neighborhoods elsewhere in Istanbul or Christian neighborhoods in Galata. But Christian and Muslim residents often resisted their encroachment and turned to legal authorities and the court to banish Jews from their new residences. For example, the imam and several muezzins of the neighborhood of Hamamcı Mühiyeddin in the Fener district testified in court against Avraham son of Isaac.[100] They accused this Jewish innkeeper of renting his rooms out to Jews despite the fact that Muslims had always inhabited the neighborhood. These Muslim men of learning petitioned the representative of the grand vizier and received a decree ordering the expulsion of Jews from the quarter. They displayed it to the magistrate, who warned the owner of the inn to expel the Jewish tenants. In another example, Armenian and Orthodox Christians complained to the magistrate of Galata that Jews who had lost their homes in Istanbul settled on Christian properties in Galata by deceitful means.[101] The Christian petitioners wanted their land back and for the Jews who settled in this matter to be expelled by imperial decree. Considering the interreligious tension after the fire, it was logical to send Jews from Eminönü to the predominantly Jewish village of Hasköy.[102]

After the fire Christians also attempted to settle where they previously had not resided, to the discomfort of Muslims, who accused them of ruining community morals. The billeting commander Hasan Agha from Hacer Kadın neighborhood near Samatya Gate testified that the neighborhood had previously been inhabited by Muslims.[103] Because many homes had recently been sold to people who were not Muslim, Christians, Jews, and thieves became dominant. Night and day "Gypsies" drank wine and spirits, played the horn, listened to storytellers, and engaged in lewdness and debauchery, including having sex with prostitutes. Muslims complained to the magistrate that because of the bawdy racket in their neighborhood they could pray neither in the mosque nor at home. Thieves had even entered the plaintiff's home. In another case, an imam and muezzin along with nine other Muslims of the Hajji Hüseyin neighborhood, also near Samatya Gate, complained to the magistrate of Istanbul that although Christians had never previously resided in their neighborhood, several Christians had rented or leased Muslim homes there, even near the mosque.[104] The men complained that their "shameful words, evil acts, and loud voices" hindered them from praying and reading and chanting from the Qur'an in their own homes. They requested that the Christians be expelled. Based on their testimony and affirmation of their claims by inspectors, it was decided that the Christians had to be expelled from the Muslim homes in which they resided.

Local Muslims also sought to Islamize neighborhoods on their own initiative. The clerk of the imperial payroll register petitioned the sultan, stating that when the great conflagration occurred all churches and synagogues that burned accrued to the portion of state lands. A Muslim school and rooms to rent to pay for the upkeep of the school were to be built on the lands of a church confiscated in this way. The church had been located in the neighborhood west of Eminönü, where the fire had started. But a sheikh who resided in the neighborhood, emboldened by a fatwa, urged the construction of a mosque in addition to the school.[105]

Muslims turned to the sheikhulislam for his legal opinion concerning the expulsion of Christians from Muslim neighborhoods. An entry in the Shariah court records of the magistrate of Galata includes the following question: "If a Christian should perform Christian rituals in the home in which he resides in a Muslim neighborhood, is it legal for him to be compelled to sell the aforementioned home to a Muslim when the people of the neighborhood notify the Shariah expert?" The answer was affirmative.[106] The same issue was raised in the Bosporus village of Yeniköy. There the deputy magistrate recorded a similar fatwa, asking, "If a Christian or Jew buys a home in a Muslim neighborhood and resides in it, when the people of the neighborhood make the situation known to the magistrate, is it appropriate for him to say that he must be compelled to sell the home to a Muslim?" The response was again affirmative. In relation to this fatwa, the court scribe of Yeniköy recorded that a Muslim in Yeniköy petitioned the sultan to have a Christian or Jew who bought a Muslim's home near the Yeniköy mosque and resided in it to appear before the magistrate of Galata.[107]

What changed the attitude of Muslim commoners in Istanbul? Had they not been frequently sighted at the city's thousands of taverns, rubbing shoulders with Christians and Jews and enjoying themselves before the fire? The anonymous author of *A Treatise on Strange Events*, composed in the second half of the seventeenth century to describe what was strange, wondrous, and even shocking about Istanbul society, mentions how Muslims drank wine, caroused with Christians and Jews on their holidays, conversed with Christians and Jews in their languages, visited in their homes, greeted them saying "My dear," and accepted their greetings in turn.[108] It was not as if Istanbul Muslims were unfamiliar with Christians and Jews, who made up nearly half the population of the city.

Muslim discomfort at the arrival of Christians and Jews in their neighborhoods after the fire may have arisen from several causes. First was the obvious contrast with the way things had been. They turned to judicial officials to reinstate the religious status quo. Second was the potential for economic competition from their new neighbors. Especially galling was the money to be made from selling alcohol and flesh. Finally, sensitivity to wine, women, song, and secret churches speaks to another trend. Muslims complained that they could not concentrate on their prayers while in their own homes. While it cannot be discounted that this was a rhetorical device used to gain the sympathy of those hearing the plaintiffs' testimony, it also signals a turn to Muslim piety. In a city as mixed and diverse as Istanbul, they could not have been witnessing wild carousing or hearing Christian liturgy recited for the first time. Whereas in the past Muslims might have joined these Christians in having a good time or ignored their prayers, in the 1660s a new wave of Kadızadeli-inspired piety rolled over the city, compelling Muslims to shape their lives in accordance with Islamic ethics and encourage their neighbors, whether Muslim or not, to do the same. This trend was especially reflected at the court of Mehmed IV.

5

Conversion to Piety

Mehmed IV and Preacher Vani
Mehmed Efendi

This chapter explores several of the major themes of the book, including why people attempt to bring others of the same religion to their understanding of that religion (the motivation of Vani Mehmed Efendi), the link between piety and proselytization, and the significance of the advocate or mediator of conversion. I focus on the changed religious scene in the 1660s following the fire and Islamization in Istanbul and the appointment of Fazıl Ahmed Pasha as grand vizier. The crucial individual is Vani Mehmed Efendi, a preacher who became closer to the dynasty and administration and more influential than the previous Kadızadeli leaders Kadızade Mehmed Efendi and Üstüvani Mehmed Efendi. This advocate of a reformed Islam free of innovations and Sufi accretions, who compelled the enjoining of good and forbidding of wrong in Istanbul by attacking Sufis and dissenters, ending the trade in wine and spirits, and razing taverns, mediated the conversion of the valide sultan, grand vizier, and sultan to his way of Islam through charismatic preaching.

To explore Mehmed IV's conversion to piety, one has to also discuss the sultan's simultaneous move to the old warrior capital of Edirne and the appointment of an official chronicler. It is mainly through the work of Abdi Pasha that we learn of Mehmed IV's religiosity, his relation to Vani Mehmed Efendi, and his enjoining good and forbidding wrong. Women overshadowed the sultan during the first eight to twelve years of his reign, while he was a boy. But by the early 1660s, when Mehmed IV was in his early twenties, and for a period lasting over two decades until the siege of Vienna, Mehmed IV is the subject of chronicles, the author, or at least narrator, of his life. The writing of history and induction into active sultanate went together for Mehmed IV. Thereafter he was depicted as a pious convert maker promoting a purified Islam to Muslims, Christians, and Jews.

Preparing a Pious Legacy

In 1663 the sultan abandoned Istanbul and established himself in Edirne, appointing Abdi Pasha to be court historian, even naming the work, in order to mark his attainment of control over the sultanate.[1] Abdi Pasha, a Muslim from Istanbul, was probably the same age as the sultan; both were educated in the palace. The historian was trained to administer the empire and rose to the offices of deputy grand vizier in Istanbul, imperial chancellor, and, toward the end of his career and life, governor of provinces in the Arab world (Basra), southeastern Europe (Bosnia), and the Mediterranean (Crete). Just as the trajectory of Abdi Pasha's official appointments follows the expansion of the empire, he had an opportunity not only to have a hand in making history, but also to produce it, to write about the affairs of the empire, shaping its history as it was to be remembered.

Although Abdi Pasha relied on the accounts of others to compose the history of events between the enthronement of the sultan and the time he was appointed court historian, the last twenty years of the chronicle are based on his firsthand knowledge of events contained therein or the knowledge of events as related to him by the sultan or his preacher. The sultan closely followed the chronicle's composition, written in straightforward Turkish, largely without the ornamental Persianate touches found in sixteenth-century official chronicles. Abdi Pasha was constantly at the sultan's side, which limited his critical stance yet placed him in an intimate position to follow events, many of which he witnessed or learned of from those who experienced them, or in which he played a role, as, for example, when he compiled the compendium of statutes including that concerning procedure to follow when a Christian converted to Islam before the court. It is an invaluable work for presenting views of events from the sultan's perspective and how he wished to be remembered, and provides insight into which events were deemed important for posterity and which were passed over in silence. Because he was appointed to write a work that praises the sultan to posterity, Abdi Pasha chose the format of the book of kings (*Shahname*), unlike earlier writers who selected the advice to kings genre.

Especially because it was modeled along the line of a book of kings, one cannot uncritically use Abdi Pasha's chronicle as a biographical source. As Denise

Spellberg writes, a life and a legacy are not the same thing; the latter is usually considered a vision of reality shaped by those who thought and wrote about the subject, for their own reasons, after the life to be retold had ended.[2] In this case, the legacy was shaped in the narrative of the sultan's life mediated by his official historian in part by the sultan while he was still living. His story is also about the construction and presentation of a sultan's historical persona by a select group of elite men, many of whom were partners in power, promoting their patron, who shaped the meaning of his life for fellow Ottomans.

The spatial and symbolic move away from Istanbul and his mother confirmed the coming into being of the sultan as ruler. For this reason he brought Abdi Pasha to Edirne and ordered him to compose a history of his reign in consultation with him. According to Abdi Pasha, "While your humble servant [Abdi Pasha] was among the servants of the royal ward under the sultanic gaze in the harem, when his eminence our majestic sultan settled in illustrious Edirne, the Abode of Victory, he appointed this slave of little worth or knowledge to the duty of recording events" (3a). Abdi Pasha's history, though penned by the able writer, emerged dialogically with its patron. It is difficult at times to distinguish the sultan's voice from that of his chronicler, nor is it possible to separate the imagined sultan from the real. In this situation it is tempting to agree to some extent with Derrida, who argues that language constitutes reality and does not merely reflect it.[3] At the same time, it would be too extreme to consider everything written in texts such as Abdi Pasha's to be only literary tropes and rhetorical devices, to claim, for example, that no conversion or conquest occurred. Instead, it is safer to claim that it did not necessarily occur as described. The aim is to discuss experience and meaning together as they can be reconstructed primarily from Ottoman chroniclers.

Abdi Pasha's text functioned first as an oral address. As he relates in the narrative, he was ordered to tell the sultan everything that he wrote about him. The author frequently read back to the sultan what he had written, the work's strength and weakness. In the summer of 1665, when Abdi Pasha fell ill and was not able to be with the sultan for several days to write the *Chronicle*, the sultan visited him to ask, "Why are you lying down? Get up and write about events!" (180a). He did not want any affair to be missed.

In the chronicle, when Mehmed IV reached his early to mid-twenties in the 1660s, following the fire and conversion of Jewish and Christian places, Abdi Pasha begins to note the sultan's piety. The sultan did not want Abdi Pasha to be remiss in making sure that posterity would remember his patron for his devoutness. Abdi Pasha included some of the sultan's favorite Qur'anic verses (165b–166a). They include "God enjoins justice, kindness, and charity to one's kindred, and forbids indecency, wickedness, and oppression" (Al-Nahl, the Bee, 16:90), which calls to mind the structure of the phrase "Enjoin good and forbid wrong," which served as the motivating idea for the Kadızadeli preachers.

Chroniclers and commentators noted the sultan's religiosity. According to Abdi Pasha, Mehmed IV celebrated the birthday of Muhammad each year beginning in the early 1660s. He would wipe his face before the cloak of Muhammad during the reading of the prayers recited for Muhammad on his birthday (186b–187a, 223b). Whether traveling or at his favorite palace in Edirne, Mehmed IV did not neglect his Friday prayers (197a–b). Mehmed Halife concurred. Describing the sultan's hunting expeditions, he claims that Mehmed IV would not go on the hunt if it meant skipping Friday prayers and the Friday sermon and admonition.[4] Abdi Pasha claims that although he traveled a great deal to hunt, Mehmed IV never postponed a single prayer time and would render prayers with other Muslims. With his preacher and sheikhulislam the sultan frequently discussed the finer points of Islam, ranging from people close to God (228b) to religious knowledge (234a) and Islamic law and custom (262b–263a, 268a–b). Whether on the hunt or on a military campaign, the sultan often invited his preacher to join him in the imperial tent for prayers and to expound upon the meaning of the Qur'an (237a). The two discussed Beyzavi's popular Qur'anic exegesis together with the sheikhulislam a couple of times a week.[5] Mehmed IV even ritually cut the throats of two animals with a sharp knife while saying "God is great" for Id al-Adha, the feast of sacrifice.[6]

Kurdish Preacher Mustafa's narrative of Mehmed IV's reign provides insight into the piety and religious practices of the sovereign and his court. He described the sultan as the "refuge of religion." On Fridays Kurdish Preacher Mustafa served as the sultan's imam.[7] He had to be present along with the sultan's servants and palace pages in whichever mosque the mobile sultan decided to visit. He had to be prepared to give a sermon and then listen to Vani Mehmed Efendi and his disciples give commentary on Hadith and the Qur'an, and preach and admonish.

The following is an example of Kurdish Preacher Mustafa's interaction with the sultan that demonstrates the way writers depicted his piety. One Friday night in the spring of 1664, Kurdish Preacher Mustafa saw the sultan sitting on a bejeweled throne at a fountain in a rose garden in Edirne, leading him to compare Mehmed IV's splendor favorably to that of fabled non-Islamic sovereigns, the emperor of China and the Sassanid shah. He then quickly returned to the ruler's Islamic credentials. The sultan was holding a Qur'an in his hands and was reading and chanting from it. After having a brief conversation with the preacher, the sultan said, "Let us draw an augury from the Qur'an." He "opened the Qur'an and after looking at the leaf, sheet by sheet he counted nineteen leaves, and on the first line of the nineteenth leaf was the verse from the Chapter of Mary (19:7). Our felicitous sultan recited and chanted the verse as is proper and said to me 'what is the noble meaning, the gracious import of this Qur'anic verse, and what does it indicate?'" Kurdish Preacher Mustafa explained that the prophet Zachariah was childless, and he and his wife old and ailing. They were horrified at the thought of the line of the prophet ending after them, so they fervently prayed to God that they would have a son eminent in prophecy and unique in devotion to God. God answered their prayers and gave them a son. Turning from prophetic times to his own era, Kurdish Preacher Mustafa relates that the verse means that God would bestow upon the sultan an intelligent son. In fact, nineteen days later, as he predicted, Prince Mustafa was born.[8]

Contemporary writers also noted that Mehmed IV had exerted himself and persevered in his studies, reaching perfection in reading and writing and all the sciences taught to sultans (92b). In the midst of devoting space to the sultan's piety, Abdi Pasha was careful to depict Mehmed IV as intelligent, and even skeptical. When an astrologer gave an overly optimistic reading, the sultan, by then in his early twenties, asked, "I wonder if he interpreted the alignment of the stars in that way considering that he was to appear before me and acquire some gold?" (164a). We can imagine Mehmed IV taking the advice of his Chinese contemporary, Qing Emperor K'ang-hsi (1661–1722), that "the emperor has to withstand the praise that showers upon him and fills his ears, for it is of no more use to him than so-called 'restorative medicine'; these banalities and evasions have all the sustenance of dainty pastries, and one grows sick of them." The same emperor claimed that his diviners "have often been tempted to pass over bad auguries, but I have double-checked their calculations and warned them to not distort the truth."[9]

Vani Mehmed Efendi, Influential Mediator of Religious Conversion

At the same time that Abdi Pasha begins to note the sultan's piousness in the early to mid-1660s, the third major Kadızadeli leader and preacher, Mehmed son of Bistam of Van, known as Vani Mehmed Efendi, also begins to play a substantial role in the narrative. If the sultan was wise enough to understand that some of those around him would say whatever they thought he wanted to hear, surely he was discerning enough to judge whether preachers were trying to use him for their interests. The sultan commanded Abdi Pasha to dine twice a week with Vani Mehmed Efendi in 1669, and it is likely that the preacher also influenced what went into the chronicle (287b). Vani Mehmed Efendi's charismatic preaching and incredible impromptu Qur'anic exposition had caught the attention of Fazıl Ahmed Pasha when the latter was governor in the remote and sometimes snowbound northeastern Anatolian city of Erzurum. The grand vizier deserves credit for bringing the preacher, who had been railing against practices at Sufi lodges and tombs there, to the attention of the sultan, which in turn had a large role to play in the sovereign's turn to piety.

Kurdish Preacher Mustafa clearly articulates the importance of the role of the mediator in conversion and the chain reaction of religious change set in motion when the grand vizier met the preacher. After Fazıl Ahmed Pasha arrived at his post in Erzurum he "observed the power of Vani Efendi's excellent virtues. Seeing his perfect piety, asceticism, and abstention from sin, he sent him to the sultan where he became glorified, honored and a pillar of the religion." The author asks, "[Had] that virtuous [fazıl] one of the age and glory of the world not seen the scholar and perfect one's perception, who would have known the value and worth of the four sacred books [Torah, Psalms, Gospel, and Qur'an]," and how could "the sultan's heart been inspired by the blessing and favor of the lord and manifestation of the light of the divine and look of divine favor?" As a result, God made Mehmed IV "the lover of men of excellent, perfect virtue."[10]

During Mehmed IV's reign many of those virtuous men were not Ottomans properly speaking, but provincials, not the products of palace or even capital schools. Like the Kadızadeli Kurdish Preacher Mustafa, who was among the palace preachers, and many other members of the movement, Vani Mehmed Efendi was most likely Kurdish since Ottoman historians referred to the Kurdish-speaking preacher as being "among the religious scholars of Kurdistan."[11] He had migrated to Erzurum from Van, a city known for its Kurdish population. He thus came from a far less cosmopolitan city than the imperial capital to which the new grand vizier took him.[12] By 1664 at the latest he had arrived in Istanbul en route to Edirne, where he took up the post of spiritual guide and preacher to Mehmed IV.[13] In 1665 he became the first preacher in the new imperial showcase mosque of the valide sultan in Eminönü. It was a suitable appointment; according to Rycaut, Vani Mehmed Efendi persuaded the grand vizier that the fires in Istanbul and Galata, which paved the way for the completion of the mosque, the plague, and the empire's lack of military success against Christians, also on the mind of many Muslims in Istanbul, were "so many parts of Divine Judgments thrown on the Musselmen or Believers, in vengeance of their too much Licence given to the Christian Religion, permitting Wine to be sold within the Walls of Constantinople, which polluted the Imperial City, and ensnared the faithful by temptation to what was unlawful."[14]

The early twentieth-century scholar F. W. Hasluck, who depicted Christians and Muslims sharing the same sacred spaces and was hostile to the antisyncretistic Kadızadeli interpretation of Islam, terms Vani Mehmed Efendi "the religious counterpart" of the Köprülü grand viziers, a preacher who "opposed lawlessness in religion as they in politics."[15] In fact, it is not so easy to distinguish religion and politics. Mehmed IV faced rebels who banded together in militant brotherhoods with semireligious initiation formulas mirroring those of dervishes, thus expressing lawlessness in disobedience to authority. Nevertheless, it is clear that Vani Mehmed Efendi was considered by many to be, like Kadızade before him, "the enemy of innovators and the beloved of those who believe in the oneness of God [Muslims]."[16]

Vani Mehmed Efendi became the confidant of the sultan, valide sultan, and grand vizier. Contrary to conventional wisdom, the Kadızadeli movement had not disappeared with the banishment of Üstüvani Mehmed Efendi to Cyprus.[17] The movement reached its greatest level of influence under Vani Mehmed Efendi, not his predecessor. In the early 1660s, Mehmed IV began to rely on, confide in, and bestow rewards on Vani Mehmed Efendi, whose preaching style was one of the reasons for his fame. The sultan never missed a Friday sermon delivered by his preacher and enjoyed spending time discussing Islam with him. The preacher had a reputation for cheering his listeners with glad tidings, frightening them with warnings, and enlightening them through his sermons (197a–b).[18] Invited to pray at Dimetoka in 1667 before the sultan and his retinue for the Ottoman army besieging Candia, Vani Mehmed Efendi ascended the pulpit after morning prayers at the imperial tent and "scattered such precious jewels from the treasure of Qur'anic truth that eyes became tearful and hearts filled with amazement" (234a–b).[19] Afterward he and the sultan had a private conversation about the commentary. In another sermon at the imperial tent, his preaching, admonishing, and Qur'anic explanation again filled his audience with admiration (237a).[20]

His stirring preaching and relationships with the most important figures in the dynasty and administration made him extremely influential. His bond with the sultan was observed by contemporary Ottoman historians such as Abdi Pasha, who relates how in 1665 the sultan bestowed on the preacher one hundred sheep (168b). In 1666 he noted that Sultan Mehmed IV even honored the preacher with a visit to his household (228a–b).[21] At the beginning of 1668 the sultan asked Vani Mehmed Efendi to pick up a bow and try his luck hitting a target. Mehmed IV had been bestowing gifts on his servants who hit the mark with bullets or arrows. Vani Mehmed Efendi picked up the bow and arrow and hit a bull's-eye, which earned him "much gold and a matchless golden bow" (262b–263a).

The preacher stayed by the sultan's or the grand vizier's side during military campaigns. This included traveling with the sultan on the second campaign against the Commonwealth of Poland in 1673, for which the commissary general was ordered to provision Vani Mehmed Efendi with foodstuffs, and accompanying the grand vizier to the front in Çehrin in 1678 and Vienna in 1683.[22] Attesting to his value to the sultan, he may have received as much as 1,000 akçe per diem from the state treasury.[23] Sultan Mehmed IV's powerful mother, Hatice Turhan, also had close relations with the Kadızadeli leader: she had included a lodge for him in her new mosque in Eminönü, and when she journeyed from Istanbul to Edirne she was accompanied by the preacher.[24] The preacher also was appointed the first teacher of Prince Mustafa (285b–286a), and then Prince Ahmed (414a); his son-in-law Fayzullah Efendi continued in this position (295b). His family also became intimately connected with the palace and earned many benefits from this relationship. His wife spent most of her time in the harem socializing with the royal ladies; his sons and sons-in-law became university professors in Bursa.[25]

Before Vani Mehmed Efendi became the sultan's personal preacher, Mehmed IV was on good terms with some orders of dervishes. He especially favored the Mevlevi, although he was later to ban Mevlevi practices, including whirling to music and repeatedly reciting God's names. As late as 1665 the sultan visited the Sufi lodge of Nefes Baba near Edirne (171b) and gave pensions to dervishes he came across in his travels, such as the "dervish free from care and worry" he met in Thrace in 1668. From 1667 until the end of his reign, Mehmed IV employed Ahmed Dede, a Mevlevi, as his chief astrologist, a man who opposed the Kadızadeli movement.

Yet the sultan's relations with Sufis changed as dynastic attitudes toward Sufis generally reflected Kadızadeli interests after 1660 (261a–b). As had other Kadızadeli leaders before him, so too did Vani Mehmed Efendi aim to eradicate what he considered illicit Muslim behavior and to strengthen the rule of Shariah and the way of Muhammad against innovation. His wrath primarily targeted "innovating" Sufis. Allying with the sultan, whom he viewed as the defender of the Muslims against the threat of heresies, he aimed to suppress the political power and religious influence of Sufis, especially Bektashis, Halvetis, and Mevlevis, the three orders that historically had had close ties with the military and the dynasty.[26] Kösem Sultan had been supported by these orders and the Janissaries; Hatice Turhan sided with the Kadızadelis against them when Fazıl Ahmed Pasha acted to dampen Janissary power. Whereas Murad IV's alliance with Kadızade was a marriage of convenience, Vani Mehmed Efendi's theological arguments concerning the danger of Sufis and innovative religious practices swayed the opinion of the religious scholar and statesman Fazıl Ahmed Pasha.

Vani Mehmed Efendi expressed his Kadızadeli views of the danger of religious innovations and of the necessity of religious obligations based on the
practice of Muhammad in two treatises written in Arabic, *The Truth of Religious
Obligations and the Practices of Muhammad and Innovation in Some Practices*
and *The Abomination of Public Recitals of God's Praises*.[27] In these treatises, he
makes forceful arguments against the Sufi way and incites others to cease engaging in Sufi practices.[28] He claims that although in his age many Muslims
believed such practices were religious obligations, public performance of reciting God's names is an abomination. Vani Mehmed Efendi was not opposed to
individual, private practice, as he promoted interiorization and rational Islam,
but he attacked ecstatic group performance of prayer accompanied by music.[29]
He also argued that recitations performed on the nights of Muhammad's conception, the revelation of his mission, and revelation of the Qur'an, as well as
at funerals, are unacceptable innovations that are not part of the Sunna and
go against the Shariah. He claimed that in opposing these practices he was
combating evil.

Vani Mehmed Efendi also denounced sheikhs who lead people astray and
those who follow them. He claims that those sheikhs who engage in such acts
have left the fold of Hanefi Sunni Islam, as have the people who follow them
and who are in fact excessively devoted to their sheikhs. Moreover, from his
perspective, those who call themselves Sufis are innovators of evil intention.
Concerning Sufi sheikhs, he argues that people follow ignorant sheikhs who
do not understand the religion out of an extreme devotion that exceeds even
their love for Muhammad. To illustrate this point he uses the metaphor of two
doctors. Imagine, he writes, two doctors: one, the skillful doctor, represents the
prophets and learned scholars. The second one, the unskilled doctor, represents Sufi sheikhs. Each treats a patient suffering from high fever: the skillful
doctor removes the blood, the unskillful doctor applies a salve that provides
temporary amelioration of symptoms. An intelligent patient will understand
the necessity of removing the bad blood, no matter how painful. The rest will
choose temporary comfort and will despise the skillful doctor. They will love
the unskillful doctor who they think is their friend who makes them feel better
and hate the skillful doctor who could really cure them.[30]

Vani Mehmed Efendi Inspires Attacks on Sufis and Dissenters

The arguments of these treatises—that Muslims must live in accordance
with the model set by Muhammad and not be misled by the false claims of
Sufi sheikhs—were persuasive. As their arguments were disseminated by the

preacher's teaching at the palace and orations in public, the grand vizier sup-
pressed Sufis and dissenters. He prohibited the public performance of Sufi
whirling in 1665–66, even forcing the Mevlevi lodges in Beşiktaş and Galata
and other dervish lodges to cease meetings, executing the Muslim scholar Lari
Mehmed Efendi in 1665, and destroying shrines frequented by the populace
in 1668, another means of Islamizing the landscape.[31] All these acts served as
moments of public edification, theaters in the instruction of right belief and
practice.

Lari Mehmed Efendi was an important Muslim in Istanbul society. He
was wealthy and a member of the religious class. He was also an imam and
respected for his knowledge and intelligence. But Abdi Pasha, who was given
the report requesting the execution of Lari Mehmed Efendi by the sultan, relates that he was notorious for his heretical beliefs (158a–b).[32] More than forty
witnesses ascertained that Lari Mehmed Efendi denied the raising of the dead
for the Last Judgment and the religious obligations of prayer and fasting, all
the while deeming the consumption of wine lawful.[33] He gathered a number
of Muslims around him who shared his views. He did not deny his beliefs.
A fatwa was decreed permitting his execution, which was duly carried out.[34]
Mehmed IV approved his execution and insisted that Abdi Pasha include it
in his chronicle; he wanted to make an example of a Muslim who denied core
principles of the sultan's pious faith. After exposing him to public view at Parmak Gate, where the patriarch had been hanged less than a decade earlier, they
decapitated him.

Displaying more boldness than Kadızade Efendi or Üstüvani Mehmed
Efendi, in 1668 Vani Mehmed Efendi targeted a shrine affiliated with the Janissaries' Bektashi order. He convinced the grand vizier to issue orders to destroy
the shrine of the Bektashi sheikh Kanber Baba located on a hill overlooking
Edirne because it had become a site of pilgrimage.[35] Abdi Pasha emphasizes
the role Vani Mehmed Efendi played in the destruction of the shrine. In an
example of the intimacy of the sultan and his chronicler, Mehmed IV spoke
to his historian one day while being shaved: "Today at prayers Preacher Vani
Mehmed Efendi said during his sermon that near Hafsa there is a grave of a
certain Kanber Baba to which some people come with bad convictions and slip
into polytheism. The sultan issued an imperial decree ordering the destruction of the shrine. Abdi Pasha praised the sultan: "Just as his eminence our
pious emperor guards the people of Islam from their enemies, so, too, does he
protect them from infidelity, error, and polytheism" (239b–240b).[36] A foreign
observer claims the shrine was razed because it was a notorious spot for illicit
sexual liaisons.[37] Other tombs that were the scene of inappropriate practices
received more lenient treatment: rather than destroying the tomb of Hüsam

Shah in 1671, which he had visited, Mehmed IV issued a milder decree outlawing practices at the shrine that contradicted Islamic law (307b).

Vani Mehmed Efendi also incited Fazıl Ahmed Pasha to send the leading Halveti sheikh of the age, Niyazi Mısri, into exile. Niyazi Mısri (1618–94) was a Sufi and a poet, the son of a Sufi of the Nakshibandi order.[38] He became a Halveti, was eventually named the successor of the Halveti sheikh Ümmi Sinan, and opened his own Sufi lodge in Bursa in 1670. Fazıl Ahmed Pasha invited him to Edirne, but due to the Sufi's persistent faith in onomancy, his host exiled him to Rhodes in 1673. He is also famous for declaring, "The name of Jesus pleases me and I am his loyal servant."[39] Followers of the sheikh claim that the real reason for his exile was because when Mehmed IV invited Niyazi to travel from Bursa to Edirne to participate in the campaign against the Commonwealth of Poland in 1672, the Sufi so quickly collected a large group of armed followers that officials feared the man's power, echoes of the Kadızadeli call to arms in 1656 that predated their leaders' exile.[40] Nine months later he was pardoned, but again exiled to Limni between 1676 and 1691.[41] A fierce enemy of Vani Mehmed Efendi and Bayrami-Melami Sufis, he linked the two in a treatise claiming that Vani Mehmed Efendi was the leader of atheists and the Bayrami-Melami Sufis. He accused Mehmed IV of being a member of the order as well.

Signaling Vani Mehmed Efendi's importance and contributing further to the shaping of a more Islamic landscape in the capital, in the 1660s the sultan gave the preacher a forest preserve on the Bosporus north of Üsküdar called Priest's Preserve. Vani Mehmed Efendi restored a small mosque, which still stands although in altered form, and built a madrasa and more than a dozen seaside mansions, most of which also still exist, including his own, in the adjoining village. A wealthy Jewish Hasköy vintner family was evicted from the village, which became known as Vaniköy (Vani's village).[42] According to the mid-twentieth-century scholar and Sufi Abdülbaki Gölpınarlı, who was partial in his writing toward antinomian dervishes, Vaniköy was one of only two areas in Istanbul where Sufis, especially Hamzavi Mevlevis, never set foot. They blamed Vani Mehmed Efendi for the murder of ninety-year-old Beşir Agha and the drowning of forty of his disciples at Kadıköy Feneri in 1662. For this reason they cursed him and his village and called him "Vani the Murderer" (*Vani-i cani*).[43]

Enjoining Good and Forbidding Wrong: Razing Taverns and Ending the Alcohol Trade

Along with members of certain Sufi orders, others, particularly those who enjoyed the good life, had reason to curse the imperial preacher. Already by 1665, in an attempt to emulate Suleiman I's first acts after he was enthroned, Mehmed IV prohibited the playing of the saz and other musical instruments, including the lute, and the singing of wandering minstrels.[44] Contemporary miniatures of young women musicians hint at other sins. They appear in racy outfits showing cleavage as they pluck phallic-shaped instruments held across their bodies.[45] Prohibiting the consumption of alcohol was a step Suleiman I had not taken. According to Vani Mehmed Efendi, taverns and the wine trade caused moral corruption, especially when located in neighborhoods that were predominantly Muslim. Another miniature from that epoch shows an amorous young couple, a lover and his beloved, sitting and embracing while looking intently into each other's eyes; the woman clutches a cup of wine to her breast as the man places his right hand on her right thigh. Their turbans touch.[46] Accordingly, at least twice during the 1660s and 1670s, orders were issued to destroy all taverns in Istanbul and end the legal trade in alcohol in order to enforce Islamic morality. Reducing or eliminating the consumption of alcohol in the imperial capital was an important attempt at putting Muslims back on the straight path, the empty space of taverns further contributing to a more Islamic landscape.

It was only natural for an Islamic dynasty to forbid the consumption of wine and spirits by its Muslim subjects. In the sixteenth century, for example, an imperial order had been issued that hindered Christians and Jews from selling wine to Muslims and openly selling and consuming alcohol themselves.[47] But at that time the pragmatic sultan did not ban the wine trade: instead, he appointed a commissioner to collect a tithe and thus benefit the imperial treasury as he tried to prohibit taverns being opened where Muslims resided, particularly near mosques.[48] Christians and Jews were allowed to produce and consume alcohol for their own purposes. But bear in mind all the complaints of Muslims concerning the wine drinking of their new Christian and Jewish neighbors following the fire in 1660. Muslims were concerned that consumption of alcohol led to immorality and vice and even prostitution in their neighborhoods.

Some Muslims enjoyed drinking and the company of prostitutes. The anonymous author of *A Treatise on Strange Events* noted that Muslims drank wine, caroused with Christians and Jews, and owned taverns. Tavern owners sold wine in Muslim neighborhoods.[49] Shariah court records demonstrate that other Muslims were upset by this situation. Muslims from the neighborhoods of Soğan Agha, Yakub Agha, and Emin Bey in Istanbul complained that Christians had rented three stores from Muslim endowments and turned them into a tavern in 1664.[50] Notable Muslim men of the neighborhood attested to the sale of wine and spirits. An imperial writ was issued warning Christians not to sell alcohol.

Warning Christians not to sell alcohol did not deter Muslim drinking. According to this mind-set, taverns had to be razed to the ground to limit their deleterious effects on the Muslim community. Accordingly, at least twice during Vani Mehmed Efendi's period of influence, Fazıl Ahmed Pasha issued orders to raze every tavern in Istanbul and prohibit the Christian and Jewish alcohol trade. For this reason western European observers such as Covel considered Vani Mehmed Efendi "the greater preacher who prated down all the coffee houses and Taverns," and the one who "preach'd down all publick Tavernes and ale-houses, and the Dervises' publick meetings."[51] Abdi Pasha relates that in 1670, within a month after the sultan returned from Greece, where he closely followed the campaign for Crete and spent a great amount of time with Vani Mehmed Efendi and the sheikhulislam, an imperial edict was issued to demolish the taverns in the city, prohibit the sale of wine, and abolish the position of wine controller (302a).[52] This action demonstrated a direct link between waging war abroad and enjoining the good and forbidding wrong at home. The decree was copied into the Shariah records of the city:

> At the present time an imperial edict has been issued stating that
> the taverns located in the city of Istanbul and Eyüp and Galata and
> Üsküdar and in all those districts attached to them are to be demol-
> ished and eradicated. Lawful landed properties are to be constructed
> in their place. After that no person is to bring wine from within or
> without the city, and is not to buy and sell and drink wine. Those who
> do so are to be given severe punishment. . . . It is to be proclaimed
> throughout the city that the taverns in Istanbul and the districts
> attached to it be demolished and eradicated and that wine not be
> bought, sold, or consumed and that severe punishment is to be given
> to those engaging in these activities.[53]

These actions had financial consequences. The office of wine controller was a great source of income for the treasury. Abolishing it would have been a financial mistake for a dynasty and empire facing difficult economic straits. But whatever the dynasty and administration lost financially from its abolition, it gained in support from the Kadızadelis. Christians and Jews must have suffered graver financial consequences. The entire lucrative trade of the import, production, sale, and export of wine and spirits was controlled by Christians and Jews. Extensive vineyards, such as those in Hasköy, Beşiktaş, and Arnavutköy, were also in their hands. The power of these vintners among Christians and Jews was a social fact as well. In a petition signed "the poor Christians of Arnavutköy" and recorded at the Shariah court of Beşiktaş, the petitioners claimed that tavern owners demanded money from them and made them sell their gardens under threat.[54] This case demonstrates that efforts to stop their activities failed.

A petition from the customs controller of Bandırma, located across the Sea of Marmara from Istanbul, recorded in the Register of Complaints from 1671 reflects the Ottoman failure in stemming the trade and the ongoing concern that it be stopped.[55] Seyyid Mehmed wrote that contrary to Islamic law and imperial edict, wine and spirits were being bought and sold in towns and villages that possessed Friday mosques and whose inhabitants were predominantly Muslim. Although the sale and purchase of wine and spirits had been forbidden by imperial decree, infidels (Christians) publicly brought wine and spirits to the quay of the town of Erdek, loaded the contraband onto ships, sold it, and delivered it elsewhere.

Christians, Jews, and Muslims rubbed shoulders in hundreds of taverns across the city. The Shariah scribe often recorded the Muslim presence at taverns in a matter-of-fact manner, such as in a case concerning another issue: murder and the payment of blood money.[56] Ibrahim Çelebi son of Ali and his wife came to court to demand blood money from Nikita Merkuri, the Orthodox Christian owner of a tavern in an unspecified Christian neighborhood of Beşiktaş. Knife-wielding Ahmed had murdered their son Mehmed while the two were sitting at the tavern with Abdullah, Mustafa, a velvet carpet dealer named Mahmud, and the stonemason Amr. The fact that five Muslim men were sitting at a tavern in a Christian neighborhood before the conversation became heated and knives were drawn is not commented on by the scribe, nor does it appear to concern the magistrate. We also know from the Shariah court records that Janissaries, who should have limited themselves to the fermented millet drink known as *boza*, a frothy and slightly sour, vinegary drink favored in winter, often frequented taverns in Hasköy.

The prohibition on alcohol was extended throughout the imperial domains in every town where mosques existed. Rycaut attributes the wider effort to Vani Mehmed Efendi as well. He quotes the decree to the magistrate of Izmir, at the time a relatively new, buzzing port city where fortunes were made or lost on the trade in legal and illegal goods. In that Aegean city, wine was banned along with games of dice, cards, and divination arrows as part of enjoining the good and forbidding the wrong, or, in Rycaut's language, "The observation of lawful Precepts hath been confirmed, and unlawful things have been prohibited."[57] Yet the effort at quashing the consumption of and trade in alcohol amounted to merely short-lived, symbolic measures that failed like Prohibition in the United States in the 1920s. High demand for a lucrative product, the creation of alternative venues for its consumption, corrupt enforcement agents who took a share of profits rather than punish lawbreakers, and stubborn and clever resistance to enforced piety ultimately doomed efforts. Nevertheless, the Kadızadeli-inspired effort was seen as a symbolic act to rid the city of a forbidden product that raised the ire of religious Muslims because it was openly consumed, often by Muslims, where other Muslims resided. Swayed by Kadızadeli preaching, Mehmed IV wholeheartedly supported the efforts to outlaw Christians' and Jews' most profitable monopoly.

6

Converting the Jewish Prophet and Jewish Physicians

Not all Muslims were pleased with the religious turn in the palace and the more rigorous policing of public morality. But not only Muslims were affected by the conversion to piety at court. In that era Muslim piety was manifested in the conversion of Christians and Jews. Accordingly, conversion moved from the sultan's inner circle outward and involved Jews closest to it. Like fire half a decade earlier, the messianic movement of Rabbi Shabbatai Tzevi in 1665 provided an opportune moment for the pious Muslim elite to promote conversion to Islam. This chapter first explores how the attempt of the sultan, his preacher, and the grand vizier to stamp out what they considered heterodox, illegitimate practices among Muslims, to root out heresy and dampen religious ecstasy, and to destroy places where rapturous religious practices were performed coincided with the outbreak of Shabbatai Tzevi's preaching, which aimed to reform Jewish life and convert Jews to the rabbi's understanding of God's prophecy. The movement culminated instead in Jewish conversion to Islam as the sultan's preacher, Vani Mehmed Efendi, instructed the rabbi in Kadızadeli tenets of Islam. Hundreds of the rabbi's followers followed suit. The Islamic reform movement that promoted a rational religion preferred by the sultan prevailed at the time over the competing ecstatic conversion movement of the rabbi.

The second part of the chapter analyzes Hatice Turhan's conversion of other Jews at the sultan's court, especially the group of Jewish palace physicians, the most visible and influential Jews in the empire.

Chronicles reveal that Hatice Turhan's unprecedented policies toward Jews reflect a change in the formerly favorable dynastic attitude that had allowed Jews to hold prominent positions in the palace for over two centuries. As with the construction of the valide sultan's mosque in Eminönü, a link between conversion and change in religious space is made: whereas at the beginning of the 1660s Jews had a privileged position with the royal family and resided mainly in the heart of the city, by the end of the decade the geographic position of the Jews reflected their fall from importance. Most Jews in Istanbul resided on the Golden Horn and the Bosporus, and those who remained in the most important palace positions were compelled to convert to Islam.

The chapter thus concerns the book's themes of why people attempt to bring others of the same religion to their understanding of that religion (Shabbatai Tzevi converting Jews to his path to God) or try to ensure that people of completely different religions join the tradition (the sultan converting Shabbatai Tzevi to Islam), the link between piety and proselytization, the central role of the mediator of conversion, and the role of changing power relations in conversion (the decline of Jews' power at court).

Rabbi Shabbatai Tzevi's Competing Conversion and Reform Movement

Prophecies about Rabbi Shabbatai Tzevi led to the eruption of the greatest Jewish antinomian movement in millennia, the culmination of widespread Jewish belief in the renewal of prophecy, a phenomenon noticed by Ottoman writers, and the dawning of the messianic age.[1] When observing authorities' response to the movement in Istanbul and Egypt, two scholars have suggested that Kadızadeli zeal and the policies of Grand Vizier Fazıl Ahmed Pasha conditioned their reaction.[2] But how should we interpret the way the sultan reacted? Just as the calamitous fire in Istanbul afforded an opportunity to remake a substantial part of the city in Islamic form, the prophetic propaganda surrounding Rabbi Shabbatai Tzevi of Izmir provided an opportunity for the sultan and his court to publicly articulate how one should properly express religious faith, to convert a prominent Jewish scholar to Islam, and to instruct him in the true religion. Just as the gaze of the valide sultan and her son from their mosque lodge in Eminönü was directed over a newly Islamized landscape on the historic peninsula, and viewed converted space across the Golden Horn in Galata, the sultan's gaze at his palace in Edirne presided over the end of a movement led by a rebellious, even treasonous rabbi, which also served as one of the most significant factors in the confirmation of the changed dynastic attitude toward Jews.

Shabbatai Tzevi's messianic calling could not have come at a worse time for the Jewish elite in Istanbul. It confirmed for the Ottomans that Jews were untrustworthy and helped convince them to turn to the Jews' rivals, Orthodox Christians, as the two groups struggled for positions of power and influence. Jews appeared to be a volatile and untrustworthy group because they so whole-heartedly endorsed Shabbatai Tzevi. Their actions threatened to undermine the social order and directly challenged the sultan's uncontested rule when he was facing serious military and financial problems, including the siege of Venetian Crete, a fact noted by a late Ottoman historian.[3] Shabbatai Tzevi's attempt to dethrone the sultan and his inciting Jews to sedition worsened already nega-tive palace opinion of Jews. The decade of the 1660s was thus a crucial turning point for the fortunes of Istanbul Jewry. Shabbatai Tzevi's mission to the city, initially met with such hope and even cockiness on the part of some Jews who felt their persecutors would soon taste their just reward, ended with most of the rabbi's original followers in despair and many eventually converted to Islam. It benefited Orthodox Christian physicians, translators, diplomats, and advisors, to whom Ottomans would thereafter entrust their lives and political affairs.

Due to the dissemination of prophecies concerning Shabbatai Tzevi, many Jews in Istanbul expected a "quick transfer of the sultan's power" to the rabbi.[4] Especially those from Iberia believed Shabbatai Tzevi would dethrone the sul-tan and crown himself king sometime in the autumn of 1665 or winter of 1666: "Jews printed prophecies of rescue from the tyranny of the Turk, and leading the Grand Signior [the sultan] himself captive in Chains." He referred to himself as "the High King, above all the kings of the Earth," and told the Jews not to fear, "for you shall have Dominion over the Nations."[5] According to the Frenchman Chevalier De La Croix, Jews expected "the imminent establishment of the kingdom of Israel" and the subsequent "fall of the Crescent and of all the royal crowns in Christendom."[6] Christians such as the Armenian historian and priest Arakel of Tabriz feared the Jews would then destroy other peoples.[7] A French Catholic priest wrote that Jews threatened Christians "with dire disaster if we failed to join them as soon as possible, and of our own good and free will walked in front of the king who would rule over them, acknowledging his kingdom and submitting to the religion and the laws which he would establish in the world." As a result of this fervor, Jews exhibited a "peculiar atmosphere of feverish expectation" that was a "psychological and social reality."[8]

The man who created such expectations was born in 1626 to a Jewish family of Greek origins in the new, bustling Ottoman port city of Izmir. His parents had immigrated to this relatively new city, a rough-and-tumble town of Armenians, Jews, Muslims, Orthodox Christians, English, French, and Dutch that began to rival Istanbul as international entrepôt.[9] In this brash, diverse environment, where western European millenarianism mixed with ecstatic Sufism, at the age of eighteen the charismatic rabbi began to lead his own group of students of Kabbalah, or Jewish mysticism. His erratic behavior led modern scholars to label him manic-depressive.[10] Because of his strange powers and magical and ascetic practices, he became the spiritual guide for many Jews. They believed that the messiah would appear in the year 1648. In that year Shabbatai Tzevi pronounced the holy name of God (the Tetragrammaton) and engaged in other scandalous practices. The rabbis of Izmir placed the ban on him sometime between 1651 and 1654. He left Izmir and began a tour of Ottoman cities with large Jewish populations, including Salonica, one of the most important centers of Jewish learning and Kabbalah. Scandalous activity there caused him again to be banished. He traveled to Istanbul in 1658. There, too, his blasphemy, offenses against tradition, strange acts, antinomianism, and elevation of sin to a holy act again compelled him to flee the wrath of the rabbis, but also attracted the attention of like-minded Muslim Sufis, including Niyazi Misri. Around 1660 Shabbatai Tzevi returned to Izmir. De La Croix claims that the heavy suffering of the Jews during the great conflagration in Istanbul pleased Shabbatai Tzevi "because he saw in it the finger of God, calling his people to repentance."[11]

In 1662 the rabbi set off for Jerusalem by way of Egypt. There he established good relations with wealthy, important Jews. When he arrived in Jerusalem he found Jews in financial and spiritual despair since the Ottoman government apparently taxed them to finance the ongoing campaign for Crete. The leaders of the community in Jerusalem sent Shabbatai Tzevi back to Egypt to raise funds for their survival. While in Egypt in 1664 he married Sara, an orphan of the Chmielniki massacres of Polish and Ukrainian Jews, who, while being raised a Christian in Livorno, proclaimed she would one day marry the messiah. On Shabbatai Tzevi's return trip to Jerusalem he revealed himself as a messiah in May 1665.[12] A well-known Kabbalist named Nathan of Gaza, whom Jews also described as a miracle-working charismatic man of God, not unlike a Sufi sheikh, took upon himself the burden of being his public relations man.[13] He was the first to recognize Shabbatai Tzevi's messianic claims. Nathan's letters to western European and Ottoman Jewry informing them of the acts of a miracle-working messiah led to widespread acceptance of his mission because Jews at the time were accustomed to claims of prophecy.

No matter that Shabbatai Tzevi was persecuted, or because of it, his following continued to swell. He promptly received the ban in Jerusalem and was expelled from the city. He arrived in Aleppo in July and was favorably received, and in September returned to his birthplace, Izmir. In December 1665 he publicly showed himself after a period of seclusion by storming Izmir's important

Portuguese synagogue with hundreds of his supporters and leading a prayer service, during which he proclaimed the coming of the redeemer and messianic king. Because they believed that the end of days had arrived, Jews engaged in purifying rituals and special prayers to mark the age, inciting a fervent response especially from Jews in the lands just beyond the frontiers of the Ottoman Empire, as far away as Morocco, Germany, and Yemen.[14]

Whereas during Shabbatai Tzevi's earlier visit to Istanbul he had received little interest from Jews and no attention from Ottoman authorities, seven years later many Jews welcomed his mission with enthusiasm, and authorities treated him as a real danger. The messianic age was proclaimed in Izmir one month prior to the first Friday prayers in the Valide Sultan Mosque in Istanbul. The Valide Sultan Mosque on the waterfront that greeted Shabbatai Tzevi in February 1666 symbolized how much the city had been transformed since he left it in 1659. As a result of Hatice Turhan's building program, he encountered a dramatically different city. Before 1660, one approaching Eminönü would have seen a skyline dominated by tall Jewish apartments. When he arrived in the city in 1666, the presence of the new mosque proclaimed that profound change had occurred, which augured well for him. Many Jews greeted him ecstatically. Their previous experience may have led them to look favorably on his perceived aims. The Jewish elite and commoner alike had suffered greatly over the past five years. They lived in crowded conditions on the fringes of the city, having recently faced a horrible fire, plague, and much death, the transformation of properties that had once housed synagogues into an imperial mosque complex, the loss of synagogues of diverse rites, and expulsion from the heart of the city on pain of death and the prohibition of their return.

Alerted by Jews opposed to Shabbatai Tzevi's calling, the Ottoman authorities became concerned when he announced himself to be king of the world, delegated the kingdoms of all empires to his followers, and declared through these actions that Ottoman rule was illegitimate. The Ottomans at the time were engaged in an endless campaign to conquer Crete and could not brook more upheaval in the empire, especially by one attempting to convert others to a competing vision of the true interpretation of God's desire and claiming that his authority superseded that of the sultan. The juxtaposition of subjects in the narratives of Abdi Pasha and Silahdar draws our attention to the Ottoman context of the movement that shaped the court's reaction. In Silahdar's text, for example, the narrative of the rabbi's rebellion is placed in the midst of a detailed discussion of the campaign for Crete, which covers almost the entire entry for 1666. This includes articulation of the emotional desire to conquer the last citadel on the island and the frustration of this desire; the delicate state of honor of the dynasty, empire, and religion; the wartime footing in the capital; and how all minds were focused on a final push to take the citadel. While the sultan sent writs to the grand vizier urging him to exert all energy to conquer the citadel as part of a jihad of those fighting in the path of God against accursed infidels, reminding him to give his heart and soul in the effort, which he desperately hoped would end in victory, and informing him that he prayed night and day for the Muslim warriors to succeed, suddenly a rabbi appeared claiming to be a prophet and acquired a large, potentially threatening following.[15] They could not be expected to react any differently when facing what appeared to be a religious insurrection.

Shabbatai Tzevi enjoyed considerable success among Jews. In February 1666 he was arrested and imprisoned after his boat was intercepted by authorities en route to Istanbul. Jews from around the empire and the world sold their houses, lands, and possessions, packed their things, and headed to Istanbul to greet their prophet. Jews in Istanbul, who had no need to sell their property and pack since the prophet would replace the sultan on his throne in that city and reward them with the material goods of Christians and Muslims, flocked to the dungeon where the rabbi was held. Because large crowds gathered where Shabbatai Tzevi was incarcerated, in April he was banished to Kilidbahir/Seddülbahir, Hatice Turhan's newly repaired fortress on the Rumelian side of the Dardanelles. There he received many pilgrims. From prison he continued to instruct his followers. He abolished the fast of the ninth of the Hebrew month of Av, the date Jews commemorate the destruction of the First and Second Temple, ordering Jews to instead celebrate a festival on that day for the dawning of the messianic age.

That day would have to be postponed. Perhaps incited into action by complaints from Shabbatai Tzevi's Jewish enemies, in September 1666 Sultan Mehmed IV, troubled by an illness that caused him and Vani Mehmed Efendi to pray before Muhammad's mantle asking for a quick recovery, ordered Shabbatai Tzevi to be interrogated beneath his gaze in Edirne by the members of the imperial council. This included the sultan's preacher, Vani Mehmed Efendi, and Grand Vizier Fazıl Ahmed Pasha's deputy, Mustafa Pasha. Because the grand vizier was campaigning in Crete, he deputized a man much experienced in facilitating conversion at the grand vizier's court.[16] Another person present was the supreme Muslim legal authority in the empire, Sheikhulislam Minkarizade Yahya Efendi, who did not support the Kadızadeli movement and may have resented the fact that Vani Mehmed Efendi acted almost as if he were a shadow sheikhulislam.[17] A legal opinion appears in his collection of opinions, however, that gave legal authority to pressured conversion to Islam. It states that a Muslim official could say "Be a Muslim" and compel a Christian or Jew to convert.[18] Not surprisingly, these men gave Shabbatai Tzevi the option of conversion or death.

Abdi Pasha wrote the only contemporary Ottoman account of Shabbatai Tzevi's movement and conversion:

> Previously a rabbi from Izmir appeared. When the Jews showed
> excessive inclination toward him, he was banished to the fortress
> of the straits in order to repulse disorder. But Jews also gathered
> there. Since according to their false beliefs, their saying "this is our
> prophet" reached the point of being the cause of social corruption
> and disturbance of the peace, the rabbi was summoned to appear in
> Edirne by order of the sultan. On Thursday the sixteenth a council
> was convened in the New Pavilion under the imperial gaze, and there
> the deputy grand vizier, sheikhulislam, and Vani Efendi interro-
> gated the aforementioned rabbi. His eminence, our majestic sultan,
> watched and listened to the proceedings secretly from a window.
> After all the talk, the rabbi denied all the nonsense said about him.
> They proposed that he embrace Islam. When they ended their speech
> saying "after this council there is no possibility for escape: either
> come to the faith, or you will be immediately put to death. Become
> a Muslim at last, and we will intercede for you with our gracious
> sultan," the rabbi, with the guidance of God, the King who forgives,
> at that time became shown the right path, ennobled with the light of
> faith and a believer responsible to God. From the exalted gracious-
> ness of the Chosroes-like sultan a salaried position at the Middle Gate
> valued at 150 akçe was deemed proper for him. At that time he was
> placed in the bath of the inner palace pages where he was given new
> clothes. He was dressed in a fur and a cloak of honor, and a purse of
> aspers was also bestowed upon him. His companion who came to
> Islam with him at this time was given the gift of an usher position
> from the exalted imperial favor.[19]

The rabbi, who at the beginning of the story appears as the prophet of Jews, becomes by its end a palace gatekeeper who firmly believes not his own prophecy,
but in Muhammad's calling. At first he was banished for false belief, but when
he acquired true belief he was brought into the most intimate space of the empire, the inner palace. His journey on the right path took him from Izmir, to
the Dardanelles, to the sultan's side. Along the way he exchanged the dress of
a rabbi for the garments of the most esteemed members of society. And he did
not convert alone: of those disloyal, seditious Jews who disrupted public order,
one joined him in royal service. The two journeyed from being rebels against
the sultan and religion to members of the faith who were trusted to serve the
sultan in his residence.

Writing at the beginning of the eighteenth century, the historian Raşid Mehmed Efendi narrates Shabbatai Tzevi's adventure in a much more succinct fashion, emphasizing his conversion. He titles the account "Making the Famous Jew Appear before the Sultan and His Conversion to Islam":

> Previously a Jewish person from Izmir called a rabbi appeared in whom the Jewish people believed. He was banished and exiled to the fortress of the straits since signs of disorder were seen from those who gathered around him. Since even there he spread disorder among the Jews, he was made to appear at the imperial stirrup [before the sultan] in Edirne on the sixteenth of the month of Rabia al-Ahar. The aforementioned Jew was brought forth while the sheikhulislam, Vani Efendi, and the deputy grand vizier were in the imperial presence. When he was interrogated about that which had occurred, he denied the nonsense attributed to him, which had earned him fame. Because he knew that his execution was certain, he showed an inclination to become Muslim.[20]

Abdi Pasha used the story of Shabbatai Tzevi's conversion to emphasize Mehmed IV's exertions on behalf of Islam, his central role in the period, his piety and magnanimity, as illustrated by his distribution of cloaks and furs. For this reason Mehmed IV is compared with Chosroes, the ancient Persian who serves as the archetype of the just ruler. This is another opportunity for the sultan to display his credentials as a worthy Islamic ruler and for his chronicler to magnify them. Raşid, on the other hand, writing years after that sultan had been deposed, stated much more bluntly that Shabbatai Tzevi converted to save his life. Although that fact is also apparent in Abdi Pasha's account, he emphasized the rewards that accrued to converts: sumptuous robes, coins, and palace positions. It is another chance for the sultan to display his munificence. At the same time, the "nonsense" and "false beliefs" of irrational Jews are ridiculed and contrasted with Islam, deemed enlightening and ennobling since it is God's truth.

We can imagine how Mehmed IV must have looked during that meeting of the council; an Ottoman miniature, the original lost, serves as the basis for a drawing of the sultan published in Paul Rycaut's *The History of the Present State of the Ottoman Empire* (1668).[21] The ruler has thick eyebrows and large, melancholy eyes. His gaze is central to Ottoman narratives of the conversion of Shabbatai Tzevi. His eyes hovered over the proceedings leading to the prophet's conversion, scanning the room and all gathered within, as he sat concealed behind a screened and barred window high above the assembly. The sultan was in control, not Shabbatai Tzevi with his preposterous claims. Mehmed IV's curiosity was piqued, mingling with outrage.

As the twenty-five-year-old ruler gazed down at the forty-year-old rabbi, whose beliefs and practices were similar to those of the type of Sufi that the sultan and Kadızadelis were attacking, he may have asked how a man could proclaim himself a prophet. How dare he state that he could perform miracles? If he had divine powers, he would have to prove it. Stories circulated that the rabbi was told that if he was the messiah he would surely be able to defy death. He was asked to remove his cloak so that the imperial bowmen could use him as target practice, but Shabbatai Tzevi asked what his other choice was. As it turned out, it was the religion of Islam. Making him a Muslim, and keeping him around the palace as a reminder of his conversion, and humbling him, would serve to remind others of the truth of the religion. After all, if even a Jewish man who proclaimed himself a prophet could accept the truth revealed by Muhammad, who could resist it? And if the rewards were so great—a palace sinecure, the sumptuous garments forbidden to be worn by those who were not Muslim—who could not see the rewards accruing to those who changed religion? What could be better than a daily visible reminder that confirmed the superiority of the sultan's religion?

These narratives illustrate that even a seditious rabbi could become a Muslim, adopt a new name, and be cloaked in the dress of Muslims. To Abdi Pasha there was no contradiction in juxtaposing a choice between death and conversion and writing that the rabbi, "with the guidance of God, the King who forgives, at that time became shown the right path, ennobled with the light of faith and a believer responsible to God." A Christian or Jew who was compelled to become a Muslim was considered a sincere believer. Even though Shabbatai Tzevi committed the crime of *fesad*, a Qur'anic term meaning sedition or rebellion against both the moral and political order, a crime punishable by execution, yet the lives of rebels could be spared, as explained in Qur'an 5:33 (Al-Ma'ida, the Feast): "Those that make war against God and His apostle and spread disorder in the land shall be put to death or crucified or have their hands and feet cut off on alternate sides, or be banished from the country. They shall be held up to shame in this world and sternly punished in the hereafter: except those that repent before you reduce them. For you must know that God is forgiving and merciful."[22] The offer of conversion to save his life was meant to illustrate God's forgiveness and generosity manifested by his shadow on Earth, the sultan. Jews thought it miraculous that Shabbatai Tzevi was not executed.

Yet this episode illustrates how Muslims perceived two opposite natures of God: justice and mercy. God can be vengeful, angry, and capable of crushing His enemies. We have already seen that Ottoman writers explained how divine wrath, manifested in the great fire of 1660, destroyed the Jewish neighborhoods in Istanbul. But God is also merciful, compassionate, and forgiving.

Ottoman writers depict this aspect of God in the way the sultan handled Shabbatai Tzevi's punishment.

It was long-standing Ottoman practice, moreover, to co-opt rebels. An example from this period is Abaza Hasan Pasha, an Anatolian commander turned rebel who was given a military governor position. By bringing men such as Abaza Hasan into the system authorities hoped to control their actions and turn their ambitions, energy, and arms away from the empire and toward its enemies. This was true for prophetic and messianic claimants as well as ordinary rebels. Approximately one year after Shabbatai Tzevi arrived in Istanbul, a Kurdish dervish from southeast Anatolia, Sheikh Seyyid Abdullah, proclaimed his son Seyyid Mehmed the redeemer or rightly guided one and raised a Kurdish army in Diyarbekir in rebellion.[23] The two were captured and brought before the sultan in the environs of Vize near Edirne, where he was on the chase. When the boy was questioned about his status, he denied the call to being the redeemer. Because Seyyid Mehmed was descended from Muhammad, the Kurdish boy-redeemer was awarded a palace gatekeeper position, like Shabbatai Tzevi. After being interrogated in Arabic and Kurdish by Vani Mehmed Efendi and the sheikhulislam, his elderly, learned father was provided with a wool cloak and sumptuous garments and a Sufi lodge in Istanbul even though he had undertaken armed insurrection. It is presumed that the dervish lodge was not of an order that was targeted for its innovative practices. Authorities intended to keep an eye on them, and creating martyrs would only lead to worse problems. This also may have motivated them to bring Shabbatai Tzevi into palace service.

The transformation of another prophet or redeemer into a person who served the interests of the sultan has some striking parallels with the narrative of Shabbatai Tzevi's conversion. The Jewish rabbi Shabbatai Tzevi, the Kurdish descendant of Muhammad, Seyyid Mehmed, and his father, Sheikh Seyyid Abdullah, were religious men who proclaimed divine callings far from the center of power. But when Shabbatai Tzevi, who set out from Izmir, and the two Kurds, who appeared in Diyarbekir, were made to appear before the imperial council, officials made them explain the claims that had been made about them. Both Shabbatai Tzevi and the Kurdish boy denied what others had proclaimed and received cloaks and coins in reward. The father of the proclaimed redeemer of the age, also cloaked in new garments, was even awarded a Sufi lodge closer to the sultan, where he could continue his religious practices. Both the rabbi and the descendants of Muhammad were accused of sedition, and the latter had actually engaged in armed rebellion. Despite this, Shabbatai Tzevi, and not the two eastern rebels, was threatened with execution. Perhaps the fact that Vani Mehmed Efendi and many of the Kadızadelis hailed from Kurdistan militated against harsher treatment of the two religious Muslims from the region.

In both the Shabbatai Tzevi and Seyyid Mehmed narratives, the same process overcame the threat of religious insurrection, whether in the guise of a new prophet or the savior of the age. The rebels were brought to the palace, interrogated by Vani Mehmed Efendi, made to deny their claims, and subsequently rewarded. Lavish sultanic liberality could overcome any threat and make even powerful religious figures and rebels into subservient members of the sultan's retinue, signs of the victory of what he and Mehmed IV considered purified, authentic, rationalized Islam vis-à-vis the ecstatic eschatological excesses of Jew and Muslim alike. Moreover, it was assumed that the converted would serve as a model of religious transformation and bring others to the sultan's form of piety.

Shabbatai Tzevi was renamed Aziz Mehmed Efendi, the name of the sultan, his preacher, and the final prophet, given a salaried position in the palace, and taught the fundamentals of Islam by Vani Mehmed Efendi so that he would in turn convert other Jews with Kadızadeli tenets. For this reason he used a rabbinic formulation when explaining that he converted to Islam "to permit what it permits, and forbid what it forbids," which is a translation of the Islamic phrase "Enjoin good and forbid wrong" so central to the ideology of Vani Mehmed Efendi.[24] Just as the sultan's preacher mediated the rabbi's transition to Islam, the rabbi became the convert maker of his wife, Sara, who joined him in the palace as Fatma, and many of his followers. The new convert Shabbatai Tzevi reportedly became an advocate of Kadızadeli Islam and converted many Jews between 1666 and 1672. Western European observers noted that after his conversion Shabbatai Tzevi strolled through the streets of Istanbul with a large retinue of turban-wearing Jewish converts to Islam and preached in synagogues to win more converts.[25] According to Jewish sources, Shabbatai Tzevi, accompanied by Vani Mehmed Efendi's men, urged Jews to convert to Islam, and many were given turbans at the royal preacher's residence. Jews also wrote that Shabbatai Tzevi invited rabbis to dispute with him in the imperial audience hall in the palace in Edirne as the sultan and his preacher observed the proceedings. Western European and Jewish sources claim that many Jews converted before the grand vizier.[26] On the face of it, the sultan had successfully converted a force of disorder and sedition into a proselytizer for the truth.

Shabbatai Tzevi was made a Muslim when he was stripped of his old clothes and enrobed in new, sumptuous garments reserved for elite Muslims. By this act he was distinguished first from other Jews and then from common Muslims by a fur cloak. This point confirms the centrality of clothing in conversion and the important role that the sultan and his court played in dressing new converts. A Shabbatean account of the conversion also emphasized the importance of cloaking Shabbatai Tzevi in the dress of Muslims: "A royal attendant came to him bringing a robe which the sultan had worn, and another attendant with one of the sultan's turbans, and they clothed him with these and called him Mehmed, in the name of the sultan."[27] This is inaccurate but significant, for the Jewish writer understood the symbolic weight of the robe and turban. Though not actually items that the sultan had worn, they represented the sultan. For the believer in the rabbi's messianic calling, Shabbatai Tzevi's donning of the sultan's garments and adopting his name as his own may have been understood as if the rabbi had become the sultan and inherited his domains as predicted. But from the sultan's perspective, enrobing the prophetic rebel tamed him, literally brought him within the fold of the cloth of the right religion, and marked him as a successful spiritual conquest.

Hatice Turhan's Conversion of Jewish Court Physicians

Shabbatai Tzevi was but the first of a number of well-known Jews to be compelled to convert to Islam before the sultan or sultana at court in the 1660s. We have already observed Hatice Turhan's predilection for Islamizing Jewish spaces in Istanbul. Following Shabbatai Tzevi's conversion from provincial rabbi to Muslim palace gatekeeper, she was instrumental in offering other prominent Jews who were nearest to the sultan, such as privy physicians, the choice of converting to Islam or losing their coveted palace positions. The head of the privy physicians was the most important medical figure in the empire because he appointed all physicians, oculists, and dentists, and he treated the sultan, with whom he was on intimate terms. In fact, his residence and laboratory at Topkapı Palace were located in the intimate, private space beyond the third gate, making him practically a member of the royal family.

In the sixteenth century the position of privy physician was usually held by a member of the Jewish elite.[28] Some scholars, such as Stanford Shaw, have made the mistake of assuming that Jewish physicians remained in a prominent position in the palace until the eighteenth century.[29] In fact, during the seventeenth century the number and proportion of Jewish physicians decreased greatly, and many of those who wished to remain in office converted to Islam, in part due to sentiment in the palace. In previous centuries some individual Jews had faced hostility in the palace because of their views concerning foreign affairs, but it was not until the late seventeenth century that the group as a whole lost its once significant place.[30] İsmail Hakkı Uzunçarşılı was the first to point out the decreasing number of Jewish physicians.[31] Ottoman treasury records, although written in an almost indecipherable shorthand script, at least make it easy to follow the trend since the register of the daily salaries of those paid by the treasury contained two separate lists of court physicians by name, title, and salary. These were the group of Jewish privy physicians, usually recorded on the last page of the register, and the group of privy physicians, who were Muslim.

The palace salary registers show that the number and proportion of Jewish physicians declined. In 1603–4 there were sixty-three Jewish and twenty-one Muslim physicians.[32] In 1607–8 there were forty-one Jewish and twenty-one Muslim physicians.[33] By the mid-seventeenth century, the overall number of palace physicians decreased to eighteen: fourteen Muslims and four Jews.[34] Sultan Mehmed IV cut the number of physicians drastically, but then the numbers rose again at the end of the century. Salary is also an important measure of the fading prestige of the Jewish physicians. The highest paid Muslim head of the privy physicians saw his daily pay decrease 20 percent, from 100 akçe in 1653 to 80 akçe in 1672, where it remained for the rest of the period. The daily salary of the highest paid Jewish physician, however, decreased 56 percent, from 45 akçe in 1653 to 25 akçe in 1666, before rising back to 30 akçe in 1670, only to fall back to 25 akçe in 1687.[35] Muslim physicians earned two to three times the salary of Jewish physicians.

In the register of 1666 the following note appears at the end of the document listing the salaries of privy physicians: "The salary of the new Muslim physician Mehmed was ordered to be added to that of the group of privy physicians. The reason for the imperial writ joined to felicity is that he became ennobled by the honor of Islam in the imperial presence of the sovereign, and became a faithful servant entitled to reward according to the requirement of an imperial writ affirming the promotion on the seventh of Ramadan, AH 1077."[36] It is important to note that the conversion is validated by stating that it occurred under the gaze of the sultan. The man adopted the name Mehmed, Turkish for Muhammad, the name of the prophet and the sultan. This conversion occurred in the same year as that of Shabbatai Tzevi, who also adopted the Muslim name Mehmed.

Radical changes affected the corps of privy physicians in the seventeenth century. At the beginning of the century, a Jewish head of the privy physicians presided over a large staff of Jewish physicians and a smaller staff of Muslim physicians. By the end of the century, a converted Jewish head of the privy physicians led a staff of physicians mainly composed of converted Christian or Jewish and Muslim physicians. Whereas Jewish physicians outnumbered Muslims three to one at the beginning of the century (63/21), by its end Muslim physicians outnumbered Jewish seventeen to one (34/2).[37] Muslim physicians outnumbered Jewish physicians one and a half to one at the beginning of the reign of Mehmed IV (17/12), and five to one at its end (20/4).[38] The number of Jewish physicians shrank as the number of convert and Muslim physicians grew. Jewish physicians in earlier centuries had occasionally converted and become chief physicians while in palace service; for example, Hekim Yakub, physician to Mehmed II, converted soon after the accession of Bayezid II to keep his position and became known as Convert (Mühtedi) Yakub Efendi.[39] But in the seventeenth century the practice became the norm. In 1669 there were as many converts as Jews serving as palace physicians (five), and in 1697 the number of converts (not including the head of the privy physicians) surpassed the number of Jews (two Jews, three converts).[40] By the end of the century, twice as many converts as Jews served as privy physicians alongside the converted Jewish head of the privy physicians, Nuh Efendi: two Jews and four converts.[41]

Modern researchers in Istanbul use archival sources today because they seem to provide hard data that when read sequentially narrate historical trends. These sources demonstrate that over the course of the seventeenth century Jewish physicians disappeared from the ranks of the most important physicians in the empire as converted Christians and Jews joined a proportionally larger staff of Muslim physicians. Basing their opinions on these documents, scholars have made Jews the agents of their own decline or cited economic reasons for their loss of office. Some have surmised that fewer Jews were educated in western European universities, which offered the most sophisticated medical training, and thus fewer were qualified to be among the pool of potential physicians. Others have speculated that financial difficulties may have caused the palace to reduce the bloated staff of palace physicians during the reign of Mehmed IV.[42] What these numbers cannot reveal, however, and what archival sources fail to provide, are the ideological reasons for and context of the trends they capture, in this case why Jews no longer became leading physicians.

To understand the story behind these bits of information, we have to turn to narrative sources. Evidence from a treatise written by a palace preacher from Vani Mehmed Efendi's inner circle reveals that in order to preserve their position at the sultan's court it was a necessary but not sufficient condition for Jews to maintain their educational edge in the medical profession. The sufficient condition for Jews to remain as physicians was for the sultan's court to maintain its sixteenth-century attitude, which allowed Jews to treat the sultan as head physician without converting. When this attitude changed, so did the Jews' ability to function in office as Jews. The circumstances surrounding the conversion of the Spanish Jewish physician Moses son of Raphael Abravanel illustrate how this happened. In the case of this physician, conversion was a necessary step to remain as privy physician and be allowed access to the sultan's body. He became Hayatizade Mustafa Fevzi Efendi and head physician in 1669.[43]

By narrating the circumstances behind the physician's conversion, Kurdish Preacher Mustafa, who links Hatice Turhan's conversion of place (Eminönü) and people (Jewish physicians) in Istanbul, provides the context sorely lacking in the archival record. In the midst of his history of the Valide Sultan Mosque in Eminönü he juxtaposes two stories about Jews in palace service. After discussing Safiye Sultan's first attempts to build the complex in the late sixteenth century, he launches into a tirade against Esperanza Malki, referred to by the Greek term *kira*, meaning "lady."[44] Like others before her, such as Sultan Murad III's mother Nurbanu's lady-in-waiting Esther Handali, Esperanza Malki served as purveyor of goods and services to the harem and an intermediary with foreign embassies in the late sixteenth century.[45] She established a close relationship with Safiye Sultan, the favorite of Murad III and mother of Mehmed III. Kurdish Preacher Mustafa claims that "strangers and foreigners" mixed in the affairs of the valide sultan and stirred insurrection. The most dangerous among them was an evil, malicious, "accursed Jewish woman," Esperanza Malki, who "unjustly caused many people to be oppressed and transgressed."[46] Having recourse to the holders of office had no effect.[47] Ultimately, her wealth, influence, and control of the Customs Office led to her murder on the staircase of the house of the Istanbul deputy of the grand vizier Halil Pasha at the hands of rebellious sipahis, who blamed her for their pay of debased coins in 1600.[48] She was the last Jewish agent to serve the harem. Kurdish Preacher Mustafa narrates her harmful exploits but does not include the detail of her murder.

Following a riff concerning the danger of Jews in palace service, Kurdish Preacher Mustafa segues into a moral tale about how the dynasty should best treat such servants. Before returning to his narration of the history of the Valide Sultan Mosque, he praises the piety of Hatice Turhan, the valide sultan who completed the mosque in the author's day. To illustrate the "advanced degree" of her uprightness and piety, he explains that she did not permit Moses son of Raphael Abravanel, another Jew in palace service, to remain as physician to the sultan until he became a Muslim.[49] The reader does not expect this sudden juxtaposition of bad and good Jews and is not prepared for the abrupt change in the narrative. Suddenly the reader learns that

at the present time the uprightness and piety and forebearance and protection of her excellency the valide sultan [Hatice Turhan], God grant her long life, are such an advanced degree that when the noble temperament of his excellency the sultan [Mehmed IV], the refuge of the universe, became disturbed, and his subtle element became weak and languid, he who is now the head privy physician, known as Hayatizade [the former Moses son of Raphael Abravanel], distinguished

by his skill, matchless in the canons of medicine, and unequalled
in its arts, who used to prescribe health-giving tonics designed for
the inhabitants of the hospital of the world, for the young and the
old, the diseased and the ailing, was brought to the attention of her
excellency, the sultana [Hatice Turhan], whose mark is chastity. Yet although Hayatizade was renowned for his high degree of skillfulness
in medicine, because he had not become ennobled and graced by the
honor of Islam, and was not exempt from and absolved of the filth of
infidelity, she was not pleased that he should take the noble pulse and
diagnose the maladies of his excellency, the sovereign whose justice
is vigilant. Therefore, she ordered that as long as Hayatizade did not
wear the crown of Islam on his head, or don the cloak of the faith on
his shoulders, he was not granted permission to give medical treatment to that sultan whose extraction is pure and who is full of justice.
In fact, treatment of the sovereign was not permitted to Hayatizade
as long as he did not ennoble himself with the teaching of Islam and
distinguish himself from among the Jews with the banner of Islam.[50]

This narrative declares that it was brought to the attention of the valide sultan
that the most renowned physician in the palace was Jewish. She determined
that no matter how superior his medical knowledge and experience, he had to
first become a Muslim to be allowed to continue having access to the sultan
and to treat him. He had to literally look like a Muslim, wearing a Muslim turban and cloak, and figuratively be clothed in the teaching of Islam. His mind
and body had to be transformed. Only after spiritually cleansing himself of his
Jewishness could he be allowed to again touch the skin of the sultan, examine
his body to determine what ailed him, and be trusted to prescribe tonics and
cures that would restore his health. The Jewish touch, which had once been
considered life-giving, was becoming taboo.

In the seventeenth century a Jewish person could convert and erase all
Jewish "taint." Early modern anti-Jewish sentiment was not modern racial
anti-Semitism that posits an "eternal Jewish biology," which can never be purified, even by religious change. Hayatizade served as head of the privy physicians once he converted. One grandson, Hayatizade Mustafa (d. 1733), became
head of the privy physicians. Another grandson, Hayatizade Mehmed Emin
(d. 1748), became the sheikhulislam, the leading Muslim religious authority in
the empire and head of the religious class's hierarchy. And displaying an intimacy with the sultan's preacher, until the mid-twentieth century his descendants resided in a seaside mansion in Vaniköy, Vani Mehmed Efendi's Islamized
village on the Bosporus in Istanbul.[51]

In the late seventeenth century the sultan's Jewish privy physicians felt pressure to convert to Islam because they had their hand on the pulse of the sultan; they had to figuratively "don the cloak of Islam" before being permitted to continue in that office. Despite being "unequalled" in professional skill, the physician Hayatizade was pressured to convert to Islam in order to continue serving as Mehmed IV's physician. According to this palace view, the Jewish physician had to become a Muslim in order to "clean" himself of the "filth" of infidelity and "distinguish" himself from the Jews. Even if more Jews had received the best education in Italian medical colleges, Hatice Turhan's insistence on conversion mitigated any educational edge Jewish physicians had over others. In contrast to the mid-sixteenth century, when Jews such as Joseph Nasi rose to the highest medical post in the empire and played an active role at the Ottoman court while remaining practicing Jews, and even convinced Suleiman I to intervene with the pope on behalf of Portuguese Jews who were Ottoman subjects imprisoned in Ancona, the leading physicians at court in the mid- to late seventeenth century, such as Hayatizade and Nuh Efendi, had to be converted Jews.[52] While their declining opportunities for medical education may have decreased the pool of skilled Jewish physicians, the fact that some Jews continued to rise to the top illustrates that this generalization is not entirely valid.

The political position of Jews had become so weak that none could intervene to change the decision to banish them from much of the peninsula of Istanbul following the fire and construction of the Valide Sultan Mosque and the compulsory conversion of physicians. Those Jews who remained best positioned in the palace, such as Hayatizade, were involved in their own struggle to retain their posts. Hayatizade eventually lost that battle in 1691 and died a Muslim imprisoned in the infamous Yedikule, located on the Marmara along the seaside wall of the imperial capital.[53] One Ottoman historian claimed that Hayatizade was dismissed because he did not take proper care of Mehmed IV's successor, Suleiman II.[54] Another wrote that Muslim physicians engineered his downfall when Mehmed IV died. They approached the sheikhulislam, who was Vani Mehmed Efendi's son-in-law Feyzullah Efendi, and stated, "Until now we had doubts about whether the chief physician was truly a Muslim; now we know he is a [practicing] Jew."[55] The physician had lived for over two decades as a Muslim by that point, but for his rivals, who claimed he did not fast or pray, this did not suffice to prove his sincerity as a Muslim. The son of a Jewish tailor who learned medicine from Jewish doctors was quickly replaced by a madrasa-trained Muslim.

Elite Jews in the Ottoman Empire were not able to recover the formerly privileged economic and political position that they lost during this period.[56]

The list of physicians who were licensed to practice in Istanbul in 1699 demonstrates that Orthodox Christians became the predominant group.[57] Only one Jew, a Venetian, made the list. Whereas Christian physicians practiced their trade in Eminönü, the location of Hatice Turhan's mosque, an area formerly heavily populated by Jews, the Venetian Jewish physician had an office in Galata, across the Golden Horn. A century earlier Jewish physicians treated the sultan and were trusted by him to negotiate international treaties, but by the late seventeenth century this role was taken by Orthodox Christian physicians.[58] Their careers serve as good examples of the new power and influence of Orthodox Christians. Whereas a century earlier Venetian Jewish physicians had represented the Ottomans in international diplomacy, at the end of the seventeenth century Orthodox Christians represented the Ottomans and Venetian Jews served Venice.[59]

Just as the construction of the Valide Sultan Mosque complex was couched in the language of the conquest and conversion of Jewish space, so too is there a subtle reference to the same theme in the articulation of Hayatizade's conversion. He was said to have distinguished himself with the banner of Islam. Though merely literary flourish, this phrase suggests a link between conversion and conquest: the banner of Muhammad was the standard that accompanied the Ottoman military on campaign.

7

Conversion and Conquest

Ghazi Mehmed IV and Candia

Islamizing space in the imperial capital and converting false prophets and errant dervishes such as Shabbatai Tzevi and people in the sultan's inner circle, including the physician Hayatizade, were two ways of displaying the dynasty's virtues. As has been seen, even the valide sultan could engage in such practices, since by the late seventeenth century she represented the dynasty to the populace. Only the sultan, however, could embark on other activities necessary to restore the reputation of the male head of the imperial household. This chapter analyzes how Ottoman historians writing after a mature Mehmed IV moved to Edirne depict him as a model, active sultan. In their accounts he is a pious, strong, manly, warrior (ghazi) sultan, who reclaimed power taken by royal women and, with his preacher at his side, converted people and places in Ottoman Europe. The perspective of contemporary chronicle writers allows us to revise how scholars have depicted Mehmed IV as well as the evolution of the sultanate and the figure of the sultan in the seventeenth century. According to the authors of books of kings and conquest books (*Fethname*), works written to extol the virtues of the sultans and grand viziers who conquered infidel citadels and cities, sultans could still matter, and Mehmed IV certainly did.

The chapter focuses on the link between conversion and conquest during the successful final siege of Candia, Crete. The next chapter concerns how the sultan led his troops in person on two campaigns against the king of the Commonwealth of Poland and

Lithuania in central Europe and during the Russian campaign. These victories enabled Mehmed IV to expand the empire to its greatest limits, leaving in his wake bell towers converted into minarets and Christians circumcised as Muslims, which in turn increased the morale of Muslims in the imperial capital. Just as it is claimed in the Qur'an that the light of Islam abolished the pre-Islamic age of darkness and ignorance, Ottoman chroniclers boasted that the shadows of Christianity (substituting for paganism) manifested in churches were dispersed by the light of Islam spread by its faithful soldiers.[1] In this view, soldiers cleared a path allowing knowledge to be transmitted, which led to true revelation being accepted by Christians, who gained eternal salvation.

The soldier may not be a proselytizer, but his actions are a precursor to conversion.[2] Speros Vyronis Jr. demonstrated how conquest sets the stage for conversion because the defeat of a Christian enemy allows Islamic institutions to replace Christian institutions, which eventually serve to convert the defeated population absorbed into an Islamic state.[3] Here the focus is not on impersonal institutions such as dervish lodges and madrasas crucial for conversion in earlier centuries, but on the personal role of the martial sultan as convert maker.[4] The chapter thus addresses the major themes of the book concerning the link between piety and proselytization, the central role of the advocate of conversion, how conversion affects religious geography and sacred space, and the role that war, violence, and changing power relations play in conversion.

Depicting Mehmed IV as a Ghazi

There is a stark contrast in the way Mehmed IV is portrayed in the writing of Ottoman historians who finished their works while he was still a minor and the state was ruled by his regent, first the previous valide sultan Kösem Sultan, and then his mother, Hatice Turhan Sultan, and those written when the sultan became an independent ruler after he was in his twenties and moved the capital from Istanbul to Edirne, where he could spend his time hunting and launching war. Chronicles composed in the former period harshly criticize his father's reign and express much anxiety about the rule of women. Histories written during the latter period, however, rarely discuss Ibrahim or royal women, but instead praise the main subject, Mehmed IV, for his martial activities. The former mainly consisted of writing that consciously aims to warn the ruler to heed the mistakes of his predecessor and not repeat them, works that fit the genre of advice to kings, whereas the latter writers chose to compose largely uncritical works of praise, including a book of kings, and numerous books of conquest.

Early modern chronicle writers composed their works in a dialogic relation to the works of their predecessors, as their works were often explicitly labeled continuations. Here I am influenced by the recent study of Gabriel Piterberg, who examined the intertextuality of four accounts of the 1622 deposition and murder of Ottoman Sultan Osman II. At the same time, I have heeded Piterberg's call, echoing that of Dominick LaCapra, rare in the field of Ottoman history, of entering a dialogue with these historical texts to see what early modern authors were trying to tell us. By looking at not only the choice of genre they selected as the medium for narrating their stories (which carries a lot of the work for the story), but also the story in their works, I examine the interplay between historical experience and the accountings of that experience.[5]

In this book, the intertextuality of the works of four writers also stands out: Karaçelebizade, Katip Çelebi, and Solakzade, who wrote on Ibrahim and the first decade of Mehmed IV's rule, and Abdi Pasha, who as official chronicler wrote about almost the entire reign of his patron, Mehmed IV. Writing in part in response to the other three historians' barbed critiques of Ibrahim, and based on the premise that "the realm reflects the ruler," Abdi Pasha and other writers connected to the court, specifically those who wrote conquest books, promote the view that Mehmed IV was a mobile, active military leader and warrior breaking out of the harem cage in the palace of Istanbul and spending most of his reign in Edirne and Rumelia, the heartland of the empire, motivated by religious zeal, bringing war to the Christian enemy and promoting the image of a worthy Islamic sovereign.[6]

Mehmed IV reigned during a period of social and economic change leading to a loss of men's control over women and women's attendant gaining of more power, an age in which understandings of the sultanate had been greatly transformed, which is reflected in the critiques and anxieties of contemporary chronicles.[7] By the time Ibrahim was enthroned, the Ottoman Empire was no longer a frontier-oriented realm whose motivating force was warfare and territorial expansion. Instead, it was a bureaucratic, sedentary empire. The sultan had been removed from the operations of government and "the cut and thrust of decision-making."[8] He withdrew from subjects and servants and from public view. Because ordinary speech was considered undignified for sultans to use, they communicated by sign language. Unable even to speak, the sultan became out of touch, and was visible only on rare, carefully staged processions through the capital. The sultan had become a showpiece and sat silently on his throne in a three-foot turban, like an icon, immobile.[9] He appeared to be aloof, secluded, and as sublime as a Byzantine or Persian emperor. This was reflected in art as it became convention for miniaturists to depict the sultan on the throne and not on horseback leading a military campaign.[10]

The sultan was less likely to engage in military campaigns or command armies as he was usually not trained in the arts of war; instead, he was compelled to live deep in the palace, literally in the cage of the harem, surrounded by eunuchs, boys, and women. Ever after Mehmed II refused to stand at the sound of martial music, the primary component of a sultan's identity had become less ghazi and more a Caesar.[11] Abolishing a frontier custom symbolizes how the imperatives of rule had changed during the transition of the sultan from the head warrior of a march principality to the emperor of an imperial state that ruled continents yet marginalized warriors. While Mehmed II's son Bayezid II and grandson Suleiman I would still campaign in person—Suleiman I took his last breath at the age of seventy-two while laying siege to Szigetvár in Hungary—after Mehmed IV's predecessor in name, Mehmed III, at the end of the sixteenth century, the male head of the Ottoman dynasty usually was more sedentary than mobile, more often engaged in ceremony than battle. And on the rare occasion that they were compelled to head the imperial army, the weaker constitutions of sedentary sultans guaranteed that they usually did not last long. Ahmed I, for example, was felled by fresh springwater; he "was happier in his garden than in Anatolia where wolves prowled."[12]

The lives of sultans had been marked by mobility, the childhood of sultans by a princely governate. Living in small towns in Anatolia, future sultans were taught the arts of war and governance. Once a sultan died, his sons raced to the capital in order to be enthroned, battling and ultimately killing their brothers in the process. Mehmed III had been the last prince sent out to train in the art of war and governance in the provinces and the last to enforce the law of fratricide, killing his nineteen brothers when enthroned. Thereafter the throne passed from prince to prince, brother to brother, in descending order of age.[13] Beginning at the turn of the seventeenth century more often than not sultans were passively placed on the throne or even against their will rather than fighting for it or actively claiming it. While mercifully left alive, Ottoman princes were neutralized in the palace, hermetically sealed from the world, confined and condemned to a life of isolation. There they waited for death, or a chance to rule without having been trained for the position.[14]

Sultanic reigns were inevitably shortened by the age of the sultans upon accession since they had spent decades isolated and inactive.[15] The two men who succeeded Mehmed IV each died in the fourth year of their reign. Whereas the early sultans had been quite mobile, after Mehmed II they began to travel only for military campaigns or pleasure.[16] Instead, residing in the palace, they spent the dynasty's wealth but not the empire's because the two treasuries were separated. In these circumstances, in which the dynasty and the empire became distinct yet connected, loyalty was owed to the dynasty and not individual sultans, who became far less significant figures than in the past. The royal household was separated from the state, although the state still earned its legitimacy from being affiliated with the dynasty. Sultans "were needed to reign: ruling became the prerogative of others."[17] Sultans were not needed as warriors.

For some sultans, the only sword they would ever unsheathe was the ceremonial one that accompanied their accession. And if they were mad or minors they did not hold it long. Because they became dispensable, seventeenth-century sultans were the first in Ottoman history to be executed. Some sultans attempted to break this pathetic mold. Mehmed IV's grandfather Murad IV has a more robust reputation, for he conquered Yerevan and Baghdad and built victory kiosks at Topkapı Palace in the fourth courtyard overlooking Istanbul to commemorate the successes. He was broken down by these campaigns, which caused him poor health and an early death at the age of twenty-nine. Murad IV did not have the reputation of being a just ruler, for although Katip Çelebi writes that he was the "greatest of sultans to have reigned since 1000 [1590]," as a result of his "using the sword of execution to frighten and terrify the rebellious, taking the reins of state in his able hands," most of his commands went against sultanic statute and "completely terrorized everyone with his oppression" and shedding of blood.[18] Moreover, he is not considered a pious sultan. He never endowed any mosques of his own, instead installing open-air places of prayer at archery grounds.[19] Osman II attempted to make himself into a warrior-sultan who engaged in battle with the Christian enemy and left the palace in order to not appear "more a persona than a person" to his subjects.[20] His effort was resisted violently and he paid the ultimate price. Nevertheless, sultans realized that "the original justification of a sultan's right to rule was as a leader in war." Accordingly, to acquire political and religious legitimacy and counter criticism, they had their chroniclers emphasize their martial exploits.[21]

Changes in the royal household led to the passing of power from strong sultans to royal women such as the valide sultan, who became the most powerful and authoritative figures in the dynasty during the "age of the queen mother," along with the chief eunuch of the harem, who had access to both male and female members of the dynasty, serving as liaison between the harem and the sultan.[22] This figure rivaled the grand vizier for control of imperial policy in an era when sultans were raised in the harem and the valide sultan was the most influential figure of the dynasty. Prior to Mehmed IV's reign, a frightening number of sultans, including his father, were dethroned and executed. Sultans seemed irrelevant and were treated as if disposable. The Ottoman court witnessed an era dominated by women. With the decreasing importance of the sultan and the increasing role of Ottoman royal women, it is not surprising that at the beginning of Mehmed IV's reign, when the boy was enthroned at a tender age, first the previous valide sultan and then Mehmed IV's mother competed to be the boy's regent and struggled for power in the palace along with the chief eunuch of the harem. As in imperial China, eunuchs, unlike virile men, were able to staff the imperial harem and wield considerable authority; castrated men and women who gave birth to sultans exercised power to the detriment of sultans.[23] This situation troubled Ottoman chroniclers for whom, similar to writers in contemporary Qing China, it seemed a violation of the ideal of the "hegemony of the imperial phallus," since "the only penis in the palace was that of the emperor—enjoying sole access to countless female vessels, who were guarded by thousands of emasculated attendants."[24] In response, not dissimilar to depictions of the Manchus during debates at the Chinese court, Ottoman writers promoted the martial qualities of the ruler.[25]

Those who wrote after the 1660s when Mehmed IV had matured responded to Karaçelebizade, Katip Çelebi, and Solakzade, chroniclers who had passed away in 1657–58. Among historians there was a real changing of the guard. The new writers paid less attention to the valide sultan, made the sultan the center of the narrative, and wrote conquest books devoted to boasting of the martial successes of the ruler and inserted poetic panegyric in the text where they described the conquest of citadels.[26] They composed accounts glorifying the sultan as military conqueror of territories in central Europe and Mediterranean islands, hoping to shape his legacy as a warrior for the faith. A key narrative also written with this intention is the *Chronicle* of Abdi Pasha, who relied on Karaçelebizade, Katip Çelebi, and Solakzade when composing his history. Contrary to these works, which were written as part of the advice to kings genre, the official historian chose to situate his account of the reign of Mehmed IV in the genre of the book of kings, meant to glorify, not give advice to, the ruler, although with perhaps less of the exaggerated praise that usually characterizes such works and written in plain language so the sultan could understand it.[27] Similar to those writing conquest books, this choice of genre and omission of discussion of Ibrahim's reign by Abdi Pasha make his work an "amnesiac text" that expends "much labor and ingenuity in the service of forgetfulness," including forgetting the fate of Mehmed IV's father and predecessor.[28] This forgetfulness did not make his text free of the specter of the problems during Ibrahim's reign against which he was writing. For this reason his strategic choice also allowed Abdi Pasha to write a work that lays out a model of sultanic behavior.

In a sense, Mehmed IV's own personal history begins with the beginning of the writing of the chronicle, for he marked his attainment of or wish to attain maturity by producing a history that conveniently skips over his father's reign, the absent yet never forgotten foil illustrating the negative consequences of improper rule. For the next two decades, as Abdi Pasha composed his history in the genre of the book of kings, with the active participation of his near coauthor and audience, Mehmed IV, other writers penned conquest books, which promoted an image of the sultan's martial attributes. Instead of being the puppet of his regent, the valide sultan, when he matured Mehmed IV is depicted as having recaptured power from women, as he was able to evoke an earlier age when sultans were military leaders. Mehmed IV did so largely by turning his back on Istanbul and holding court in Edirne, a city referred to as "the hearth of the ghazi," the launching pad for war into the heartland of the Christian enemy.[29] The spatial and symbolic move away from Istanbul confirmed the coming into being of the sultan as man and ruler. He was compelled to break away from his mother's regency if he were to develop into a full-fledged man. He expanded the palace at Edirne so it could become the main royal residence for the first time since the conquest of Constantinople two centuries before.[30] There he passed most of his reign in the legendary pursuits of hunting, feasting, and banqueting, as well as hosting archery competitions, horse races, and javelin and wrestling matches.[31] Unlike Topkapı Palace, this royal residence afforded the sultan easy escape. There was ample space for him to pitch the imperial tent outside the palace at the start of military campaigns or royal journeys. When he did alight in the environs of Istanbul, he most often stayed in the palace and hunting lodge at Davud Pasha or at Kağıthane on the Golden Horn, which was well known for its empty spaces, ideal for archery competitions and military processions.

In an era when Muslim sovereigns were kept from the battlefield where they could engage in activities considered to be crucial for the performance of sultanic virtue, and were considered to be utterly lacking in the attributes of a strong ruler, Mehmed IV was depicted as an earthy, rough, simple leader more comfortable on horseback than sitting on a throne. Hunting caused him to become "vigorous and robust due to riding about outdoors."[32] Mehmed IV's chroniclers highlight the diverse prey that he ordered killed or killed with his own bow or gun, and other, sometimes cruel entertainments that he enjoyed watching. Far from being presented as a font of peace and reconciliation or sedate, a peripatetic Mehmed IV is depicted as eagerly promoting war, overseeing battle, dealing harshly with prisoners, and executing and displaying the heads of those who dared to challenge his monopoly on violence. Unlike most other seventeenth-century sultans, the Mehmed IV of Ottoman chronicles pursues conquest. His armies penetrate enemy territory with swords and missiles, humiliate the enemy by selling their wives and families into slavery, symbolically violate men and women, and replace the signs of their existence, such as churches, with those of the conqueror, including mosques, to demonstrate potency and give his subjects a vicarious sense of invulnerability.

Fahri Derin has pointed out that when Abdi Pasha began to compose his work he primarily relied on the histories of Karaçelebizade, Katip Çelebi, and Solakzade to write about the period from Mehmed IV's birth in 1641 through the first decade of his reign in 1658.[33] However, while pointing to slight changes Abdi Pasha made to the texts he transmitted, such as by shortening accounts or correcting names, dates, and places, Derin does not comment on the radical change in tone. Ibrahim hunted and launched war, but these actions were not emphasized by earlier writers. In contrast to chronicle authors who structure their narrative as diachrony, each entry marked by a date, Abdi Pasha uses a strategy of temporal discontinuity, which is antisequential—skipping from Mehmed IV's birth in 1641 to his enthronement in 1648—to pass over the troubled reign of Ibrahim and to inscribe on a tabula rasa the model of manliness that he promotes. He does not find Ibrahim's reign to constitute a usable past vis-à-vis his apparent authorial intentions or his seeming strategy.[34] Instead of heightening the contrast between the two reigns by mentioning the first, Abdi Pasha's amnesia-prone text selectively skips ahead to concentrate on the reign of his main subject.[35] As Paul Strohm notes in a medieval English context, "A wrinkle in the text's time opens a door through which we potentially pass to the utopian—a space between what is and what used to be or might be."[36]

For Abdi Pasha, benefiting from the luxury of fifteen years' retrospection following Ibrahim's disastrous reign, that ideal or normative vision consists of Mehmed IV waging war abroad, reviving jihad, and sending his military forces abroad, setting out on campaign in person as well. In this way, the author can represent the sultan, enthroned while a child, as a man with a thin beard but thick mustache, a brave who, unlike his father, can prove himself as sultan. Abdi Pasha linked the sultan's hunting to waging war and Islamic zeal.[37]

Mehmed IV and his handlers, Hatice Turhan and Abdi Pasha, were not unaware of the potential of ghaza for improving the sultan's image at home. Mehmed Halife notes that already in 1658, after the conquest of Yanova and following a week of celebrations in the capital, "as the felicitous sultan arrived in Edirne from Islambol with the intention of waging a military campaign, which caused the army to become confident [in his warlike intentions], a noble fatwa was issued declaring Mehmed IV a ghazi, and thereafter it was decreed that at the Friday sermon his name was to be read as 'Ghazi Sultan Mehmed Khan.'"[38] The sultan made warfare against the Republic of Venice, the Commonwealth

of Poland, and the Habsburg Empire into a major feature of his reign. At the
very end of 1665, the Ottoman Imperial Council secretary Mehmed Necati
completed the *History of the Conquest of Yanık* and presented it to Mehmed IV.
Necati's work is devoted to the sultan's heroic deeds of ghaza and jihad in the
early 1660s. He writes that the sultan was motivated to wage war in central Europe, first because "God commanded 'wage jihad on the path of God'" (Qur'an
22:78), and second because the sultan aimed to follow the example of Muhammad, who strove to carry out this divine directive Accordingly:

> In the auspicious year 1073 [1662–63], the illustrious, good fortuned,
> felicitous, and magnificent sultan of Islam, shadow of God, caliph
> of the age, master of the auspicious conjunction, custodian of the
> two noble sanctuaries [Mecca and Medina], most holy lands, and two
> directions of prayer [Mecca and Jerusalem], kingdoms of the West and
> East, eye of humanity and pupil of the eye, sultan son of a sultan, the
> Sultan Ghazi Mehmed Khan son of the Sultan Ibrahim Khan son of
> the Sultan Ahmed Khan, may God cause his fortune to endure until
> the end of time, his excellency, directed himself toward the Venetian
> infidels, and on the eighth day of Shaban the great [March 18,
> 1663] departed the protected city of Istanbul, the abode of sultan
> and residence of the caliph, the kings' and sultan's desire, and with a
> tumultuous army like the sea, settled in Davud Pasha field.

In order to "make known to the Christians the strength and vigor of Islam,"
the council had decided it was necessary to conquer the citadel of Yanık (Raab).[39]
At the end of the sixteenth century Ottoman historians had explained the attempt to take the same citadel of Yanık in more practical terms: the governor of
Bosnia had been defeated and killed in skirmishes with the Habsburgs.[40]

In the words of court chroniclers and in the actions of the sultan, constant
reference was made to Muhammad. After the sultan and his representative
the grand vizier had arrived in Edirne, and one day prior to setting out on
the military campaign, Mehmed Necati writes, "In accordance with Ottoman
ceremony and befitting sultanic pomp and display," Mehmed IV handed Fazıl
Ahmed Pasha the banner of Muhammad (5a). The outcome of this campaign of
the "ghazi monotheists" or "ghazi Muslims" or "army given God's help and victory in battle" against the "infidels destined for Hell," or "accursed ones firmly
fixed in Hell," and "evil-acting Caesar," seemed obvious to the author (16b, 22a,
22b, 36b). In one clash, of 4,300 infidels only twenty-eight "accursed ones" had
been spared the sword, but they were wounded (33b). Half dead, they threw
themselves into a river, and "like hooked fish, with a thousand torments and
trials," crossed to the other side and were saved. During this campaign, when

defense works and citadels were conquered, the Ottoman side immediately killed all ordinary enemy troops found within and read the call to prayer (33a). Commanders and other leading defenders, however, sometimes were brought before the presence of the grand vizier and converted to Islam. For example, after conquering one fortress, eleven leading men, former "accursed ones," displaying on their foreheads the sign that they were "guided to the path of the all-merciful and all-compassionate," became "honored by the glory of Islam" before Fazıl Ahmed Pasha (37a). Following the successful conquest of Yanık and the signing of a peace treaty with the Habsburgs, the grand vizier returned to Edirne from the battlefront and the sultan returned from Belgrade, arriving in Istanbul with great ceremony and a grand procession (48b–49a).

Ghazi Sultan Mehmed Khan had both successfully campaigned against the enemy in only two years and brought about a favorable peace. This contrasted favorably with over a century earlier when it had taken Suleiman I eighteen years of war and negotiations to arrive at a suitable settlement (50a). Mehmed IV thus carried out God's order to "act upon his religious zeal" and wage jihad, "sending in all directions braves and famous brave commanders who forbade to themselves what is forbidden or the least comfort or rest, battled with heart and soul, and sacrificed their lives as martyrs."[41] The brave commanders included "the hero" Fazıl Ahmed Pasha (30a). Because Mehmed IV exerted the appropriate zeal, unlike his father, historians claimed that affairs of religion, empire, and sultanate were successful (50a).

When Mehmed IV was in his twenties and had commanded his grand vizier to complete the conquest of Candia in 1666, he again displayed a historical consciousness. As he had when he invited Abdi Pasha to accompany him to Edirne to serve as the sultan's chronicler in his new residence, he had Abdi Pasha read him narratives of the jihads of sixteenth-century sultans, including Selim I's defeat of the first Safavid Shah Ismail at Chaldiran in 1514, Suleiman I's conquest of the citadel of Rhodes from Venice, and the same sultan's taking of Belgrade from the Habsburgs.[42] Belgrade was a gateway to Vienna, "the Bulwark of *Germany*, and consequently of all Christendom," the city to which Suleiman I traveled while en route to an attempted conquest of the Habsburg capital.[43] Having Abdi Pasha read him these military exploits demonstrates Mehmed IV's interest in great land and sea victories of previous ghazi sultans over the three main Ottoman enemies in the previous century and his sensitivity to how he wanted to be remembered in the future. He participated in several campaigns and cheered on the troops at others. Long lost to the silences of history, he made a mark through his personal desire to combine piety with presence on the battlefield.

Christians in central and western Europe got the message. Prints of Mehmed IV made between 1663 and 1683 present him before burning citadels and horrifying scenes of battle. For example, in a work entitled in Latin "Mahomet the Fourth of This Name, Emperor of the Turks and of All the Orient, the Worst Enemy of the Christian Religion," Mehmed IV sits beneath a cloud-filled sky astride a magnificent, powerful horse.[44] With front legs raised, an open mouth, and fixed gaze—a typical pose for a conqueror's horse—the animal is ready to charge. It wears a feathered headdress held in place with a diamond aigrette under which a frightening, lionlike face descends, partly obscuring the horse's face. A winged-lion clasp that holds its ceremonial dress sits across its

FIGURE 7.1. Mehmed IV in the eyes of his enemies. Anonymous, "Mahomet Istivs Nominis IIII Tvrcarvm et Totivs Orientis Imperator Infestissimvs Christianæ Religionis Hostis" (Mahomet the fourth of this name, emperor of the Turks and of all the Orient, the worst enemy of the Christian religion), Österreichische Nationalbibliothek, Vienna, Porträtsammlung, Bildarchiv und Fideikommißbibliothek, Pg 26 25/1, Ptf. 30: (28). Reproduced with permission.

breast. The sultan, who holds a scepter in his right hand, wears a turban with an oversized ghazi aigrette and sports a mustache whose tips are upturned, cocks his head to the right, his large dark eyes beneath slightly raised eyebrows looking sternly yet dully and calmly just into the distance beyond the viewer. He wears a many-pleated heavy garment beneath a spotted, fur-lined cloak. His luxurious garment is rolled up his right leg, revealing a mighty, meaty knee and thick calf, demanding comparison with the muscular yet slightly smaller legs of the horse. Man and beast seem to share the same threatening body. Mehmed IV's left hand firmly holds the reins of the vigorous horse. In the background a battle rages between charging Ottomans on horseback with raised sword, arrow, and lance, and the banner-waving defenders of a citadel lying in a plain. Contorted corpses are strewn across the foreground. Just behind Mehmed IV a group that may be citadel defenders is moving toward the Ottoman forces, giving the Christian viewer some hope for victory.

The prayers that Vani Mehmed Efendi composed for the sultan in the mid- to late 1660s offer insight into both the religious motivation and the legitimation of such military campaigns.[45] Vani Mehmed Efendi depicts the sultan as the defender of the domains of Islam, repelling threats to the empire. This was not new, since previous sultans had also been called the defenders of Islam and the protectors of the holy cities of Mecca and Medina. But articulated along with calls for reinvigorating Sunni Islam within the empire, this terminology emphasizes dynastic concern with shoring up its moral defenses, waging the jihad of the soul and the jihad of military campaign. Ottoman writers referred to foreign Christians in ways that revealed the struggles were not merely depicted as geopolitical: they were described as a clash between Christendom and Islam.

Vani Mehmed Efendi's prayers provide a glimpse into the image of a pious sultan and strong leader that the preacher favored, the chronicler echoed, and the sultan and valide sultan promoted. Vani Mehmed Efendi encouraged the sultan to defend the empire from the attacks of the infidels, Catholic Venetians and Habsburgs, while at the same time strengthening Sunni Hanafi Islam and Islamic law against the threat of religious innovation within the empire, shorthand for the Sufi practices that he condemned. Foreign Christians and Ottoman Muslims who did not agree with the tenets of the Kadızadelis were the external and internal enemies against whom the sultan was encouraged to battle. A prayer composed in 1664 on the occasion of the sultan's leaving the palace in Edirne to Yanbolu refers to him as "the defender of the lands of Islam from the assault of infidelity and rebels, the protector of the dominion of the illustrious Shariah from the evil of innovation and sinners" (1b). In the same prayer, the sultan is lauded for being "the guardian of the pillars of the Shariah" and "the keeper of the armies of the people of the Sunna" (2a). Vani Mehmed Efendi composed another prayer on the occasion of the sultan's journeying from the palace in Edirne to Çatalca the following year, in which he praises the sultan for being "always guided to success by God over the enemies of religion and state, infidels and innovators" since "those enemies of bad laws and customs are overwhelmed and utterly destroyed (2b). In a prayer composed in 1665, the year Vani Mehmed Efendi became the preacher at the Valide Sultan Mosque, whirling by dervishes was banned, and Lari Mehmed Efendi executed, the preacher credits the sultan for being "true-hearted in proclaiming the true religion to unbelievers, faithfully resolved to reinvigorate the practices of the messenger of God" (2b). Other prayers composed in those years for when the sultan traveled or during public holidays praised him for "driving away the infidelity of polytheists" (3b), defending Shariah and Sunni Muslims (6a), protecting the borders of Islamdom and saving Islam (7b), since he was "the one who strengthens the building of Islam and its pillars" while also being "the one who proclaims the true religion to unbelievers and humiliates the word of the infidels and sinners" (8a–b).

The Campaign for Candia, Crete

The best contemporary source for an Ottoman view of Mehmed IV's role in military campaigns in the 1660s, including the final stages of the war over Crete, is a work that is explicitly labeled a book of jihad and ghaza. *The Essence of History*, by the imam Hasan Agha, Fazıl Ahmed Pasha's private secretary and seal keeper, was begun in 1675 and completed in 1681, when the sultan was at the height of his power. It was dedicated to narrating the grand vizier's conquests.[46] Already on the first folio in the invocation written in Arabic the author uses the Arabic terms for warrior in God's cause (*mujahid*) and struggle in God's cause (*jihad*) eight times to describe the pious grand vizier who modeled his life on that of the prophet, waging war against unbelievers and hindering Muslims from engaging in error. He is "the most superior of mujahids," "commander of the army of the believers," "crusher of the enemies with the sword of the mujahids," "destroyer of the idols of the infidels," "cutter of the roots of vice," and "one who exalts the call of the victorious jihad." While Fazıl Ahmed Pasha led the actual campaign against Venice, Mehmed IV offered moral support from the European mainland, traveling to the ports from which the Ottoman navy embarked to besiege the island. This action alone allowed Hasan Agha to refer to the sultan as a ghazi since he was "the distinguished one of the Ottoman dynasty, the heir of the sovereignty of Suleiman, the Alexander of the age, the one who spreads justice and faith, the one aided with the victory of God, the sovereign who has recourse to God, his eminence Ghazi Sultan Mehmed Han son of Sultan Ibrahim Khan, may God strengthen him and confirm victory over the enemies with the sword of jihad until the Day of Judgment."[47]

Hasan Agha depicts the sultan in a way that counters modern historiography on his reign. Rather than characterizing him as a childish fool who had no concern for affairs of state, the author of *The Essence of History* bases his narrative on what he witnessed and the correspondence between the grand vizier and the sultan to depict him as intimately involved in war and diplomacy. The sultan waits impatiently for news from the front and offers advice for the campaign. He appears especially concerned that his grand vizier exert himself for jihad and ghaza and glorious conquests for Muslims while at the same time recognizing that all assistance comes from God, thus demonstrating his piety. Mehmed IV consistently tests Fazıl Ahmed Pasha to see how much he is striving in the name of the religion since the sultan entrusted him and the army to God. Thus, for example, the author includes many of the written exchanges between the sultan and his grand vizier during the 1660s, including the campaigns in central Europe undertaken prior to the renewed effort for Candia. Thus during the Uyvar campaign in October 1663, the grand vizier received an imperial writ stating in part:

> What state are you in now, and what is the condition of the soldiers of Islam? It has been a very long time. I am waiting for joyful news. By the grace of God, it is nearly November. You know how quickly winter arrives in that region. Reflect upon it accordingly and deny yourself sleep and rest. Gird your loins. Being in the service of the manifest religion, pay attention to exerting yourself in the matters of ghaza and jihad. It is hoped that the eternal God and the Muslim sovereign who does not fade will be made joyful with word of numerous conquests. . . . You bear the honor of the sultanate. . . . Let me see to what extent you exert effort for the auspicious, manifest religion. I have entrusted you and the soldiers of Islam to God. May the exalted God be your protector and one who watches over you. My grand vizier, God willing after the conquest and subjugation, consult with the ministers of my state and present to the imperial stirrup [the sultan] the wise and reasonable plan. (32b)

The sultan then proceeds to make notes on commissions, personnel changes, and promotions, demonstrating a knowledge of precedent, procedure, and protocol. He was intimately involved in war readiness and wanted to keep control of the military registers. At the end of the decree he again presses his representative to prove how much he is striving in the name of the religion.

When the sultan learned of the conquest of the citadel, he sent another writ to his grand vizier. In it he expressed how ecstatic and joyous the news of the defeat of "the infidels of Hell" made him. He congratulates the successful ghazis and mujahids and sends the grand vizier a jeweled aigrette, an "enemy-destroying saber of the master of the conspicuous conjunction" with a jeweled hilt, and a fur with silver brocade and kaftan:

> By the grace of God, the Opener of all ways, the citadel of Uyvar was
> conquered and made captive. Praise and glory were given to God, the
> granter of munificence when my imperial stirrup was inspired by
> joy with the glad tidings that in accordance with my imperial heart's
> desire the infidels destined for Hell were hopelessly abandoned and
> punished. These illustrious conquests cheered my noble disposition
> and illuminated my gracious mind with joy. Humble yourself as a
> supplicant in entreaty to His eminence the Eternal Creator. Moreover,
> very many illustrious conquests have occurred. May bowed-headed
> infidels destined for Hell never be protected from the flames of Hell.
> I give benefactions to honor you and my stone-leveling and earth-
> moving ghazi and mujahid servants of the victorious campaign for
> my auspicious religion and dynasty. (38b)

After listing the favors he bestowed upon his grand vizier, the sultan then urged his men to exert themselves in a way worthy of Islam, the Ottoman dynasty, and the honor of the sultanate to repair the conquered citadel and make it part of the Ottoman bulwark in central Europe.

In the spring of 1664, another letter from the sultan to his representative demonstrates that he closely followed the unfolding military campaign in central Europe, that he was aware of its fluctuating fortunes, and that he was cognizant of the intrigues of enemies and allies (64b–65a). This writ, read aloud to all ministers and military commanders, urges Fazıl Ahmed Pasha to not only plan the campaign well, but to act following the path of godliness, to take great pains exerting every effort to avenge the enemies of Islam and the Ottoman dynasty. The letter stresses that his ghazi and mujahid servants who give life and soul should know that the sultan prays to God to be their helper and guide, and that they are not merely on a military campaign, but are serving the religion as well. They are the troops of the monotheists who will destroy the polytheists abandoned by God. Those who undertake ghaza and jihad will obtain a blessing and their conquests will make God, the sultan, and Muslims joyful and glad.

That summer the sultan continued to write passionate, pious letters urging on his grand vizier (74b–75a). He asks him how he is faring "against the atheist enemy" and announces the birth of prince Mustafa, an auspicious sign that he hopes will be accompanied by glad tidings from the ghazis and mujahids fighting on his behalf in the struggle between the forces of good (Muslim ghazis) and evil (the miserable infidels destined for Hell). He repeatedly emphasizes that it is only reverence for God that will cause matters to turn out well. In the Ottoman version of the twenty-year peace treaty offered to the Habsburg emperor in 1664 at the end of the campaign, which would be unwisely broken by Grand Vizier Kara Mustafa Pasha when he launched the invasion ending with the failed siege of Vienna, Fazıl Ahmed Pasha is referred to as the "opener of the gates of jihad" and the "ghazi on the path of God" (88b). The sultan at the time was in Edirne enjoying a manly round of javelin; he later journeyed to the Dardanelles, hunting along the way (90a). Having attained peace with the Habsburgs, Fazıl Ahmed Pasha and Mehmed IV decided to immediately turn their attention to Venetian Crete.

Let us examine how the commentator narrates the campaign against Crete. According to Hasan Agha, following the settling of matters with the Habsburgs the previous year, in the winter of 1665, Fazıl Ahmed Pasha proposed a major campaign to finally conquer the last holdout of Candia, an effort initiated twenty years before, which was still unresolved. To Ahmed Dede, the stubborn resistance of the defenders was increasingly troubling as Venetians battled Ottomans with the swords of slain Muslims inscribed in Arabic with the phrase, "Oh God, the Conqueror and Victor."[48] The grand vizier met with the sultan in Edirne to ask for authority to launch a campaign for the citadel of Candia, desiring to take revenge on the Venetians in the name of the dynasty, for it was the perfect time to "completely exert ourselves on this greater jihad so God may liberate the citadel for the community of Muhammad" (95a). The grand vizier appealed to the sultan's honor: "For how many years has the citadel of Candia caused great tumult and confusion to the sultanate of the House of Osman, and [this failure] is on everyone's tongues. Give your blessing right away, my sovereign, and we will also see this concluded in a peace treaty" (95a–b). The sultan agreed. Allowing Candia to remain in infidel hands did not befit sultanic zeal.[49]

The grand vizier personally led the siege efforts. In accordance with Ottoman statute, Fazıl Ahmed Pasha first appeared before the sultan wearing a short-bodied fur coat brocaded with silver thread, red velvet pants, and a Selimi turban.[50] After he kissed the ground before the sultan, the latter placed two jeweled aigrette pins on his turban and dressed him in two sumptuous fur cloaks. The sultan then handed the grand vizier the black banner of Muhammad and honored him with a benediction. The grand vizier took the standard upon his shoulder and exited the palace grounds. As he set off for the front, the sultan gave him an imperial writ emphasizing the imperial gaze, stating that he would see how well laid were his plans and follow from afar how intelligently he would proceed (99b).

Vani Mehmed Efendi and Grand Vizier Fazıl Ahmed Pasha exchanged feverish letters during the renewed siege efforts in 1667 that illustrated their desire to defeat the Venetians in the name of Islam.[51] Vani Mehmed Efendi praised the grand vizier for battling in the cause of God and leading the Muslims to (the not yet achieved) victory over infidels. Because of his frequent leading of military campaigns, Fazıl Ahmed Pasha is explicitly referred to as a ghazi, "the one who raises the banner of jihad, repels infidels and obstinate deniers, is the ruler of the victorious and the rightly guided, and the combatant on the path of God."[52] The grand vizier had not merely a military mission, but a religious one as well. Throughout the letters the two men referred to the Venetians as "accursed," whereas the Ottomans were "warriors of Islam," combining the geopolitical with a religious contest.

This first renewed siege effort was unsuccessful. Vani Mehmed Efendi comforted the grand vizier by writing that no one has ever heard of such a well-fortified citadel falling in only one battle. He wrote that God always supports and protects His servants, and prayed for conquest "which would gladden all of mankind—save infidels and sinners—who will face the tip of the sword of victory." He assured him that "God destroys what is false," and signed the letter, "the sincere friend who calls others to religion, Mehmed al-Vani."[53]

Fazıl Ahmed Pasha was also instrumental in bringing others to Islam, testifying to Vani Mehmed Efendi's claim that he was "true-hearted in proclaiming the true religion to unbelievers, faithfully resolved to reinvigorate the way of the messenger of God."[54] In the spring of 1667, the grand vizier left Chania to besiege the citadel of Candia. Along with the entire army he paraded before it. Suffering from lack of water, hunger, and fear, perhaps terrified by the Muslim battle cry, some fled the citadel and converted to Islam before Fazıl Ahmed Pasha.[55]

The commentator Hasan Agha continues to depict the sultan as a concerned sovereign dedicated to matters of state. He boasts, "Giving his complete attention to the matter of the conquest of the islands, and ordering the necessary troops and equipment to be sent to the front, the sultan decided to journey to Eğriboz."[56] Evliya Çelebi also assigns Mehmed IV a key role in the final effort in the conquest of Candia. He writes that the Muslim soldiers before the citadel of Candia, learning that the sultan was traveling in person to Eğriboz and intended to then pass over to Crete, "became frightened" and incited by his impending arrival, then used all possible force to take the citadel, ultimately conquering it in this way.[57] According to Hasan Agha, in the summer of 1667, the sultan continued to watch events closely and sent a concerned writ to his grand vizier and commander in chief. Again he desired to know the exact status of his deputy and armed forces. He constantly humbled himself in prayer for God's assistance, confident that because his men followed the model of Muhammad they would be victorious in their efforts for Islam, the House of Osman, and God, and that the enemies of Islam and the Ottoman dynasty would be utterly frustrated. He urged Fazıl Ahmed Pasha to gird the "saber associated with victory from the sovereign's swords possessed of victory," and with the advantageous costume of a sumptuous sable fur from the sultan's own furs, "with heart and soul use every effort without pause for religion, my dynasty, and the honor of my sultanic reign."[58]

The sultan did not want to be, like his father, deposed for waging an inconclusive military campaign for Crete. His honor was on the line. For this reason he took personal interest in the outcome of the campaign, in this writ claiming to have read the letter the grand vizier sent to him, and pledging, "God willing in no time I will personally set out and day by day try to draw near to that region and my servants who are the ghazis of Islam. I pray night and day that God the Creator does not turn my hope to disappointment."[59]

He would not be disappointed. By the fall of 1668, after fifteen months, Ottoman forces reached the walls of the citadel. According to his writ, this made the sultan excessively joyous and demonstrated that he was following events closely. He expressed pleasure that the effort was going well, since victory was as close as the walls of the fortress. Delighted at the good news, he thanked and praised God, and he wished to reward his ghazis and mujahids on the great, blessed ghaza. He hoped that very soon illustrious conquests would gladden all Muslims and that all enemies would be crushed by irresistible might and end up suffering in Hell. Then the sultan challenged the grand vizier to display his martial manliness to the sultanic gaze: "Complete courage means the spilling of blood, and manliness and bravery are commended. When you bestir yourself to manly bravery and display your total zeal, the citadel's conquest will be divinely facilitated."[60]

Urging the grand vizier to victory for the sake of the sultan's honor, Mehmed IV wrote, "Be vigilant to strengthen the ghazis who are sacrificing heart and soul in ghaza." The sultan then informs his grand vizier that he too has joined him on the path of jihad: "In order to aid the manifest religion, and resolving to join in ghaza, I too, set out on campaign from Edirne in state with my complete retinue during the month of Rabia al-Awwal on a blessed Thursday, preferring to suffer hardship on the path of God." He had reached the plain at Dimetoka and was prepared for victory: "May God not deprive me on this road."[61]

The sultan exchanged more letters with the grand vizier regarding how to treat the Venetian ambassador in Yenişehir. In an anxious letter to Fazıl Ahmed Pasha, he asked him what to tell the Venetian based on news from the front: "My grand vizier, what do you say, when the ambassador arrives, what response do I give him? If you are of the opinion that you are about to conquer the citadel, I will tell the ambassador we want the Venetians to turn it over to us. But if not, and it will be required to prolong the siege for another year, then it means the empire has been rendered weak, powerless, and impotent in sending soldiers, munitions, and other necessities of war to the island."[62]

The letters exchanged between the sultan and his grand vizier often referred, explicitly or implicitly, to connections among manliness, victory in battle, and propagation of the faith. This metaphor of sexual impotence is tied directly to the empire's honor and by extension to that of the sultan. Comprehending the import of the writ, the grand vizier wept for three days and nights and became greatly distressed. It took him days to write a response. He wrote letters to all key men of state, including the sheikhulislam and Vani Mehmed Efendi, hoping they could help assuage the sultanic anger. Finally he informed the sultan that the army was fatigued but that the citadel would soon be theirs. He asked God to be on their side, to not let the citadel remain in infidel hands. Using the language of manliness, he wrote that it was necessary to give the ambassador a manly response. The sultan acted accordingly, but the Venetian ambassador gave what was considered a "swinish response," wanting the citadel to remain Venetian. His honor as a man at stake, the sultan declared that his forces would not withdraw.[63]

In February 1669, the grand vizier held a great divan at which all military and administrative leaders gathered to hear the writ of the sultan. When it was read, as Silahdar writes, "the eyes of the ghazis of Islam, which were filled with blood, flowed with tears like a flood."[64] All cried, except for the traitorous head of the bombardiers, who, because he said "I am going to the Franks [western Europeans]," was dressed in chains. Hasan Agha relates how the sultan's writ called on all gathered soldiers and commanders to personal discipline and bravery, to give no respite to the enemy of religion.[65] He told them that their perseverance was honorable and worthy of reward in this world and the next. He urged them to show him their zeal, battling the enemy like manly braves, sacrificing heart and soul, struggling together, subjugating Candia after great effort. He wrote that it would be a shame upon Islamic zeal if any among them fled the battlefield or if his army simply withdrew. The subjugation of the citadel was his uttermost imperial desire; accordingly, he would do whatever was necessary to be successful, and he wanted to see their effort increase many-fold.

The sultan followed the siege efforts closely from mainland Greece. His journey from Edirne to Dimetoka, Gümülcine, Serres, Salonica, Yenişehir, and Eğriboz was considered an effort to exalt Islam based on the resolve and intention of ghaza.[66] He was praised for leaving aside his normal comfort and instead inviting hardship as he passed through cities, alighting in his imperial tent facing the field before which rebellious officials from far-flung parts of the empire were executed. It was a journey of justice littered with the bodies of the unjust.

In June 1669, over two years after the siege of Candia had begun, Ottoman forces launched a massive battle to take the fortress. As Hasan Agha writes hyperbolically, "Never before had anyone seen such a tremendous battle and use of treasure and never will anyone see it again."[67] The Ottomans sacrificed more than thirty thousand Janissaries alone in the final siege efforts, which is to say more than one thousand per month, and used several thousand tons of ammunition, bombs, and hand grenades.[68] Other sources estimate the total losses during those two years at more than seventy-five thousand soldiers.[69] Despite the losses, the sultan still wanted to conquer the citadel. Because he demanded its conquest ever more fervently, his military was urged to act as manly braves, to strive even more to conquer it, so that the soldiers would be blessed on Earth and in the hereafter, the martyrs to go to paradise and the living to see its conquest.[70] The sultan pressed the grand vizier, and the grand vizier pressed the commanders to show greater effort. Fazıl Ahmed Pasha served his commanders coffee despite its recent ban and sent them back to continue the siege.

An omen of conversion presaged the fortress's fall. In September 1669, the chief physician Salih Efendi died. After converting, Hayatizade was appointed in his place and ordered to appear before the sultan. Then came the good news that finally Candia was conquered. The commander and ministers again wept when they kissed the skirt of Fazıl Ahmed Pasha. The grand vizier rubbed his face in the black earth. Relieved, exhausted, ecstatic, and thankful, he finally cried uncontrollably and continued to weep day and night for ten days.[71] He may have had a secret weapon, his pious mother, who mirrors the pious Hatice Turhan. The next day he went to a nearby citadel and met with his mother, kissed her hand, and the two cried together before she set off for the hajj.[72] The grand vizier called for massive celebrations in the citadel and in the harbor, with the army blasting their cannons from within the fortress and the navy firing its guns over the water. The grand vizier then composed a summary report submitted to Mehmed IV that the jihad was successful: "For twenty-seven years the Muslims' honor had been trodden underfoot, but now, because of the zeal, manliness, and bravery in battle of the sultan's servants, the citadel has been conquered."[73]

The citadel of Candia, in the words of Rycaut "the most impregnable Fortress of the World, strengthened with as much Art and Industry, as the human Wit of this Age was capable to invent," surrendered to the Ottomans after twenty-seven years of war, ending a twenty-seven-month and twenty-seven-day siege on September 27, 1669.[74] September 27 was an important date in Ottoman history: in 1529 the forces of Suleiman I arrived before the walls of Vienna for the first unsuccessful Ottoman siege of that city. The day marked by failure had been converted into a day of pride. The Ottomans had finally gained control of the eastern Mediterranean. People had believed the citadel would never be conquered. Its defenders had devoted much effort to fortifying it and had reinforced it for twenty years, encircling it with water and fire by means of mines, bastions, and a moat. But for two years and nearly four months, summer and winter, night and day, combat and killing over the citadel never ceased, and in the end, the Ottomans were victorious.[75]

The populace of Istanbul greeted news of the conquest with great joy, tears of relief, and even disbelief, and celebrated the conquest for three days and nights. The Ottomans finally could clear the shipping lanes of hostile navies and end the blockades of Istanbul. Venetians at Candia would no longer harass and capture ships of Muslim pilgrims and merchants. Abdi Pasha relates how the sultan received the news: "My sovereign, good news! The citadel of Candia has been conquered! The sultan responded, 'Is it true? Has the grand vizier's report arrived?'"[76] After the sultan took the report from Abdi Pasha, his weeping hindered its reading. Seeing the sultan burst into tears, all present wept tears of joy together. A stoic scribe was compelled to read the report to the sobbing group. After the miraculous news arrived, the sultan decided not to cross over to Crete, but to winter in Salonica and return in spring to Edirne, where Fazıl Ahmed Pasha would return to him the banner of Muhammad.

Although he had a hand in Islamizing the island, Mehmed IV's contribution to the display of martial manliness came in the hunt. He had not taken a direct military role in the siege of Candia because Ottoman sultans did not engage in naval battles. After learning of the conquest while out hunting, the sultan decided to winter in Salonica with his favorite concubine.[77] Rycaut claims that she knew how to hunt as well: "Like *Diana*, or some Mountain Nymph, she became a Huntress after her Prince, as he a Ranger after his Game."[78] The sultan (and perhaps his favorite) engaged in hunting and riding and did not return to Edirne until the following spring, when he held a grand ceremony before the Hunting Gate. As Abdi Pasha informs us, during Mehmed IV's hunting trips en route in exhilarating valleys full of the cries of nightingales, he killed nearly eight hundred prey, half deer, half rabbits.[79] One of his hunting trips took him to the forbidding, emerald green island of Samothraki (Samothrace).[80] Mehmed IV wanted to go up the steepest mountain, but his retainers told him they would suffer death rather than allow it because the mountain was impossible to climb. This tale of the sultan's almost reckless bravery prepares the reader for his future exploits on the path of ghaza. After the successful campaign, which led to the conversion of the Cretan landscape, Mehmed IV was prepared to turn his attention to waging ghaza in central Europe.

Conquest and Conversion on Crete

Taking Candia converted much of its religious geography by marking its landscape as Muslim-inhabited and Muslim-ruled. Not only did Christians become Muslims over time, but churches were transformed into mosques.[81] Minarets became the most prominent and visible sign of the citadel's transformation. First the great cross was taken down from the wall. Then the fourteen churches and monasteries found within the citadel of Candia, which were Maltese, papal, Spanish, and Venetian, became Friday mosques; bell towers were capped with spires, and galleries transformed into minarets were added for muezzins, the first being the litterateur Evliya Çelebi, to call the faithful to prayer.[82] The greatest church and monastery, San Francisco, apparently bigger than Hagia Sophia and more spacious than the Suleimaniye, was named for Sultan Mehmed IV; the others were named for Hatice Turhan, the only woman so honored; Grand Vizier Fazıl Ahmed Pasha, the conqueror of Candia; Sultan Ibrahim, who had launched the initial invasion; and the rest for the military commanders and palace officials. Seventy-four other churches were converted into smaller mosques for daily use.[83] According to Silahdar, these places, formerly "filled with polytheism and error," became "illuminated by the light of Islam" as they were "purified of idols," sprinkled with rose water and musk, and *mahfil* (royal gallery), *mihrab* (prayer niche), and *minaret* were put in place.[84] This is language similar to that used in the construction of the Valide Sultan Mosque in Istanbul, completed a few years earlier. The citadel of Candia had been full of monk cells. To replace them with mosques, the soldiers first destroyed the "idols" and "images" they found so that "those ancient abodes of idols became, like the luminous heart of the believer, free of the filth of polytheism; and those abodes of graven images darkened by the gloom of infidelity became, like the heart of the people of firm belief, purified and stripped of the marks of error."[85]

In his writ in response to his victorious grand vizier, the sultan praised the conversion of churches into mosques: "Those Muslim warriors fighting on the path of God, by utterly destroying and crushing by irresistible might the polytheist infidels, converted the places of assembly and abode of despicable infidelity into places of manifestation of the lights of the signs of Islam, and converted churches of polytheism which are temples for worshipping idols into the place of prayer of the community of Muhammad."[86]

Christian places would also be altered elsewhere in a reflection of earlier Islamization of the Cretan landscape. When Chania was conquered in the summer of 1645 at the beginning of the campaign for the island, the ancient Hagia Nikola church was converted to a mosque with the addition of prayer niche and pulpit. Muslims rendered Friday prayers in it, and it was dedicated to Ibrahim, becoming the Imperial Mosque.[87] Three other great churches with marble walls embellished and ornamented with diverse icons and mosaics were also converted and "purified of their idols."[88] Cemeteries "of rebels and the wicked" were destroyed by cannon. Similar resacralization of space also occurred the following year after the conquest of Resmo (Rethymo), where the largest church became the sultan's Friday mosque, and in Suda where a madrasa was also constructed.[89] As churches were converted into mosques throughout the island, bell towers became minarets. Some churches became public baths. A nunnery became a Janissary barracks.[90] This was as radical a gendered and religious transformation as could be imagined: an abode of virginal Christian women devoted to a peaceful life of prayer converted into the quarters of converted Christian men who dedicated their lives to waging war on behalf of an Islamic empire.

Jewish places suffered similar transformations and gave further evidence of the decline of the Jewish elite vis-à-vis the Orthodox Christian elite. Candian Jews, many of whom expressed a desire to flee to other lands, were paid to give reports on the condition of the citadel during the campaign.[91] After the Venetians agreed to surrender, as many as eighty Jews remained in the citadel, and a Janissary commander was appointed to protect them. Despite their loyalty, the former Jewish neighborhoods and their homes and stores in Candia were endowed in their entirety to the Valide Sultan Mosque in Candia, as much of Eminönü had been Islamized in this fashion by the sultana.[92] Rather than entrusting the duty to a member of the Jewish elite, Panayiotes Nicoussias was one of the officials who received the Venetian delegation surrendering Candia in 1669 and negotiated the subsequent peace treaty. Nicoussias was allowed to buy a church in Candia, "which became the nucleus of the Orthodox community."[93]

8

Conversion and Conquest

Ghaza in Central and Eastern Europe

In Pursuit of the White Castle: The Sultan Leads His Troops in Central Europe

Mehmed IV became a ghazi who personally went on the path of jihad in the early 1670s when he journeyed to the heart of Europe to conquer a citadel, the elusive object of desire in Nobel Prize–winning author Orhan Pamuk's *White Castle*. Unlike the fictive modern version, in the seventeenth century the pursuit was successful, and today the citadel is referred to as "the Turkish fortress." Hajji Ali Efendi, like Kurdish Preacher Mustafa in the service of the deputy grand vizier Mustafa Pasha, was charged with composing a narrative of the sultan's six-month journey as he traveled from Edirne to Kamaniça (Kamenets-Podol'skiy) and back in 1672. The author depicts the sultan as a ruler prepared to wage war in person to protect the empire. First, when Mehmed IV learned that the Venetians were violating the borders of Bosnia contrary to a peace treaty, he headed toward Filibe to pacify them; then, learning that Arab bandits were attacking Muslim pilgrims and Mecca, he planned on wintering in Bursa before continuing on to Mecca in the spring.[1] If the pious sultan had ventured to Arabia, he certainly would have made the hajj, becoming the first sultan in Ottoman history to do so, or, more likely, being deposed for such a decision, like Osman II. The Ottoman Empire was a European empire, and its heartland lay in southeastern Europe, not Arabia.

When Mehmed IV was about to set out for the first Ottoman capital of Bursa, word arrived that the king of the Polish Commonwealth had broken their peace treaty. As a result, instead of setting off along the potentially dangerous path of Osman II, he decided to launch a campaign in central Europe. In the spring of 1672, despite the renewal of a 1640 peace treaty five years earlier, the grand vizier and the sultan began a campaign against the Commonwealth of Poland, desiring to conquer the Carpathian fortress of Kamaniça, located in the southeast corner of Poland (today Ukraine) bordering the northern region of Moldova. This incomparable white citadel, perched on a lofty rock like a precious jewel in a fortified ring, was the key to Poland and Ukraine.[2] Polish forces had been harassing the sultan's protégé, the Cossack military leader Doroshenko, who sided with the Tatar khan. Allied with the Cossacks of Ukraine and the khan of the Crimea, the Ottomans faced a Polish, Russian, and Habsburg alliance when war began in the spring of 1672. As Rycaut observes, the sultan was not unaware that his presence on the battlefield in the heart of Europe would mean "that the Fame and terror of the Grand Signiors motion" could "abate and bring low the spirits of the Poles, and induce them to dispatch an Ambassador with terms of peace."[3]

According to Hajji Ali Efendi, more than geostrategic concerns motivated the sultan. He aimed to conquer the citadel not only for military reasons, ensuring that the enemy no longer used it to harass Ottoman dominions, but to render it Muslim, converting its religious landscape. Mosques were to be built, churches converted, the call to prayer read, Friday prayers rendered, and Muslims incited by preachers from converted pulpits to wage jihad.[4] Just as the author of *The Conquest Book of Yanova* had linked the sultan and the divine plan, so too does this author begin his work drawing a connection between the decree of God, the life of Muhammad, the exploits of the Ottoman sultans, and Mehmed IV. According to this vision of history, God had commanded the believers to engage in struggle and ghaza. Striving to follow Muhammad's example, the Muslims had persevered in implementing God's command to wage ghaza and jihad. Among all Muslims, the sultans of the Ottoman dynasty were especially dutiful in carrying out this decree; in fact, it had become their custom to carry out this command. The current Ottoman sultan was also driven and impelled to do God's will. Providence had decreed Mehmed IV to be "the master of the auspicious conjunction who makes the world luminous with the sword of victorious effect brilliant like the sun" (1b). Because of "the abundance of strength and toughness and imperial majesty in his brave disposition," during "his felicitous era of prosperity and lucky planetary conjunction," the sultan, repeatedly referred to in the text as the "deliverer of conquest and ghaza, the powerful sultan who causes fear and dread, Mehmed Khan," devoted himself fully to striving and waging ghaza and jihad in person, becoming a sultan whose overriding aim was to launch ghaza (1b–2a).

Over midway through his narrative, Hajji Ali Efendi elaborates on Mehmed IV's unique ghazi character. "In truth," he begins, "the disposition of the mighty sultan of Islam who causes fear and dread, the deliverer of conquest and ghaza, Sultan Mehmed Khan," and his "imperial zeal did not resemble that of sultans of the past," for his pious inclination was beyond description (88a). Moreover, the author of the conquest book links the sultan's desire to wage ghaza and the incitement of his preacher, Vani Mehmed Efendi: "Night and day, as the sultan's preacher Vani Mehmed Efendi expressed the excellent, virtuous qualities of ghaza and jihad in his Qur'anic exegesis before the imperial presence, the imperial disposition was polished and made manifest. Other than ghaza and jihad, he had no other desires in the world" (88a).

For those accustomed to reading of Mehmed IV as a profligate hunter, this description must come as a surprise. Yet hunting also plays a role in the narrative. Reflecting Abdi Pasha's linking of the sultan's hunting to waging war and Islamic zeal, the author discusses how the sultan desired to wage ghaza and jihad and declare his total effort and exertion on this path, and even desire for battle, and in the next passage without irony notes that the sultan went on a hunting trip (9b, 14a–b). One such trip involved four hundred to five hundred people, including the retinues of the grand vizier and deputy grand vizier (15b–16a). As in the case of Suleiman I, writers at that time saw no conflict between waging war and killing game, in fact seeing the latter as preparation for the former. The notion that hunting is suitable for warriors, indeed necessary to keep the martial skill sharp, was also taken for granted by warriors elsewhere, such as in contemporary Japan.

Other writers shared Hajji Ali's vision of the sultan's prowess as ghazi and the spiritual role of his preacher. Yusuf Nabi, appointed to serve as a secretary for the campaign, composed a work entitled *The Conquest Book of Kamaniça*.[5] In its introduction, the writer praises the sultan as the "defender of Islam," who is the "sun of the world adorning the summit of majesty, the grandeur of the halo around the luminous moon" (3a). Because of his piety, Mehmed IV is referred to as "the zealot of the manifest religion" desiring jihad (3b). The religiosity of "the sultan son of a sultan, the deliverer of conquest and ghaza, Sultan Mehmed Khan Ghazi" incites him to be "the hero who defeats and destroys the enemy, the master of the auspicious conjunction who conquers lands," and "the one who casts fire upon the homes of rebels and floods the households of polytheists, the wicked, and the disobedient" (3b). These actions bring tranquility to Muslims because they secure the frontiers of the empire.

Yusuf Nabi praises the sultan for daring to go to Kamaniça in person, to launch a difficult and arduous campaign to a distant land untouched by "the hooves of the horses of the ghazis" (61a). Because the hooves of his horse hit the ground in Poland, it would be forevermore Ottoman territory. Previous sultans had never considered such a campaign, being content to exchange gifts of friendship with Christian kings. Who would decide to launch a campaign against the incomparable and difficult to conquer citadel, so strong and exceptional that when the "eye of the epoch gazes around the world," it fails to find its peer? (29a) To Nabi, only Mehmed IV, a sultan exalted in zeal, possessor of the overpowering might of a conqueror and falcon claws, could grasp the significance of conquering the citadel (61b).

Yusuf Nabi uses well-chosen avian imagery when describing the sultan, his preacher, and the defenders in the citadel. He refers to Mehmed IV as a falcon and hawk and Vani Mehmed Efendi as a nightingale. No longer "a blindfolded falcon" or "an inexperienced white hawk who has no knowledge of the world," or even "a lion who has not yet hunted," the sultan is "the high flying royal falcon" (6a). This apt imagery causes the reader to imagine an active, powerful, and ruthless attacker. Like a person possessed of equanimity, a falcon stays aloft in a single spot. But then, like a focused warrior, it suddenly and swiftly attacks its target. Like Mehmed IV, a falcon both hunts and kills his prey. At the same time, the interpretation and explanation of the Qur'an and Hadith of the "sultan's personal preacher, the Sheikh Mehmed Vani," is compared to a nightingale singing in a colorful rose garden (8a–b). This is also apt imagery, for it offers the reader a sense of tranquil, sublime beauty that contrasts well with the violent image of the falcon sultan swooping down upon his prey, joined by his soldiers who are also described as men like falcons on the field of ghaza, or Janissary falcons (33b, 51a). They attacked a citadel that was an abode of irreligious infidels and "the nest of polytheist crows and kites" (38b).

Finally, the author of *The Conquest Book of Kamaniça* also deploys gendered language and concepts which again display the links between manliness, warfare, and conversion. Kamaniça is "an impregnable citadel" (28a). But it stood no chance, being attacked by thousands of manly braves who staked their lives for the cause of ghaza, sacrificing and exerting religious zeal, never considering the possibility of dying (38b). When they beheld the city within the citadel, they felt a sense of wonder and disgust. They marveled at the strange public buildings, curious monasteries, eminent homes, unassailable palaces, and wide plazas (29b). Accordingly, they converted those areas into "places of beauty of the ghazis" and "places of worldly pleasure of the believers" (38b). The terms the author uses for "places of beauty" also mean the bride's apartment where the virgin unveils herself for the first time to her husband after the wedding ceremony. Switching from Ottoman to Persian, the author alludes to soldiers taking their pleasure on the women they found within Kamaniça (44a).

Abdi Pasha's account of the sultan's participation in this lesser known campaign also offers much insight into Mehmed IV's character and vision of the sultanate. He emphasizes his glittering appearance in ceremonial armor designed to dazzle and overawe spectators. Because the sultan had effectively moved the capital to Edirne, an excellent starting point for campaigns in Otto-man Europe, all military forces invited to participate in the imperial campaign as well as members of the administration and religious class, including Vani Mehmed Efendi, lined up outside of Hunting Gate at the palace in Edirne to receive sumptuous cloaks and kiss the ground before him. After a sign from Mehmed IV, they all raised their hands as Vani Mehmed Efendi prayed, then all saluted "the shadow of God." The sultan presented Arabian horses to the leading men of state, Vani Mehmed Efendi, and the sheikhulislam. When he left the palace the sultan and his pure Arabian horse were decked out in jew-eled armor "radiant as the light of the sun."[6] Hajji Ali Efendi also notes that the sultan favored golden armor.[7] Over his "master of the auspicious conjunc-tion helmet" the sultan wrapped a green imperial shawl on which were two ghazi aigrettes (his horse also had an aigrette plume on its head). Mehmed IV was girded with a jeweled "world-conquering imperial sword" and an "enemy-extinguishing Rustemian quiver of arrows" that glittered like lightning, daz-zling the eyes of all who beheld him.[8] Dressed in this awesome fashion, the sultan led an ostentatious procession with bravery and manliness.[9] Although dressed more luxuriously than fourteenth-century ghazis, with his glittering, golden armor and ceremonial weaponry, which seemed to confirm Hajji Ali Efendi's claim that the sunlike brilliance of his victorious sword of the master of the auspicious conjunction illuminated the world, the combination of ghazi military energy and imperial lavishness articulated the same message.[10] Meh-med IV was not stuck in the harem deep within the palace but was an active, mobile, martial sultan who waged war in person for the sake of the religion and empire. After all, Nihadi notes in relation to this campaign that it is written (Qur'an 61:4), "Verily God loves those who battle on God's path."[11] The sultan handed the "horsetail blazing with God's assistance in battle" to Fazıl Ahmed Pasha, and the campaign was under way.[12]

The sultan and his forces had to overcome daunting natural obstacles to reach their goal. They set out optimistically, with great ceremony, but a dogged rainfall soon hindered their advance. The constant rain created so much mud that the legs of their horses became stuck. They had to use ropes to pull them out and even to force them to move forward.[13] At some points it became nearly impossible and inconceivable for the army to continue on its march toward Kamaniça. According to Abdi Pasha, the muddy, swampy conditions continued for weeks, and some of the sultan's men were lost to lightning.[14] Worse, on some evenings the heavy rain hindered the sultan from making it to the imperial tent, which was carried separately. Worse still, the silver carriages of the sultan's favorite concubine and mother of future sultans, Gülnuş Emetullah, got stuck in the thick mire, and the imperial couple were separated as well (322b–323a). The grand vizier and his men had to devote their energy to helping the favorite concubine's carriage get out of the thick muck. She and the prince were left to wait out the campaign in Hacıoğlu Pazarı while the sultan and the army continued their journey. This was not the only bad omen. The campaign was plagued by heavy thunderstorms and rains during the three months it took to travel from Thrace to Moldavia to cross the Danube and Dneister, and finally to enter Polish territory and alight before Kamaniça.

Accompanied by Vani Mehmed Efendi, the "sovereign whose badge is courage" (334a) played a direct role in the battle, making his presence known, even determining when his forces should fire their cannons. At the beginning of August, when he arrived before the citadel of Kamaniça, Mehmed IV sent a firm message to its defenders, saying, "Turn over the citadel without a fight, and I will grant the protection of your lives and property. You are free to go wherever you wish to go. Otherwise, if with the assistance of God I have to take the citadel by force, afterwards I will decimate you" (334a–b). The defenders responded to the sultan by saying, "Other than the builder, no hand had ever touched the citadel since the day it was built. It is a virgin citadel. Because of this, we prefer to spill our blood [like a virgin who has never been touched]" (334b). On the sultan's command, Ottoman forces bombed the citadel. When the citadel's bastion was taken and the flag of Islam planted, Janissary suicide squads became ghazi martyrs while planting mines at the walls of the citadel (336b). After a huge effort and constant barrage, and great loss of life on both sides, Ottoman forces took the citadel.

The defeated defenders sent men articulating five conditions for surrender (337b–338a). First, those men along with their wives and children who wanted to remain in the citadel and town could remain without being badly treated; second, those who desired to leave with their families would not be mistreated; third, a sufficient number of Catholic, Armenian, and Orthodox Christian churches could be maintained within the citadel, Christians could practice the rites of their "false" religion within them, and their priests would not be ill-treated; fourth, Ottoman soldiers would not be billeted in the homes and rooms of Polish noblemen, princes, and priests who remained; and finally, concerning those soldiers who leave, taking only their own weapons, they and their families and goods would not be harmed. If these conditions were met, they promised the gates to the city and citadel would be turned over. The sultan granted these conditions and the Ottomans took over the citadel and city. While the defeated soldiers were divvying up the ammunition in the arsenal, however, there was a great explosion and several hundred lost their lives (338b). A tower and the palace were destroyed, seen as punishment for their not keeping their word. This caused the Ottomans to distrust the defenders' intentions and suspect a ruse. They quickly consolidated control over the citadel.

In his first Polish campaign, in which the sovereign participated in person, Mehmed IV proved himself a ghazi. Abdi Pasha is proud to refer to him as the one who "illuminates the world with the light of jihad" (342b). He is "the brave conqueror of the age," signified by a phrase in Arabic (*Ebu al-fath*), and "the sovereign conqueror" in Persian (*Kishvar-kusha*), as well as master of the auspicious conjunction whose imperial ghazas and conquests are marked by victory (339b). Mehmed IV rode around the entire citadel, both to see it and to be seen.

The sultan could be satisfied, returning to Edirne in triumph for conquest and the capitulations that came with it enhanced his image as a fighter for the faith. Amassing a larger number of "manly and brave" troops than had Murad IV during the Baghdad and Armenian campaigns, he soundly defeated the "accursed ones destined for Hell." The campaign ended in triumph, promise to God fulfilled. Thus having satisfied his religious zeal, Mehmed IV had time to hunt at least eight times on his return, going on the chase with his grand vizier or engaging in massive hunting drives with local commoners conscripted for the occasion.[15] Three days and nights of celebrations were ordered throughout the empire. In addition to Kamaniça, the Polish king ceded to the empire several dozen fortresses and defense works in Podolia. Christian holy space was Islamized. Whole garrisons had been put to the sword, townsmen and women had been retained as domestic slaves, Armenian and Jewish merchants had been deported to large cities and ports elsewhere in the empire.[16] The sultan returned to Edirne that fall after a victorious campaign, "arriving at the seat of the throne of the abode of divine assisted victory with an overwhelming concourse of attendants, and world-conquering imperial majesty."[17] When commoners who lined the city streets and servants of the sultan who waited along the route to the palace gate to kiss the ground before him beheld their ruler, they understand that he was indeed the "powerful sultan of Islam who causes fear and dread, the deliverer of conquest and ghaza, Sultan Mehmed Khan."[18]

The Second Polish Campaign and the Death
of Fazıl Ahmed Pasha

The following year Mehmed IV had to wage a second campaign to ensure the Treaty of Buczacz that guaranteed Polish tribute. Silahdar, echoing Abdi Pasha, depicts the first campaign as but a warm-up, for the zeal of the sultan had not been dissipated. He was aching for battle and bloodshed, and to make the Polish king "taste the sword of fire" in order to uphold his honor and that of the religion and dynasty he represented.[19] He was like a champion falcon or a tough horseman; one campaign was not enough to satisfy the hunger of his zeal. He journeyed as far as Isakçı on the Moldovan frontier with Vani Mehmed Efendi and did not return to Edirne for almost a year and a half. Due to the heavy snow, the campaign was suspended for winter, which gave the sultan ample time for hunting, such as one trip lasting thirty-three days. The journey was taken up again on the day of the vernal equinox. During that time, the opponent of the Kadızadeli movement, Sheikhulislam Minkarizade Yahya Efendi, lying sick in bed in Edirne, was replaced by the more compliant Çatalcalı Ali Efendi.[20]

Mehmed IV passed into Cossack territory and again presided over the bloody capture of numerous defensive works after offering the defenders terms of surrender. Abdi Pasha notes that the troops fighting for the sultan often killed or imprisoned the enemy after ignoring white flags asking for quarter. He watched as hundreds of others who waved the white flag were put in chains and sent to the galleys. Of prisoners remaining in defense works, the sultan took scores for himself to serve in a variety of palace roles. As we have seen before in the case of Shabbatai Tzevi, this sultan liked to surround himself with converts. After the long journey from Isakçi, the sultan, in the words of Abdi Pasha, arrived in Edirne "with the splendor of the master of the auspicious conjunction conquests."[21]

After several more years of off-and-on battles with the Commonwealth of Poland, which saw the Ottoman army advance as far as Lvov, by 1676 the Ottomans had conquered Podolia in Ukraine. In that year it turned out that not everyone around the sultan seems to have been on the same page of the book of correct morals. The learned, virtuous ghazi Fazıl Ahmed Pasha, who had otherwise exalted morals and had left in his wake mosques in Uyvar, Crete, and Kamaniça, a man who defeated Habsburgs, Poles, and Venetians, could not overcome the bottle. Some unnamed close associates had helped convert him into an alcoholic.[22] Because of his declining health, in autumn 1676, rather than travel overland from Istanbul to Edirne with the sultan, he went by skiff to the quay of Ereğli, and from there to Çorlu.[23] After a stroke his condition worsened, and a little over two weeks later "he departed from this lower world and migrated to the world to come." Despite his piety, alcoholism ultimately caused his death at age forty, several years after the last decree outlawing wine consumption was issued.[24] A couplet written as his obituary (recorded in a palace archival document) relates that for many days he led a life of pleasure in a place of mirth, but in the end, all living creatures are separated from this world; with a painful separation he, too, went away.[25] As Evliya Celebi writes, tongue in cheek, "At the estate of Karabiber [Black Pepper] he drank his final cup."[26] His years in office were not easy, but were quite successful. He had continued his father's mission of restoring the empire to greatness. Others have written how Fazıl Ahmed Pasha's fifteen years in office was one of the longest terms held by a grand vizier in Ottoman history, marked by a concern for improving the political, economic, and military strength of the empire.[27] What is emphasized in this book is his role in promoting piety.

With the able assistance of Fazıl Ahmed Pasha, Mehmed IV had propelled the empire to the northernmost limit of Ottoman expansion, which also turned successes in battles throughout Europe to economic advantage by filling the depleted treasury with taxes from eastern European provinces. Tribute was imposed on all of Poland. The Cossacks were subjected. These victories put an end to decades of spending on military endeavors that saw no return. More important than the economic benefit was the religious significance. These wars were not seen merely as battles over broken treaties and alternating military alliances. The boy sultan had become a victorious ghazi and battles between the Ottomans and the Venetians, Poles, and Habsburgs were depicted as struggles between Islam and Christianity, played out in the contest over sacred geography.

The Russian War: Vani Mehmed Efendi at the Front

In 1678, Mehmed IV again went on campaign, this time against the Russian Empire. The cause was the Cossack Doroshenko, who double-crossed the sultan and joined the Russians, who occupied parts of Ottoman-controlled Ukraine. Vani Mehmed Efendi was at his side, although the sultan never crossed the Danube and alighted in the plain of Hacıoğlu Pazarı in Silistre while the preacher continued to the front with the grand vizier. The sultan presented Grand Vizier Kara Mustafa Pasha a brocaded fur, a jeweled sword, a velvet shalvar, and jeweled aigrettes and personally handed him the black wool banner to lead the campaign against the Russians.[28] Hüseyin Behçeti composed *Ascent of Victory* within a year of the campaign. According to the author, Mehmed IV was the caliph of Islam, the shadow of God on Earth, a brave hero, and, most important, "the Ghazi Mehmed Khan, deliverer of conquest and ghazi."

He praises the sultan for having waged ghaza and jihad for three decades, for battling against the miserable infidels on divinely assisted ghazas. In the eyes of the author, Mehmed IV is the luminous sun king whose movements are like the rising of the star and whose light nourishes the seven climes. The natural disposition of that sun king also inclined toward the chase, and his favorite, so Mehmed IV made sure to hunt en route and bring his favorite along as well.[29] Abdi Pasha adds that the battles were quite bloody as the Ottoman forces put all enemy combatants to the sword and killed up to thirty thousand. The Ottoman soldiers "bravely battled for the honor of the state and religion," and Mehmed IV ordered a week of celebration after victory was assured.[30]

Vani Mehmed Efendi played a key role in inciting the troops to fight. In the view of contemporary writers, his words may have been as important as Ottoman weapons in securing victory. Hüseyin Behçeti records that the "luminous preacher of pleasing speech" gave sermons after noon worship before the grand vizier, Janissary commander, and entire assembled army. His peerless sermons "gave out a light which polished the mujahids and illuminated the ghazi braves." In his sermons he explained and expounded on the Qur'anic verses concerning the Battle of the Ditch, here referred to as a ghaza, and the treachery of the Jewish Banu Qurayza tribe at Medina. First he included Qur'an 33:9–25, verses from The Clans (Al-Ahzab), which derives its name from the tribes that Jews were accused of trying to incite against the Muslims. A main theme includes how faith is rewarded with divine assistance on the battlefield. Vani Mehmed Efendi then discussed verses 25–27.[31] They are as follows: "God turned back the unbelievers in their rage, and they went away empty-handed. God helped the faithful in the stress of war: mighty is God, and all-powerful. God brought down from their strongholds those who had supported them from among the People of the Book and cast terror into their hearts, so that some you slew and others you took captive.[32] God made you masters of their land, their houses, and their goods, and of yet another land on which you had never set before.[33] Truly, God has power over all things." According to Hüseyin Behçeti, these words inspired the soldiers to wage ghaza and jihad in the name of the one God, the true religion of Islam, and God's messenger, Muhammad.

Desiring to inspire the soldiers to jihad, Vani Mehmed Efendi again repeatedly discussed the Battle of the Ditch, the betrayal of the Jews and their brutal end.[34] This time he quoted verses in The Spoils of War (Al-Anfal), which derives its name from the first verse: "The spoils of war belong to God and God's messenger." He recited the following verses (Qur'an 8:55–63):

> The basest creatures in the sight of God are the faithless who will
> not believe; those who time after time violate their treaties with you

and have no fear of God. If you capture them in battle discriminate between them and those that follow them, so that their followers may take warning. If you fear treachery from any of your allies, you may retaliate by breaking off your treaty with them. God does not love the treacherous. Let the unbelievers not think that they will escape Us. They do not have the power to do so. Muster against them all the men and cavalry at your disposal, so that you may strike terror into the enemies of God and the faithful, and others besides them. All that you give for the cause of God shall be repaid you. You shall not be wronged. If they incline to peace, make peace with them, and put your trust in God. God hears all and knows all. Should they seek to deceive you, God is all-sufficient for you. God has made you strong with God's help and rallied the faithful round you, making their hearts one.[35]

The succeeding verses refer to how twenty steadfast men will vanquish two hundred, and a hundred steadfast men may rout a thousand unbelievers since God is with those who are steadfast in faith and battle.

Hüseyin Behçeti gives Vani Mehmed Efendi a central place in his narrative and leads the reader to believe that his preaching led to the successful conquest and Islamization of Christian places in central Europe, linked to Muhammad's exploits in Arabia against Jews a millennium before. This claim echoes the earlier connection made between Muhammad's and Hatice Turhan's expulsion of Jews. In many ways the campaign for Çehrin appeared a warm-up to the attempt to take Vienna five years later. Mehmed IV set out on campaign but remained in a city along the campaign trail; he sent Grand Vizier Kara Mustafa Pasha and Vani Mehmed Efendi ahead to the front, where they served to conquer and convert people and places.

Conquest and Conversion in Central Europe

The alleged treachery of the Polish defenders at Kamaniça gave the sultan the excuse to stamp out what Kadızadeli zealots considered idolatry. He ordered that all churches be converted into mosques. To do so, Abdi Pasha records, churches had to be "purified of the images and idols that are the signs of infidelity and polytheism." They also had to be purified of the dead: "As many as three to four thousand infidel corpses buried in the cellars, some decomposed, others whole with their clothes on their backs in accordance with their false rituals, were excavated with their coffins and thrown into the dunghills."[36] An eyewitness Catholic account records, "All the dead had been dug up from the tombs and graves and taken away from the city, and the holy images removed from the Catholic and Orthodox churches had been laid in the mud on the streets" on which Mehmed IV entered the city.[37] The practice had also been followed elsewhere after conquest, such as at Chania, Crete, and was based on a much earlier precedent.[38] According to the *History of Mehmed the Conqueror,* written for its namesake by Kritovoulos, an Orthodox Christian appointed governor of the island of Imbros, when the Ottomans conquered Constantinople "the last resting places of the blessed men of old were opened, and their remains were taken out and disgracefully torn to pieces, even to shreds, and made the sport of the wind while others were thrown on the streets."[39]

When Mehmed IV, continuously referred to by Hajji Ali Efendi as the "mighty sultan of Islam who causes fear and dread," decided to enter the city and engage in religious devotions, including Friday prayers, a church had to be readied for the occasion.[40] The Catholic cathedral St. Peter and St. Paul was renamed "Conquest" (*Fethiye*). Yusuf Nabi boasts, "Immediately on that day, in order to convert their lofty monasteries into mosques for the community of Islam and places of worship for the people who are the best of humankind," a decree was issued permitting "the filth of paintings of human figures and idols and crucifixes and organs to be annihilated with the tip of an axe, and gilded statues, idols, and hanging crosses to be destroyed by illustrious swords."[41] The arrival of the radiant sultan, compared to the rising of the sun and the golden rays of the sun at dawn, is juxtaposed in Yusuf Nabi's account with the darkness of unbelief. Christian holy space, "like the luminous heart of believers, became free of polytheism, and those abodes of idols dark and gloomy with the darkness of infidelity became, like those of firm religious belief, purified of traces of error and going astray. In place of crucifixes, [they added] low reading desks for the Qur'an; in place of organs, the sounds of the reading of the verses of the Lord; and in place of crosses and censers, an imperial gallery [*mahfil*], a niche indicating the direction of Mecca [*mihrab*], and a pulpit [*minbar*]."[42] The author could also have added the other "m," *minaret.* The Ottoman dynasty, led by the zealous Mehmed IV and represented by the *mahfil*, and Islamic religion, led by Vani Mehmed Efendi and manifested in *mihrab, minbar,* and *minaret,* together transformed the main Catholic church of Kamaniça.

Vani Mehmed Efendi, the grand vizier, the sheikhulislam, and the chief justices of Anatolia and Rumelia and other officials arrived in a great procession to pray together with the sultan. The sermon delivered after the prayers "was read in the name of the mighty sultan of Islam who causes fear and dread, the deliverer of conquest and ghaza, Sultan Mehmed Khan."[43] Hajji Ali Efendi writes that after "the noble mihrab and minbar became adorned with the noble eulogies of the companions," as he prayed for all the ghazis and mujahids who sacrificed their hearts and souls for the cause, Vani Mehmed Efendi delivered "a sermon and admonishing suitable for ghaza, jihad, and illustrious conquests," which "incited the soldiers of the army of monotheists to strive and thank God in their hearts, minds, and souls."[44] Yusuf Nabi adds that Vani Mehmed Efendi's discussion of the merits and virtues of jihad and conquest, verified by Qur'anic verses, was so beautiful it was as if his words spread perfume that rose to the dome of the mosque.[45] Then the grateful congregation of Muslims and the army prayed heartily for the sultan and dynasty, since "the powerful sultan who traverses the world causing dread" was among them.[46]

Along with Fethiye, all the great churches, referred to as soiled or contaminated abodes of the idols of polytheism, were converted to mosques. According to Yusuf Nabi, the zeal of Mehmed IV caused church bells in the citadel and city to be replaced by the Muslim call to prayer, and the Brahman dwellings were transformed into madrasas for Muslim students (taliban) and scholars and places for chanting the Qur'an. Although there were no Hindus in that Polish citadel, the term "Brahman" is used to make explicit the claim that Christianity is polytheistic. Thus, in addition to a sultanic mosque, others were marked for the grand vizier, deputy grand vizier, boon companion, and Vani Mehmed Efendi. Each was given a church that was suitable for transformation into a mosque, "purified of infidel and polytheist rituals and illuminated with Islamic worship."[47] One mosque was also given to the valide sultan Hatice Turhan, another to the favorite concubine, Gülnuş Emetullah, consolation prize perhaps for her diligence in accompanying the sultan through the mud most of the way to this remote citadel in Poland.[48]

Ottoman chroniclers and historians praised the conversion of sacred space. Appointed to write a poem celebrating the victory, Abdi Pasha boasted, "When the group of infidels left in safety, that great citadel became full of the light of faith. A beautiful Friday mosque was built after numerous abodes of idols were purified of the filth of the marks of infidelity."[49] Yusuf Nabi, in his chronogram of the conquest of the citadel, also praises "the sultan of the religion, the king of kings of the world, the khedive of the epoch," Mehmed IV, "that strong royal falcon," for his conversion of Christian places. After the Ottomans took over the citadel, "the community of Muhammad destroyed those monasteries of soothsayers filled to the brimful with infidelity and all their places of worship, breaking and destroying the idols and crosses, not allowing any infidelity in the new Muslim citadel," as "the light of Muhammad fell upon the fortress of Kamaniça."[50]

As already seen in the case of the conversion of the landscape in Istanbul, Ottoman writers viewed the conversion of churches to mosques as a conquest of infidel space. The light of Islam is said to replace the darkness of infidelity. According to Kurdish Preacher Mustafa's account of the Ottoman reconquest of Bozca Island, the candle of Islam illuminated every corner of the churches.[51] A common way authors of conquest books expressed the successful completion of ghaza and jihad was to note that churches were converted to mosques and the Muslim call to prayer chanted from bell towers, drowning out church bells. Often this conversion of places was articulated on the very first folio of the manuscript, such as in the work of Vecihi Hasan Çelebi.[52] A typical example is the prose of Mehmed Halife, who writes that the Ottoman forces "cleaned and purified the citadel [Varat/Várad in Hungary] filled with infidelity and error; their churches and temples became masjids and mosques; places where church bells had rung became places where God was exalted and God's unity declared as the five daily prayers were called from them, and they became the place of Friday prayers."[53] In addition, Ottoman troops damaged the fourteenth-century statues of saint kings, including Saint Stephan holding a golden apple in his hand, considered the talismans protecting the town, and later transported them to Belgrade, where the remains were converted into cannons.[54] When describing the conquest of Uyvar, the same author writes, "Praise God that now in this marvelous city, which for so many years has been filled with infidelity and error, the call to prayer is chanted; in place of the wicked sound of the church bell is the felicitous call to prayer of the righteous; the infidels' churches and monk cells were converted into the masjids and madrasas of the men of religion."[55]

Such imagery is common in Ottoman writing. The sixteenth-century historian Sa'deddin described the conquest of Constantinople in the following terms:

> The evil-voiced clash of the bells of the shameless misbelievers was
> substituted [with] the Muslim call to prayer, the sweet five-times
> repeated chant of the Faith of glorious rites, and the ears of the peo-
> ple of the Holy War were filled with the melody of the call to prayer.
> The churches which were within the city were emptied of their vile
> idols, and cleansed from their filthy and idolatrous impurities; and
> by the defacement of their images, and the erection of the Islamic
> prayer niches and pulpits, many monasteries and chapels became
> the envy of the Gardens of Paradise. The temples of the misbelievers
> were turned into the mosques of the pious, and the rays of the light
> of Islam drove away the hosts of darkness from that place so long
> the abode of the despicable infidels, and the streaks of the dawn of
> the Faith dispelled the lurid blackness of oppression, for the word,

irresistible as destiny, of the fortunate sultan became supreme in the governance of this new dominion.[56]

Likewise, after Buda was conquered in 1541, Suleiman I's *Conquest Book* declares that the sultan made it into an abode of Islam in part by converting the large churches into mosques where his soldiers could render their Friday prayers.[57]

Whereas Buda, Constantinople, Uyvar, Varat, Bozca Island, and Kamaniça were all military conquests, and the treatment of their religious buildings was a given, the same cannot be said of the churches and synagogues in Istanbul. What is new is the linkage made in the late seventeenth century between lands taken after overcoming resistance and those destroyed by natural disaster. Evliya Çelebi juxtaposes the sultan's participation in ghaza, the conversion of churches to mosques within conquered citadels, and the construction of the Valide Sultan Mosque in Istanbul. Before narrating the construction of the mosque in the formerly largest Jewish neighborhood of the city in Eminönü, he concludes the section on "the wars in which the sultan participated in person" by writing, "Thank God! The aforementioned citadels [Candia, Kamaniça] being conquered, they were added to the domains of Islam, and all churches within were converted into Muslim places of worship where Muslims worshiped and rendered the five daily prayers. Praise the Creator! These conquests occurred during the just reign of Sultan Mehmed IV Khan. May God grant him a long life and permit many more ghazas."[58] Using similar language to legitimize the conversion of churches, synagogues, and enemy territories contributed to the production of Mehmed IV's image, and that of other members of the dynasty, including his mother, as warriors for the religion or at least its defenders.

Not only spaces were converted during these wars; so were soldiers. Ottoman narratives of the period discuss conversions to Islam during or following battles. Enemy soldiers converted after defeat, imprisonment, and being sent before the sultan. According to an archival document, in 1661–62 the keeper of the main citadel on the Dardanelles, Mustafa Pasha, sent to the sultan four men, including a Venetian, who had all deserted the enemy's battleships and gone over to the Ottoman side.[59] Although the men's subsequent fate was not recorded, one wonders why the pasha did not detain them and enroll them on the Ottoman side, as did other commanders. Instead, he sent them to the sultan, where it is most likely they converted to Islam and served in the palace. At that point, after having deserted the battlefield and submitted to a new leader, nothing less could be expected of them.

Civilians also converted to Islam in the context of war. When women and children were found in citadels, they were sold into slavery. Besieged Christians feared the Muslim battle cry used to intimidate them.[60] Many were starving, wounded, surrounded by corpses, missing arms and legs, witnessing their churches attacked and burned to the ground or blown sky high from explosive mines dug beneath them on the pretext that soldiers hid in them. More frequently, Christians saw their churches being made into mosques and the graves of their comrades and saints destroyed. Some saw conversion as their only chance of redemption, such as during the campaign to the central European citadel of Uyvar and elsewhere in central Europe.[61] But they did not have to convert. They could refuse surrender and fight to the death. As a result, they faced death, slavery, or imprisonment. Or they could surrender, accept status as protected Christians and Jews and Ottoman sovereignty, and usually remain in place. Or they could convert to Islam to be released from the siege.[62] Overall, Christian soldiers were more likely to starve in a siege, drown in a moat or river while fleeing a citadel, or battle to the death. When captured, they would usually face the tip of the sword, not an offer to put on a turban. When the Ottomans captured massive numbers of prisoners, they "would run their enemies through with the tips of well-tempered swords."[63] It was better to kill enemy combatants and convert civilians. The Ottoman army did not have a policy of converting Christian soldiers on the frontier. As will be seen in the next chapter, Mehmed IV was often the instigator of the conversion of civilians.

9

Hunting for Converts

Individual and group conversions of noncombatants occurred most often before the sultan in the forests of Rumelia when he was on campaign or the chase. As numerous chroniclers relate, like other early modern monarchs, Mehmed IV preferred hunting as his favorite pastime, but rather than being merely a frivolous activity, as modern historians have claimed, the sultan's contemporary chroniclers argued that hunting demonstrated his bravery and courage, hence manliness, and trained him for warfare. Reading archival records together with the chronicles we learn that in addition, hunting allowed Mehmed IV close contact with thousands of his subjects, and in these circumstances he personally converted Christians, in particular, to Islam. Hundreds of men and women changed religion at his feet during conversion ceremonies in which the sultan displayed his magnanimity by re-dressing the converts head to toe.

Conversion ceremonies suggest a hint of modern rulers' interest in promoting (a new) life rather than death, the decentering of power, and the creation of new interiorities and subjectivities that discipline the body of the individual.[1] The sultan first directly intervened in commoners' lives, not to end them, but to promote a new way of being. Ceremonies before the sultan mirrored birth, as the convert, similar to a naked newborn, was named and clothed. Converted to a Kadızadeli interpretation of Islam, which also emphasized new interiorities, the new Muslim was encouraged to play an active role in self-governance, regulating his or her behavior from within and disciplining others by enjoining the good and forbidding the wrong of neigh-bors. A hint of a turn to governmentality is inferred from the fact that three to four times more people converted to Islam before Mehmed IV than were executed before him. This chapter thus demonstrates the uniqueness of the pe-riod and its convert-making sultan while utilizing the book's themes of the link between piety and proselytization, the key role of the mediator of conversion, and the context of war and conquest in conversion.

Sultans and the Hunt

No modern scholar depicts Mehmed IV as a ghazi. He is damned, when men-tioned at all, for his alleged "addiction to the hunt," which acquired "a patho-logical nature."[2] To his chroniclers, however, there was nothing pathological about hunting. If a sultan aimed to demonstrate his martial skill and prac-tice for war, the struggle between man and beast was the best arena. This was the case in Japan and other cultures where martial virtues dominated, such as Qing China, as well as in western Europe, where monarchs also hunted. Mehmed Halife writes that when the sultan returned to Edirne following his trip to pacify the Anatolian countryside in 1658, that winter and spring "with complete pleasure he spent his time riding, hunting on the chase and drive, throwing javelin, and engaging in preparations for war."[3] Riding, hunting, and javelin throwing recapitulated war. For this reason Abdi Pasha wrote that the sultan shot arrows at targets in the plaza before the New Pavilion in the palace in Edirne not merely for target practice or entertainment, but "with the de-liberate intention of waging ghaza" while also impressing the spectators and proving his manliness (merdānelik).[4]

The term the Ottoman chroniclers used for "manliness" in the seventeenth century relates to the Islamic culture of chivalry signifying bravery. The Ot-toman term is derived from Persian. In Persian, mard means a man, a hero, brave, bold, and capable. The plural connotes heroes and warriors. Mardāna means brave, manly, courageous, and vigorous; the term for field of battle, arsa-i mardānagī, where manhood is proven, stems from the same term. In Ottoman, merd is used for a man, a brave, and a manly man; merdāne is brave. Merdānelik, then, is bravery and courage, manliness.

Hunting appears as a defensible practice to Mehmed IV's chroniclers. Prowess in hunting demonstrated courage in facing death and magnanimity in either sparing a great animal or distributing the rewards of the hunt. When hunting, one comes across commoners. There was no better opportunity for bringing Christians into the fold. Modern historians attack Mehmed IV for being frivolous without recognizing what would be considered in the seventeenth century to be a positive. Since the eighteenth century, naysayers have viewed his frequent pursuit of the chase as wasteful activity and luxury.

Earlier sultans with far greater reputations engaged in exactly the same practices, and this may have been the precedent that Mehmed IV's court mimicked. Ottoman miniatures depict Mehmed IV's predecessors hunting: Bayezid II (reigned 1481–1512), who had a reputation for being a peaceful Sufi, strikes a deer as hounds pursue rabbits; Selim (reigned 1512–20) clobbers a tiger in the head with a mace as hounds pursue deer and cuts a crocodile in half on the banks of the Nile; and Suleiman I (reigned 1520–1566) hits a bull with his arrows while falconers watch the scene.[5] Suleiman I was not criticized for temporarily moving his court to Edirne and engaging in the hunt while on campaign. His successor, Selim II (reigned 1566–1574), who was an avid hunter, is remembered for building the splendid Selimiye mosque in Edirne and not for his hunting passion. Ottoman writers discuss Ahmed I (reigned 1603–17) hunting while traveling between Edirne and Istanbul, but do not criticize him for that practice; in fact, he has a favorable reputation for putting down the widespread rebellions in the Anatolian countryside. Mehmed IV's father, Ibrahim, also left Istanbul on occasion in favor of Edirne's open air, an ideal place for a relaxing diversion.[6]

All Ottoman sources attest that hunting was Sultan Mehmed IV's passion. Mehmed Halife explains that before Mehmed IV's constant devotion to ghaza and jihad, he became excessively fond of falcons and javelin. A miniature from an Ottoman costume album depicts a falconer with red-gloved hand on which sits a bird of prey with a rope around its legs.[7] The miniature calls to mind the thirteenth-century Holy Roman Emperor Frederick II von Hohenstaufen's beautifully illustrated *De Arte Venandi Cum Avibus* (The Art of Falconry). The Ottoman miniature of the falconer was placed near the front of the album, illustrating the position's importance at the time. According to Mehmed Halife, Mehmed IV had a zeal for the chase (*sayd ü şikar*) and the drive (battue, *sürgün avı*) "that not a single one of his sultanic predecessors had ever possessed."[8] Going on the chase summer and winter he is said to have developed the disposition or temper of a lion and brave man. Mehmed IV may have begun his reign a tiny child, but beginning at the age of twenty, hunting made him strong, tanned, and manly according to contemporary writers. When he rode, "he became a horse swift as the wind and a cavalryman like the wind."[9] He was "big-bodied, had a solid chest, was broad-shouldered, and broad-backed, but of average weight, and long-legged.

He was tall like his father. His arms were thick and his hands wide as a lion's paws."[10]

Contemporary chroniclers take a positive view of Mehmed IV's fondness for the hunt. The reader of Abdi Pasha's *Chronicle* discovers that during his reign Mehmed IV engaged in at least fifty hunting expeditions, the earliest in 1658, when the sultan was seventeen years old, and the last in 1681, soon before the chronicle ends.[11] Naima narrates his first hunting trip much earlier, in autumn 1650. In this account, the sultan went to a pavilion on the edge of Kağıthane stream in Istanbul, where the chief palace guard released foxes and rabbits; Arabians were dispatched after them, and the sovereign watched the spectacle. Finding itself cornered when chased by a horse, one rabbit threw itself into the river and swam to the other side. Seeing that it had been saved from the horse, the palace guards wanted to send a hound after it. But the sultan declared, "Free the rabbit!" A hound attacked the rabbit anyway, so the poor creature turned and threw itself again into the water. But the hound caught it and brought it back to the pavilion. The palace guards made it release its prey, and they brought it before the sultan, who had it let go on a mountaintop where it would be safe, at least from his hounds. Naima writes that this was seen as an omen that the sultan's life and reign would be long and prosperous. He then narrates another episode during which the sultan prevented his falconers from releasing their birds of prey on other birds considered harmless.[12] Naima considered this further evidence that the sultan, who demonstrated compassion for living creatures and made sound judgments concerning life and death, had reached the age of discretion and sagacity and displayed intelligence. Thus Mehmed IV's earliest hunting trip is used by an Ottoman historian to prove the ruler's wisdom, not profligacy. Yet modern novelist Orhan Pamuk, who takes this scene from Naima and includes it in his novel *The White Castle*, adds a redheaded dwarf, has the sultan ask about bulls with blue wings and pink cats, and ignores the sentiment of the contemporary Ottoman writer because it would upset the conventional depiction of the sultan as a buffoon, which is what his audience expects.[13]

The sultan's mighty hunting trips lasted from one day to two months. Mehmed IV hunted while residing in Edirne and Istanbul; while journeying between the two cities; before, during, and after military campaigns; while wintering with the army on campaign; and while journeying for other purposes. Abdi Pasha's chronicle informs us that he spent fifty-five days in the environs of Yanbolu hunting in 1666 (226b); thirty-five days in Eğriboz while en route to Crete in 1669 (292a); twenty-five days in Yanbolu and environs in 1664 (149a); three weeks while wintering in Salonica following the conquest of Crete in 1669 (295b); fifteen days in Uzunköprü in 1667 (250b); and two weeks and another week in the environs of Yenişehir while traveling to Crete in 1668 (278a). Military campaigns were opportunities for more hunting. Mehmed IV made sure to hunt in 1672 in the vicinity of Kamaniça immediately after the citadel was conquered and during his return to Edirne (342a). In 1673, while on the second Polish campaign wintering in Hacıoğlu Pazarı, he spent thirty-three days on the chase in the vicinity of Ester, and then two weeks in Kavarin at the beginning of spring (368a). Again in 1674 at the end of year following the second Polish campaign he hunted at Kurt kayası (Wolf Rock; 384b). The sultan spent forty-five days hunting while in Silistre after sending the grand vizier to conquer Çehrin in 1678. En route to Istanbul after the citadel was taken, he engaged in a massive eighteen-day hunting expedition, including the drive, in the environs of Burgos (412a–b).[14] If hunting had been something shameful, or an activity Mehmed IV wanted to hide from posterity, Abdi Pasha and other chroniclers favorably inclined toward their subject would not have devoted so much space to recording the dates, locations, length, and prizes of so many chases.

In Eurasian societies, great leaders engaged in extraordinarily large hunting parties. Mehmed IV sometimes enjoyed armchair or sedan hunting, or had his falconers release prized Circassian falcons or hawks to hunt birds, and once even tried bringing an elephant and its Indian trainer along for the sport, but fearing the yelping hounds the elephant ran away (157a–b). But his preferred method, in which the hunting party formed a great ring and drove the game before it like a flock of sheep, then contracted the ring and sent hunters into it to kill the game, was the same method practiced by the great Mongol leader Genghis Khan.[15] This is significant, because one element in the Ottoman dynasty's legitimizing propaganda concerned its connection with the great dynasties of central Asia. This is why the sultan was titled "khan." Mehmed IV's Chinese contemporary, Emperor K'ang-hsi, also peripatetic, frequently engaged in the hunt, which he linked to war and defense of the empire, and ruled during a period of territorial expansion, becoming the conqueror of the island of Taiwan, perhaps for the Chinese the equivalent of Crete. He was more articulate than the Ottoman sultan and left thousands of pages of autobiographical writing. The following poem, entitled "Hunting in the Ordos, the Hares Were Many," expresses his love of hunting:

> Open country, flat sand
> Sky beyond the river. Over a thousand hares daily
> Trapped in the hunter's ring. Checking the borders
> I'm going to stretch my limbs; And keep on shooting the carved bow
> Now with my left hand, now my right.[16]

Emperor K'ang-hsi and Sultan Mehmed IV favored the drive, or battue, a hunting technique that brought them into close contact with commoners. In these hunts hundreds or even thousands of local villagers moved through the forest beating bushes, making noise, scaring animals, and flushing the game in the direction of the waiting sovereign and his retinue, who would be either on horseback or on foot, bearing arrows, axes, blades, and bullets. A miniature from early in Mehmed IV's reign depicts a hunter using his left arm to hold a rifle to his left shoulder; the hind legs of a large gray hare are wrapped around the barrel of the weapon, and the animal's heavy carcass points head-first toward the ground.[17] The commoners assembled for the hunt, such as this armed hunter, would also bring the prey to the sultan. Mehmed IV's involving commoners in the chase and having personal contact with them is another reminder of how his reign harkened back to those of earlier ghazi sultans who were mobile and visible.

Massive numbers of peasants were assembled. For example, Abdi Pasha relates how on one Sunday in 1667 the sultan used as many as thirty-five thousand peasants to drive animals through a forest preserve near Filibe (247b).[18] In 1670 Mehmed IV drafted twenty-five thousand and ten thousand commoners into hunting duty for two other massive hunts in Eski Zağra (Stara Zagora; 304b). During the first chase in Eski Zağra, 265 deer were killed. This was not a great ratio of peasant to prey, and was more akin to shooting fish in a barrel than engaging in battle between man and beast. It was less exciting than the capture of a deer by a panther that Mehmed IV observed and insisted Abdi Pasha record ("If you did not write about it, immediately write it down!"), but impressive nonetheless (172a). The drive could cover very large distances: while traveling from Edirne to Istanbul in 1661, the sultan set aside time to engage in a drive hunt that began in Çatalca and stretched as far as Davud Pasha on the outskirts of Istanbul.[19] John Covel wrote in 1675 that the sultan's physician told him Mehmed IV engaged in "exercise, especially hunting, which he followes still most extravagantly, many times going out two or three houres before day[light], and it may be not returning till as late at night; sometimes (as this last winter) summoning in all the *Villánes* in 20 mile compasse to drive a whole wood or forest before them."[20]

Like other rulers, Mehmed IV killed stupendous numbers of animals. Several thousand deer and hares were killed during all the hunting expeditions, along with hundreds of bears, elk, foxes, leopards, lynx, wild boars, wolves, and extinct animals that no longer appear in modern dictionaries. In typical entries from Abdi Pasha's chronicle, we learn that in one hunting expedition in April 1666, 2,200 rabbits and eighty foxes were killed (204a–b). During a three-day span in November 1667, the sultan engaged in battue hunting, killing ninety-four deer, four elk, and three wolves, and in sedan chair hunting, targeting eleven deer and three wild boars (244a). The following April two battue expeditions netted seven deer, seventeen elk, six wolves, and two lynx (257a). Mehmed IV may not have killed any Venetians during his journey toward Crete in 1669, but he did kill 364 rabbits over five days and 143 deer over another two during his lengthy hunting expeditions after the campaign (296a). As K'ang-hsi relates, in a fashion similar to Abdi Pasha's writing style though in first person, "Since my childhood, with either gun or bow, I have killed in the wild 135 tigers and 20 bear, 25 leopards, 20 lynx, 14 tailed *mi* deer, 96 wolves, and 132 wild boar, as well as hundreds of ordinary stags and deer. How many animals I killed when we formed the hunting circles and trapped the animals within them I have no way of recalling—most ordinary people don't kill in a lifetime what I have killed in one day."[21] The sultan was as boastful as the Chinese emperor and delighted in giving especially large prey, such as massive stags, as gifts to the royal family and members of the administration. It is not clear whether they shared his enthusiasm, although his favorite concubine and his mother may have noticed that these gifts were symbols of the sultan's manliness.

Hunting and Conversion

Mehmed IV's contact with commoners compelled to join the hunting party had other outcomes. Historians have overlooked how this sultan's mobile court served as a traveling conversion maker. While on the hunt or campaign, while actually riding on horseback through the forests of Rumelia or holding court in the imperial tent set up on the march or in palaces in the provinces, Mehmed IV was responsible for either compelling Christians to join the fold or facilitating their conversion to Islam by staging conversion ceremonies at which new Muslims declared the Islamic credo, were re-dressed in Muslim clothing, and were given Muslim names.

Abdi Pasha makes a link between hunting, ghaza, and the conversion of Christians. He notes that even while hunting in the environs of Edirne, Mehmed IV had the *Biography of the Prophet* read to him in his privy chambers. When he "heard of the way infidels cursed the companions of the prophet, his religious fever boiled over" (228b) Abdi Pasha juxtaposes Mehmed IV's enjoying having his chronicler read to him about the martial exploits of Muhammad and previous Ottoman sultans on the path of ghaza and jihad and narrate how they exerted themselves on behalf of the religion with the sultan's personally converting a peasant while out hunting (162b). The sultan's chronicler narrates how Mehmed IV compelled a Christian to become Muslim while he was on the chase in the spring of 1665 at a favorite hunting ground less than two days' journey from Edirne, a place where the sultan made it a point to hunt for two days while returning from his first Polish campaign:[22]

> On Thursday the twenty-fourth [of Shaban] his eminence, our sov-
> ereign, rode in state to Pasha Köy. On the return journey, as he was
> passing through the countryside and engaging in the hunt, from
> his own imperial hand he let loose a hound after a rabbit, then he
> rushed after it, giving his horse free rein. He went quite a distance
> on that path. Then one of his servants informed him that in that
> place a cow was about to give birth. At once he reined in his horse
> and halted at that place and viewed the spectacle and awesome
> wisdom of God the Creator of All Things. Out of his royal compas-
> sion, his imperial majesty wished to assist that cow in giving birth,
> and so he had the cow's drover brought into his presence. And the
> sultan remained there until the cow gave birth. Afterward, with no
> intermediary he addressed the drover: "are you a Muslim?" When
> the cattle drover made his Christian status known, out of royal com-
> passion the sultan called him to the true religion and guided him to
> the straight path with complete gentleness and softness. "Come,"
> he said, "become a Muslim. Let me give you a means of livelihood
> and God will forgive all your sins. In the afterlife you will go straight
> to Paradise." The sultan offered Islam to him more than once, but
> the Christian refused. Yet when the sultan's servants present in that
> place made him aware of the situation saying, "The one speak-
> ing with you and saying to you, 'be a Muslim,' is none other than
> his eminence the majestic emperor, the Refuge of the Universe in
> person," at that moment the cattle drover became guided onto the
> right path and with alacrity he accepted Islam and his son followed
> him. The convert related that previously he had been offered the
> faith in his dreams several times. Everyone was amazed at these
> events. Out of the exalted royal favors he was given many excel-
> lent coins and a gatekeeper position at the pay scale of fifteen akçe
> per day. The sultan issued an order to his servant, deputy grand
> vizier Mustafa Pasha, that the man and his son be attached to the
> gatekeepers of the Old Palace in Edirne. After the sultan returned
> from his ride and rested in his palace [in Edirne], he related this
> event, with his own blessed imperial tongue, to this humble servant
> [Abdi Pasha]. "Today," he said, "I did not, in truth, simply go on the
> chase. Rather, by divine wisdom, while pursuing a rabbit I chanced

upon a cow giving birth, and while watching the spectacle, in my
presence Islam became divinely facilitated to that fellow. Therefore,
that is a cow of divine guidance." He ordered that they purchase the
cow with its suckling calf, and place it in the palace's privy garden.
(161a–162b)[23]

The narrative combines two sultanic processions, one riding in state and the
other pursuing game. The first, from Edirne to the village, could not have failed
to stir notice among the populace as the sultan and his retinue made a showy
procession through the area with their magnificent horses and carriages and
lavish outfits. The sultan often rode in state in a red velvet and sable fur cloak.
On the return to Edirne the sultan engaged in the hunt. These two trips combine two dimensions of this sultan's persona that would endear him to the
populace and promote his image as a strong ruler: the first, the display of his
majesty; the second, the demonstration of his martial skills and generosity.

The main thrust of the narrative involves wildness, loss, shock, and wonder followed by confusion and ultimately a resolution satisfactory to all parties.
The cattle drover failed at first to understand before whom he was standing.
Even more surprising, if we consider the way sultans of the period are usually
described, Mehmed IV spoke to the man without an intermediary. He neither
communicated through sign language nor passed on his wishes to an aide, but
came face-to-face (although it is improbable that he would have dismounted)
with the lowly commoner. Given what we know of how the sultans' near sacred
status generally required that they wrapped themselves in a cocoon of silence,
this was a signal departure from the norm.[24]

The sultan is depicted as one capable of seeing in mundane daily life and
endlessly repeated events the miraculous finger of God. Mehmed IV appears
as a sensitive, gentle man, concerned about all creatures, the same sultan described elsewhere as being touched by the beautiful song of nightingales in a
valley in Thrace. In other parts of his chronicle, Abdi Pasha juxtaposes the sultan's witnessing of an execution outside his imperial tent with his protection of
a swallow and its young when the bird built a nest on a column inside the imperial tent (236b). The sultan apparently refused to strike the tent until the young
birds could fly. This is another occasion for Abdi Pasha to invoke the motif of
the sultan's compassion and generosity. Mehmed IV also appears in this narrative of the converted commoner as being so pious that even while deep in the
forests of Rumelia he can think of no more important question to ask the man
before him than whether he has been called to the true faith. Considering the
ruling circle's turn to piety it is not surprising that he personally attempted to
convert the Christian.

The narrative also raises some questions. The reader wonders why the peasant was unable to recognize the sultan as sultan. Although Mehmed IV would not have been wearing the ghazi aigrettes and very tall turban that served as dress on ceremonial occasions, he would have been mounted on a fine Arabian, wearing a sumptuous fur or fur-lined cloak and surrounded by many retainers and guards. Sudanese harem eunuchs were a rare sight in Bulgarian villages. The second question that comes to mind is how the sultan communicated with the drover. Mehmed IV spoke the relatively simple Turkish that Abdi Pasha uses to write his chronicle. The commoner, who was probably an Orthodox Christian, most likely spoke Bulgarian as his mother tongue. Perhaps the peasant knew Turkish, or enough Turkish to understand that conversion was occurring, or perhaps the sultan employed locals to act as hunting guides who could also speak both languages.

The sultan takes on a remarkable persona in the narrative, speaking as both the head of a powerful and patrimonial dynasty offering the man a sinecure in the palace in Edirne, and as God's representative on Earth, the shadow of God, who can assure converts that they will attain the best of the afterlife. But the commoner still does not comprehend the situation and refuses to convert not once, but twice, which makes for a better conversion story. The sultan withdraws, astounded that the man failed to accept the offer, surprised that he was unsuccessful in confirming that Islam is the true faith. The man quickly changed his tone and demeanor only after the sultan's servants, and in particular the African eunuchs, told the man that it was the sultan who offered him these benefits, the sovereign to whom he owed his liege. According to this construction of a conversion narrative, the power, majesty, and might of Islam as represented by Mehmed IV were impressive enough to cause conversion. Some social scientists might explain the rational choice made by the drover facing extreme alternatives; others may claim the motivation was based on financial compensation; to still others, the promised rise in social status may have been the cause. But considering Abdi Pasha's chronicle to be a piece of literature, it is important to examine how the story is narrated and how the author depicts the disposition of the main subject, including his pietistic demeanor.

Let us examine the drover's claim that he had previously dreamed of being offered the chance to convert. It is well known that Sufis communicate with people through dreams, where they appear to offer advice, tell the future, or admonish people to change their ways. It is remarkable that at a time when the sultan and his court and administration were cracking down on Sufi practices, the sultan acts in this story like a Sufi sheikh. Mehmed IV, who took his own and the dreams of others seriously, materializes in real life after appearing in a man's dream and becomes the realization of the subconscious or primordial (the event occurs deep in the forest) longing of the Christian. The most effica-cious Sufi way of communication enables the sultan whose court was cracking down on some forms of Sufi practice to ensure his will. The dream connects the sultan to the divine plan and allows him to fulfill God's design.

This is a remarkable turn in the narrative. It leavens a tense moment when the Christian man refuses the offer of the representative of the dynasty and religion. Remember that his resistance to the will of the sultan is the second moment of shock in the narrative, the first being the sultan's initial surprise at seeing a live birth. Until he reveals the dreams he had had, the commoner ruins the moment and the mood. One might be tempted to argue that this narrative is less about conversion than the munificence of the sovereign. Abdi Pasha, how-ever, could have chosen any act of giving to represent the sultan's munificence and generosity. He could have written that the sultan said "Be a Muslim" and the man converted. Instead, the dream motif is a critical device that allows Abdi Pasha to emphasize the sultan's magnanimity and his role as God's representa-tive on Earth executing God's will. Sunni Muslims who are not Sufis also em-phasize the importance of dreams, and offer a prayer asking for moral guidance to be delivered during sleep. The drover dreamed of Muhammad or spiritual guidance; the sultan is the manifestation of that guiding to the right path. In this period, the idiom for expressing magnanimity is bringing another to the correct interpretation of Islam through religious conversion. Tension resolved, the story ends with an illustration of the sultan's benevolence and magnanimity.

For the sultan, the royal way of telling about conversion links hunting with fulfillment of the divine plan. In this narrative, Mehmed IV becomes not only the representative of the dynasty and religion, but also the agent of reli-gious change. That this sultan wanted to be surrounded by converts and "holy cows" is not surprising considering that the following year both the Jewish messiah Shabbatai Tzevi and the Kurdish savior Seyyid Mehmed would also be given gatekeeper positions at his palace, and gatekeepers tended to support the Kadızadelis.

The converted drover was only one of hundreds of Christians who con-verted at the feet of the sultan during the second half of Mehmed IV's reign. An Englishman who resided in Istanbul during the 1670s as the chaplain to the British ambassador recorded in his diary the circumcision festivities of Princes Mustafa and Ahmed in Edirne in 1675. John Covel wrote that during this fes-tival, which came in the wake of successful campaigns in central and eastern Europe,

I saw many 100es of them (there being about 2,000 in all the
13 nights) cut, and the Turkes would be so farre from hindring your

seeing, as they would make way for you. There were many of riper
yeares, especially renegades that turn'd Turks. I saw an old man
which they reported to be 53 yeares old, cut. The common way there
of turning was (as I saw severall) to go before the G. Sr. [Mehmed IV]
and Vizier [Grand Vizier Fazıl Ahmed Pasha], and throw down their
cap, or hold up their right hand or forefinger; then they were immediately led away by an commander (who stands by on purpose), and
cut with the rest. I saw a Russe of about 20 yeares old, who, after he
had been before the Vizier, came to the tent skipping and rejoicing
excessively; yet, in cutting he frowned (as many of riper ages doe).
One night we met a young lad, who askt us the way to the Vizier.
Being a country boy, we askt him what he would with him. He told
us his brother turn'd Turk, and he would goe find him, and be cut,
too; and two dayes after he was as good as his word. It is very dangerous meddling in these cases here. There were at least 200 proselytes
made in these 13 days. It is our shame, for I believe all Europe have
not gained so many Turkes to us these 200 years.[25]

Once we get past the early modern Christian confusion of circumcision with
castration and emasculation, Covel's observations of the pomp and ceremony,
serving as prelude to pain, provide an example of public conversion of Western
and Eastern Christians before the sultan.[26]

The sultan provided a banquet for tens of thousands of people and bestowed a set of clothing on each circumcised child as well as a purse of coins,
thus symbolically becoming the generous father to several thousand sons.
Covel notes that among the thousands of Muslim children being circumcised
there were a couple of hundred Christian converts to Islam, mostly from Christian empires, and smaller numbers of Ottoman subjects.

What is especially significant for our purposes is how Ottoman chroniclers
and foreign observers depict Mehmed IV's central role in the process. The first
crucial moment of actual religious conversion, the public transformation of
Christian into Muslim, literally occurs at his feet. According to Covel, the intending convert would appear before the sultan and grand vizier in the imperial
tent set up for the occasion, exchange the headgear of a Christian for that of a
Muslim, or at least throw away the Christian headcovering in anticipation of
receiving a Muslim turban, raise one finger in order to state *Allahu akbar*, that
God is most great, and be whisked away for immediate circumcision.

Covel's observations are significant for he served as witness to the implementation of a statute that describes how the court of Mehmed IV responded
normatively when a Christian male voluntarily sought to become Muslim.

Conversions before the sultan that required bestowals of cloaks and white turban cloth were so frequent in the 1660s and 1670s that the court wanted to clarify matters and ensure that it was following correct procedures. Finally in 1676,
after Fazıl Ahmed Pasha had passed away and was replaced by his fifty-year-old
former deputy and nephew, Kara Mustafa Pasha, the grand vizier ordered Abdi
Pasha, who in addition to being official chronicler also served as imperial chancellor between 1669 and 1678, to codify the statute outlining correct procedure
while compiling all known Ottoman statutes into a single collection of Ottoman
law. Abdi Pasha finished it the following year. According to "The Statute of the
New Muslim":

> If an infidel [Christian] should desire to become Muslim in the
> presence of the grand vizier in the imperial council, at once he is
> instructed in the articles of the faith of Islam. After a command is or-
> dered to the imperial treasurer for a handful of coins and clothing as
> gifts of kindness to be bestowed upon the convert, an usher takes and
> delivers him to the imperial surgeon on duty that day in the council.
> The surgeon immediately takes him to the designated corner and cir-
> cumcises him [right then and there]. It is an ancient statute for one of
> the imperial surgeons to be on call every day in the imperial council
> and in the palace of the grand vizier.[27]

This archival document allows us to verify what Covel observed, to fill in or
correct the details, and to then compare this statute with the actual practice of
conversion as it occurred in the period by reading other archival and narrative
sources. First, however, it bears scrutiny.

Several parts to "The Statute of the New Muslim" immediately strike the
reader. Just as Covel mentioned only male converts, so too is this document explicitly written to prepare for the event of male Christian conversion. The term
"infidel" was routinely used in the seventeenth century to designate Christians;
Jews were usually labeled "Jews." Though, theoretically speaking, the term
could include Jews, the emphasis on circumcision leads one to the conclusion
that Christian males are the group the court imagined converting. The fact
that an imperial surgeon who performed the operation was on call every day in
both the imperial council and the grand vizier's quarters also informs us of the
court's understanding that mainly Christian men would be seeking religious
change there and of the frequency of its occurrence. It is an interesting but
unanswerable question whether the surgeon himself was Muslim, Christian,
or Jewish, or a convert. In this period in all likelihood he may have been Jewish,
but more likely was a convert to Islam.

The statute makes no mention of the sultan. Moreover, emphasis is placed on the conversion occurring in the imperial council and the palace of the grand vizier, which were in Istanbul. The imperial treasurer also plays a role in the process. The statute thus emphasizes the role of those who ran the day-to-day affairs of the empire and ignores the presence of any dynastic figures. This illustrates the bureaucratization trend that had become so prevalent by the seventeenth century, in which we can begin to speak of the operations of an Ottoman administration. Again we see the routinization of office, the bureau-cratization of function, and the ritualization of ceremony that mark a sedentary bureaucratic empire.

At the same time, this archival source illustrates how misleading it is to rely exclusively on such documents (some might even say, engage in document fetishism) and to ignore literary sources. The wording of the statute, although compiled and first recorded in the reign of Mehmed IV, was anachronistic when it appeared, for it did not take into account the reality of the age, both the fact that the sultan held court in Edirne or on the hunt or military campaign in Rumelia, and that the sultan was very much present at conversion ceremonies. This fact serves as a warning to researchers who believe that reading archival sources alone as repositories of factual data can provide an accurate picture of an age. There are other elements of the statute, such as the reward the convert received, which alert us that the statute was first articulated prior to Mehmed IV's reign. The handfuls of coins delivered to the convert were Ottoman akçe, not the western European coins actually in use in the markets of the empire at the time.

More interesting still are the elements that signify conversion as conceived in this statute. Primary is the emphasis on desire. A Christian man had to want to become Muslim, had to voluntarily intend to change religion. Nothing in this statute would allow for a coerced or compulsory conversion. Abdi Pasha compiled "The Statute of the New Muslim" prior to completing the *Chronicle*. In his history, his making a dream serve as the cause of the drover's conversion makes even that change of religion appear voluntary. Second, agency is given to the intending convert. According to this law, the court is not seeking converts, but converts are seeking the court. The grand vizier acts after the Christian approaches his palace or the imperial council. This leading minister of the empire is not out in the countryside drawing Christians into the fold. After the Christian has arrived expressing his wish to convert, the court then has the duty to instruct him in his new faith. This raises the question of what the convert thought he was converting to, and why the court saw itself as necessarily having to teach the Christian about Islam. This assumes that the Christian man desired to become Muslim without having much of a clue about what it entailed.

Was the circumcision news to him as well, and if so, is that why "immediately" he is circumcised, "right then and there"? One imagines that the Islam taught to the convert reflected Kadızadeli interests in promoting an Islam stripped of what were considered evil accretions. Vani Mehmed Efendi had instructed the ecstatic mystic Shabbatai Tzevi in the faith after his conversion at court and accompanied the sultan and grand vizier on imperial campaigns and meanderings. Covel noticed something not articulated in the statute: converts stated that God is most great, affirming the unity of God. Although this phrase has been a central pillar of Islam in all periods, it was emphasized in the late seventeenth century as practices labeled innovations were labeled polytheistic.

This brief look at the statute still leaves many unanswered questions. How was the statute implemented? Were only Christian men converted at the court? How often was the sultan involved? Where did the conversions actually occur? And what type of clothing was distributed? Answering these questions will demonstrate the necessity of reading archival documents together with narrative accounts.

The most recent published accounts of conversion in the Ottoman Empire are based primarily on archival documents, Islamic law court records, tax surveys, or petitions addressed to the sultan.[28] They advance our knowledge by presenting detailed studies based on careful reading of one type of Ottoman documentary source. Relying on records of the distribution of cloaks and purses of coins to new converts, Anton Minkov's study concludes that most converts were motivated by the hope of financial reward and, to a lesser extent, social advancement. This concurs with Heath Lowry's thesis that Christians converted to Islam in Trabzon in part because it was considerably cheaper to be a Muslim than to be a Christian, since Christians paid higher taxes. Lowry and Minkov attribute motivation to the converts based on sources composed by bureaucrats not primarily interested in conversion. In the case of court records they needed to make sure only that Islamic and sultanic law were properly followed, in tax surveys recording taxable households, and in the case of petitions, accounting for expenses of the treasury. In all such documents the officials made sure to record that proper procedure was followed. Thus, in the case of petitions, because Sunni Hanefi Islamic law stipulated that conversion must appear to be voluntary, no matter the actual circumstances in which Christians or Jews became Muslim, the scribes had no other choice but to record that it was so.

Minkov takes the documents at face value and tautologically claims that because there is no indication in the petitions of involuntary conversion to Islam, the Christians voluntarily converted, as they stated.[29] Minkov can come to this conclusion only because he did not read narrative sources together

with archival documents, failing to understand the context of power relations in which the latter were recorded. By reading the archival sources alone,
without the benefit of contemporary chronicles, he is misled about the circumstances in which scribes depicted these items being bestowed. This is
not surprising in a work that covers an enormous, diverse region during the
reigns of a number of different sultans in a time frame selected for its archival documentation rather than historical cohesiveness. The documents depict
the giving of new clothes to converts who willingly change religion in "the
capital city" at the palace. Minkov concluded that most conversions probably
took place at the meeting of the imperial council and that the sultan was not
present.[30] But he does not match the dates of these documents with the movements of Sultan Mehmed IV as recorded in the official history of his chronicler,
Abdi Pasha. Had he done so, he would have realized that these conversions
occurred at conversion ceremonies before the sultan in Thrace and Bulgaria
while he was en route to a military campaign or on the hunt.

One is compelled to acknowledge that the best option is to read Ottoman
archival and narrative sources together to understand the context of conversion
and Ottoman understandings of conversion and to examine how the intentions of the converters are depicted. This is the most responsible course to
take considering that the converts lived more than three hundred years ago
and their experience is available to the historian only filtered through Ottoman
officialese and literary flourish. Flesh-and-blood characters are drawn in black,
gold, and red Ottoman ink. Archival recordings of their actions are not merely
mines of information to be culled and recorded in satisfying tables and charts.
They cannot be simply displayed like gems shorn of their muddy origin. This
is not to say that narrative sources are without their problems, to turn the tables
and go to the opposite extreme, ignoring archival documents and fetishizing
chronicles. It is best to avoid document fetishism and chronicle positivism,
instead reading both archival and literary sources as traces of the past that not
only reflect lived experience, but reveal how writers conceived of the era in
which they lived.

Let us examine archival documents concerning the cloaking of new Muslims. They exist for the reigns of earlier seventeenth-century sultans, Ahmed I
and Murad IV, but they are few and far between.[31] During the second half of
the reign of Mehmed IV there is a large increase in documentation of the distribution of clothes to new Muslims. Although one cannot discount the fact that
the period after 1650 saw a massive increase in scribal documentation, the
change is remarkable nevertheless. Ottoman archival sources provide evidence
that hundreds of Christians and Jews converted to Islam in the presence of

Mehmed IV between 1654 and 1686 and requested Muslim clothing and head-gear. Correlating the petitions of new converts recorded by the imperial scribe and the narratives chronicling the sultan's movements, especially the chronicle of Abdi Pasha, it emerges that converts appeared especially in Rumelia and Silistre, primarily while the sultan was on hunting trips and secondarily while he was passing through the province en route to military campaigns, thus belying the bureaucratic, static nature and narrative of the archival documents. The fill-in-the-blank nature of petitions for new clothes for converts reflects more the routinization of the practice than the actual circumstances in which conversion occurred.

The conversion of commoners along Mehmed IV's hunting trail becomes traceable around the middle of the 1660s.[32] Places such as Vize, which is situated east of Edirne less than halfway along the route to Istanbul, is one such location. During the end of the 1660s and the beginning of the 1670s converts also were collected while the sultan was traveling to Yenişehir by way of Dimetoka and Tırhala to support the imperial campaign against Crete, or participating in two military campaigns against the Commonwealth of Poland.[33] Other than one conversion in Moldova, most conversions during the latter campaign again occurred in Bulgaria. It should be borne in mind that even while on campaign Mehmed IV devoted time to the hunt. Thus, Hajji Ali Efendi, who recorded all the resting stations on the sultan's first campaign in 1672, noted that while in Kozluca, less than ten days' journey north of Edirne in the district of Silistre, the sultan set out to hunt after a number of peasants were prepared to drive the game toward him during the chase. The conversions during the second campaign mainly occurred at imperial rest stations in the province of Silistre. The halting grounds of Kozluca (ten days), Hacıoğlu Pazarı (fourteen days), Karasu (seventeen days), Hacıköy (twenty-one days), and Isakçı (twenty days) were all within three weeks' journey from Edirne in the province. The journey followed a northeastern path along the Black Sea in the direction of Moldova and the Commonwealth of Poland.[34] In 1672, one of the imperial halting stations was Karinabad (Karinova/Karnobat), which was a six-day journey north of Edirne. That town was the home of a group of adults and children who converted together in Istanbul at the court at the end of Mehmed IV's reign (124b).[35] From the mid-1670s to the end of Mehmed IV's reign in 1687, one finds that converts appeared wherever the sultan hunted in Edirne, Istanbul, and their environs, especially Kurd kayası near Edirne; Silivri, which is near Istanbul; and Davud Pasha, just outside Istanbul, a well-known assembly point for Ottoman armies, where the sultan often held court at the Pavilion of the Standard while on hunting outings. That kiosk possessed "a broad rectangular vaulted bay with a sofa," which made it "a pavilion for reviews, for the room is full of large casements with grilled windows above them."[36] It was an ideal position from which the sultan's gaze could take in conversion ceremonies.

The archival evidence of conversion at court has come down to us in three formats. Despite their differences, all three express the sultan's power to grant wishes as well as his attitude toward converts and conversion. The first type, documents produced between 1671 and 1675, a period that included the two Polish campaigns, begin with praise to God and consist of a terse order to the treasurer to provide for bestowal of the necessary garments to a convert or converts present at the imperial council, followed by the date and a proportionally large signature of the grand vizier. From these documents we infer that after a Christian or Jew appeared at court before the sultan or grand vizier with the intention of converting, his or her request for reward was submitted in writing to the secretary of the imperial council, who then sent the petition to the treasurer with the grand vizier's command to bestow the clothing on the new converts. The treasurer of the palace was an essential figure in conversion. He never separated from the sultan, not even on campaign, because he was the official responsible for providing the ceremonial robes and clothing bestowed as an honor on officials, as well as on converts. An example of this format follows: "God is everlasting! To the Treasurer of the Palace, may his power and glory be increased! Give new garments to a new Muslim man upon receiving the document [to be exchanged for clothing or coins] of the imperial council. Recorded on August 30, 1673. (Signature)."[37]

The second format is far more interesting to the historian because it sometimes provides additional information about the converted and the location of their change of religion. These documents, mainly composed in the last several years of Mehmed IV's reign (1685–87), when the sultan spent most of his time hunting in the environs of Istanbul, are longer, addressed to the sultan, and appear as the humble supplications of his devoted subjects. They were recorded in three stages. First, at the center of the paper, one finds the exposition of the petition proper. It invariably contains salutations consisting of praise of the sultan's generosity and magnanimity, followed by a statement that the following person or persons converted to Islam and therefore requests that the sultan order clothing bestowed on the converted. The petition was then "signed," giving the number of people petitioning, their names, and relations. At the top of the paper appeared the second part of the petition, consisting of an invocation to God and the fact that the petition was accepted and acted on by the grand vizier. Finally, beneath these lines yet above the petition proper, came the third part, the action taken in response to the request, namely, clothing bestowed by the treasurer and the date given. Action was taken based on the decision of the sultan or his grand vizier and usually stamped with the seal of the latter. A typical example follows:

> (Second part, acceptance of request and action of grand vizier) God is everlasting!
> It has been recorded.
> (Third part, action of palace treasurer) It was commanded that garments be given according to custom on September 4, 1686.
> (First part, text of petition) Long live his eminence my felicitous and generous sultan!
> Let it be the order of my sultan that garments be bestowed according to custom to this humble servant who became honored by the glory of Islam yesterday at the imperial stirrup [before the sultan's presence] at Davud Pasha.[38]

These documents, in which cloth for turbans, like the sultan, was in motion, commended the sultan's generosity and fatherlike attributes.

The following document, which includes the information that five new Muslims received material for turbans, is an example of how conversion at the court was recorded in the third format:

> May it be registered in its place.
> Benefactions.
> An exalted order is commanded to be given to the treasury on the eleventh of Dhu al-Qa'da, 1076 [May 15, 1666] concerning new Muslims who became ennobled by the honor of Islam in the presence of his eminence the sovereign, who is the Refuge of the Universe, and at the threshold of his eminence the deputy grand vizier in Edirne.[39]

Again we see that although "The Statute of the New Muslim" did not mention the sultan and foresaw religious change being carried out in a prescribed manner before the imperial council or at the grand vizier's palace in Istanbul, conversion actually occurred before Mehmed IV wherever the sultan traveled, as well as before the grand vizier's deputy and in the palace at Edirne. The sultan's entourage always contained officials who stored, maintained, and were responsible for bestowing precious cloaks lined with fur. And wherever conversion occurred and was recorded, the imperial secretary often sprinkled gold dust on the black ink, a surprising burst of enthusiasm and normative judgment, particularly when the glittery ore covers petitions of the first, most business-like kind, the least expressive or celebratory. Again, like the trust deed for the Valide Sultan Mosque and labels in the margin of the Shariah court records highlighting the conversion of churches and synagogues to mosques, gold dust signals celebration of the religious change of Christians and Jews and their sacred geographies.

Because sumptuary hierarchies distinguished Muslims from members of other religions, changing the body by dressing in new clothing was fundamental to transforming Christians and Jews into Muslims. "The Statute of the New Muslim" does not mention what type of clothing would be crucial in the transformation of a Christian or Jew, but legal opinions from the leading Muslim religious authorities concerning valid means of conversion demonstrate how a mere change of headgear could be the first step in causing a Christian or Jew to become a Muslim. A turban of white cloth served as a mark of religious affiliation. Three legal opinions from late seventeenth-century Sheikhulislam Yahya Efendi Minkarizade emphasize the central role it played in the conversion of a Christian or Jewish man to Islam:

> Question: If a Christian or Jew should wear a white turban on his head and henceforth say, "I became a Muslim," is his or her conversion to Islam considered valid? Answer: It is.
> Question: A Christian or Jew wears a white turban on his head. After he became completely embellished by Islam, when two Muslims ask, "what are you?" if he should say, "I am a Muslim," is his conversion to Islam considered valid? Answer: It is.
> Question: When a Christian or Jew wears a white turban on his head he is asked, "why did you wear it, have you become a Muslim?" If he should say, "I have been a Muslim for a long time," is his conversion to Islam considered valid? Answer: It is.[40]

Therefore, a Christian or Jew could change his status to Muslim when he wore a white turban, a good type of muslin used for a turban, or a type of high headgear with a cotton interior over which a turban is wrapped, and then declared himself to be a Muslim.[41] An indication of the trend arises from the fact that Rycaut included the illustration of an unadorned white turban of a convert in his history. It is most likely that converts also recited the Muslim credo in Arabic, before two Muslims, declaring that there is no God save God and that Muhammad is God's messenger.

Commoners who appeared at court to convert removed their former dress and donned garments of Muslims to symbolize their passage into the empire's privileged religion. The process of conversion was thus in part garment-centered. The sultan inscribed his authority on the symbolic surfaces of bodies when he cloaked Christians and Jews in Muslim dress at his court.[42] It was an elaborate performance of supplication rewarded by a display of royal benevolence. Petitions depicted the sultan as the benefactor to his supplicating servants, who referred to themselves as his humble slaves. These ceremonies were staged to impress upon participants the great wealth and power of the sultan. The ceremonies also represented and generated bonds between subjects and sultan linked by cloak or turban.[43]

The ritual of distributing turbans and cloaks reaffirmed the principle that the sultan, acting on behalf of Islamic law and Ottoman statute, regulated all social relations and articulated the religious, social, and political order of Ottoman society. It marked both his control of the process and his role in concluding the transformation with a symbolic and public affirmation of the religious change of the convert. By distributing the component parts of white turbans to new Muslims, he dispensed his power as projected through the medium of garments over space, time, and distance. Turbans and cloaks flowed from southern Rumelia to the Commonwealth of Poland, Ukraine to Istanbul. By repeating this same ritual hundreds of times, he aimed to construct community, to provide a means of connecting with his subjects. The intention was to use the distributions to link the subjects more closely to the sultan and warn others of his awesome reach and power. It was hoped that the effect of the ceremony would be that long after he left the hunting grounds near Edirne or pavilions on the outskirts of Istanbul, the new Muslim was reminded by the turban received at court that he had become a Muslim. After participating in the ceremony and receiving its message, he was then free to imagine himself belonging to a larger community of like Muslim men wearing similar white turbans across the empire.

The documents ordering the treasurer to bestow new clothing on new Muslims list the items that were actually bestowed. The new Muslim received the obvious sign of conversion, the cloth and base of a white turban. Converts could also be given leather footwear, linens, trousers, short trousers that reached the knees, and waistbands. If the convert was an individual whom the Ottomans viewed as important, he would receive a short, sable fur cloak brocaded with silver and gold thread. Thus, whereas Covel and sheikhulislams mention only headgear, converts were also re-dressed from head to toe, inside and out. For example, a brief document dated September 23, 1673, reads, "God is everlasting! To the Treasurer of the Palace, may his power and glory be increased! Give new garments for a new Muslim male and a new Muslim female upon their arrival at the secretary of the imperial council."[44]

This document would mislead a researcher who read it alone without consulting the literary sources of the period. The sultan is not mentioned, but the imperial council is, and one might therefore assume that the change of religion occurred before the grand vizier in Istanbul. But people often converted before the sultan while he was on the hunt or military campaign. Rather than name the imperial treasurer, as in the statute, the man responsible for imperial finances, this document instructs the palace treasurer to provide the garments to the converted couple. As Rycaut notes:

> The *Haznadar Bashi*, or Lord Treasurer of the *Seraglio* [*saray*, pal-ace], who commands those Pages that attend the Treasury; I mean not that which is of present use, as to pay the Souldiery, or serve the publick and present occasions of the Empire, for that is in the hand of the *Tefterdar*; but that Riches that is laid apart for the expences of the Court, and that which is amassed and piled up in several rooms of the *Seraglio*, of which there have been collections and additions in the time almost of every Emperour, distinguished and divided by the names of the *Sultans*, through whose industry and frugality they had been acquired, but this Wealth is conserved as sacred, not to be used or exposed, unless on occasions of extreme emergency.[45]

When Rycaut mentions "Riches" that are "amassed and piled up," he is refer-ring to the precious cloaks such as sable furs of honor kept under the watchful eye of the palace treasurer.[46] Rather than being used only during emergencies, it is more correct to say that the garments were circulated on significant oc-casions, including conversion ceremonies. More important, Rycaut mentions that the palace treasurer accompanied the sultan wherever he traveled. In Sep-tember 1673, the sultan had alighted on the plain of Isakçi during the second Polish campaign where these conversions occurred.

A researcher can be misled in other ways. Despite the implication of the statute that only men would convert at court, numerous archival documents mention women who became Muslims. Treasury records reveal that in ad-dition to turbans for men, the sultan's court distributed a wardrobe full of clothes to women who converted to Islam. These included women's slippers and cloaks.[47] According to the petitions recorded by the secretary of the impe-rial council concerning the bestowal of new dress today housed at the Prime Ministry's Ottoman Archive in Istanbul, nearly two hundred people converted before the sultan and grand vizier. Of the people receiving new clothes, most were men. Based on the location of conversion, it can be assumed that they were predominantly Orthodox Christian, although some Jews in and around Salonica also may be included in these petitions. Two-thirds of the people ap-pearing at these courts consisted of groups of men ranging in size from two to fifty. The second largest category of converts consisted of single men. Fewer groups of men and women, likely married couples, and sometimes families with children converted together. A similar number of small groups of women, usually two, including mothers and daughters, also came to the courts of the grand vizier and sultan to receive Muslim clothing. A handful of women and a girl came alone.

The sources located in Istanbul are but the tip of the iceberg. Many petitions were probably made orally and never recorded and never made it into the modern archive. There may have been other informal conversions as well. Other studies corroborate the finding that mainly men converted to Islam at the traveling courts of the sultan and grand vizier in Rumelia. This included some who converted while the sultan was hunting. Ottoman archival sources located at the Oriental Department of the National Library in Sofia, copies of which do not exist in Istanbul, provide further evidence of this type of conversion. For example, from autumn 1679 to winter 1680, twenty-two men, two women, and a girl became Muslim in the presence of the sultan when he was on the hunt in Thrace.[48] An extraordinary document records the conversion of 379 people over the course of a single year, the period from summer 1679 to late spring 1680.[49] Most were men (193), although there were 146 women, eighteen boys, and twenty-two girls who also became Muslim. These conversions are further evidence of the link between conquest, Kadızadeli preaching, hunting, and religious conversion, for they occurred in the wake of what is referred to as Kara Mustafa Pasha's successful ghaza leading the men of the religion of the beloved of God (Muhammad) on behalf of the monotheists against the evil crucifix-worshipping crusader forces of Muscovy during the conquest of Çehrin in 1678.[50] The sultan's Kadızadeli preacher Vani Mehmed Efendi had accompanied the grand vizier on the campaign and again played a key role inciting the troops. The sultan had ventured as far as Hacıoğlu Pazarı and then returned to spend a great deal of time hunting in Davud Pasha (412b).

Cloaking converts provided Mehmed IV a link to his prophetic namesake and to a millennium of Muslim leaders. Abdi Pasha presented Mehmed IV with a commentary on the "Mantle Ode," memorializing Muhammad's bestowal of his cloak on a convert.[51] At the same time, cloaking converts was a means of displaying Mehmed IV's legitimacy, power, and prestige at a time when sultans had become marginal, isolated, and symbolic figures. As a writer at the court of Louis XVI observed, "Ceremonies are the most important support of royal authority. If one takes away the splendor that surrounds him, he will be only an ordinary man in the eyes of the multitude, because the populace respects his sovereignty less for his virtue and rank than for the gold that covers him and the pomp that surrounds him."[52] Mehmed IV's supporters and chronicle writers believed virtue was important. With his piety and public ceremonies, the sultan aimed to impress his subjects, those in the ruling class who opposed his rule because they thought he was a do-nothing sultan, new wealthy civilian constituents of the ruling class who were vying for power, and foreigners present in the empire. In a period of acute anxiety, caused by economic crisis, political instability, and the ever-changing fortunes of the military, the sultan desired to assert normality, order, and social balance and publicly celebrate those Christians and Jews who joined the faith, articulated in the form of cloaks and turbans. In this way religion played a part in regulating the social order by contributing to the semiotics of clothing.

One more item bestowed by the sultan demands comment: the purse of coins. Here it may seem as if we are speaking of a truly recognizable commodity in the common understanding of the term as something intended for exchange. But the sultan offered no more than a handful of Ottoman aspers at a time when daily transactions were conducted with western European coins. By the middle of the seventeenth century, as the Ottomans practically ceased producing Ottoman coins, the only coins that issued from Istanbul mints were used primarily in court ceremonies. The purse of coins thus had more symbolic than real value. This is similar to the situation in early modern Europe where the *sparsio*, the distribution of coins at coronations, involved not coins currently in use, but new ones minted for the occasion.[53] Coins distributed by the sovereign had extramonetary, not actual, value for the sultan, elite, and commoners alike.

Mehmed IV as Convert Maker

Mehmed IV was a convert maker in the first sense because he and his court facilitated the conversion of Christians and Jews to Islam through a ritual changing of mind and body. At the same time, this sultan was a convert maker in a more literal sense because, like his mother, he also compelled people to enter Islam. Numerous examples of the second meaning of convert maker appear in the pages of Ottoman historical narratives, especially Abdi Pasha's *Chronicle*. The earliest successful conversion occurred when Mehmed IV was only thirteen years old. A foreign admiral, probably Venetian, was captured in 1654 (57b). When he appeared before the imperial council, the admiral "became distinguished among his peers by becoming honored by the glory of Islam." He was taken into the sultan's private quarters and settled in the great room. During that chaotic time, when everything seemed to be going wrong, it must have made an impression on the teenage sultan to have a mighty foreign military leader who had guided successful attacks on the imperial domains become subservient to him and a believer in the one true God. The admiral was but the first of enemy combatants to change religion at his feet. The drover with the magic cow converted in the spring of 1665. That summer "an edict was sent to the palace in Edirne concerning the Cossack prisoner of war seized by the governor of Silistre, Vizier al-Hajji Hüseyin Pasha. [The prisoner] was sent to the imperial presence where he acquired the honor of Islam" (176a). The following summer, the governor-general of Bosnia Sohrab Mehmed Pasha brought 170 severed infidel heads, fifty-six prisoners, and ten banners, which the sultan viewed at the Justice Pavilion in the palace in Edirne. Two of the prisoners became Muslim and the sultan awarded them each gold coins (216b–217a). That fall Shabbatai Tzevi became a Muslim under the sultan's gaze. In the summer of 1667, "since three male servants from the infidel ambassadorial retinue of Poland became numbered among those who find honor in Islam, an order was issued in this matter that they be adorned in Muslim garments and be appointed to the group of palace pages attached to the external palace service" (236a). Finally, in autumn 1668, the sultan and Vani Mehmed Efendi were en route to Yenişehir in Greece in support of the renewed efforts to conquer Crete and had alighted in Tırhala, where the sultan had just bagged forty-three deer. As reports of the conquest of Candia seemed imminent, eighty Habsburg and French soldiers sent to assist the Venetians were taken captive and brought to the sultan. One or two became Muslim before him (286a–b).

The conversion of the Venetian admiral, the Cossack, French, Habsburg, and other Christian prisoners of war, and the members of the ambassadorial retinue of the king of the Commonwealth of Poland demonstrate that no matter the wording of "The Statute of the New Muslim," sometimes other forces, such as the fear of death or impressment into servile status, or even the sultan's anger, were probably involved in religious change than merely the volition of the Christian or Jew who desired to convert. Prior to the conversion of the Polish pages, the sultan had been angered when the royal gatekeepers failed to make the Polish ambassador kiss the ground. This ambassador had a reputation for being of violent temper and rude.[54] The sultan retired the head of the gatekeepers and may have demanded the conversion of the pages to appease his outrage (235b). In all these situations, as when the rabbi Shabbatai Tzevi appeared before him, Mehmed IV compelled men in captivity to change religion, being, like his mother, a convert maker.

10

The Failed Final Jihad

After the conquest of Constantinople, Mehmed the Conqueror made a glorious entrance into the city at Edirne Gate and rode through the streets en route to Hagia Sophia. He hoped to crown his reign with the conquest of Rome. En route to Vienna, Suleiman I paraded through streets decorated in classical triumphal arches in the manner of Roman triumphs after commissioning Venetian artisans to produce a marvelous crown similar to a papal tiara, emperor's mitre crown, and ceremonial Habsburg helmets, uniting symbols of Christian imperial regalia.[1] Convert maker Mehmed IV's exodus from his imperial capital and journey to Serbia en route to an anticipated triumphal horseback ride through Vienna was reminiscent of the processions of his two illustrious predecessors. What better way to promote the greatness of the Ottoman dynasty than by defeating its greatest rival, the empire that controlled lands bordering Ottoman Europe? What other action could justify the effective move of the imperial seat to Edirne, the abode of the ghazis? Taking the Habsburg city would cause Mehmed IV to be remembered among the preeminent ghazis in Ottoman history. And by taking his son out of the cage and along on campaign with him, to show him to the people, Mehmed IV, by this point over forty years old, was also breaking with tradition. He was giving his son a lesson in ghazi warfare, as he had on the Kamaniça campaign, and promoting him as his rightful successor through his presence on what would be an illustrious campaign leading to the conversion of people and places in central Europe.[2]

This chapter analyzes the Ottoman siege of Vienna in 1683 in the framework of several of the book's interrelated themes: the links between conversion and conquest and between piety and proselytization, the centrality of the mediator in conversion, how conversion affects religious geography and sacred space, and the role war, violence, and changing power relations play in conversion. As is well known, the siege did not go as planned and the Ottoman forces were routed. The rest of the chapter explores the fallout. While the sultan continued to hunt and convert peasants, a gathering storm of opposition coalesced to banish Vani Mehmed Efendi and dethrone Mehmed IV.

Vani Mehmed Efendi's Incitement to Conquest and Conversion

Vani Mehmed Efendi authored an important Qur'anic commentary in 1679–80 that explicitly linked conversion and conquest.[3] The commentary offers the preacher and Kadızadeli leader's theory of the process of conversion, which mirrors the practice of religious transformation at Mehmed IV's court: conversion of self, others, and sacred space. According to his historical model, for which he cites the Islamization of central and southern Asia and Anatolia as evidence, Turkish leaders converted and they and their descendants were then compelled by piety to conquer territories, including Constantinople, changing religious geography in the name of Islam.

His understanding of history also promoted the idea that when those of true faith go to war, their piety is rewarded. Thus according to Vani Mehmed Efendi, Constantinople was conquered merely by the Ottomans saying "There is no God but God and God is most great" three times. For the preacher, conversion and conquest have additional import. Conversion of the Turks to Islam followed by their successful conquests fulfilled God's destiny not only for Turks but for all Muslims, and thus humanity.

He begins the crucial section concerning conversion and conquest using a Qur'anic passage (9:38–39, At-Tawba, Repentance) to promote the idea that the Arabs failed to fight on the path of ghaza. First he quotes the Qur'anic passage: "'Believers, why is it that when it is said to you: 'March in the cause of God,' you linger slothfully in the land? Are you content with this life in preference to the life to come? Few indeed are the blessings of this life, compared to those of the life to come. If you do not fight [the ghaza in Rum] He will punish you sternly and replace you by other men" (542b). He then begins his commentary on the passage, using the opportunity to claim that Turks do not resemble Arabs, for they willingly take up the cause of jihad.

"If you do not fight." Oh Arabs, you do not fight on the campaign for Byzantium [Rum]. . . . But the Turkish people do not in any way resemble the Arabs. Because for a long time the Turks have been the ones who are the mujahids waging ghaza against the Byzantines and Europeans [Efrenj] by land and sea in the East and West. It is the Turks who have conquered all of the lands of the Byzantines and settled in them. They have made all of the lands of the Byzantines, Armenians, and Georgians, and some of the lands of the Europeans and Russians into Turkish territories. . . . Most Christian peoples from all different sects became Muslim with the blessing of the Turks; after first being Byzantine, European, and Russian they then became Turkish. This is also another sign of the great grace and kindness with which God blessed the Turks. (543a)

He then discusses the Hadith concerning the conquest of Constantinople, explaining that Muhammad predicted that Turks would conquer the city. First he quotes the Hadith:

Muhammad asked, "have you heard of a city surrounded on one side by water, on the other by land?" They said "yes." Muhammad continued by prophesying: "the Final Day will not occur until 70,000 sons of Isaac arrive to conquer it. They will enter without shooting an arrow or firing a weapon. The first time they say 'there is no God but God and God is most great' [la illaha illa la wa allahu akbar] the sea side of the city will fall to them. The second time they say the same phrase the land side will fall. When they say it for the third time, their way will be cleared, they will enter the city, and take its booty." (543a)

To Vani Mehmed Efendi, the meaning of the passage is clear: "I say that the people who were prophesied are the Muslim Turks . . . their campaign will reach as far as the city. Because of this, it was expected that the city's conquest would be achieved by the Turks." Consequently, "the Turks conquered Constantinople, their commander Sultan Mehmed son of Sultan Murad the Ottoman conquered Constantinople after a 54 day jihad in 857 [1453]" (543b). This fact allows Vani Mehmed Efendi to contrast Ottoman success with Arab failure. Arabs were not "destined to conquer the city. It is as if the Turks' merely declaring 'God is most great' was enough to conquer the city without even resorting to arms or battle" (543b).

Before returning to his main argument that the Turks replaced the Arabs in fulfilling God's intent to spread monotheism at the expense of the

polytheists known as Christians, he offers a genealogical explanation proving that the Turks are the (unnamed group) predicted not only in Hadith, but
also the people about whom God speaks in the Qur'an. It is put forward that
because Oghuz Han married Isaac's daughter, "Turks are the sons of Isaac on
the mother's side. Just as Jesus is of the sons of Israel, Turks are of the sons
of Isaac. . . . The name 'Turk' is given to the sons of Oghuz Han. They are the
Turkmen" (544b–545a). The message is simple: Abraham had two sons, Isaac
and Jacob/Israel. Those descended from Jacob/Israel, including the Jews,
Christians, and Arabs, have failed in their mission. The sons of Isaac, on the
other hand, represented by the Turks, have succeeded.

Having established through his genealogical discussion that the Turks are
mentioned in the Qur'an, he begins to narrate a history of the conversion of
the Turks to Islam, which is always coupled in his mind with conquest. First he
sets the stage: "[Where the Turks settled] people were Zoroastrians. Muslims
[Arabs] did not fight against them, but Turks attacked them. Around 350 [961]
the [Ismaili Shi'i] Rafizi heretics occupied Egypt and Syria, and other than the
Abbasid caliphs, Rafizied all Muslim rulers. The Byzantines, benefiting from
this split among Muslims, occupied Muslim lands and reconquered lands previously conquered by the Muslims" (545a). The entire Muslim world except for
those areas controlled by the Abbasids was in the hands of the Shi'is. The Shi'i
Fatimids controlled northern Africa, the Levant, and the Holy Cities. The Shi'i
Buwayhids controlled Iran. Sunni states were very weak; the Abbasid caliph
was but a figurehead. Muslims were in a woeful state, so God made the Turks
Sunni Muslims in order that Turks and Muslims could fulfill their destiny:
"Because of this, God completed his bestowal of good upon Muslims and made
the Turks into Muslims with his favor and grace. In 349 [960], Cenk Khan, sovereign of all Turks . . . became a Muslim. Because he converted, over 200,000
other Turks also converted with his blessing. As a result, learned scholars and
miracle-working sheikhs appeared among them" (545a). But in keeping with
his Kadızadeli ideology, Vani Mehmed Efendi makes no other mention of Sufis
and makes them equivalent in importance to scholars. Thus he chooses to over-
look the crucial role that Sufis played in the Islamization of the Turks and lands
conquered by Turks, this vision of Islamic history fitting in with his generally
anti-Sufi interpretation of Islam. He would not boast of Sufi successes when he
opposed many of their orders and practices. His vision of conversion is linked
to conquest, not Sufi preaching.

Vani Mehmed Efendi continues by explaining the arrival of Turkish Is-
lamizers, "the people of the Sunna" (545b), in India and Anatolia, precipitating
the significant battle at Manzikert, which was the key enabling the Islamization
of lands conquered by Turks: "Then one of the Byzantine emperors named

Urmanus [Romanos Diogenes] gathered all Byzantines, Europeans, Georgians, and Armenians to pray according to their corrupted rites at the largest church in Istanbul, Hagia Sophia, and in 456 [1064] set out. This cursed one set out with 400,000 Christian infidels and 2,400 carriages loaded with weapons and arrived at Malazgirt setting foot upon Muslim territory. Sultan Alparslan was in Tabriz and his army was dispersed. He only had an army of 14,000 Turks and Kurds" (545b–546a).[4] With God's intercession, "they defeated the infidels, killed or took their soldiers prisoner, and took their belongings as booty" (546a).

Vani Mehmed Efendi argues that Alparslan's victory at the Battle of Manzikert was a watershed for conquest and conversion. The triumph opened the gates of Anatolia to Turks, who migrated in mass numbers, radically changing the demography. They carried the ghaza and jihad in which they had engaged in the East, sacrificing their lives for Islam against Turks who had not yet become Muslim, to the West against Byzantium and the rest of Europe, replacing the Arabs who had begun the struggle. Rather than being an ally of the Arabs carrying the battle east, they eventually conquered Arab as well as infidel territories. Conquest went hand in hand with conversion. Following the victory at Manzikert, Sultan Danishmend Ghazi and many Turks settled in Anatolia. With the arrival of the Danishmendids, people and places were soon converted in Byzantine cities, mosques replacing churches and monasteries.[5]

Vani Mehmed Efendi connects his narrative of Turkish conversion and conquest to the early Ottomans, the last branch of the Turkish genealogy. When the Mongols ("infidel Tatars") defeated the Muslims, "the Ottoman sultans' ancestor Ertuğrul came to Greek [*Yunan*] territories and settled near Söğüt. Later most Turks fleeing the Tatars settled there and waged ghaza against infidels pursuing them. . . . Later, they conquered Constantinople and countless European lands and cities" (546b). He then switches again to first person and returns to his main point concerning the Ottomans heeding God's call to pursue conquest in the name of conversion: "This is my analysis of 9:39. That is to say, 'Oh Arabs! If you do not go out on the ghaza in Rum against Byzantium, God will punish you and your enemy will occupy your lands.'. . . Now Turks have become victorious over Arabs in the East and in the West. 'And another people will take your place!' Indeed, the Turks have taken your place and wage ghaza against the Byzantines" (547a). Thus it is now the Ottomans who serve the religion, waging war against the Habsburgs and Romanovs, the successors to the Byzantines, having inherited this duty from the Arabs and earlier Turks.

Vani Mehmed Efendi's Qur'anic commentary produced convincing arguments that may have incited Mehmed IV and Kara Mustafa Pasha to continue launching war in central and eastern Europe against Christian powers. This is significant, for conventional wisdom presents the latter as being responsible for the siege of Vienna while overlooking the articulation of conversion and conquest in the writing of Vani Mehmed Efendi and the role it may have played in the fateful campaign. The religious scholar was at the height of his influence and popularity. After writing this text he had many opportunities to preach its thesis to eager audiences of military leaders and viziers during Friday prayers and in private audiences with the sultan. Fitting for his advocacy of war and the conversion of Christians and Christian places, Vani Mehmed Efendi was named campaign preacher during the siege of Vienna in 1683 so that he could exhort troops at the battlefront as he had on the Russian campaign.

The Second Ottoman Siege of Vienna

Not since Suleiman I, who attempted to take the seat of the Habsburg throne in 1529 at the beginning of his illustrious reign, did an Ottoman sultan attempt such a bold undertaking. To take Vienna, the "Golden Apple" of the age, would have meant conquering central Europe, and western Europe might not have been able to resist the Ottoman advance. In short, most of Europe would have become another Ottoman province, or at least a tribute-paying region of the last great Islamic empire. Two portraits of the sultan were made in 1683, the fateful year of the siege, by Musavvir (Painter) Hüseyin, the only Ottoman portraits to have survived from the period between 1666 and that year. The first today is in Ankara, the capital of the Republic of Turkey, the much truncated successor of the Ottoman Empire. Mehmed IV, who appears with his predecessors Murad IV and Ibrahim, is labeled "Sultan Mehmed Khan Ghazi."[6] He sits tensely on his throne, gripping it with his right hand. Rising behind the throne and perfectly enframing the sultan is a large golden orb that calls to mind the sun. The star of the sultan seems to still be rising. Indeed, the miniaturist also included the chronogram from the sultan's birth year referring to him as a light.

The second miniature ended up in Vienna as part of the defenders' war booty.[7] There are also three miniatures on one page, from top to bottom: Murad IV, Ibrahim, and Mehmed IV. The uppermost representation is of Murad IV, labeled "Sultan Murad Khan Ghazi," who appears battle-ready. He wears jeweled armor as well as a jeweled quiver of arrows on his left hip, clutches a jeweled sword in his right hand, and forms his left hand into a fist placed over his chest. The middle miniature is a depiction of Ibrahim. The artist has given him a sumptuous fur-lined, billowing, red velvet cloak over a pink garment. The lowermost miniature on the page presents Mehmed IV and is labeled "Sultan Mehmed Khan Ghazi." Also referred to as "the shah and sultan

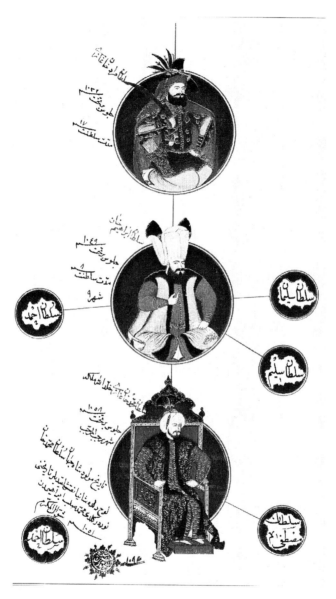

FIGURE 10.1. Three sultans: Murad IV, Ibrahim, Mehmed IV. Musavvir Hüseyin, *Silsilenâme*, Vakıflar Genel Müdürlüğü, Ankara, Kasa no. 4-181 4, fol. 40a. Reproduced with permission.

of the world," he is seated on a high, ornately patterned gold throne. He looks directly at the reader. He confidently clasps the end of the armrest with his left hand while pressing firmly downward with his palm on the other armrest. He wears a tall, white turban ornamented with three ghazi aigrettes. His eyes are bright and active, his eyebrows slightly raised. His sumptuous fur-lined cloak, which consists of large red and yellow diamonds on a blue background, is opened, revealing a green and yellow garment and jeweled sash. He looks ambitious, his feet turned to the right as if he is about to stand up, balancing his weight on the armrests.

The text that accompanies the miniature celebrates his military triumphs. It claims that Mehmed IV is "the powerful and glorious sultan, the sovereign of the world, and king of kings of humankind, sultan of two continents and khan of two seas, custodian of the two noble sanctuaries [Mecca and Medina], the sultan son of a sultan son of a sultan, the conqueror and ghazi Sultan Mehmed Khan son of the Sultan Ibrahim Khan."[8] Following this introduction, after praying that God grant him continued strength and power and numerous conquests, the author immediately launches into a discussion of the conquests and peace treaties obtained during Mehmed IV's era. These include Yanova by Köprülü Mehmed Pasha (1657), Vardat by commander Ali Pasha (1660), and Uyvar (1663), Yeni Kale (1664), peace with the Habsburgs (1664), Candia and the island of Crete (1669) by Fazıl Ahmed Pasha. Then the author notes that in 1672 the sultan went in person to conquer Kamaniça, the linchpin of Poland and Cossack territories, and successfully completed the mission with overpowering force. Then again the sultan turned his attention to the state of the frontiers and campaigned in person against the Cossacks at the unapproachable and impregnable citadel of Ladezrin in 1674. Finally, the author mentions that Kara Mustafa Pasha used this citadel as a launchpad for conquering Çehrin from the Poles, Russians, and Cossacks. He concludes by praying that the world's master of an auspicious conjunction will be honored by many more conquests. This miniature had been commissioned by Kara Mustafa Pasha and presented to the sultan shortly before the grand vizier set out for Vienna.

The Ottomans could have learned from the mistakes of the previous campaign to take the Habsburg capital. A major campaign in central Europe was a severe test of Ottoman military capabilities. The campaign season lasted from spring to autumn, yet it would take until midsummer for the army to even reach Belgrade. Along the way the Ottoman commander would confront storms, winds, and rain. He would also face the difficult problems of provisioning his troops and transporting them along roads and across streams and rivers to the battlefront. Most war matériel had to be carried overland on animals, but the harsh conditions caused a high attrition rate. Winter weather also frequently began during autumn. In 1529, Suleiman I did not arrive before Vienna until the end of September, slowed by rain and flooded rivers, facing a well-garrisoned city, running out of time, lacking in provisions. In the middle of October the sultan called off the siege: "'Snow from evening until noon next day,' 'much loss of horses and men in swamps,' 'many die of hunger'—so ran the story of the grim march to Belgrade."[9]

Unlike his uncle Fazıl Ahmed Pasha who had spurned the requests of the leaders in the part of Hungary under Habsburg rule to break the peace treaty with the Habsburgs and campaign to "liberate" the area, Grand Vizier Kara Mustafa Pasha played the leading role in the debacle. Writing just before the Vienna campaign, Evliya Çelebi considered him "a strong vizier whose opinion and counsel are adopted, who is intelligent, and wise."[10] Showing some acumen, he had commissioned the translation of the Hungarian and German sections of Willem Janszoon Blaeuw's *Atlas Maior*, presented by the Dutch ambassador in eleven volumes to Mehmed IV in 1668, not yet completely translated.[11] His predecessor had ended twenty-seven years of warfare with Venice, subjected the entire island of Crete by conquering an invincible fortress, added Ukraine to the empire, and subjugated the Poles and Cossacks. But contrary to the efforts of Emperor Leopold I, he refused to renew the peace treaty with the Habsburgs, which had one year remaining. Instead, in 1682 he began preparations for war.

Not all members of the administration supported renewed war. Kara Mustafa Pasha asked Sheikhulislam Çatalcalı Ali Efendi to issue a fatwa on the question of whether it was canonically valid to wage war against those desiring to surrender or refusing to join battle.[12] The sheikhulislam did not give him the answer he wanted, and opined that war was not licit. Nevertheless, because of the grand vizier, war was unavoidable. The Habsburgs thought the Ottomans would campaign against Yanık, so they fortified it, leaving Vienna less protected and seemingly an easy target. Seeing the new situation, they even offered to give up Yanık, but Kara Mustafa Pasha set his mind on Vienna. As a result, a chronicler from a generation later considers the grand vizier to have been "a courageous and strong person," but "he had the disposition of a merchant."[13] Why settle for Yanık when he could have better goods: Vienna? While on the march Kara Mustafa Pasha received news of a bad omen: his palace in Istanbul had nearly burned to the ground.

The best Ottoman perspective of the events that followed is the *Events or Calamities of Vienna* (*Vekāyi'-i Beç*), composed by the grand vizier's secretary of imperial protocol Ahmed Agha, who accompanied the army on the march to Vienna, served at headquarters during the siege before the citadel, and withdrew with the defeated Ottoman forces.[14] The author refers to the campaign as a ghaza and those involved as ghazis and raiders (akıncı). Although he uses the latter term, it is clear from other statements that he viewed the campaign as war on the path of God. He hoped the siege would be successful and never lost faith in the grand vizier, viewing him favorably until his execution. What is most noticeable about the text is its physical state: it is poorly written and full of crossed-out words; it is water-damaged, the top lines of many pages are blurred, and red ink bleeds across many pages. It is symptomatic of the fate of the campaign. In fact, it is in such fragile condition that researchers at Topkapı Palace Museum Library are no longer permitted to read the original. Unlike the endowment deed of the Valide Sultan Mosque from 1663, or the presentation copy of Kurdish Preacher Mustafa's treatise of 1675, which appear flawless and are embellished with gold, the condition of this narrative mimics the hasty, chaotic flight of the grand vizier and the deteriorating state of Mehmed IV's reign following the siege.

The campaign began with a bad omen and ceremony. The sultan, referred to still as a ghazi, his sons Mustafa and Ahmed, his favorite concubine, his commander in chief the grand vizier, and Vani Mehmed Efendi left Edirne in April and led the army through portentous rain and a sea of mud to Belgrade. The sultan remained in a tent outside the city, the favorite and princes were sent to a palace within, and Kara Mustafa Pasha and the preacher continued on after a massive military procession and ceremony. During the ceremony, the sultan sat on his throne in the head tent, his legs stretched out, his knees covered with a red shawl.[15] The princes stood on his right, their shoulders leaning against the throne. The sheikhulislam and Vani Mehmed Efendi were present when the palace treasurer and turban bearer, after being given the sign by the sultan, each pinned a jeweled round aigrette on the turban of the grand vizier, who also received a jeweled sword and quiver and was cloaked in a sable fur. That year nearly 10 percent of the Ottoman budget would be spent on nearly 2,500 robes of honor.[16] The sultan then took Muhammad's black wool banner in his hands, kissed it, and handed it to the grand vizier, telling him he entrusted the noble banner to him, and he entrusted the vizier to God.[17] Kara Mustafa Pasha kissed the ground and the sultan's preacher prayed.

Despite the bad omen of overcast weather, within two months more than one hundred citadels and redoubts had been captured by the army of Islam. When they captured the enemy's positions, the Ottoman forces killed those who had fought against them, offering no quarter, and rolled their heads on the ground before the grand vizier. In the second week of July, with an insufficient force, the grand vizier and his armies arrived before the well-defended gates of the Habsburg capital to wait for its surrender. The first skirmishes in the environs of Vienna went well as the Muslim ghazis captured heads, prisoners, and much booty.[18] In the meantime, the Polish king, long a thorn in the Ottoman side, and a significant army also headed for the city.

The grand vizier's secretary was in high spirits, believing that the defeat and destruction of the enemies of religion was becoming as clear a reality as the light of day. He displays historical consciousness by linking Mehmed IV with his famous predecessor when he mentions that on July 13 the grand vizier arrived at the spot where Suleiman I had pitched his tent in 1529. He remained convinced of imminent victory because of the piety of the grand vizier, whose forces are constantly referred to as ghazis. According to the author, because the heroic grand vizier was implementing God's commands, such a country had been seized and become a place where the horses of the army of Islam galloped. He continued claiming that to those who know history it was unnecessary to show any more proof that until then no military commander had been shown such clear signs of imminent conquest.[19]

On July 14 the Ottoman forces arrived before the citadel of Vienna and demanded its surrender. In an act illustrating the link between religious conversion and conquest in that era, Kara Mustafa Pasha sent a letter in Ottoman and Latin to the inhabitants of the city, referred to as being located in a country made for Islam, and the forces guarding it.[20] The grand vizier states in the letter that his innumerable, divinely assisted soldiers have arrived before the citadel with the intention of taking it and propagating the word of God.[21] Following the custom of Muhammad, he offers the citadel's defenders the option of converting to Islam to be spared being put to the sword, or they could give up the citadel without a fight, and without changing religion they could still find safety. If, however, they neither converted nor surrendered without a battle, they would be wiped out in the name of God, their wealth and goods pillaged, and their children made into slaves. He thus urged them first to submit to Islam and surrender, or second, to at least surrender peacefully, either way agreeing to live under Islamic sovereignty, whether with eternal salvation in the first instance or temporal stability and prosperity in the second.[22] He warned them that if they refused to submit to the shadow of God on Earth (Mehmed IV), who had sent him to take the city and propagate Islam, they faced death and enslavement.

The inhabitants prepared to fight rather than become Muslims. The Habsburg emperor at any rate had already fled to Linz. The Croatian who had relayed the original letter and the response told the grand vizier's messenger to hurry up and go, otherwise he would be filled with bullet holes. When the Orthodox Christian Alexander Mavrocordato, who served as Divan translator, relayed the information, the grand vizier roared for the cannons to be ready and the battle to begin.[23]

Let us listen again to his secretary of protocol. He describes the war between the "enemies of religion," "accursed and miserable infidels," and "herd
of rabid pigs," the most ritually unclean of animals, destined to "burn in the
eternal flames of Hell" on one side, and on the other the soldiers or "army of
Islam" or "ghazis of Islam" fighting on the path of God, who were attentive to
their prayers and led by a commander "brave as a lion."[24] He continued to be
in high hopes during the early stage of the siege, thanking God that it could
not be any other than a sign of victory that the infidels found themselves cut
off in every direction and besieged, giving such a blow to Islam's enemies that
it cannot be described. For him, the reason for the impending victory was un-
doubtedly the piety of the commander leading the Ottoman forces. He wrote
that if God willed it, the citadel of Vienna, the object of the grand vizier's desire,
would certainly be conquered and added to the domains of Islam thanks to this
illustrious man's sincere religious zeal and obedience to God's decrees.[25]

To prepare for battle and victory, the Ottoman forces engaged in customary
ritual practices. The grand vizier and all commanders and officials listened to
the Ottoman military band play until late at night, and again first thing in the
morning. The drums, reed pipes, trumpets, and cymbals played at the same
time, making a great noise, startling the inhabitants of Vienna, and combined
with the booming sound of cannons and guns seemed to make the heavens
fall. When the sumptuous cloaks, jeweled sword, dagger, and imperial decree
sent by the sultan arrived, a great ceremony began before the tent of the grand
vizier, the representative of the sovereign whose presence was felt. The tent
was opened and the grand vizier was seen sitting in his tent wearing a tall
turban and fur cloak. The Janissary commander was on his right arm and the
imperial treasurer on his left. Ali Agha held the imperial writ with both hands.
He passed it to the grand vizier and kissed his hem. The grand vizier took it
respectfully with both hands, kissed it, and while the heralds shouted "May it
be auspicious!" and cheered, he took it to his breast. This time Ali Agha presented a cloak embroidered with gold and covered in ermine fur. The heralds
again shouted "May it be auspicious!" and cheered. The grand vizier took the
cloak. He took and kissed the sword. The sword bearer came and girded him
with the sword. Then he took and kissed the dagger. The sword bearer girded
him with that as well. As he took each gift the halberdiers cheered. Radiant and
glowing with proud joy, the grand vizier stood bolt upright and took out the
imperial writ. He kissed it. He took it from its pouch and gave it to the imperial
secretary. He took a few steps to the middle of the tent and read each word of
the writ one at a time with a loud voice so that all present would understand
it well. Finally, he read the monogram of "his eminence the world-ruling emperor" that he had affixed "with his own blessed hands" to the top of the writ.

Then the decree was again presented to the grand vizier. He took it, kissed it, and put it in his breast as the halberdiers shouted and cheered. Soon after, the Ottoman forces held a military procession in the entrenchment with generals, soldiers, and the military band, proof to the secretary of imperial protocol of the sincerely religious grand vizier's unconditional submission to God and the approaching magnificent victory.[26]

Throughout July the narrative of *The Events of Vienna* maintains its confident tone, although elements of doubt make a subtle entrance. The author begins to pray that the attacks of the Habsburgs fail, the strength of the besieging forces increase, and the battle plans be successful. Yet it was learned by the end of the month that the defenders of the citadel had bulletproof armor. At the beginning of August, the author tried to keep his spirits up, claiming that the Ottoman side was continually conquering more land, and not timid step by step, but freely. The infidels understood, he thought, what a catastrophe they faced. But he noted that because of this they defended themselves with all their might. At the end of the first week of August, the author's tone turns pleading, asking God to allow the Ottomans to conquer the citadel quickly. As Kara Mustafa Pasha ceased sleeping, desperately waiting for victory, the author continued to fervently pray for the misery of the infidels and victory of the Muslims. In early August, the tone of the narrative improves as its author learns that the Habsburg ambassador claims if only he had given up the fortress of Yanık his side would not have to face such devastation. For the author it was too late, for God had set on fire the sparkling flames of divine wrath. Now God knew no pity, and no compassion.[27] The days of the Viennese defenders were numbered. The chronicler gains confidence, convinced that God was on the Ottoman side. Yet by the end of the month, he had cause for concern once more.

The campaign was waged for the dynasty and religion, but soon word arrived that the former head of the dynasty was no more. The chief eunuch of the harem sent news, along with a gold sword and diamond-covered dagger, of the valide sultan's death in Edirne.[28] When Hatice Turhan died, she ended a remarkable period of over four decades on the Ottoman political stage. According to a historian writing after Mehmed IV's reign had ended, when they realized the extent of their loss, recognized how she had represented the dynasty, and understood her role in keeping the dynasty afloat, the public mourned: "Alas, woe to us, the greatest pillar of the dynasty has gone."[29] The valide sultan was buried in her immense tomb in Istanbul across from the imperial mosque she built. It is the largest royal tomb complex in the city. God's names are written in large, white, cursive calligraphic letters on a navy blue tile background above the lower windows on the mausoleum's exterior. Suitable for the tomb endowed by a pious Muslim, "Our Lord! Grant us good in this world and good in the hereafter, and save us from the chastisement and torment of the fire" (Qur'an 2:201) is written in large cursive calligraphic letters of gold leaf on a black marble background above the main door. The entrance door is one of the most beautiful examples of mother-of-pearl and ivory work. "Oh my Lord, the opener of doors, open auspicious doors for us" is written in large cursive calligraphic letters in mother-of-pearl relief style on the leaves of the door (half the verse written on each leaf). In the mausoleum, decorated with the period's most beautiful tile panels up to the level of the upper windows, one sees the best examples of masterful stained-glass work. As in the Valide Sultan Mosque, the first thirty verses of the Sovereignty (Al-Mulk) sura of the Qur'an are written as a tile band in large white cursive calligraphic letters on a blue background above the lower windows within the tomb. These verses warn of the horrible consequences for heedless unbelievers in the hereafter and the reward for those who shun heedlessness and think of the many admonitions about the blazing fire of Hell.

The capital of the Habsburgs was supposed to be suffering such a fiery fate. The Ottomans made a major attack on Vienna, but the city would not fall. By the last week of August, some soldiers began speaking ill of the grand vizier. Although it was Ramadan, others were caught drinking wine, receiving as punishment two hundred lashes of the whip before the assembled troops. Kara Mustafa Pasha had to bring his commanders together to urge them to exert all effort to bring the campaign to a successful finish. In the final days of August, the defenders of the besieged city fired one hundred rockets from the tallest and most central cathedral in the city, Saint Stephan, which the author interpreted not as a sign of their strength, but as a sign of their weariness and depressed state. He implored God to completely remove these infidels from the face of the earth. Yet, though the author gloats when he learns that the defenders of the citadel were suffering from hunger, he also has to acknowledge the serious problems of feeding Ottoman animals and troops, the inflation of prices, and difficulties getting needed supplies.[30]

Conditions were worsening, and an end to the siege was nowhere in sight. To raise the morale of the troops, on the first of September the sultan's preacher exhorted them to fight in the path of God. As The Events of Vienna relates in language similar to that of Abdi Pasha, repeating his important role played at Çehrin five years previously, Vani Mehmed Efendi preached to the army of Islam while making his frequent rounds in the trenches. He gave them such wonderful admonition and incited them in such an effective way that everyone who had knowledge of the art of speech was greatly astonished. But the preacher's words did not stay in people's minds for long. Within a couple of days of his impressive oration, an official refused to accept an appointment. The angered grand vizier grabbed him by the beard and hit him twice, then had him arrested for disobeying orders.[31]

While the grand vizier, like the sultan's preacher, visited the trenches to cheer on the troops or discipline his commanders, Ottoman forces learned that the French, Habsburg, and Polish forces had united. Christian forces had arrived to save the besieged city. The author of *The Events of Vienna* prayed that God would grant the army of Islam strength and victory and cause the enemies of religion to face utter defeat and rout. Kara Mustafa Pasha faced a continual barrage of missiles, which his secretary of protocol interpreted hopefully as demonstrating that the defenders no longer knew what to do and were in desperate need of help, which actually more accurately described the Ottoman side.[32]

On the sixtieth day of the siege, September 12, Kara Mustafa Pasha gave orders for the final attack. Thirty thousand Ottoman troops faced a combined Christian army four times its size. To the astonished master of ceremonies, Christian forces seemed to have flowed like a flood of black tar that smothered everything in its path, and also seemed like threatening storm clouds or an immense herd of furious boars that trampled and destroyed everything.[33] The defenders of Vienna were able to outmaneuver the Ottoman soldiers because the troops of the Crimean Khan Murad Giray did not carry out orders and cover the others. As an anonymous western European eyewitness relates:

> The Duke of *Lorain* Order'd the Chevalier *Lubomirski* with the *Polish*
> Horse to advance toward the Enemy; and in case he found them
> too strong for him, to retire, and draw the Enemy after him. Which
> Orders he accordingly executed with good Success; for the Enemy be-
> lieving the *Poles* had fled, follow'd them with great fury and eagerness
> so far, till the D. of *Lorain*, who was prepar'd to receive them, easily
> surrounded them, and cut the greatest part of them in pieces: The
> rest fled in so great confusion, that they who escap'd the Sword, were
> drown'd in the River *Mark*.[34]

Fuming to be repulsed so vigorously, the grand vizier attempted to mine the bastion, but this too was foiled.[35]

The siege was doomed. Confederate forces joined under the leadership of the king of the Commonwealth of Poland Jan Sobieski attacked the grand vizier's position. The soldiers around him, seeing that the coalition forces attacked and advanced from two sides, and that the Ottoman forces were being defeated, lost their will to fight.[36] It was not possible to resist the overwhelming number of enemy forces, and the Ottoman soldiers were routed, as Nihadi relates, "some drowning, others having to drink the sherbet of martyrdom."[37]

Yet the grand vizier mounted his horse when the Polish king and his troops marched toward the black banner. He made battle-ready his retinue, Vani Mehmed Efendi, and the sword bearers and cavalry. As the generals on each flank were beginning to lose, the grand vizier and his troops at the heart of the military formation held their ground. But the opponents' attacks increased, and the furious battle waged for five to six hours. Knowing that his failure would lead to his execution, the grand vizier refused to flee his position even as the enemy occupied the Ottoman military camp. The defenders' cannon fire and rockets fell on the army of Islam like rain. At that point the Muslims understood it was too late, that there was no chance of being saved from defeat. The troops around the grand vizier were both fighting and trying to flee. The grand vizier and his closest men withdrew to the tents, carrying the banner of the prophet. At this point, the "enemies of religion" entered headquarters and the treasury. The grand vizier continued to do battle. He took a lance and with a few of his men began again to fight.[38] He did not want to withdraw due to his courageous zeal and mad stubbornness. Yet he saw the writing on the wall. Saying that it was better to die than see that day, he decided to die on the battlefield. But the men around him disagreed. Pained for his brother in religion and wanting to save the banner, sipahi commander Osman Agha began to plead with Kara Mustafa Pasha. He told him that it was too late, that he was the heart of the army; if he was sacrificed, the entire army of Islam would cease to exist. He begged him to withdraw at last. The grand vizier and Vani Mehmed Efendi fled with the banner.[39]

In the words of the book of miniatures he had commissioned, Kara Mustafa Pasha was the representative of a fortunate dynasty that made the world bow to its commands, but he lost his tent and the miniatures to the forces of the Polish king. As the anonymous western European source relates, "In a short time the *Turkish* Guards of their Trenches giving way, put all the rest into confusion: Upon which the *Grand Vizier* fled with his Horse, leaving all his Foor [force], to the number of 25000 to be cut in pieces, together with all his Artillery, Baggage, and Treasure, with the Spoil of his own Pavilion, to reward the Courage of the Victor."[40] The forces allied with the Habsburgs took three hundred cannons and even the grand vizier's treasury, which included the sumptuous cloaks, daggers, and swords used in the elaborate ceremonies prior to the ultimate battle, as well as the book of miniatures containing the striking portrait of a bold Mehmed IV. Osman Agha took Muhammad's banner and the survivors of his routed army began to withdraw toward Buda by way of Yanık. They took only what was light, leaving the rest; utterly defeated and in mourning, saving only their souls, "spilling bloody tears," they withdrew. They arrived at Yanık exhausted, in shock, destitute, and ashamed. Most had no tents; they slept in the open.[41] What had happened to the triumphant grand vizier? What of Vani Mehmed Efendi's exhortations, which had apparently worked so well at Çehrin but failed to produce the same effect at Vienna? How could the "army of monotheists" be defeated by the "infidels without religion"?

It was time for the Ottoman enemies to boast. The following day, September 13, 1683, the triumphant Polish king wrote a letter in Latin from the captured grand vizier's tent:

> For the *Turkish Gran Vizier*, swell'd bigg with the entire Force of the East, and of the *Crim-Tartars*, already swallowing in hope, not only what (without Relief) was within three days of its Fate, *Vienna*; but with that, even all *Christendom*; was notwithstanding in one day's Battle and Onset, entirely Routed and put to Flight. Their Infantry (in the common style *Janizaries*) as being a slaver Force, and no wayes equal in Flight to their Horse, was left behind in the Tents, and abandoned to the Direction of the Conqueror. The Tents themselves, taking up well nigh two Miles in length and breadth taken. Their Cannon, all their Powder, and Ammunition, with the Richest of their Spoils, became the just Reward of the Victors Arms. *Vienna* freed thus from so hard a Siege, and from such Dangers as had almost proved Fatal, and the Imperial Seat restored to its own *Caesar*.[42]

Mehmed IV would not be able to call himself the Caesar of Christendom. He had come as far as Belgrade, and had even brought along Gülnuş Emetullah as he had to Kamaniça over a decade previously, in anticipation of the triumphant conquest of the Habsburg city. Learning of the course of events, how the soldiers of Islam had been routed, and then "half naked and in wild disorder, falling and rising like a wounded fugitive, they fled to Yanık," the sultan returned to Edirne following a difficult journey in heavy rain.[43]

Political and Religious Aftermath

Unfortunately for the dynasty, defeat before the walls of Vienna, the Golden Apple, proved costly. Following the crisis of Vienna, Mehmed IV's proclivity for hunting was criticized, as was his mobility; no longer desiring Abdi Pasha's imagined ruler whose "footstep covered the world from end to end," his opponents demanded a sedentary sultan enthroned in Istanbul, and some chroniclers ceased to apply the ghazi label to him.[44] The failed siege served to "shake the Ottoman state at its foundation and cause its power to become so weak it could never again be compared to its former might."[45] It was a mighty gamble that failed, ending the Kadızadeli movement's dominance at court and leading to the dethronement of Mehmed IV.

After failure, scapegoats were sacrificed. When the Ottoman forces routed at Vienna assembled at Yanık, Kara Mustafa Pasha decided to first make an example of Vizier Ibrahim Pasha, the governor-general of Buda. His forces gained notoriety for being the first defeated in battle and the first to arrive at Yanık. When the governor-general arrived before him, apparently shaking like a yellow leaf in the fall wind, the grand vizier called the man an accursed unbeliever and blamed him for the defeat. He had told the grand vizier that the citadel of Vienna would be easily conquered, for it had a very small garrison, but in the end the governor-general cut and ran.[46] He was executed. Abandoning the triumphalist, pious tone of the earlier part of the narrative, and failing to come up with any plausible explanation for why his sincere prayers were not realized, the author of *The Events of Vienna* finds that only violent, gendered language could express his outrage. The "bitch" known as the Tatar khan, who did not even have as much courage as a woman, fled the siege of Vienna and arrived a day earlier and alighted before Yanık. In his view, no Tatar khan had ever engaged in such treachery. Gathering courage after ejaculating misogynist rhetoric, the grand vizier's secretary of protocol then had the unenviable task of first relating some more convincing reasons for the calamity of Vienna, and then describing the execution of his patron.

The chronicler offers four moral reasons why it was God's desire that the Ottomans suffer such a defeat. The first three had to do with the lack of religious zeal of the troops and poor planning, the final reason was a lack of piety.[47] First, despite Vani Mehmed Efendi's spellbinding speeches, in the end, the soldiers were only after booty. At this point in Mehmed IV's reign, perhaps the term *akıncı*, or raider mainly concerned with obtaining booty, had become more accurate than *ghazi*, or warrior fighting against the infidel on behalf of the religion, which entailed sacrifice. On the day of battle, when some at headquarters began to load up goods and flee, soldiers at the front decided to do the same. Second, the Ottomans gathered all their forces in one place in the trenches and expected Tatars to fight like others instead of using them to harass the enemy. In fact, the Tatars failed to fight because they too only considered the gains to be made and were not willing to sacrifice themselves in battle. Third, the horses of the cavalry were underfed and incapable of attack. The planners of the campaign had failed to devise a way to provide for proper fodder. Fourth, Ottoman soldiers failed to understand that all success and victory is proof of God's grace. They neglected to praise and thank God for successes small and great. Instead, they acted ungratefully and suffered punishment as a consequence. This sentiment clashes with the narrator's earlier depiction of the soldiers and commanders engaging in prayer and being motivated by religious conviction, which, according to his logic, should have resulted in God's favor.

Trying to explain the cause of such disaster, and echoing earlier claims about the causes of the greatest conflagration in Istanbul's history, other commentators repeated these sentiments. Nihadi claimed that rather than enjoining good and forbidding evil, the commanders permitted what is inappropriate, the soldiers engaged in immoral acts disapproved of by God and excessive amounts of various types of debauchery, and all armed forces were blinded by vanity and their transgressions.⁴⁸ What began as a bad decision compounded by poor planning, an insufficient numbers of troops, and the unfortunate arrival of the defender's allies was doomed by the morally corrupt actions of the army itself. Eighteenth-century chroniclers stressed the immorality of the Ottoman forces, but in greater detail: "When the Muslims found wine, even those who had never drunk, drank it and engaged in vice and debauchery. Although the siege occurred during the holy months of Rajab, Shaban, and Ramadan, not fearing God, they did not give up fornicating and pederasty. They became so accustomed to drinking and being constantly intoxicated they forgot to praise and thank God for His blessing. Accordingly, they incurred God's wrath."⁴⁹

The debacle cost the grand vizier the sultan's favor. Mehmed IV's mother had passed away during the campaign, but her ally, the chief harem eunuch, still had influence. Yusuf Agha convinced the sultan that the grand vizier was responsible for the defeat, again highlighting the divisions between those interests running the seventeenth-century dynastic household (the valide sultan and harem eunuchs) and those responsible for the administration of empire (grand viziers in general, and the Köprülü men who served as the last three viziers in this period in particular).⁵⁰ After the sultan had the person who submitted the report of the defeat killed for bearing bad tidings, he ordered that Kara Mustafa Pasha be executed in Belgrade, the city for the second time host to a sultan impatient to take the biggest immediate prize in the Christian world after Constantinople, and that failed again to witness a triumphal sultanic departure.

The grand vizier is depicted as being resigned to and eager to meet his fate. On Christmas Day, he was stripped of his imperial seal, the banner of Muhammad, and keys to the ka'aba which he hung around his neck, all signs of his being the representative of the sultan and leader of jihad. When he was told of his impending end while engaged in afternoon prayers, he declared that what God wills happens. He finished his prayers and told his pages to leave but not to forget him in their prayers. He took off his turban and ordered the executioner to enter. To be considered a martyr, he had the rug removed so his body would fall in the dust. The executioner raised the dismissed grand vizier's beard and passed the noose around his neck. The grand vizier admonished him to tie it well.[51] The executioner tugged at the ropes two or three times, and the former grand vizier expired. The body was taken out to an old tent, where they prepared the corpse for burial, performed the funeral prayers, and then cut off the head, buried the body in the courtyard of the mosque opposite the palace, and sent the head to Mehmed IV in Edirne. First it was placed at the palace gate to serve as a warning to others, then it was buried in the courtyard of a local mosque. Hüseyin Behçeti, who had written the *Ascent of Victory* in celebration of Kara Mustafa Pasha's conquest of Çehrin and in praise of Vani Mehmed Efendi's incitement to jihad four long years before the rout at Vienna, died soon after in Belgrade after having retreated from the front with the army and his patron.

One of those who safely returned with the army to Edirne after setting out with the sultan to Belgrade was a twenty-five-year-old who served in the royal laundry as one of those in charge of the sultan's linen.[52] Before his retirement from royal service in 1703, he became the sword bearer (*silahdar*) of Ahmed III, and that is the name attached to the history he wrote as a continuation of Katip Çelebi's narration of Ottoman history. Although Silahdar used *The Events of Vienna* as a source for his account, he adopted a critical tone toward the grand vizier (2:42–94). With the benefit of many years' hindsight, when discussing the beginning of the campaign he complains that Kara Mustafa Pasha failed to bring large cannons and mortar and enough firepower to conquer the citadel, the same mistake Ottoman planners had initially made during the Candia campaign. This was particularly inexcusable to the author at a time when the empire was at the peak of its economic and military strength with enough wealth and matériel to sustain a larger campaign. Silahdar infers that the grand vizier thought he could conquer Vienna without the requisite war and bloodshed. In his entries for the last weeks of August, Silahdar argues that the grand vizier had already been told that the army did not have enough ammunition to subdue the citadel, that Vienna was especially well fortified, and that the longer it was besieged the harder it would be to take it, especially because the enemy was being reinforced while Ottoman forces faced deprivation. He complains that the grand vizier could have avoided the fiasco if he took Yanık and stopped there; doing so would have made the emperor desire a peace treaty. Or he could have surrounded Vienna in all directions rather than going straight before its citadel. Silahdar claims that if the Ottoman military had put pressure on the city in that fashion, Vienna would have fallen without a battle. He also puts words to this effect in the mouths of the grand vizier's commanders, who at the end of August stated that they were badly outnumbered and requested tens of thousands of additional troops; yet Kara Mustafa Pasha failed to fulfill his promise to send more troops, leaving the beleaguered Ottoman armed forces to their fate. Silahdar vents his rage when he describes the last days of the siege and final battle of the campaign. For him, "a sixty day siege went to waste" since "the atheists in the citadel" were incited by seeing the arrival of reinforcements (2:84). He wanted God to "damn and destroy them." But on the day of the final battle, "the imperial army left everything and all was taken by the accursed infidels. . . . God forbid! It was such a rout and great calamity; such a crushing defeat had never been suffered in the history of the dynasty" (2:87).

Silahdar's history reflects how the tide turned for Mehmed IV. Following his description of the failed siege of Vienna, he ceases to call the sultan "ghazi," opting instead to simply refer to him as "his excellency, the sovereign," nor does he make the sultan the central agent in the narrative. At the meeting of his council at the beginning of 1684, Mehmed IV learned that the Habsburgs had been aided by all Christian nations, including Muscovy, the Commonwealth of Poland, Sweden, France, Spain, England, the Netherlands, the Papal States, Genoese dukes, and Venice (2:126–27). Christian armies were on the march in the Crimea (Muscovy), Kamaniça and Moldova (Commonwealth of Poland-Lithuania), Bosnia, Crete, the Greek islands and coasts (Venice). It was as if all the enemies Mehmed IV had defeated earlier in his reign were coming back to haunt him with a vengeance. The sultan asked his council what to do about the situation. The viziers, commanders, and religious class were all in agreement: they did not want the sultan to campaign anymore, but remain in the capital and send men, munitions, and matériel and experienced commanders to fight on all fronts. This was the end of Mehmed IV's freedom to be a mobile ghazi.

The plan did not work, and soon rebellion was couched again in gendered language. Territorial losses accelerated from the Peloponnese to central Europe (2:139). Even Buda was besieged. In 1685 a group of ten thousand sipahis openly rebelled against the idea that their mobile ghazi leader could not lead them in campaign (2:201). They refused to go on campaign without him at their head, without the grand vizier, and without the banner of Muhammad, all of which they considered to be contrary to the law of Suleiman I. They asked how those who died could be considered martyrs and those who killed the enemy be considered ghazis if they fought on their own without sultan, grand vizier, and holy relic. The sheikhulislam responded by asking them whether Suleiman I was a prophet and his word equivalent to Hadith (2:202). As the answer was obviously negative, a statute from that era was annulled. Those who die are assured of their manliness because they are martyrs, he assured them, and those who kill are ghazis; yet those who do not obey commands are to be crushed like infidels and loose women. The sipahis were not persuaded and gathered at dawn at the bank of the Tunca pledging to attack the homes of the grand vizier and Janissary commander. Edirne's public baths and markets were closed and the city prepared for battle. A commander and a thousand Janissaries were sent against them. The ringleaders were captured and some banished to Limni Island, others to the galley, but the rebellion continued.

The reputations of those responsible for the calamitous situation suffered. Vani Mehmed Efendi was not punished as was the grand vizier, yet the debacle at Vienna, which he had spurred Kara Mustafa Pasha to undertake and in which he had played a major role inciting the troops to battle, served to end the influence of the one who brought his vision of a reformed Islam to the sultan's court as well as dampen support for his followers, the Kadızadelis. Nihadi later blamed Vani Mehmed Efendi for impudently inciting the sultan to launch the campaign.[53] As was seen at the beginning of the chapter, in his work completed just a couple of years before the ill-fated attempt, Vani Mehmed Efendi had interpreted Qur'anic verses and Hadith in a way that promoted religious war for it led to conquest and the conversion of the population. He saw the campaign for Vienna as a continuation of this historical effort.

The sultan was upbraided by chroniclers for placing his trust in Vani Mehmed Efendi. The preacher had been appointed spiritual guide of the army. But after the defeat, Vani Mehmed Efendi, who had never separated from the sultan or grand vizier for over two decades, journeying with them on the hunt and military campaigns, was banished. Apparently no one could any longer stomach his goading to jihad or his harsh criticism of contemporary Muslim practices. He was sent to his estate, which apparently was a citadel converted into a palace in the village of Kestel, near Bursa. It is said that he brought many Kurds there to be near him.[54] There he died soon after. The inscription on his tomb in the cemetery adjacent to the village mosque included the lines "Angels composed a chronogram for the death of that eminent one of high rank. 'Vani Efendi ascended to the Throne in Paradise,'" 1096 (1685).[55]

With the passing of Vani Mehmed Efendi, Mehmed IV again turned to Mevlevi Sufis for spiritual guidance. The sultan considered going to Istanbul for a few days, but he abandoned that wish, saying, "Without taking vengeance on the enemy of religion, how can I show my face in Istanbul?" (2:192). In 1685 when he did finally return to Istanbul, the sultan likely accompanied his chief astrologer, the Mevlevi Ahmed Dede, twice a week to the reopened Mevlevi lodge in Beşiktaş, where the two listened to the reading of Rumi's great work the *Mesnevi* and observed the whirling of the dervishes, again practiced in the capital. While in Davud Pasha the sultan probably also visited the Yenikapı Mevlevi lodge twice a week. Expenditures from the sultan's and public treasuries show that the palace again began to favor Mevlevis. Cloth was cut from the sultan's own treasury, and meat, bread, oil, and rice were provided to Mevlevi lodges from the public treasury (2:244). During this period, religious disputes among Muslims again intensified. Invited to appear before the sultan at the Beşiktaş pavilion, the sultan's Kadızadeli preachers and Sufi sheikhs disputed whether a perfect spiritual guide was to be found in that age or not. Each side cursed the other and the sheikhulislam had to come between them to make them kiss and make up. Kadızadelis were no longer prominent or largely unchallenged at court. At the beginning and end of his reign the sultan was surrounded by Mevlevi Sufis, those dervishes whose public practices of whirling to music and ecstatically, rhythmically reciting God's names were a central target of Kadızadeli preachers who promoted rational religion.

Mehmed IV had expanded the empire to its greatest extent during his reign; bit by bit the pieces were falling off. The years 1685 and 1686 were marked by the execution of grand viziers, military crisis and defeat, the loss of territory and citadels, shrinking empire, renewed financial crisis, and the reappearance of rebels and bandits in Anatolia, who gathered thousands of men to their side to pillage and plunder town and village from Sivas to Bolu (2:215–28). Exhilarated by their successes against the Ottomans, Polish forces attempted for the next four years to retake Kamaniça, but were unsuccessful. They applied constant military pressure nonetheless. Venice, allied with the pope, Spain, Genoa, Florence, and Malta in the Holy Alliance of 1684, tried to reconquer Crete, also without success, but was able to make serious inroads, particularly in the Morea, where the defeated Venetian defender of Candia Francisco Morosini was able to exact some revenge, and Venice even took Athens in 1687.

Conversion of Christians and Jews at the End of Mehmed IV's Reign

How did the sultan respond during these dark years that called to mind the crisis-ridden 1650s? In part, he went hunting while going back and forth between Edirne and Istanbul, where he finally settled beginning in the spring of 1686. Sometime in this period Abdi Pasha, sent perhaps partly in exile to remote Basra to serve as governor, presented Mehmed IV the final version of the history of his reign, which mercifully covered events only up to 1682, completely avoiding the siege of Vienna and his loss of ghazi status.

Despite an end to ghaza and jihad, the sultan continued to facilitate the conversion of Christians and Jews to Islam in public conversion ceremonies. Archival sources housed in Istanbul record that in 1685, fifty people converted together to Islam before the sultan when Mehmed IV had traveled from Edirne to Istanbul. It was at the Yapacağı estate near Silivri where most presented themselves before him and became Muslims. Forty-three people converted during one month in 1686 while the sultan was hunting night and day, his tent pitched either at the grounds of the imperial dockyards in Istanbul or in Davud Pasha. This included two Orthodox Christian men, acting separately. The first converted to Islam and changed his name to Ali. He then petitioned for garments and alms to be bestowed on him according to statute. The second man, the new Muslim named Osman from Yaylakabad (Yalova), located across the Marmara Sea from the Ottoman capital, also appeared in court requesting the clothes of a Muslim. Soon after, the new Muslim Mustafa appeared to request the same Muslim garments, namely, materials for a turban.[56] Many men came alone to convert and became servants to the sultan, such as the new Muslim Ali, "honored by the glory of Islam in the imperial presence," who came "to wipe my face in your felicitous presence so that I may be attached to the group of chamberlains of the privy tent" in the summer of 1686, and the new Muslim Abdullah, who in early autumn requested "that I become a soldier in the artillery regiment."[57]

The sultan also continued to be a convert maker of women. A typical document from fall 1686, the autumn of Mehmed IV's reign, reads as follows:

God is everlasting! The document has been registered.
It was commanded saying, "let women's garments be bestowed according to custom." September 18, 1686.
Long live his eminence my illustrious and gracious sultan!
This woman servant came humbly to your noble foot-dust to become honored by the glory of Islam. It is entreated that according to statute clothing and alms be commanded with gladness. The remaining decree belongs to my sultan.
Your humble servant Fatma and her grown daughter Ayşe.[58]

Two other examples of petitions involving women converts at court are representative of the process:

God is eternal!
The document has been registered.
It was commanded that garments be given according to custom.
August 23, 1686.
Long live his eminence my felicitous and gracious sultan!
We have come from Karîn-âbâd and become honored by the glory of Islam at the imperial stirrup [before the sultan], two women, two men, and two boys. It is requested that garments be bestowed. The remaining decree belongs to my sultan.
New Muslims

6 people

2 new Muslim minors 2 new Muslim women 2 new adult Muslims.[59]

The sultan had frequently passed through this town in Bulgarian Thrace while on campaign and the hunt during the preceeding two decades. Because the sultan would no longer come to them, compelled as he was to remain in Istanbul, people from the provinces intending to convert before him had to journey to the imperial capital. In another archival document one reads:

> God is eternal!
>
> The document has been registered.
>
> It was commanded that garments be given according to custom.
>
> Long live his eminence my felicitous and generous sultan!
>
> This orphan slave woman desired to become honored by the glory of Islam. That which is hoped for from my sultan's exalted compassion is this: since the articles of the faith of Islam have been repeated, my clothes, gifts, and alms be bestowed according to statute. The decree in this matter belongs to my sultan.
>
> Your humble servant,
>
> The new Muslim women, Ayşe and Emine.[60]

Modern historians and his contemporaries in Istanbul did not notice that the sultan was instrumental in bringing Christians and Jews to Islam and were thus unaware of this meritorious activity. There is no evidence that the religious classes observed, praised, or even knew about his efforts.

II

Mehmed IV's Life and Legacy, from Ghazi to Hunter

Hunting to Excess and the Downfall and Death of the Sultan

Once the sultan returned to the capital, he sought to resuscitate his reputation as a pious, just sovereign, but as Silahdar relates, circumstances did not permit him to improve his image. The numerous conversions at his feet were overshadowed by his hunting habit. Mehmed IV visited Eyüp as he had at the very beginning of his reign. He upbraided his servants who did not bring rebels to justice, decrying their femininity in an imperial writ: "Why did you not attack the bandits as you were ordered, why do you instead saunter and stroll about like women?"[1] Silahdar was eyewitness to a renewed campaign against rebels, the fruit of which was scores of rebel heads arriving before the gaze of the sultan. That fall, the sultan watched from the Alay Pavilion at the edge of the palace walls as a brigand was paraded through the city in a humiliating and torturous fashion and then hanged at Parmak Gate (2:244). At the same time, in the spring and summer of 1686, the sultan was in, but not within, Istanbul. He preferred Davud Pasha Palace and the gardens near the dockyards for hunting, riding, and promenading, and Üsküdar garden and the village of Çengelköy on the Asian side of the Bosporus, where he amused himself among the cherry blossoms along with half of the people of the harem (2:241, 244). Yet while the sultan was enjoying the delights of the city on the Bosporus, the empire had entered the second year of a ruinous drought and famine. Since the failed military campaigns there had been a dearth of rainfall. The price of wheat and grain skyrocketed. In some places in Anatolia, oak and plum root and walnut shell were ground into meal; because the combination was indigestible, many died (2:242).

Dire straits for commoners, lawlessness in the capital, and military failure turned commoners, the military, and factions in the administration against Mehmed IV. The sultan's constant hunting earned the wrath of the religious class and united commoner and elite alike in opposition. All anyone could see was that Mehmed IV was in the environs of Istanbul, pitching his tent where he pleased and hunting; no one seemed to have appreciated his proselytizing behavior.

Hunting practices defended before 1683 failed to win approbation thereafter, when he was no longer considered a ghazi (1:160).[2] The sultan was like a vampire, going to the hunt either before daybreak and returning at night, or going at night and returning the following night, seemingly without concern for the empire (2:245). It seemed that he entirely neglected his subjects and his own religious obligations. He traveled from Üsküdar to Beşiktaş only three times for prayers. Malicious rumors and reports began to spread. People learned that the Commonwealth of Poland besieged Kamaniça and attacked the borders of Moldova. As Silahdar, writing decades later, notes, his indifference caused "all the people to hate him, and gossip increased." The religious scholars and Janissaries began to openly criticize his apparently indifferent behavior when the empire's dominions were being lost: "When will he abandon the hunt? For how long will he continue to hunt? Is he not ashamed? Does he not fear God? What good has he been for the past forty years, other than not oppressing the commoners? Don't all the evils that the empire is suffering now stem from the shameful act of hunting?" (2:245).

An archival document drawn up by the palace treasurer reveals that there was justification for these critiques at the end of Mehmed IV's reign. A document from the summer of 1685—after Hatice Turhan Sultan, Vani Mehmed Efendi, and Abdi Pasha were no longer on the scene—details the income and expenses of the inner treasury.[3] Whereas the army expenses for the Hungarian campaign of Commander in Chief Ibrahim Pasha were 182 loads akçe, and the army expenses for the Polish campaign of Commander in Chief Suleiman Pasha 100 loads (plus an additional 50 loads given to the soldiers), the remainder of the expenses for the sultan's hunting trips in 1685 amounted to 91 loads. That is to say, expenses for the sultan's hunting excursions were at least exactly half as much as expenditures for war with the Habsburgs, over twice as much as that sent to those defending the forts and redoubts on the road between

Belgrade and Buda, almost as much as the income sent by the governor of Wallachia (Romania), and nearly one-fifth of the total loads spent by the inner treasury. By 1685, therefore, the sultan's hunting habit had indeed become an incommensurate burden to bear. It is not surprising that these critiques did the most to shape the unfortunate sultan's legacy.

Finally, the religious scholars took it upon themselves to upbraid Mehmed IV. They desired a sedentary sultan in Istanbul and began to openly denounce the sultan's lifestyle. Silahdar narrates that on a Friday at the beginning of autumn in 1686, the sultan invited Hajji Evhad dervish lodge Sheikh Hüseyin Efendi to give the sermon at Davud Pasha Mosque. But the sheikh refused, saying, "The one who wants to hear a sermon should come to Istanbul like other people to be present at the mosque. It is not our duty to go there; let him come here. Besides, he should abandon the hunt, come and sit on his throne, and be occupied with worship and piety, obeying the ordinances of God. The empire is in ruins. Protect the subjects! It is not lawful to go to the foot of a man who does not accept counsel. The truth goes in one ear and out the other" (2:245). Himmetzade Abdullah Efendi was brought to Davud Pasha, but he also fearlessly stated criticism similar to how the religious class had criticized Ibrahim nearly forty years earlier. A pious sultan who had devoted much of the second half of his reign to converting Christian holy space into Muslim sacred geography was accused of allowing the opposite to happen: "Muslims and the state are without a leader. Because of this, territories and citadels of Islam are taken by the enemy of religion. Countless mosques and masjids have become temples filled with idols and places of pagan worship. Change your actions! Repent from your sins! Ask for God's pardon and forgiveness! What is this inordinate appetite for mounting and dismounting? . . . For how long have you been lying in the sleep of heedlessness? Sovereigns go hunting regularly, I understand. But now is not the time. There is a time for everything" (2:246). The members of the sultan's entourage, their eyes full of tears, threw him out. Just as Hüseyin Efendi predicted, the sultan did not heed the advice. While the sheikh was speaking he proclaimed, "Let there not be sermons at the mosques I attend while I am out riding and on the hunt." The chief justice went to the sheikhulislam to ask why the sultan did not attend Friday mosque and prayers. They asserted that while he engaged in his nighttime adventures, following his whim for the hunt and chase, the empire's condition had become dire. Without his fixed gaze, the whole thing fell apart: important matters of the Muslims were ignored. They urged the sultan to abandon the hunt in order to save the religion and empire, to sit on his throne, attend mosque like every other Muslim. In short, "We do not want him to go on the hunt, and not come to prayer" (2:246).

Mehmed IV tried to appear as if he had changed his behavior as his court continued to suffer the withering criticism of the populace. A summary report submitting the religious class's complaints was sent to the sultan. This time, seeing that the entire religious establishment had turned against him, and fearing its unity and seriousness of purpose, he abandoned the hunt and attended prayers at the highly visible mosque his mother had built. A great crowd, including religious scholars, Janissaries, and city folk, gathered at the Valide Sultan Mosque and surrounded Sheikhulislam Çatalcalı Ali's carriage when it arrived. According to Silahdar, they shouted, "The sheikhulislam does not fear God and is not ashamed before the prophet." Then they turned to blame him for being vain and corrupt and abandoning his higher calling: "Because of fear of losing your great position, you do not tell the sultan the truth. Can't a man be found to replace you? For fourteen years, because you humored his whims, you defiled legal opinions and put the state in this situation. After such guilt and sins, in order to be secluded from the commoners you have begun to come to prayers in a carriage. How many of your predecessors did the same? Only priests ride in carriages!" (2:246). They were ready to break the carriage into pieces. That day Vani Mehmed Efendi's son-in-law Mustafa Efendi gave the sermon in which he spoke about the military campaigns, but most in the assembly wanted to bring him down from the pulpit.

Soon after, word of Buda's fall reverberated through the sultan's court and the empire. The army had been routed again in the heart of the Ottoman province of Hungary, first seized by Suleiman I at the beginning of his reign. Buda was a more tragic loss than Vienna for it was an important, long-held possession. Its loss, coupled with that of Belgrade, triggered Ottoman panic. In consequence, Çatalcalı Ali was banished to Bursa. The new sheikhulislam, Ankaravi Mehmed Efendi, met with the sultan at Davud Pasha and told him to give up hunting for a few days or go to Topkapı Palace to end the gossip. If he did not abandon the hunt, the scholar warned, scandal would increase. Because the commoners and elites alike were brokenhearted at the military situation, if a rebel should appear he would gain a large following and it would be difficult to put down insurrection. The sultan agreed: "I have abandoned the hunt, God willing, for a few days I will cross to the dockyard" (2:247). But it was too late. Whatever action he took could not decrease the anger people felt toward him.

The adverse environmental situation did not help the sultan at all. The winter of 1686–87 was one of the harshest in memory and reflected its being the little ice age. Huge snowstorms caused much hardship and difficulty. The weather's unprecedented severity closed roads for up to two months, and snow filled homes in many cities and villages. In Istanbul, the Flea Market was filled with snow, which then melted over the stores; the fruit in gardens—lemons, oranges, pomegranates, figs—was pickled; Kağıthane stream froze as far as the garden of the dockyard; and one could walk on the ice over the Golden Horn (2:263). Silahdar had great difficulty crossing by boat using an ice paddle from Eyüp to the dockyard garden where the sultan had alighted. In Istanbul roofs collapsed from the weight of the snow, which may have caused as much damage as a massive fire.[4]

The economic situation also began to reflect the gloomy state of the military. Because of the campaigns, the treasury had again been emptied. Few akçes remained, commoners were in terrible shape, and the grand vizier decided on the extraordinary measure of raising a tax among the already seditious religious class (2:262). The response to the unprecedented auxiliary tax was unsurprisingly negative, and the religious scholars and officials blamed the sultan for emptying the treasury during forty years of building superfluous pleasure palaces. They proclaimed that they might as well burn their books, for the sultan honored priests and not Muslim scholars. The ringleader of such criticism was banished to Cyprus and the tax was taken by force, quarter by quarter, house by house, from every member of the religious class save those with the rank of sheikhulislam (2:263).

Mehmed IV's days were numbered because the army, administration, and religious class united against him. In the autumn of 1687 the Ottoman army was routed at Mohács, the same Mohács that had been the scene of a great Ottoman triumph during Suleiman I's day. The soldiers rebelled against Grand Vizier Suleiman Pasha and desired to install in that office another Köprülü in his place, the Köprülü son-in-law Siyavuş Pasha, who favored putting the sultan's brother Suleiman on the throne (2:278–82). Their actions were heeded. The new grand vizier Siyavuş Pasha exchanged letters with Sheikhulislam Ankaravi in which they discussed how religion and faith and honor had disappeared, that the Ottomans would have a bad name among infidels so long as Mehmed IV, once the terror of central Europe and the Mediterranean, remained on the throne, and that there was no unity in the army. The religious scholars argued that the sultan must be replaced for he acted against the Shariah and did not accept their advice. The only solution was to dethrone him. Desperate, Mehmed IV executed Suleiman Pasha and vowed "to completely abandon hunting, to banish his greyhounds to other places, to keep only one hundred of his horses in the imperial stables and disperse the rest, and limit his expenses."[5] These extraordinary pledges alert us to the ultimate failure of Abdi Pasha, Hatice Turhan, and Mehmed IV to sell an image of a pious ghazi sultan. By this point, with Abdi Pasha in Basra and Hatice Turhan buried beneath her tomb, the sultan was commonly viewed as a playboy.

Mehmed IV had come to power in an age characterized by the intervention of the military in political affairs, and he would lose power because of a military coup. What had begun as an insurrection of a few soldiers had turned into a great rebellion of the imperial army. Soldiers ordered to winter in Edirne instead marched on the capital. As Silahdar relates, the grand vizier sent a summary report to the sultan, submitting to him the information that the army disobeyed his command to winter in Edirne. Instead it rose up, raided his tent, raised the horse tails of campaign by force, and set off for Istanbul intending to enthrone the sultan's brother (2:290). The sultan responded in a fashion that demonstrated that he understood his reign was effectively over. Although resigned to his fate, he remained defiant:

> Three times I sent a noble writ assigning them to take winter quarters between Belgrade and Edirne. . . . In reality, you did not take notice of it, it is clear from your language and thoughts that you did not obey and submit. If your desire is to remove me from the throne, then I desire that my son Mustafa, may he be entrusted to God, passes to my place; and little Ahmed, may he also be entrusted to God. After this if you resolve to do me harm, I take refuge in God from evil. God, whose majesty be exalted, has one noble name and it is overwhelmingly powerful. My wish from God is that all of you be overpowered and subjugated. (2:291)

In November the sultan sent a writ to the sheikhulislam complaining that four times he had written to his grand vizier without response (2:295). The silence was his clue that his reign was about to end. He asked the sheikhulislam to let him know if the army reached Istanbul. He received no response. The leaders of the military, administration, and religious hierarchy gathered in Hagia Sophia to hear the decree read by the deputy grand vizier Köprülüzade Fazıl Mustafa Pasha, who "asked whether there were any doubts about it being canonically valid to dethrone a sultan who was occupied with the chase while the enemy was attacking and occupying the lands of the empire, a sultan who destroyed and turned everything upside down by trusting a few men of evil intention, while distancing himself from those who had the ability to understand the solution for these problems."[6] The "few men of evil intention" may be a reference to the Kadızadeli preacher Vani Mehmed Efendi and the chief harem eunuch, Yusuf Agha; the men who "had the ability to understand" were the Köprülü viziers. The assembly agreed to enthrone Mehmed IV's younger brother Suleiman. They established the throne at the Gate of Felicity and took a reluctant Suleiman from the cage.

Like Ibrahim (who years before had witnessed the first murder of a sultan in Ottoman history, the deposition of sultans, and the execution of his three brothers who had spent sixteen years locked in a room, and who feared for his life every time he heard footsteps in the hall), Suleiman was also terrified of being killed.[7] He had refused to come out of his own accord. Told they did not come to frighten him or hurt him, but to make him sultan, he expressed doubt. He had been imprisoned for over forty years since childhood. Suleiman, completely breaking down from decades of anxiety about this very moment, asked whether they could possibly understand what it was like to spend a life in terror, or know "what is it for a soul to face what I faced." He concluded from his experience that "it is better to die at once than to die a little each and every day," and began to cry (2:297). As was the case for Mehmed IV nearly forty years before, Suleiman had nothing suitable to wear, so the eunuch put his own sable over his robe.

The transfer of power went smoothly. When he was informed that he had been deposed, Mehmed IV stated, "This must be God's desire" (2:298). The sultan was not aware that he was merely to be imprisoned. Never forgetting the fate of his father, he inquired, "Are you going to kill me?" The forty-seven-year-old ruler was replaced by his forty-five-year-old brother, Suleiman. After Suleiman "was released from the prison [of the cage], he was placed down in the cradle of the sultanate like an ignorant, young, and tender child."[8] Although a mature man, he was recast as a child, not able to escape the actual status of Mehmed IV when he was enthroned at the age of seven. The new Sultan Suleiman II imprisoned his brother and his two sons, first in the sword room in Topkapı Palace, from whence he had been brought out, and then in Edirne in 1689. Following Mehmed IV's deposition, criers spread the news, the weekly sermon and coinage were changed to reflect the name of the new sultan, and word was sent to all the lands of Islam.

Along with the more explicit reasons given for pressuring Mehmed IV to step down, one can also cite the underlying tension that the sultan and his mother had managed to control until the very end: the struggle between those who wanted Istanbul to be the capital and those who demanded Edirne or other cities in its place. Mehmed IV's choice of capital and lifestyle reflects how, throughout Ottoman history, there was a tension of "Istanbul versus another city," especially Edirne in Thrace, which served as the Ottoman capital prior to the conquest of Constantinople and was perceived as the center of warfare and raiding in Europe.[9] This tension between competing cities—the one the pride of autonomous ghazis, the other the seat of the central bureaucratic state—stood for competing visions of the nature of the state (frontier ghazi

ethos versus imperial ethos of a sedentary state) and erupted several times between the fifteenth and eighteenth centuries. Janissaries deposed and murdered Osman II because that sultan had plotted to destroy the sultan's servants
recruited from Christian youth and replace them with a new army drawn from
Turks and Kurds from eastern Anatolia and Arabs from Syria and Egypt, and
move the capital away from the Ottoman heartland in southeastern Europe
to Bursa, Damascus, or Cairo.[10] Members of the Ottoman administration and
military rejected the project of "going in the direction of Anatolia," perhaps because it ran counter to the Ottoman myth of formation, the water-crossing into
southeastern Europe that allowed the Ottomans to succeed as a world empire
based in Europe. Crossing the water in the other direction back to Anatolia
would violate the political imagination and serve as countermyth.[11] Mehmed IV, however, crossed into southeastern Europe and remained there for the
majority of his reign; he moved there in part to wage war in Europe, engaging
in ghaza and jihad.

One can interpret the coup against Mehmed IV as another instance of the
clash between the former Byzantine capital, orphaned by Mehmed IV until the
end of his reign, and Edirne, the launching pad into Ottoman Europe, where
he spent most of his life. The sultan's absence from Istanbul had been filled by
the symbolic acts of his mother, including the construction of her mosque in
Eminönü, but these were ultimately inadequate substitutions for those who favored the real thing in place of a substitute dynastic leader. In the end the pen-
dulum swung back in favor of the last Ottoman capital, although Suleiman II
and Ahmed II, remembering the many long years in captivity in the cage, spent
as much time outside of Topkapı Palace as possible. Ahmed II spent his entire
brief reign in Edirne out of fear of what awaited him if he returned. Suleiman II
soon realized that Mehmed IV had to be banished from Istanbul, for he could
not represent it, did not speak for its interests. Mehmed IV was condemned
to spend the rest of his days in the ghazi capital. Yet at the same time, his successor had learned that campaigning in person was crucial to being seen as
a worthy sultan. Soon after taking the oath of allegiance, he set out to retake
Ottoman Hungary.

When Musavvir Hüseyin made another portrait of Mehmed IV in 1692–93,
he simply labeled it "Sultan Mehmed Khan son of Sultan Ibrahim Khan." The
only text accompanying the portrait offers the information that he "was enthroned in 1058 [1648] and served as sultan for forty years, five months, and
thirteen days."[12] In the portrait, Mehmed IV, who wears a brown sable fur-lined
cloak, appears deflated, defeated, worn out, even depressed. He is no longer
the shadow of God on Earth, or the sun spreading its rays about its surface. He
has been desacrilized. His heavy eyebrows are slightly raised, and he has two

rows of deep lines or bags under his puffy, sorrowful eyes. He wears a brown beard spotted with flecks of gray. His shoulders are slightly hunched forward. Placed on the right side of the page, Mehmed IV stares dully ahead, facing his successor's portrait. Musavvir Hüseyin names several of Mehmed IV's predecessors as ghazis and depicts them as warriors. They include Osman Ghazi, the eponymous thirteenth-century founder of the dynasty, who wields a sword in his right hand; Ghazi Murad I; Sultan Mehmed Khan Ghazi the Conqueror; Sultan Selim Shah Ghazi, who holds a scepter; and the sword-wielding Sultan Murad IV Khan Ghazi. All wear high white turbans with red tips and two black and red ghazi aigrettes, along with open cloaks revealing colorful garments beneath their fur-lined cloaks. Mehmed IV, on the other hand, is not labeled a ghazi, is painted with a humble turban and a single aigrette, and wears a cloak completely buttoned up, adding to his tired, weary look.

Unlike Suleiman I, an avid hunter and ghazi who has a much better reputation, Mehmed IV did not have the fortune to die on the battlefield while called "Sultan Ghazi Mehmed Khan," nor while still on the throne. After leading or sending thousands of ghazis to their deaths on the battlefront, he died a private death of natural causes in 1693, six years after being forced to abdicate the throne, a year after his chronicler passed away in Crete. Only then was his body allowed back into Istanbul. The dynasty that again made Istanbul its seat could

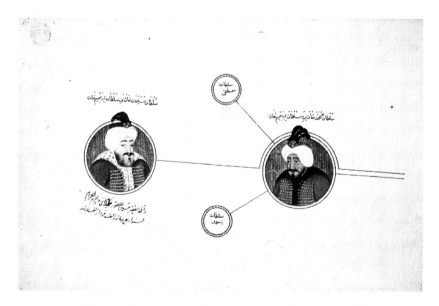

FIGURE 11.1.   Mehmed IV at the end of his reign. Musavvir Hüseyin, *Silsilenâme*, Österreichische Nationalbibliothek, Vienna, Bildarchiv, Handschriftensammlung A.F. 17, fol. 36a. Reproduced with permission.

tolerate reclaiming only a lifeless Mehmed IV. By bringing his corpse to Istanbul and burying it in the tomb that was part of the mosque complex his mother made, Sultan Suleiman II could create a public ceremony that would add to the pomp and circumstance of the dynasty. As its centerpiece was the body of a sultan who "had cheeks burned by the sun" and "was a little bent forward in stature since he frequently rode horses," hardly the type of man one would have imagined to have been Ottoman sultan in the late seventeenth century.[13]

Mehmed IV probably would have preferred to have been buried in his beloved palace in Edirne, whose Hunting Gate offered easy access to the fields and forests of Thrace that he so loved. Like his Chinese contemporary, Mehmed IV loved the sense of liberation that travel and hunting afforded him. As K'ang-hsi, who enjoyed riding and shooting every day he could outside Peking, relates, "But it is when one is beyond the Great Wall that the air and soil refresh the spirit: one leaves the beaten road and strikes out into untamed country; the mountains are densely packed with woods, 'green and thick as standing corn.' As one moves further north the views open up, one's eyes travel hundreds of miles; instead of feeling hemmed in, there is a sense of freedom."[14]

During his reign, the former sultan was repeatedly compared to the sun and his comings and goings to the rising and setting of that celestial body. When writing of Mehmed IV's death a generation after it occurred, Silahdar also marks his passing with references to the sun (2:690–91). He does not call him a ghazi, or mention ghaza or jihad. Instead, Silahdar claims that Mehmed IV died in the harem at sunrise. A man who spent his life breaking free of the harem institution ends his life in it. His death is coolly noted by another comparison to the sun, this time separating the man from the star. At the start of a new day, the world-illuminating and all-seeing sun rises, but the mobile conqueror Mehmed IV does not.

Mehmed IV's Posthumous Reputation

Within a decade of Mehmed IV's death, writers reinterpreted his reign. Already at the turn of the eighteenth century, everything positive that Mehmed IV had achieved for his dynasty, empire, and religion, namely, a restored name, greatest territorial extent, and hundreds of conversions of people and places, seemed to have been forgotten. A harsh anonymous chronicle, written from a post-1684 point of view, which repeatedly refers to Mehmed IV simply as "Sultan Mehmed," devotes but four of 158 folios to the period between 1661 and 1675, an era that witnessed the conquests of Uyvar, Crete, and Kamaniça.[15] It describes Crete and Kamaniça in one folio without using the terms ghaza, ghazi, or jihad. It never gives the sultan any agency and dismisses his military exploits. Concerning Kamaniça, all agency is given the grand vizier, who "took the sultan" to Poland where, after an easy campaign, the citadel was taken, only to be retaken by the infidels several years later (51b–52a). Writing about the siege of Vienna, the critical anonymous author claims that the grand vizier "went out on campaign against Austria and even took the sultan out of Istanbul and from there wintered in Belgrade" (60b–61a). When the grand vizier set out for Vienna in the spring "with an infinite army and complete pomp and circumstance, he left Sultan Mehmed in Belgrade and set out himself" (61a).

Instead of Mehmed IV's military conquests, the anonymous author devotes detailed attention to his hunting habit at the end of his reign, particularly its absurd dimensions and extravagant waste (74b–76b). He begins the section by claming that in general, Mehmed IV was interested in the chase, javelin throwing, and wrestling, but also sometimes would call together an assembly of religious scholars who would lecture on important topics and engage in disputes and discussions. Even while hunting he continued the practice, Vani Mehmed Efendi being given the place of honor. The sultan is given credit for understanding some of what they said and even from time to time making appropriate learned comments. But over time he allegedly reduced the number of learned gatherings, limiting them to a couple of days per year, and "became so addicted to the hunt and had such a passion for it" that he would hunt whether in Edirne or Istanbul, winter or summer, leaving two to three hours before dawn and returning one to two hours after sunset (75a). And every day a couple of hundred of the grand vizier's or deputy grand vizier's men would have to wait at the palace gate in the predawn dark and set out whenever the sultan appeared, returning only at sunset. The author then launches into a tirade against the battue. Astonished, yet at the same time unimpressed by the sultan's actions, he claims that Mehmed IV would gather thousands of drovers from numerous districts who would gather countless animals and kill them before the watchful gaze of the sultan. No mention is made of the hundreds of drovers who converted to Islam before the same gaze. Instead, we read about the miserable commoners who froze to death in the winter chases, especially in the awful winter of 1686–87. Again in summer the sultan engaged in his whim and fancy. Although "so many men became disgusted and bored of hunting, he never became tired of the habit he so loved" (75b).

The anonymous author set the hunts in a larger pattern of extravagance. He claims that the sultan would take several hundred slave girls along with him on the hunt, also alleging that Mehmed IV had nearly two thousand concubines in his palaces (76b). Large carriages of the concubines required four to six horses to pull. This meant that a massive number of horses and carriage drivers had to be hired, fed, and supplied, and hundreds of palace pages were also needed. The pages demanded thoroughbreds. Others could not pass up an opportunity for a day in the country. The chief eunuch and the palace eunuchs, royal grooms, and palace treasurer also joined the sultan's retinue, leading to exorbitant expenses to supply hundreds of carriage horses and thoroughbreds (76a). Not only the animals had to eat. Cooks were sent into the forests to bring firewood to the next day's halting ground, light a fire in the snow, and cook meals for the sultan and the hundreds of people who accompanied him, his companions, slave girls, eunuchs, pages, carriage drivers, and saddlers. As a result, Mehmed IV had become a ruler in name only: "The only signs and marks of his sultanate that remained were the reading of his name at Friday prayers and the striking of coins in his name" (76b).

Sir Paul Rycaut reflected the view of the anonymous chronicler. Rycaut both criticized the sultan's personality and alluded to the damage hunting caused:

> For never was a Prince so great a *Nimrod*, so unwearied a Hunts-
> men as this; never was he at quiet, but continually in the fields on
> Horseback, rising sometimes at Midnight, to ride up the Mountains,
> that he might more easily discover the Sun in the Morning; by which
> extravagant course of Life, he wearied out his Court and Attendants,
> who began to believe the amourous humour of the Father more sup-
> portable, than the wandaring Vagaries, and restless Spirit of the Son.
> But not only were his Huntings tedious to his Court, but troublesome
> and expensive to the whole Country, which were all summoned in
> wheresoever he came, and sometimes thirty or forty thousand men
> appointed to beat the Woods for three or four days, carrying before
> them the compass of a days Journey about, inclosing all the Game
> and wild Beasts within that Circuit, which on the day of the Hunt,
> the Grand Signior [the sultan] kills and destroys with Dogs, Guns,
> or any other way, with abundance of noise and confusion; which
> Pastime, tho lawful in itself, and commendable enough in so great a
> Prince, yet the frequent use of it, was a burden and an oppression to
> his People, whilst in the Winter they passed many cold Nights in the
> Woods, and being unused to that hardship, many of them paid for
> their Emperors Pastime with their own lives.

Rycaut also complains of the sultan's stubborn and even childish nature, writing that "no difficulties and inconveniences of Weather," including driving rain and wind that overturned tents, "could give one Hour of intermission" to the sultan's hunting desires.[16]

The best example of the transformation in the sultan's reputation can be found in the successive versions of the chronicle written by Ahmed Dede. In the introduction, the astrologer praised the Ottoman dynasty's moral virtue, expressed by its establishing justice in the empire and waging ghaza and jihad against polytheists and heretics abroad. Continuing to express these themes, in the introduction to his section on Mehmed IV, written during his reign, Ahmed Dede wrote, "He was the pearl of the crown of sultans, the best silk brocade of khans, the one who brings glad tidings of justice, kindnesses and favors, who spreads security and the faith, the protector of the lands of God, East and West, the one who helps the servants of God, far or near, the pious and God-fearing sultan, the khan who conforms to the canon law, the muja-hid, ghazi king, deliverer of conquest and ghaza."[17] A generation later, when the poet Ahmed Nedim was commissioned to translate Ahmed Dede's history from Arabic into Ottoman in 1720, the image of the pious, warring proselyt-izer evident in the quotation above was deemed inappropriate to the time and replaced by the bland phrase "the greatest sultan and most honorable shah of shahs, the king who watches over the believers."[18] Mehmed IV had been trans-formed into a sedentary sultan. No mention is made of Islam, piety, jihad, or ghaza. References to Mehmed IV waging jihad, which appear in the original, are excised in Nedim's translation. Whereas the table of contents in Ahmed Dede's original labels Mehmed IV "the esteemed conqueror and ghazi, the sul-tan Mehmed Khan the ghazi, son of Ibrahim Khan," the table of contents of the nineteenth-century printed version of the Ottoman translation labels Osman and Murad IV ghazis, but Mehmed IV "the Hunter."[19] Although the "Hunter" label offers some visions of mobility, it is not the same as the mobile, manly warrior image promoted during his reign. Despite the repeated assertion of modern historians that Mehmed IV acquired the epithet "the Hunter," they do not clarify that it was actually applied centuries later; the nickname does not appear in any text written during his reign.[20]

Even though for nearly thirty years, an entire generation, every preacher in every mosque in the Ottoman Empire during his Friday sermon called Mehmed IV "Ghazi Sultan Mehmed Khan," only a generation after his death, Mehmed IV had been remade into a sedentary sovereign. Other historians writ-ing after Mehmed IV was dethroned also declined to refer to him as a ghazi, instead choosing to accentuate his sedentary nature. Nihadi, who wrote a uni-versal history of the Ottoman dynasty from its origins in 1281 to 1685, begins his work praising Osman for being the chief of all ghazis. Although he relied largely on the *Chronicle* of Abdi Pasha, he does not refer to Mehmed IV as ghazi or mujahid. When he describes Mehmed IV leading two military campaigns against the Commonwealth of Poland in 1672–73 and 1674–75, which contemporary Ottoman writers referred to as ghaza or jihad, Nihadi prefers to call the sultan the "august ruler," "the one exalted in stature as King Jem," and the "refuge of the universe," imperial titles that harken back to the glory and pageantry of ancient, pre-Islamic Iran, rather than refer to him as a pious warrior for Islam.[21]

Along with his active role in promoting military conquest of infidel lands, Mehmed IV's conversion of Christian and Jewish souls and space also disappeared from the historical record after his reign. The sultan might otherwise have been nicknamed "the Converter" rather than "the Hunter." Mehmed IV's reign lent itself to erasure, in particular because it is remembered mainly for the fact that at the end of his epoch, following the unsuccessful siege of Vienna in 1683, the Ottoman Empire began to contract territorially; this can be seen as the beginning of a process that culminated in the destruction of the empire in the ashes of World War I. It was therefore more satisfying for later generations to imagine Mehmed IV as a profligate hunter than to memorialize him as a strong ruler. It was, and is, less troubling to pin the blame for the empire's centuries-long dissolution on a few flawed leaders than to consider the actual values of that age and the complicated processes that led to the empire's dismemberment.

Conclusion

Islamic Rulers and the Process of Conversion

Conversion of self, conversion of others of the same religion, conversion of others of different religions and their sacred spaces within society, and the waging of ghaza in part to convert others and their religious geography abroad were all linked during Mehmed IV's epoch. His interest in conversion arose during a period of crisis when the empire faced religious intensification and revival. Most notable about the ideology of Mehmed IV's court was its marked religious piety: the sultan and his inner circle openly proclaimed their own piety in their writings and through their personal behavior and the policies they implemented. After experiencing their own conversion, Mehmed IV, Hatice Turhan, Fazıl Ahmed Pasha, and Vani Mehmed Efendi considered themselves devoted Muslims returning society to the right path, from which it had deviated. Mehmed IV and his circle desired Muslims to convert to their more rational approach to the religion. Reforms targeted ecstatic Muslim practices and those who did not conform to the new piety. At the same time, they aimed to have all members of society be transformed in similar fashion, including Jews such as Shabbatai Tzevi who acted like antinomian dervishes. This dimension of their piety went hand in hand with an interest in Islamization of Christian and Jewish people and places and impelled them to promote the adoption of the religion by Christians and Jews. Conversion at home and abroad, each associated with ghaza, honored those facilitating it because the conversion of others confirmed for them the rightness of their own religious change.

Correlated with the ever-widening scale of Mehmed IV's pursuit of conquest and conversion, the sultan also effectively changed the capital from Istanbul to Edirne. However, the "evocative power" of the power struggle between the ghazis and the sultan's servants, represented by the choice of imperial seat and the proper balance between ghazi, frontier sultans, and sedentary emperors, remained unresolved.[1] Already in 1703, Sultan Mustafa II, who had personally engaged in ghaza and jihad, was forced to abdicate, and his successor Ahmed III had to promise not to relocate to Edirne as had his predecessor.[2] In "the 'long durée' of Ottoman political history," the tension between Istanbul and especially Edirne "represented a symbolically potent axis that defined different sociopolitical interests, preferences, and visions."[3] Mehmed IV's reign was an initially successful effort to regain the aura of a mobile, ghazi sultan fighting for the religion and the empire, which suited his vision of an Ottoman sultan. But it was ultimately doomed to failure without frontier warriors to keep him in power. Unfortunately for Mehmed IV, he lived in the wrong era. Had he been in power in the sixteenth century, or certainly before 1453, he might have been known as "the Ghazi" today. In the end, he could not shape the outcome according to his will alone. His ability to remain in power was limited by the specific historical context (his decreasing popularity, loss of pillars of support Fazıl Ahmed Pasha, Abdi Pasha, and Hatice Turhan), the structural constraints of the late seventeenth-century empire (the fragmentation of authority between the bureaucracy headed by the grand vizier—particularly men from the Köprülü household—and the dynasty, the power of Janissaries and the religious class to make and unmake sultans), the cultural expectations of Ottoman sovereignty that the sultan be an aloof yet authoritative emperor seated in Istanbul, and the contingency of military rout and soldiers' anger at Vienna, conditions that conspired against his aims.[4]

Mehmed IV's immediate successors understood how important successful ghaza was for a sultan's career. What their chroniclers did not emphasize, however, was religious conversion. Although archival sources continue to provide a narrative of the conversion of Christians in Ottoman Europe in the eighteenth century, with magistrates appearing as the most important mediators of conversion, the process escaped the attention of writers at court. As conversion was not one of their interests, it is not surprising that they failed to mention its occurrence during Mehmed IV's or his successors' reigns. The link between conversion and conquest was sundered. In part because the mediators of conversion to piety were implicated in failure, the crisis of the 1680s did not lead to conversion at court. Of great importance during the era of Kadızadeli piety, it simply became less important in the aftermath of the debacle at Vienna and the dethronement of Mehmed IV. Conversion in and of itself had been important to the Ottomans from the beginning, including Sheikh Edebali's conversion through a dream to the realization of the role that Osman would play in human destiny, the trailblazing proselytizing path of Sufis linked with the dynasty, the formation and replenishment of the elite infantry corps of Janissaries through a levy on Christian youth, and the conquest and conversion of the Byzantine capital of Constantinople. Archival sources attest to how, to the very end of Ottoman history in the early twentieth century, Christians and Jews became Muslims in diverse circumstances. Yet the meaning of conversion, the amount of weight it is given by the ruler and his court, like the sultan's hunting habits and military conquest, was always defined by the particular ideological and historical context.

Earlier Islamic rulers facing grave internal and external threats had converted to piety, sought to purify Islam of innovations, compelled other Muslims to follow the same path, and engaged in stricter enforcement of restrictions on Christians and Jews, including those concerning churches and synagogues. Examples are as diverse as Umayyad Caliph Umar II (reigned 717–20), Abbasid Caliph al-Mutawakkil (reigned 847–67), Fatimid Caliph al-Hakim (reigned 996–1021), and Ottoman sultans Bayezid II (reigned 1481–1512) and Murad III (reigned 1574–95).[5] Whereas these rulers did not necessarily want Christians and Jews to join their ranks, as earlier pietistic movements did not go hand in hand with conversion of people of other religions, Mehmed IV's court promoted the conversion of Christians and Jews as well as Muslims.

Mehmed IV differed from his predecessors, yet several phenomena in the seventeenth-century Ottoman Empire were not unique in the Islamic world. Although their differences were also great, Mehmed IV had much in common with his neighboring Islamic sovereigns, for, like the Safavid shah in Isfahan and the Mughal sultan in Delhi, he also became a visible ruler, appearing regularly in public.[6] More significantly, as in the Safavid and Mughal empires, a reassertion of the center with the male sovereign at its head and the conversion of Christians or Jews or Hindus, and in the latter empire a crackdown on powerful Sufis and attacks on dervish centers, went together. Indeed, Mehmed IV, Abbas II, and Aurangzeb were all convert makers.

As in the Ottoman Empire, where religious conversion was a central motif in its history, beginning with the recruitment of Christians into the administration and military through conversion to Islam, so too in the Safavid Empire (1501–1722) did conversion appear as a central theme. The Safavids rode to power on the zeal of men who converted to a revolutionary, messianic, "exaggerated" version of Islam in the fifteenth century. Once in power they promoted conversion to a more rationalistic legalistic, and Shariah-minded Imami Twelver Shi'ism in the sixteenth century, converted most of the populace of

Iran from the Sunni interpretation of Islam to Shi'ism, and turned to converted Christians to serve as their core military strength.[7] Yet both dynasties
(Ottoman and Safavid) struggled in later centuries to maintain authority as the
military backbone of the empire (Janissaries or Qizilbash) began to play a role
in making or breaking the sovereign, determining who would come to power
and how long they would stay there. Initially not only king and warrior (ghazi),
but also Sufi sheikh, the shahs of the Safavid dynasty were like their Ottoman
counterparts also considered the "shadow of God" (although with a different
eschatological understanding). They ruled over a predominantly Sunni Muslim
population, yet had as one of their central aims its conversion to Shi'ism, which
they successfully accomplished.[8] Accordingly, Armenians, foreign Catholics,
Jews, and Sunni Muslims faced episodes of persecution. Jews suffered from
the whims of the shah, who more resembled a western European king, was
influenced by less-forgiving Shi'i law, and was not constrained by the firmly
grounded religious autonomy prevalent in the Ottoman Empire. According to
Iranian Jewish accounts, between 1656 and 1661, Mehmed IV's contemporary
Shah Abbas II (reigned 1642–66) compelled whole communities of Jews to
convert, resorting to violence of a sort never seen in the contemporary Ottoman
Empire.[9] As they compelled Jews to convert to Islam, the Safavids promoted
Armenian traders. This is similar to how Ottoman policies adversely affected
Jews yet benefited Orthodox Christians in the same era. It illustrates how rulers
played groups off one another within their society and favored groups that prof-
ited the administration and dynasty. In the late seventeenth century the waxing
economic strength of Armenian traders in the Safavid Empire and Orthodox
Christian merchants in the Ottoman Empire was one of the reasons these two
groups were privileged to carry out important functions in their respective
societies.

In the Safavid Empire, Mehmed IV's contemporary Shah Abbas II, unlike
his Ottoman rival, used Sufis to fulfill his conversion aims. His chroniclers
refer to him as a "dervish-loving monarch" and patron of Sufis, despite the
widespread discord among the religious class over the role of Sufis at court
and the prominence of Sufism in the empire. He encouraged conversion of
the general populace to Twelver Shi'ism in part by means of dervishes sent
to the four corners of the empire who, like Kadızadeli preachers, taught what
was enjoined and what was prohibited. He even paid for the hajj of converts.
At the same time, similar to Hatice Turhan, who had the Valide Sultan Mosque
built in Eminönü, he also demonstrated an understanding of the power of the
imperial gaze, for he constructed a pavilion on the portal of the palace facing
the main square in Isfahan, an elevated position that signaled his presence
whether he presided over ceremonies or not. This stage was "superimposed

onto the lofty gate that commanded a panoramic view of the entire square from which Abbas II could display his bravura of power." As in the Ottoman Empire, there was a backlash against the close affiliation between the ruler and Sufis. Numerous polemics against Sufism were written during his reign, and finally, twenty-three years after he was deposed (two years after Mehmed IV was dethroned), Sufi lodges were banned, and wine, singing, and dancing were prohibited; in 1694 gambling was banned and coffeehouses demolished.[10]

The rulers of the Mughal Empire (1526–1707), Sunnis with close relations with the Chisti Sufi order, also had much in common with the sultans of the Ottoman Empire. In the beginning they effectively ruled over a population that was predominantly not Muslim, in this case Hindu. And like the Ottomans, the Mughals did not aim to convert the majority of the population. Yet the Mughals presided over just such a demographic change. Charismatic Sufi pioneers received grants of land from Mughal sultans to clear forests and plant rice and propagate Islam among forest people in new settlements replete with mosques, incorporating them into a Muslim culture and political system. Over the course of four centuries, western and eastern India developed large populations of Muslim peasants.[11] The last major Mughal emperor, Aurangzeb (reigned 1658–1707), Mehmed IV's contemporary, according to some historians, attempted to Islamize Shi'i and Hindu regions.[12] And like Mehmed IV he cracked down on illicit activities such as drinking, gambling, prostitution, the use of narcotics, and the playing of music. He also was apparently the first Mughal ruler to impose the poll tax on Hindus and has a reputation for destroying Hindu temples.[13] Like scholarly attitudes toward Mehmed IV, accounts of Aurangzeb's reign may also reflect more the biases and interests of modern writers and less the concerns of those writing during his historical epoch. Some Hindu writers present this Mughal ruler as the paradigm of malicious Muslim rule in southern Asia, manifested in forced conversion and the destruction of Hindu temples. In response, some Muslim scholars have gone to the other extreme, explaining how "tolerant" Aurangzeb was and claiming that he did not coerce Hindus to become Muslim. Similarly, in some modern southeastern European narratives of the second half of the seventeenth century, Mehmed IV is depicted as the exemplar of what is considered the brutal reign of Islam, as he allegedly forced tens of thousands of Christians to convert to Islam. In great contrast, some modern Turkish accounts depict Mehmed IV as the worst example of Oriental decadence, and never mention conversion.[14]

One reason rulers in each of the three land-based Islamic empires became interested in conversion at the same time was the symbolic power of demonstrating the truth of the ruling religion by producing the visible signs of its victory. The acts of celebrating the conversion of Armenians, Orthodox Christians, and Jews, or Hindus, and even compelling some of them to become Muslim had several audiences. These included dissident or competing members of the ruling elite and dynasty, religious authorities, Muslim commoners, rulers of the other Islamic empires, and western European observers. Just as the bodies of women serve in Europe and the Middle East today as the site of contestation over the proper role of Islam and secularism in society, in the Islamic world of the Ottomans, Safavids, and Mughals Christians and Jews or Hindus served as signposts of the Islamic virtues of the rulers. For most of Islamic history, members of other religions were treated in such a way as to demonstrate the benevolence and compassion of the shah or sultan. But in times characterized by Islamic zeal, rulers sought to demonstrate their conviction by applying the letter of the law, especially concerning Christians and Jews. It usually sufficed to ensure that they were properly humbled, made distinct, and removed from positions of power. But to oversee the conversion of visible individual Jews such as palace physicians or the large-scale religious change of numerous Christian or Jewish commoners, or to Islamize the landscape, was a means of acquiring additional sanction for rule. This is one reason Mehmed IV was willing to emerge from his silent aura of sacrality, to renounce the sign language he used to communicate at court in order to speak without intermediaries and compel a cattle drover to become a Muslim. It was worth his temporary contact with the Christian commoner because it would strengthen his pious reputation.

Mehmed IV's time in power also invites comparisons with those of modern rulers. The reign of the last important Ottoman sultan, Abdülhamid II (reigned 1876–1909), who was also a throwback to another era, abandoning the Topkapı Palace in favor of a more rustic, remote abode (Yıldız Palace, within a forest preserve uphill from the Versailles-like Dolmabahçe Palace), provides insight into Mehmed IV's reign because of the surprising similarities between the two men. Mehmed IV's modern counterpart differed in that the tools at his disposal—railroads, telegraphs, factories, censuses, passports, steamships, clock towers, newspapers—that could be utilized to produce the desired propagandistic effect among political opponents, the subject populace, and foreigners alike were far superior to those available in the seventeenth century. Mehmed IV had to rely on public monuments such as imperial mosques and celebrations and ceremonies to impress rivals and supporters. And to expect Mehmed IV to share Abdülhamid II's aims, including creating a Muslim Turkish proto-citizenry and modernizing the empire, is to be anachronistic, never mind Vani Mehmed Efendi's claims of the superiority of the Turks. Nevertheless, both reinvigorated the symbolic language of the sultanate and forged links of sacrality directly with the people. Mehmed IV and Abdülhamid II encouraged a revival of piety and attempted ideological reinforcement in an effort to instill right belief and strengthen support. Both sultans invested in a recharged dynastic mythology and actively converted people—whether marginal or mainstream Muslims, Christians, or Jews—to what was considered an acceptable version of Islam.[15] Instead of compelling or facilitating conversion on the hunt or campaign trail, as had Mehmed IV, Abdülhamid II sent pious religious teachers as missionaries throughout the empire to correct the beliefs of Muslims and convert Muslim heretics (Alevi, bedouin, and Shi'ia) especially in the eastern half of the empire, to Sunni Hanefi Islam.[16] While the targeted population and geographical region of the conversion efforts may have been different, for Mehmed IV was oriented toward the western provinces, Abülhamid II's revival of piety also occurred during a period of crisis and was also linked to conversion. As he faced the crisis of territorial contraction, this sultan tried to purify the lands and people still remaining in his possession.

Abdülhamid II followed a strategy of domination based on legitimacy, whereas the rule of recent Middle Eastern leaders, such as Hafiz al-Asad of Syria, has been based on compliance. Citizen compliance during the al-Asad era in Syria was achieved "through enforced participation in rituals of obeisance." Like his modern counterpart, Mehmed IV engaged in spectacles that had voluntary participants, such as religious conversion ceremonies to represent his power and dominance. Spectacles in which those around him were re-dressed from head to toe in clothes theoretically the sultan's own mobilized bodies for political obedience and made his power plain and obvious.[17] Such body-centered spectacles demonstrated how he exercised power to control his subjects' behavior. By reasserting order through their bodies, the sultan sought to defuse the tension of the period and create an image of stability.[18] Mehmed IV also revised meaningful symbols, such as the ghazi, so as to communicate current political messages, including demonstrating real personal leadership, piety, military prowess, and male virtue in an era when the sultan was expected to be a ceremonial figure of little significance.

Young Mehmed IV as hunter. "Mehmed the Hunter's Imperial Procession: Paintings Commissioned by the 17th Century Swedish Ambassador Claes Rålamb." Exhibition, Pera Museum, Istanbul, Turkey. Photograph by author. Used with permission.

Postscript

Silences and Traces of the Past

On the explanatory panel in the mausoleum complex of Hatice Turhan in Eminönü, Mehmed IV is referred to as "the Hunter," not "the Ghazi." Entering Hatice Turhan's mausoleum one notices first how many cenotaphs fill the main room. Unlike the mausoleum of Suleiman I, with few cenotaphs in the center of the sanctuary, this tomb is chockablock with caskets of princes and sultans. Second, one realizes that the first large cenotaph is that of the mausoleum's patron and main guest, the valide sultan. One has to fully enter the main door before noticing Mehmed IV's turban-topped cenotaph a little behind that of his mother. In death, as in early life, he could not escape her shadow. Despite his years of independent action, he lies next to her in the earth beneath the tomb, the significance of his reign overshadowed by subsequent historical events and silenced by two centuries of history writers.

While in Istanbul completing the writing of this book, I came face to face with a building-size banner advertising an exhibit at the Pera Museum in Istanbul. On the banner, taken from an original 1657–58 oil painting commissioned by Swedish Ambassador Claes Rålamb, a mounted Mehmed IV is accompanied by two hunters on foot bearing bows and quivers of arrows. The sultan sits on a white horse with gold stirrups, saddle, and harness bedecked in precious jewels. Mehmed IV wears a white turban with two ghazi aigrettes, a gold garment beneath a gold and gray-blue silver-brocaded sleeveless cloak, pink trousers, and gold boots. He holds the golden reins in his right hand and looks straight ahead.

White turban, ghazi aigrettes, and weapons for hunting were the most important and intertwined symbols of Mehmed IV's reign. Yet until today only the last has been given prominence, as seen in the name of the exhibition at the Pera Museum, "Mehmed the Hunter's Imperial Procession," and the text accompanying the exhibit describing the ruler as "Sultan Mehmed IV, remembered as Mehmed the Hunter because of his passion for hunting." It is the author's aim that the reader take away a reinterpretation of the significance of hunting (bows and arrows) and an understanding of the importance of conversion (white turban) and ghaza (ghazi aigrettes) during Mehmed IV's era.

Like the sultan that he served during that epoch of constant ghaza, today in Turkey Kara Mustafa Pasha is also not a favored name from the Ottoman past. None of his effects are on display at the Topkapı Palace Museum in Istanbul. Yet today at the Museum of Vienna several remnants of Kara Mustafa Pasha are proudly exhibited. They include a portrait of the forlorn grand vizier, a painting depicting his painful execution, and his battle tent along with captured horse tail standards. Belgrade fell to the Habsburgs in 1688, and with it, the mosque where Kara Mustafa Pasha's corpse had first been buried. The mosque was converted into a church. Monks in a monastery claimed to have dug up and kept one of the grand vizier's rib bones and sent his skull to the Habsburg capital.[1]

Prior to setting out for the ill-fated Vienna campaign, Kara Mustafa Pasha had begun construction of a madrasa complex on the Divan Yolu, the main avenue in the peninsula of Istanbul. Completed in 1684, it became the final resting place of the former grand vizier's skeleton. Today the main room and dome of the madrasa appear as if about to fall down; the outside is overgrown with weeds. The dome looks like a cap placed over flowing locks of curly green hair. The madrasa is the home of the Yahya Kemal Museum and Bookstore devoted to the works of the famous poet who once served as Turkish ambassador to Warsaw, today's capital of the country whose king had been responsible for the Ottoman defeat in 1683 that caused Kara Mustafa Pasha's execution. The library was established by the Istanbul Conquest Committee, a group formed on the four hundredth anniversary of the Ottoman conquest of Constantinople. Traces of one successful conquest overshadow the unsuccessful campaign led by Kara Mustafa Pasha.

Some of the insufficiently small cannons from Kara Mustafa Pasha's siege of Vienna, whose belching smoke and dull boom had articulated the Ottoman attempt to take the city in 1683, thereafter signaled a different intention. They were melted down and reshaped into the bell of Saint Stephan's Cathedral, the massive church whose spires tower over the inner city. The tide was turning.

Rather than the call to prayer silencing the peal of church bells, as at Bozca Island, Crete, and Kamaniça, a church bell replaced the roar of Ottoman cannons, which would never again threaten one of the most important central European cities, the capital of the Habsburg Empire. Surviving the siege also is a crescent-shaped, brass, gilded ornament, which had been placed atop the highest tower of Saint Stephan's in the early sixteenth century. Its inscription reads in Latin, "This in your memory, Suleiman. Anno 1529."

Following an era in which many places were converted in Muslims' favor, by the turn of the eighteenth century the opposite process of the Christianization of Muslim spaces predominated. Little sign remained of Mehmed IV's conquest of Kamaniça. A single tall minaret that remained after the Ottomans lost the citadel and city to the Polish king was topped with a three-meter-high statue of Mary, symbolizing the re-Christianization of Islamized places.[2] Just as Muslims had disinterred the Christian dead when they took the city, Christians disgraced the buried Muslims after the citadel's reconquest. That the Ottoman Empire was a European empire and was considered one by its contemporaries, and that it had been part of the European political order for centuries, would be forgotten after late nineteenth-century treaties took away most Ottoman territory in southeastern Europe.[3]

Unlike success in battle, which is easily reversed, conversion may have had a more durable outcome, if not always the one the converters originally intended. Purification can never really succeed, for purification movements inevitably produce new hybrids.[4] The Kadızadeli interpretation of Islam condemned any sign of the reconciliation or fusion of diverse beliefs and practices. Despite the aims of these religious reformers, one of the most long-lasting consequences of Mehmed IV's era may have been the creation of communities of descendants of seventeenth-century Christian and Jewish converts to Islam that either maintained religious beliefs and engaged in practices that combined elements of the original and adopted faiths, or created new religions following their ostensible conversion experience. The converters' and converteds' aims of conversion can be radically different; conversion is not a one-way street, as converts shape their religion in light of their own interpretation. Mehmed IV thought that he had converted the messianic claimant Shabbatai Tzevi into Aziz Mehmed Efendi, a proselytizing force for Islam. His actions and those of his followers, however, provide another example of the fleeting effects and ultimate unraveling of Mehmed IV's successes.

The Shabbatean movement was not quenched. Despite being a Muslim after his conversion, Aziz Mehmed Efendi continued to engage in Kabbalah. He encouraged his followers to retain a belief in his messianic calling and practice the Kabbalistic rituals and prayers that he taught them. Antoine Galland claims that he and his converted followers visited synagogues in Istanbul and prayed in Hebrew.[5] He was even seen wearing a Jewish skullcap and phylacteries. The canonically required four Muslim witnesses testified that they observed that Aziz Mehmed Efendi continued to practice Judaism despite dressing as a Muslim, and thus again stirred trouble when the Ottomans were in the midst of a military campaign, this time in Poland. But the sultan, for the second time, despite the convert's apostasy, spared him execution. Aziz Mehmed Efendi was instead exiled to Ülgün (Dulcigno or Ulcinj) on the Adriatic in Albania in 1673.[6] Before he died several years later, he married a Jewish woman from Salonica whose brother consolidated the first community of followers.[7]

After overcoming the shock of his conversion to Islam, most of the Jewish followers converted back to normative Judaism. A second smaller group of followers ostensibly continued to live as Jews, but as late as the eighteenth century their descendants continued to believe Aziz Mehmed Efendi was a prophet and to practice the rituals he had taught. For the final group, however, which coalesced in Salonica, the radical failure of their prophet led not to disappointment, but to rationalization, confirmation, acceptance of the paradox of the rabbi's conversion, renewed confidence, and the ecstasy of knowing that one cannot know the mysteries of God's chosen. They readily accepted the messiah's explanations for his act, that conversion was a temporary punishment for Jews because they had not recognized the true God that he had discovered, and redoubled their belief in the prophet by also converting to Islam.[8] Having come this far and severing many social ties in the process, they continued the movement centered on the former Shabbatai Tzevi with a new name and new practices.

Members of this group called themselves *Ma'aminim* (Hebrew, "believers"); Muslims called them *Dönme* (Turkish, "those who turn," "converts"). They continued to possess distinct beliefs and enact unique rituals into the twentieth century. Unlike Jews, the Ma'aminim ostensibly followed the requirements of Islam, including fasting at Ramadan and praying in mosques, one of which they built. Unlike Muslims, the Ma'aminim maintained a belief that the former Shabbatai Tzevi was the messiah, practiced Kabbalistic rituals, and recited prayers in Hebrew and Judeo-Spanish. They married only among themselves, maintained detailed genealogies, and buried their dead in distinct cemeteries. As the Ottoman Empire collapsed, the Ma'aminim were compelled to settle in Istanbul.[9] Thousands of corpses lie today in their major cemetery in the city, a short minibus ride away from Vaniköy, the village on the Bosporus given to Mehmed IV's preacher. The descendants of those who found a syncretistic resolution to seventeenth-century religious trends and the heirs of Vani Mehmed Efendi reside together in modern Istanbul.

Notes

INTRODUCTION

1. The link between internal conviction and social action is made in Nimrod Hurvitz, "From Scholarly Circles to Mass Movements: The Formation of Legal Communities in Islamic Societies," *American Historical Review* 108, no. 4 (October 2003): 1001. Hurvitz quotes Max Weber, *The Sociology of Religion* (1963; Boston: Beacon Press, 1993), 164: "Religious virtuosity, in addition to subjecting the natural drives to a systematic patterning of life, always leads to the control of relationships within communal life . . . and leads further to an altogether radical religious and ethical criticism."

2. Webb Keane, *Christian Moderns: Freedom and Fetish in the Mission Encounter* (Berkeley: University of California Press, 2007), 76–77.

3. Orhan Şaik Gökyay, *Evliya Çelebi Seyahatnâmesi, 1 Kitap: Istanbul*, Topkapı Sarayı Bağdat 304 Yazmasının Transkripsiyonu-Dizini (Istanbul: Yapı Kredi Yayınları, 1996), 114.

4. Silahdar Fındıklılı Mehmed Ağa, *Silahdar Tarihi*, 2 vols. (Istanbul: Devlet Matbaası, 1928), 1:101.

5. Ibid., 1:102.

6. Karaçelebizade Abdülaziz Efendi, *Ravzatü'l-ebrâr zeyli* (Tahlîl ve Metin), 1732, ed. Nevzat Kaya (Ankara: Türk Tarihi Kurumu Basımevi, 2003), 25, 44.

7. Mehmed Halife, *Tarih-i Gilmani*, Topkapı Saray Museum Library, MS. Revan 1306, fol. 91b. Ottoman chronicle writers used the term *padishah* (emperor) to refer to the ruler. I have chosen to use the word "sultan," as it is more familiar to readers.

8. Ahmed Dede ibn Lutfullah, *Jami' al-Duwal fi al-Tarikh*, Suleimaniye Library, MS. Esad Efendi 2101–2103, fol. 772b.

9. My understanding of religious conversion has been especially influenced by the work of William James, A. D. Nock, Eugene Gallagher, Lewis Rambo, and Gauri Viswanathan, and by conversations with converts to pietistic movements within their given religion and those who have become Bahai, Buddhist, Christian, Jewish, and Muslim.

10. *Encyclopaedia of Islam*, new ed. (hereafter cited as *EI²*), s.v. "Īmān," by L. Gardet.

11. A. D. Nock, *Conversion: The Old and the New in Religion from Alexander the Great to Augustine of Hippo* (1933; Baltimore: Johns Hopkins University Press, 1998), 7.

12. Robert Hefner, "Introduction: World Building and the Rationality of Conversion," in *Conversion to Christianity: Historical and Anthropological Perspectives on a Great Transformation*, ed. Robert Hefner (Berkeley: University of California Press, 1993), 17.

13. Lewis Rambo, *Understanding Religious Conversion* (New Haven, CT: Yale University Press, 1993), 116–17.

14. Ibid., 137–41.

15. Ibid., 113–23.

16. For examples of this process, see Eliza Kent, *Converting Women: Gender and Protestant Christianity in Colonial South India* (New York: Oxford University Press, 2004).

17. William James, *The Varieties of Religious Experience: A Study in Human Nature* (1902; Cambridge, MA: Harvard University Press, 1985), 42.

18. Ibid., 381; Gauri Viswanathan, *Outside the Fold: Conversion, Modernity, and Belief* (Princeton, NJ: Princeton University Press, 1998), 83–86. See also Eugene Gallagher, *Expectation and Experience: Explaining Religious Conversion* (Atlanta, GA: Scholars Press, 1990), 11–38.

19. Kent, *Converting Women*, 241.

20. Rambo, *Understanding Religious Conversion*, 66–75, 87–101.

21. On the role of the magistrates, see Marc Baer, "Islamic Conversion Narratives of Women: Social Change and Gendered Religious Hierarchy in Early Modern Ottoman Istanbul," *Gender and History* 16, no. 2 (August 2004): 425–58.

22. John Lofland and Norman Skonovd, "Conversion Motifs," *Journal for the Scientific Study of Religion* 20 (1981): 379–80; Lorne Dawson, "Who Joins New Religious Movements and Why: Twenty Years of Research and What Have We Learned?" in *Cults and New Religious Movements: A Reader*, ed. Lorne Dawson (Malden, MA: Blackwell, 2003), 116–30.

23. Nock, *Conversion*, 77.

24. Christopher M. Clark, *The Politics of Conversion: Missionary Protestantism and the Jews in Prussia 1728–1941* (Oxford: Clarendon Press, 1995), 61, 99; Michael Khodarkovsky, *Russia's Steppe Frontier: The Making of a Colonial Empire, 1500–1800* (Bloomington: Indiana University Press, 2002), 193–96.

25. Stewart Gordon, "A World of Investiture," in *Robes and Honor: The Medieval World of Investiture*, ed. Stewart Gordon (New York: Palgrave, 2001), 15.

26. Michael Sells, *Approaching the Qur'an: The Early Revelations* (Ashland, OR: White Cloud Press, 1999), 8. As Muhammad had bestowed his cloak on an early convert, caliphs and then Persian and Turkish rulers, taking over where Sassanid and

Byzantine emperors left off, conferred their own cloaks to honor subordinates. The practice of giving one's garment eventually was replaced by the bestowal of sumptuous garments produced for the purpose that were used to appoint, promote, and reward distinguished service. Although no longer clothing that the sovereign had actually worn, these garments conferred honor and recognition on those who received them. See *EI²*, s.v. "Khil'a," by Norman Stillman; Paula Sanders, *Ritual, Politics, and the City in Fatimid Cairo* (Albany: State University of New York Press, 1994), 29–30, 78, 128, 186; Paula Sanders, "Robes of Honor in Fatimid Egypt," in Stewart, *Robes and Honor*, 225–39; Karl Stowasser, "Manners and Customs at the Mamluk Court," *Muqarnas* 2 (1984): 13–20; Carl Petry, "Robing Ceremonials in Late Mamluk Egypt: Hallowed Traditions, Shifting Protocols," in Stewart, *Robes and Honor*, 353–77; İsmail Erünsal, "II. Bâyezid Devrine Ait Bir İn'âmât Defteri," *Tarih Enstitüsu Dergisi* 12 (1981–82): 303–42.

27. Viswanathan, *Outside the Fold*, xi.

28. Clark, *The Politics of Conversion*, 88.

29. Ibid.

30. James Muldoon, "Introduction: The Conversion of Europe," in *Varieties of Religious Conversion in the Middle Ages*, ed. James Muldoon (Gainesville: University Press of Florida, 1997), 5; Richard Fletcher, *The Barbarian Conversion: From Paganism to Christianity* (Berkeley: University of California Press, 1999), 237, 242.

31. The three terms are interrelated. Place denotes a specific, definite location. Landscape denotes a site encountered as a sight. Space can be conceived either as the area defined by a network of places or a practiced place, the daily practices of people in a place. Thus Eminönü, a district in Istanbul, is a bounded place that one can find on a map, a landscape when viewed from the sea with its telltale buildings, and a space in which people engage in practices such as worshipping at houses of prayer. See W. J. T. Mitchell, "Space, Place, and Landscape," in *Landscape and Power*, ed. W. J. T. Mitchell, 2nd ed. (Chicago: University of Chicago Press, 2002), vii–xii.

32. Sufis, known more for their bringing people of different faiths together, could be instrumental in demolishing churches and monasteries. See Tamer el-Leithy, "Sufis, Copts and the Politics of Piety: Moral Regulation in Fourteenth-Century Upper Egypt," in *Le développement du soufisme en Égypte à l'époque mamelouke*, ed. Richard McGregor, Cahier des Annales islamologiques 27 (Cairo: Institut français d'archéologie orientale, 2006), 75–119.

33. Ethel Sara Wolper, *Cities and Saints: Sufism and the Transformation of Urban Space in Medieval Anatolia* (University Park: Pennsylvania State University Press, 2003); Jamsheed Choksy, *Conflict and Cooperation: Zoroastrian Subalterns and Muslim Elites in Medieval Iranian Society* (New York: Columbia University Press, 1997), 93–106; Richard Eaton, *The Rise of Islam and the Bengal Frontier, 1204–1760* (Berkeley: University of California Press, 1993), 228–47.

34. Samuel Y. Edgerton, *Theaters of Conversion: Religious Architecture and Indian Artisans in Colonial Mexico* (Albuquerque: University of New Mexico Press, 2001).

35. Ibid., 2. In medieval Anatolia, Sufis emphasized the Christian genealogy of formerly Christian sites and structures reused as dervish lodges, incorporated Christian

practices into rituals held in these buildings, and promoted Christianity as a transitional phase to the true religious path. The dervish lodge served to "assimilate different forms of religious expression and formed them into a new ideological system that allowed for a plurality of shared beliefs and practices." Wolper, *Cities and Saints*, 74–81, 98.

36. John Howe, "The Conversion of the Physical World: The Creation of a Christian Landscape," in Muldoon, *Varieties of Religious Conversion in the Middle Ages*, 67.

37. During this process, at first the new beliefs or gods or practices could be included and accepted by locals at their shrines, then over time they become identified with or merge with local ones, and finally, they displace or replace them. Eaton, *The Rise of Islam and the Bengal Frontier*, 269–90.

38. Howe, "The Conversion of the Physical World," 66, 69.

39. Here I am speaking of external societal crises, not internal psychological problems. Spyros Vyronis Jr.'s study *The Decline of Medieval Hellenism in Asia Minor and the Process of Islamization from the Eleventh through the Fifteenth Century* (Berkeley: University of California Press, 1971) is based on the premise that Muslim conquest led to crisis among the Orthodox Christians of Anatolia, which facilitated their conversion to Islam. For the relation of crisis at the societal level (social and political disintegration) to conversion in general, see Rambo, *Understanding Religious Conversion*, 44–55.

40. Nock, *Conversion*, 99.

41. Jean Comaroff and John Comaroff, "Christianity and Colonialism in South Africa," *American Ethnologist* 13 (1986): 1–22.

42. The converters may translate indigenous religious terms in contemptuous ways, or decide not to translate terms from their own religion. See Sabine MacCormack, *Religion in the Andes: Vision and Imagination in Early Colonial Peru* (Princeton, NJ: Princeton University Press, 1991); Vicente Rafael, *Contracting Colonialism: Translation and Christian Conversion in Tagalog Society under Early Spanish Rule* (Durham, NC: Duke University Press, 1993); Devin DeWeese, *Islamization and Native Religion in the Golden Horde: Baba Tükles and Conversion to Islam in Historical and Epic Tradition* (University Park: Pennsylvania State University Press, 1994).

43. DeWeese, *Islamization and Native Religion in the Golden Horde*, 23–24.

44. Rambo, *Understanding Religious Conversion*, 173; Peter Hardy, "Modern European and Muslim Explanations of Conversion to Islam in South Asia: A Preliminary Survey of the Literature," in *Conversion to Islam*, ed. Nehemia Levtzion (New York: Holmes and Meier, 1979), 98.

45. Nehemia Levtzion, "Toward a Comparative Study of Islamization," in Levtzion, *Conversion to Islam*, 7.

46. James Sandos, *Converting California: Indians and Franciscans in the Missions* (New Haven, CT: Yale University Press, 2004); William B. Taylor, "Two Shrines of the Cristo Renovado: Religion and Peasant Politics in Late Colonial Mexico," *American Historical Review* 110 (October 2005): 945–74. Apostasy is the flip side of conversion. One finds a theoretical discussion of apostasy in the legal opinions of religious authorities, and sometimes the mention of the execution of apostates in records of the imperial council. Yet one is harder pressed to find mention of apostasy in chronicles since it was so difficult for writers to imagine Muslims willingly leaving Islam.

47. Mustafa Naima, *Tarih-i Naima, Ravzat ül-Hüseyn fi hulasat-i ahbar el-hafikayn*, 6 vols. (Istanbul: Matbaa-yi Âmire, 1864); Silahdar, *Silahdar Tarihi*; *İslam Ansiklopedisi*, s.v. "Mehmed IV," by Cavid M. Baysun, 556. See also A. N. Kurat, "The Reign of Mehmed IV, 1648–87," in *A History of the Ottoman Empire to 1730: Chapters from* The Cambridge History of Islam *and* The New Cambridge Modern History, by V. J. Parry, H. Inalcik, A. N. Kurat, and J. S. Bromley, ed. M. A. Cook (New York: Cambridge University Press, 1976), 162; A. D. Alderson, *The Structure of the Ottoman Dynasty* (1956; Westport, CT: Greenwood Press, 1982), 65–66; Rifa'at Ali Abou-El-Haj, *The 1703 Rebellion and the Structure of Ottoman Politics* (Leiden: Nederlands Instituut voor het Nabije Oosten, 1984), 90; Özdemir Nutku, *IV. Mehmet'in Edirne Şenliği, 1675*, 2nd ed. (Ankara: Türk Tarih Kurumu Basımevi, 1987); İsmail Hakkı Uzunçarşılı, *Osmanlı Tarihi*, 3 (1), 3rd ed. (Ankara: Türk Tarih Kurumu Basımevi, 1983), 366; Reşad Ekrem Koçu, *Osmanlı Padişahları* (1960; Istanbul: Doğan Kitap, 2002), 315–16; Stanford J. Shaw, *History of the Ottoman Empire and Modern Turkey*, 2 vols, vol. 1: *Empire of the Gazis: The Rise and Decline of the Ottoman Empire, 1280–1808* (New York: Cambridge University Press, 1976), 219.

48. If I have erred when responding to overly dismissive and disparaging historiography, I have erred on the side of being sympathetic to the main subjects of the study, Mehmed IV and those nearest him.

49. See Gabriel Piterberg, *An Ottoman Tragedy: History and Historiography at Play* (Berkeley: University of California Press, 2003), 10–14, 148–50; Colin Imber, *The Ottoman Empire, 1300–1650: The Structure of Power* (Hampshire, UK: Palgrave Macmillan, 2002), 321–22; Gülrü Necipoğlu, *Architecture, Ceremonial, and Power: The Topkapı Palace in the Fifteenth and Sixteenth Centuries* (Cambridge, MA: MIT Press, 1991), 16, 26, 30, 102–6, 175; Nicholas Vatin and Gilles Veinstein, *Le Sérail ébranlé: Essai sur les morts, depositions et avènements des sultans ottomans (XIVe–XIXe siècle)* (Paris: Fayard, 2003), 185–92.

50. Imber, *The Ottoman Empire*, and Daniel Goffman, *The Ottoman Empire and Early Modern Europe* (New York: Cambridge University Press, 2002), like Leslie Peirce's *The Imperial Harem: Women and Sovereignty in the Ottoman Empire* (New York: Oxford University Press, 1993) before them, do not extend their analyses past 1656. Donald Quataert, *The Ottoman Empire, 1700–1922* (New York: Cambridge University Press, 2000), begins with a quick overview but devotes three quarters of the book to the nineteenth century. Mehmed IV appears in these modern texts as a hapless minor deserving of only two or three mentions.

51. Norman Itzkowitz, *Ottoman Empire and Islamic Tradition* (Chicago: University of Chicago Press, 1972), 38; Halil Inalcik, "The Emergence of the Ottomans," in *The Cambridge History of Islam*, ed. P. M. Holt, Ann K. S. Lambton and Bernard Lewis (New York: Cambridge University Press, 1970), 1:283.

52. See, for example, Feridun Emecen, "From the Founding to Küçük Kaynarca," in *History of the Ottoman State, Society and Civilisation*, ed. Ekmeleddin İhsanoğlu, 2 vols. (Istanbul: Research Centre for Islamic History, Art and Culture, 2001), 1:3–62; 6–8, in which he argues that ghaza was an Islamic military campaign against the Byzantines and that this ghaza/jihad worldview was the prevalent ideology of the first Ottomans. He does not mention Ottoman campaigns against Muslims nor Christian allies of the Ottomans.

53. Pál Fodor, "Ahmedī's Dāsitān as a Source of Early Ottoman History," in *In Quest of the Golden Apple: Imperial Ideology, Politics, and Military Administration in the Ottoman Empire*, Analecta Isisiana 45 (Istanbul: Isis Press, 2000), 9–22.

54. Cemal Kafadar, *Between Two Worlds: The Construction of the Ottoman State* (Berkeley: University of California Press, 1995).

55. Heath Lowry, *The Nature of the Early Ottoman State* (Albany: State University of New York Press, 2003). Lowry echoes Quataert, who wrote, "Christians as well as Muslims followed the Ottomans not for God but for gold and glory—for the riches to be gained, the positions and power to be won." Quataert, *The Ottoman Empire, 1700–1922*, 18.

56. Şinasi Tekin, "XIV. Yüzyılda Yazılmış Gazilik Tarikası 'Gâziliğin Yolları' Adlı Bir Eski Anadolu Türkçesi Metni ve Gazâ Cihâd Kavramları Hakkında," *Journal of Turkish Studies* 13 (1989): 144. See also Colin Imber, "What Does *Ghazi* Actually Mean?" in *The Balance of Truth: Essays in Honour of Professor Geoffrey Lewis*, ed. Çiğdem Balım-Harding and Colin Imber (Istanbul: Isis Press, 2000), 165–78.

57. Paul Wittek, *The Rise of the Ottoman Empire* (London: Royal Asiatic Society, 1938), 14–15, 38. I do not disagree with Wittek's basic assessment, although Kafadar's more nuanced reworking of his thesis is more convincing than the original argument.

58. Vryonis, *The Decline of Medieval Hellenism*; Spyros Vyronis Jr., "Religious Change and Continuity in the Balkans and Anatolia from the Fourteenth through the Sixteenth Century," in *Studies on Byzantium, Seljuks, and Ottomans: Reprinted Studies* (Malibu, CA: Undena, 1981), 137; V. L. Ménage, "The Islamization of Anatolia," in Levtzion, *Conversion to Islam*, 52–67; Kafadar, *Between Two Worlds*, 62–90; F. W. Hasluck, *Christianity and Islam under the Sultans*, ed. Margaret Hasluck, 2 vols. (1929; New York: Octagon Books, 1973); Michel Balivet, *Byzantins et Ottomans: Relations, interaction, succession*, Analecta Isisiana 35 (Istanbul: Les Éditions Isis, 1999), 53.

59. Ömer Lütfi Barkan, "Osmanlı İmparatorluğunda Bir İskan ve Kolonizasyon Metodu Olarak Vakıflar ve Temlikler I: İstila Devirlerinin Kolonizatör Türk Dervişleri ve Zaviyeler," *Vakıflar Dergisi* 2 (1942): 279–386.

60. Nathalie Clayer, *Mystiques, état et société: Les Halvetis dans l'aire balkanique de la fin du XVe siècle à nos jours*, Islamic History and Civilization, Studies and Texts 9 (New York: Brill, 1994); Irène Mélikoff, *Hadji Bektach: Un mythe et ses avatars. Genèse et évolution du soufisme populaire en Turquie* (Leiden: Brill, 1998); *EI2*, s.v. "Bektashiyya," by R. Tschudi; John Kingsley Birge, *The Bektashi Order of Dervishes* (London: Luzac, 1937).

61. Itzkowitz, *Ottoman Empire and Islamic Tradition*, 59–61.

62. *EI²*, s.v. "Devshirme," by V. L. Ménage; *EI²*, s.v. "Ghulam-Ottoman Empire," by Halil Inalcik; Itzkowitz, *Ottoman Empire and Islamic Tradition*, 49–53.

63. Ménage, "The Islamization of Anatolia," 65–66.

64. Çigdem Kafesçioğlu, "The Ottoman Capital in the Making: The Reconstruction of Constantinople in the Fifteenth Century" (PhD diss., Harvard University, 1996), 5–6. Chapters 2 ("Reckoning with Kostantiniyya: The First Years of Ottoman Rule") and 3 ("Constructing the City: The Architectual Projects") are most relevant for these themes.

65. Gülrü Necipoğlu, *The Age of Sinan: Architectural Culture in the Ottoman Empire* (London: Reaktion Books, 2005), 61–68.

66. For example, in 1587 the seat of the Orthodox Christian patriarchate was forced to move when the sultan ordered the conversion of the Church of Pammakaristos into Fethiye (Victory) Mosque following Ottoman campaigns against the Safavids. Caroline Finkel, *Osman's Dream: The Story of the Ottoman Empire, 1300–1923* (New York: Basic Books, 2005), 192.

67. Osman Çetin, *Sicillere Göre Bursa'da İhtida Hareketleri ve Sosyal Sonuçları (1472–1909)* (Ankara: Türk Tarih Kurumu Basımevi, 1994); Heath Lowry, *Trabzon Şehrinin İslamlaşması ve Türkleşmesi 1461–1583*, trans. Demet Lowry and Heath Lowry, 2nd ed. (Istanbul: Boğaziçi Üniversitesi Yayınevi, 1998); Anton Minkov, *Conversion to Islam in the Balkans: Kisve Bahası Petitions and Ottoman Social Life, 1670–1730* (Leiden: Brill, 2004).

68. Minkov, *Conversion to Islam in the Balkans*, 110.

69. Legal sources include collections of legal responses of the sheikhulislams; law codes; "The Statute of the New Muslim"; and Islamic law court records from the Beşiktaş, Galata, Hasköy, Istanbul, and Yeniköy districts of Istanbul. Archival and other sources include petitions addressed by commoners to the sultan; palace payroll registers; petitions of the imperial secretary; imperial writs; registers of the bestowals of cloaks by the court; decisions of the imperial council; and treatises composed by the sultan's preachers. Epigraphic and visual sources include tombstone and mausoleum inscriptions and the inscriptions in the main mosque and tomb complex built in Istanbul as well as other mosque inscriptions inscribed during this period. Endowment deeds of new mosques were also examined, as were Ottoman miniature depictions of Mehmed IV made over the course of the reign of the sultan, stock characters in Ottoman society, and European prints.

70. Quataert, *The Ottoman Empire, 1700–1922*, 1–12; Goffman, *The Ottoman Empire and Early Modern Europe*, 1–20, 192–234.

71. Goffman, *The Ottoman Empire and Early Modern Europe*, 233, 224–25.

CHAPTER 1

1. Katip Çelebi, *Fezleke*, 2 vols. (Istanbul: Ceride-i Havadis Matbaası, 1286/1869), 2:327; Naima, *Tarih-i Naima*, 4:305.

2. Anonymous, "Valide Sultan/la Maore Regina," Staatliche Museen zu Berlin, Preußischer Kulturbesitz, Kunstbibliothek, Lipperheide OZ 52, 68.

3. Katip Çelebi, *Fezleke*, 2:329.

4. Karaçelebizade, *Ravzatü'l-ebrâr zeyli*, 2.

5. Katip Çelebi, *Fezleke* 2:329; Ahmed Dede, *Jami' al-Duwal*, fol. 772a.

6. Naima, *Tarih-i Naima*, 4:325.

7. Peirce, *The Imperial Harem*, 263–64.

8. Karaçelebizade, *Ravzatü'l-ebrâr zeyli*, 4.

9. Ibid., 3.

10. Katip Çelebi, *Fezleke*, 2:329.

11. Karaçelebizade, *Ravzatü'l-ebrâr zeyli*, 4.

12. Mehmed Hemdani Solakzade, *Tarih-i Al-i Osman*, Topkapı Palace Museum Library, MS. Ahmed III 3078, fol. 467a.

13. Karaçelebizade, *Ravzatü'l-ebrâr zeyli*, 4.

14. Karaçelebizade, *Ravzatü'l-ebrâr zeyli*, 5; Solakzade, *Tarih-i Al-i Osman*, fol. 467a; Vecihi Hasan Çelebi, *Tarih-i Vecihi*, Topkapı Palace Museum Library, MS. Revan 1153, fol. 47b; Mehmed Halife, *Tarih-i Gilmani*, fol. 17b.

15. Solakzade, *Tarih-i Al-i Osman*, fol. 469a.

16. Mehmed Halife, *Tarih-i Gilmani*, fol. 18a.

17. Anonymous, "Sipachi/Soldato a Cavallo," Staatliche Museen zu Berlin, Preußischer Kulturbesitz, Kunstbibliothek, Lipperheide OZ 52, 52; Anonymous, "Jeniceri/Gianicaro Soldato a piedi," Staatliche Museen zu Berlin, Preußischer Kulturbesitz, Kunstbibliothek, Lipperheide OZ 52, 53.

18. Solakzade, *Tarih-i Al-i Osman*, fol. 469a.

19. Katip Çelebi, *Fezleke* 2:334–37; Karaçelebizade, *Ravzatü'l-ebrâr zeyli*, 17; Naima, *Tarih-i Naima*, 4:370; Solakzade, *Tarih-i Al-i Osman*, fol. 469a.

20. Mehmed Halife, *Tarih-i Gilmani*, fol. 18b.

21. Gökyay, *Evliya Çelebi Seyahatnâmesi*, 114.

22. Abdi Efendi, *Sur-name-i Sultan Mehmed ibn Ibrahim Han*, Topkapı Palace Museum Library, Istanbul, MS. Revan 823, fols. 16b–17a; Mübahat S. Kütükoğlu, ed., *Osmanlılarda Narh Müessesesi ve 1640 Tarihli Narh Defteri*, Enderun Yayınları 13 (Istanbul: Ünal Matbaası, 1983), 356.

23. Abdurrahman Abdi Pasha, "Osmanlı Kanûnnâmeleri," *Millî Tetebbu'lar Mecmû'ası* 1, no. 2 (Temmuz-Ağustos 1331/1912): 529.

24. Karaçelebizade, *Ravzatü'l-ebrâr zeyli*, 6.

25. Necipoğlu, *Architecture, Ceremonial, and Power*, 11–12. While the ideology behind the term was unchanging, referring to conquest of the leading Christian empire in order to rule the world, the target kept changing, from Constantinople to Rome, Budapest, and, finally, Vienna. See Pál Fodor, "Ungarn und Wien in der osmanischen Eroberungsideologie (im Spiegel der *Târîh-i Beç krâlı*, 17. Jahrhundert)," in Fodor, *In Quest of the Golden Apple*, 52–53.

26. Karaçelebizade, *Ravzatü'l-ebrâr zeyli*, 7.

27. Anonymous, "Sultan Mechemet Imp. de'Turchi," Staatliche Museen zu Berlin, Preußischer Kulturbesitz, Kunstbibliothek, Berlin, Lipperheide OZ 52, 1.

28. Karaçelebizade, *Ravzatü'l-ebrâr zeyli*, 7.

29. Solakzade, *Tarih-i Al-i Osman*, fol. 467b.

30. Vatin and Veinstein, *Le Sérail ébranlé*, 305–20.

31. Katip Çelebi, *Fezleke*, 2:329; Karaçelebizade, *Ravzatü'l-ebrâr zeyli*, 9; Naima, *Tarih-i Naima*, 4:334.

32. Ahmed Dede, *Jami' al-Duwal*, fol. 772b.

33. Robert Mantran, "Un document sur la cizye a Istanbul a la fin du XVIIe siècle," *Journal of Turkish Studies* 11 (1987): 11–15. According to Ottoman poll tax records, there were 62,000 Christian and Jewish households in Istanbul in 1690–91, of which 80 percent were Christian. If Christians and Jews made up 42 percent of the city's population, as they had in the previous century, then one can estimate that there were 86,000 Muslim households in the city. One can then approximate a population of between 600,000 and 750,000, including 200,000 to 250,000 Christians and 50,000

to 60,000 Jews. Robert Mantran, *Istanbul dans la seconde moitié du XVIIe siècle: Essai d'histoire institutionnelle, économique et sociale* (Paris: Librairie Adrien Maisonneuve, 1962), 25, 44–47.

34. Eremya Çelebi Kömürciyan, *İstanbul Tarihi: XVII Asırda İstanbul*, trans. Hrand D. Andreasyan, 2nd ed. (Istanbul: Eren, 1988), 39.

35. Gökyay, *Evliya Çelebi Seyahatnâmesi*, 193, 195–96. He used the same phrase, "*Yahûdîler ile mālā-māldır*," in describing Hasköy.

36. Halil Inalcik, "Ottoman Galata, 1453–1553," in *Essays in Ottoman History* (Istanbul: Eren, 1998), 275–99, 349–50.

37. Eremya Çelebi, *İstanbul Tarihi*, 14–15; Gökyay, *Evliya Çelebi Seyahatnâmesi*, 261.

38. Eremya Çelebi, *İstanbul Tarihi*, 15.

39. Gökyay, *Evliya Çelebi Seyahatnâmesi*, 261.

40. Stéphane Yerasimos, "La Communauté juive d'Istanbul a la fin du XVIe siècle," *Turcica* 27 (1995): 119–20, 124.

41. Lucienne Thys-Şenocak, "The Yeni Valide Mosque Complex of Eminönü, Istanbul (1597–1665): Gender and Vision in Ottoman Architecture," in *Women, Patronage, and Self-Representation in Islamic Societies*, ed. D. Fairchild Ruggles (Albany: State University of New York Press, 2000), 62–63; Kürd Hatib Mustafa, *Risāle-i Kürd Hatīb*, Topkapı Palace Museum Library, MS. Eski Hazine 1400, fols. 18a–b.

42. Oktay Aslanapa, *Osmanlı Devri Mimarîsi: Orhan Gaziden başlıyarak sonuna kadar Padişahlara göre gelişmesi* (Istanbul: İnkılâp Kitabevi, 1986), 197.

43. Imber, *The Ottoman Empire, 1300–1650*, 91; Peirce, "The Display of Sovereign Prerogative," "The Politics of Diplomacy," and "The Exercise of Political Power," in *The Imperial Harem*.

44. Alderson, *The Structure of the Ottoman Dynasty*, 42.

45. Karaçelebizade, *Ravzatü'l-ebrâr zeyli*, 13, 17–18.

46. Imber, *The Ottoman Empire, 1300–1650*, 115–18.

47. Karaçelebizade, *Ravzatü'l-ebrâr zeyli*, 11.

48. Katip Çelebi, *Fezleke*, 2:329–30.

49. Karaçelebizade, *Ravzatü'l-ebrâr zeyli*, 4, 10.

50. Solakzade, *Tarih-i Al-i Osman*, fol. 467b.

51. Katip Çelebi, *Fezleke*, 2:329–30.

52. Karaçelebizade, *Ravzatü'l-ebrâr zeyli*, 12–13, 25.

53. Naima, *Tarih-i Naima*, 4:332.

54. Solakzade, *Tarih-i Al-i Osman*, fol. 467b.

55. Anonymous, "Zelat/Carnefier," Staatliche Museen zu Berlin, Preußischer Kulturbesitz, Kunstbibliothek, Lipperheide OZ 52, 99.

CHAPTER 2

1. Rambo, *Understanding Religious Conversion*, 44, 20, 47.

2. David Lowenthal, *The Past Is a Foreign Country* (New York: Cambridge University Press, 1985), 215.

3. Gabrielle M. Spiegel, *The Past as Text: The Theory and Practice of Medieval Historiography* (Baltimore: Johns Hopkins University Press, 1997), 43, 44–56.

4. Julie Scott Meisami, *Persian Historiography: To the End of the Twelfth Century* (Edinburgh: Edinburgh University Press, 1999), 6.

5. According to Piterberg, *An Ottoman Tragedy*. But see Gottfried Hagen's review of Piterberg, http://www.h-net.org/~turk/ (accessed March 2006).

6. Paul Strohm, *England's Empty Throne, Usurpation and the Language of Legitimation, 1399–1422* (New Haven, CT: Yale University Press, 1998), xi.

7. Meisami, *Persian Historiography*, 11–12.

8. 'Îsâ-zâde, *'Îsâ-zâde Târîhi*, quoted by Naima, *Tarih-i Naima*, 6:362; Karaçelebizade, *Ravzatü'l-ebrâr zeyli*, 227, 244, 267.

9. See Cornell Fleischer, *Bureaucrat and Intellectual in the Ottoman Empire: The Historian Mustafa Âli (1541–1600)* (Princeton, NJ: Princeton University Press, 1986).

10. See Bernard Lewis, "Ottoman Observers of Ottoman Decline," *Islamic Studies* 1, no. 1 (1962): 71–87; Pál Fodor, "State and Society, Crisis and Reform, in 15th–17th Century Ottoman Mirror for Princes," in Fodor, *In Quest of the Golden Apple*, 23–44; Cornell Fleischer, "From Şehzade Korkud to Mustafa Âli: Cultural Origins of the Ottoman Nasihatname," in *Proceedings*, 3rd Congress on the Social and Economic History of Turkey, Princeton University, August 24–26, 1983, ed. Heath Lowry and Ralph S. Hattox (Istanbul: Isis Press, 1989), 67–77; Goffman, *The Ottoman Empire and Early Modern Europe*, 112–27.

11. Itzkowitz, *Ottoman Empire and Islamic Tradition*, 90–91.

12. Halil Inalcik, "Military and Fiscal Transformation in the Ottoman Empire, 1600–1700," *Archivum Ottomanicum* 6 (1980): 283–337.

13. Oktay Özel, "Population Changes in Ottoman Anatolia during the 16th and 17th Centuries: The 'Demographic Crisis' Reconsidered," *International Journal of Middle East Studies* 36 (2004): 188, 194–95.

14. The similar transformation that occurred in the Ottoman, Safavid, and Mughal empires is synthesized in C. A. Bayly, *Imperial Meridian: The British Empire and the World, 1780–1830* (London: Longman, 1989), 16–34.

15. Daniel Goffman, "Izmir: From Village to Colonial Port City," in *The Ottoman City between East and West: Aleppo, Izmir, and Istanbul*, ed. Edhem Eldem, Daniel Goffman, and Bruce Masters (Cambridge: Cambridge University Press, 1999), 79–134.

16. Karaçelebizade, *Ravzatü'l-ebrâr zeyli*, 216, 223.

17. Ibid., 249.

18. Cemal Kafadar, "The Myth of the Golden Age: Ottoman Historical Consciousness in the Post Süleymânic Era," in *Süleymân the Second and His Time*, ed. Halil İnalcik and Cemal Kafadar (Istanbul: Isis Press, 1993), 37–48.

19. Katip Çelebi, *Fezleke*, 2:361.

20. V. J. Parry, "The Period of Murād IV, 1617–48," in Cook, *A History of the Ottoman Empire to 1730*, 139.

21. Ahmed Dede, *Jami' al-Duwal*, fol. 773b.

22. Katip Çelebi, *Fezleke*, 2:369.

23. Solakzade, *Tarih-i Al-i Osman*, fol. 474a; Naima, *Tarih-i Naima*, 5:73.

24. Katip Çelebi, *Fezleke*, 2:369.

25. Robert Dankoff, *The Intimate Life of an Ottoman Statesman: Melek Ahmed Paşa (1588–1662) as portrayed in Evliya Çelebi's Book of Travels (Seyahat-name)*, translation and commentary by Robert Dankoff (Albany: State University of New York Press, 1991), 102.

26. Mehmed Halife, *Tarih-i Gilmani*, fol. 21b.

27. Solakzade, *Tarih-i Al-i Osman*, fol. 475b; Vecihi Hasan Çelebi, *Tarih-i Vecihi*, fol. 63a.

28. Karaçelebizade, *Ravzatü'l-ebrâr zeyli*, 95.

29. Nihadi, *Tarih-i Nihadi*, fol. 158a.

30. Naima, *Tarih-i Naima*, 5:112.

31. Dankoff, *The Intimate Life of an Ottoman Statesman*, 89.

32. Nihadi, *Tarih-i Nihadi*, fol. 158b.

33. Solakzade, *Tarih-i Al-i Osman*, fol. 480b.

34. Naima, *Tarih-i Naima*, 6:99.

35. Gökyay, *Evliya Çelebi Seyahatnâmesi*, 116.

36. Ahmed Dede, *Jami' al-Duwal*, fol. 775a.

37. Karaçelebizade, *Ravzatü'l-ebrâr zeyli*, 189, 191.

38. Ibid., 191–92; Kürd, fol. 5b.

39. Karaçelebizade, *Ravzatü'l-ebrâr zeyli*, 196.

40. Mehmed Halife, *Tarih-i Gilmani*, fols. 27b–29a.

41. Kürd Hatib, *Risāle*, fol. 5b.

42. Karaçelebizade, *Ravzatü'l-ebrâr zeyli*, 199; Vecihi Hasan Çelebi, *Tarih-i Vecihi*, fol. 75b; Naima, *Tarih-i Naima*, 6:98.

43. Mehmed Halife, *Tarih-i Gilmani*, fols. 1b, 35b, 36b.

44. Solakzade, *Tarih-i Al-i Osman*, fol. 487a.

45. Ahmed Dede, *Jami' al-Duwal*, fol. 776a.

46. Katip Çelebi, *Fezleke*, 2:373–74; Abdurrahman Abdi Pasha, *Vekāyi'nāme*, Köprülü Library, Istanbul, MS. 216, fols. 27a–28a.

47. Karaçelebizade, *Ravzatü'l-ebrâr zeyli*, 67.

48. Dankoff, *The Intimate Life of an Ottoman Statesman*, 76–77.

49. Karaçelebizade, *Ravzatü'l-ebrâr zeyli*, 68; Naima, *Tarih-i Naima*, 5:98, 97–98.

50. Karaçelebizade, *Ravzatü'l-ebrâr zeyli*, 69.

51. Katip Çelebi, *Fezleke*, 2:374; Karaçelebizade, *Ravzatü'l-ebrâr zeyli*, 70.

52. Karaçelebizade, *Ravzatü'l-ebrâr zeyli*, 70.

53. Mehmed Halife, *Tarih-i Gilmani*, fol. 21a.

54. Gökyay, *Evliya Çelebi Seyahatnâmesi*, 115; Dankoff, *The Intimate Life of an Ottoman Statesman*, 87.

55. Karaçelebizade, *Ravzatü'l-ebrâr zeyli*, 73.

56. Mehmed Halife, *Tarih-i Gilmani*, fol. 21a.

57. Karaçelebizade, *Ravzatü'l-ebrâr zeyli*, 78.

58. Mehmed Halife, *Tarih-i Gilmani*, fols. 23a, 26b.

59. Ahmed Dede, *Jami' al-Duwal*, fol. 774b.

60. Katip Çelebi, *Fezleke*, 2:385. The original title of the work is *Düstur ül-amel li-islah il-halel*.

61. Karaçelebizade, *Ravzatü'l-ebrâr zeyli*, 134.

62. Naima, *Tarih-i Naima*, 5:282.

63. Karaçelebizade, *Ravzatü'l-ebrâr zeyli*, 184, 187, 214, 215, 184.

64. Ibid., 213, 224, 213.

65. Ibid., 216.

66. Topkapı Palace Museum Archive, Tahriratlar (Dispatches) E. 3890.

67. Karaçelebizade, *Ravzatü'l-ebrâr zeyli*, 222; Naima, *Tarih-i Naima*, 6:341.

68. Karaçelebizade, *Ravzatü'l-ebrâr zeyli*, 213.

69. Şevket Pamuk, "The Disintegration of the Ottoman Monetary System during the Seventeenth Century," *Princeton Papers in Near Eastern Studies* 2 (1993): 67–81.

70. Şevket Pamuk, "In the Absence of Domestic Currency: Debased European Coinage in the Seventeenth-Century Ottoman Empire," *Journal of Economic History* 57, no. 2 (June 1997): 345–66.

71. Such as Ardahan in northeastern Anatolia in 1653. Topkapı Palace Museum Archive, Tahriratlar E. 10267.

72. Jane Hathaway, *The Politics of Households in Ottoman Egypt: The Rise of the Qazdağlıs* (New York: Cambridge University Press, 1997), 14.

73. William Griswold, *The Great Anatolian Rebellion, 1000–1020/1591–1611*, Islamkundliche Untersuchungen Bd. 83 (Freiburg: K. Schwarz Verlag, 1983); Mustafa Akdağ, *Celâlî İsyanları, 1550–1603* (Ankara: Ankara Üniversitesi Basımevi, 1963).

74. Sir Paul Rycaut, *The Present State of the Ottoman Empire* (London: Printed for Tho. Basset, 1687), 82; Karaçelebizade, *Ravzatü'l-ebrâr zeyli*, 115, 179.

75. Mehmed Halife, *Tarih-i Gilmani*, fol. 29a.

76. Karaçelebizade, *Ravzatü'l-ebrâr zeyli*, 33.

77. Ibid., 52; Ahmed Dede, *Jami' al-Duwal*, fol. 773b.

78. The Ottoman budget revealed debits of 687 million aspers and credits of 532 million aspers. Mantran, *Istanbul*, 252.

79. Katip Çelebi, *Fezleke*, 2:297–98, 304, 305.

80. Ibid., 314, 315.

81. Naima, *Tarih-i Naima*, 4:255.

82. Ibid., 4:441.

83. Ibid., 4:261–62.

84. Katip Çelebi, *Fezleke*, 2:319.

85. Naima, *Tarih-i Naima*, 4:265; Ahmed Dede, *Jami' al-Duwal*, fol. 773a.

86. Naima, *Tarih-i Naima*, 5:22.

87. Karaçelebizade, *Ravzatü'l-ebrâr zeyli*, 44, 142.

88. Ibid., 62, 63, 159. In 1655 forces of the governor-general of Buda, besieging an enemy citadel, thinking that fires lit by shepherds were the signs of an enemy camp, fled their positions, causing confusion in the ranks, and then suffered great losses when the actual enemy fired on them. Topkapı Palace Museum Archive, Tahriratlar E. 7645.

89. Karaçelebizade, *Ravzatü'l-ebrâr zeyli*, 64.

90. Ersin Gülsoy, *Girit'in Fethi ve Osmanlı İdaresinin Kurulması, 1645–1670* (Istanbul: Tarih ve Tabiat Vakfı, 2004), 126.

91. Karaçelebizade, *Ravzatü'l-ebrâr zeyli*, 64–65. An admiral who repeatedly failed in battle, pillaged coastal areas, and grounded his great warships on rocks or lost them and hundreds of men to accidental ammunition fires was able to avoid an order for his arrest, obtaining instead a pardon (159–60).

92. Gülsoy, *Girit'in Fethi*, 120–23; Karaçelebizade, *Ravzatü'l-ebrâr zeyli*, 266. One battle in the Dardanelles in 1655 is typical. When the Ottoman admiral gave the order to attack, the Ottoman ships crashed into each other, "leaving those on board bewildered as oar smashed against oar and sail against sail." The Venetians found a breach and attacked fiercely, winning the battle as they seized Ottoman galleons. Abdi Pasha, *Vekâyi'nâme*, fols. 81a–b.

93. Karaçelebizade, *Ravzatü'l-ebrâr zeyli*, 263.

94. Naima, *Tarih-i Naima*, 6:196.

95. Karaçelebizade, *Ravzatü'l-ebrâr zeyli*, 263.

96. Ibid., 236, 239.

97. Solakzade, *Tarih-i Solakzade*, fol. 483b; Mehmed Halife, *Tarih-i Gilmani*, fol. 32a.

98. Karaçelebizade, *Ravzatü'l-ebrâr zeyli*, 254–55, 243.

99. Mehmed Halife, *Tarih-i Gilmani*, fols. 32a–b.

100. Kürd Hatib, *Risâle*, fol. 7a.

101. Karaçelebizade, *Ravzatü'l-ebrâr zeyli*, 275, 285.

102. Naima, *Tarih-i Naima*, 6:210.

103. Karaçelebizade, *Ravzatü'l-ebrâr zeyli*, 283.

104. Katip Çelebi, *Fezleke*, 2:275–76; Naima, *Tarih-i Naima*, 4:191.

105. Karaçelebizade, *Ravzatü'l-ebrâr zeyli*, 143.

106. Kürd Hatib, *Risâle*, fol. 7a.

107. Ahmed Dede, *Jami' al-Duwal*, fol. 776a.

108. Karaçelebizade, *Ravzatü'l-ebrâr zeyli*, 283, 143.

109. Kürd Hatib, *Risâle*, fol. 8a.

110. Solakzade, *Tarih-i Al-i Osman*, fols. 470b–471a; Karaçelebizade, *Ravzatü'l-ebrâr zeyli*, 28; Katip Çelebi, *Fezleke*, 2:343–44.

111. Ahmed Dede, *Jami' al-Duwal*, fol. 773b; Naima, *Tarih-i Naima*, 6:71.

112. Karaçelebizade, *Ravzatü'l-ebrâr zeyli*, 29; Mehmed Halife, *Tarih-i Gilmani*, fol. 19b.

113. Katip Çelebi, *Fezleke*, 2:349.

114. Karaçelebizade, *Ravzatü'l-ebrâr zeyli*, 43–44.

115. Abdi Pasha, *Vekâyi'nâme*, fols. 87b–88a.

116. Karaçelebizade, *Ravzatü'l-ebrâr zeyli*, 221, 233, 61, 62.

117. Silahdar, *Tarih-i Silahdar*, 1:68.

118. Nihadi, *Tarih-i Nihadi*, Topkapı Palace Museum Library, MS. Bağdat 219, fols. 176a–b.

119. Naima, writing well after Mehmed IV's reign, did not include the conversion attempt in his narrative. He entitled his account "The Hanging (or Crucifixion) of the Patriarch." Naima, *Tarih-i Naima*, 6:264. Orthodox Christians also appear in this text as an internal enemy. The author claims that Ottoman authorities discovered dozens

of sets of Janissary clothing in the residence of the patriarch. During the uprisings and fires in Istanbul in the 1650s, "strong infidels wore Janissary dress and caps and looted, daring to betray and harm Muslims."

120. Ibid., 5:320–21.

121. Ibid., 4:397, 5:304.

122. Topkapı Palace Museum Archive, Arzlar (Writs) E. 7002/1 through E. 7002/86.

123. Topkapı Palace Museum Archive, Arzlar, E. 7002/83.

124. Naima, *Tarih-i Naima*, 5:420.

CHAPTER 3

1. Michael Cook, *Commanding Right and Forbidding Wrong in Islamic Thought* (New York: Cambridge University Press, 2000), 13–14.

2. Ibid., 473, 476, 67.

3. Rambo, *Understanding Religious Conversion*, 66.

4. Naima, *Tarih-i Naima*, 5:54–59, 6:227–41; Lewis Thomas, *A Study of Naima*, ed. Norman Itzkowitz (New York: New York University Press, 1972), 106–10.

5. Katip Çelebi, *Fezleke*, 2:182.

6. *Tarikat Muhammadiye* and *Risāle-i Birgili Mehmed*, respectively.

7. Katip Çelebi, *Fezleke*, 2:182.

8. Hurvitz, "From Scholarly Circles to Mass Movements."

9. Halil Inalcik, *The Ottoman Empire: The Classical Age, 1300–1600*, trans. Norman Itzkowitz and Colin Imber (New York: Praeger, 1973), 184. See *Encyclopaedia Iranica*, s.v. "Amr be ma'rūf," by W. Madelung. The phrase *al-amr bi'l-ma'rūf wa'l-nahy 'an al-munkar* appears several times in the Qur'an, such as 3:110: "You are the best community brought forth for mankind, enjoining what is proper and forbidding what is reprehensible and believing in God." Other references are found at 3:104, 7:157, 21:16, and 22:41, where the practice is seen as being equal to prayer in importance. It was institutionalized in Islamic societies in the office of the inspector of markets and morals. The Committee for the Propagation of Virtue and the Prevention of Vice is the Saudi Arabian government ministry employing religious police to enforce Shariah. The Taliban movement in Afghanistan and Pakistan is also based on the principle of commanding right and forbidding wrong.

10. Cook, *Commanding Right and Forbidding Wrong*, 328.

11. Ibid., 321–22; Inalcik, *The Ottoman Empire*, 184.

12. Cook, *Commanding Right and Forbidding Wrong*, 323–24, 325.

13. Madeline Zilfi, *The Politics of Piety: The Ottoman Ulema in the Postclassical Age* (Minneapolis: Bibliotheca Islamica, 1988), 135.

14. Solakzade, *Tarih-i Al-i Osman*, fol. 487b.

15. The phrase Solakzade uses is *salla 'llahu 'aleyhi ve sellam*. Solakzade, *Tarih-i Al-i Osman*, fol. 487b; *Fezleke*, 2:182; Silahdar, *Tarih-i Silahdar*, 1:58. The followers of Kadızade and the followers of Sivasi Efendi also differed on the questions of whether the pharaohs converted to the true faith; whether medieval Sufi Ibn al-Arabi's grave is

blessed; and whether it is appropriate to curse Yazid, who martyred Ali's son Hussein, visit tombs for intercession, or kiss the hand, foot, and skirt and bow to elders and religious leaders. Naima, *Tarih-i Naima*, 6:229–30.

16. Solakzade, *Tarih-i Al-i Osman*, fol. 487a.

17. Mehmed Halife, *Tarih-i Gilmani*, fol. 7b.

18. Dankoff, *The Intimate Life of an Ottoman Statesman*, 85.

19. Mehmed Halife, *Tarih-i Gilmani*, fols. 6b, 6b–7a, 7b.

20. Katip Çelebi, *Fezleke*, 2:197.

21. Solakzade, *Tarih-i Al-i Osman*, fol. 487b.

22. Katip Çelebi, *Fezleke*, 2:182.

23. Silahdar, *Tarih-i Silahdar*, 1:58.

24. Solakzade, *Tarih-i Al-i Osman*, fol. 487b.

25. Ibid.

26. Roy P. Mottahedeh, *Loyalty and Leadership in an Early Islamic Society* (Princeton, NJ: Princeton University Press, 1980), 147.

27. Such as a Nakshibendi-affiliated mosque and madrasa in Diyarbekir. Topkapı Palace Museum Archive, Arzlar E. 7008/17.

28. Robert Dankoff, *An Ottoman Mentality: The World of Evliya Çelebi*, afterword by Gottfried Hagen (Leiden: Brill, 2004), 88.

29. Rycaut, *The Present State of the Ottoman Empire*, 315. Other British writers added a positive gloss; see, for example, Steven Pincus, "Coffee Politicians Does Create: Coffee Houses and Restoration Political Culture," *Journal of Modern History* 67 (1995): 807–34. As an Englishman wrote, "It reason seems that liberty of speech and words should be allowed/where men of differing judgments crowd/and that's a coffee-house, for where/should men discourse so free as there?" Anonymous, *The Character of a Coffee-House* (London, 1661).

30. Katip Çelebi, *Fezleke*, 2:183.

31. Ibid., 2:182.

32. Peirce, *The Imperial Harem*, 24, 144.

33. The original title is *Nasīhât al-mülūk targīben li-hüsn al-sülūk.*

34. The work is entitled *Şifa' al-Mü'min.*

35. Abdi Pasha, *Vekāyi'nāme*, fols. 4b–5a; Karaçelebizade, *Ravzatü'l-ebrâr zeyli*, 13.

36. Naima, *Tarih-i Naima*, 5:54.

37. Dankoff, *An Ottoman Mentality*, 76.

38. On the history of the movement to 1656, see Ahmed Yaşar Ocak, "XVII Yüzyılda Osmanlı İmparatorluğunda Dinde Tasfiye (Püritanizm) Teşebbüslerine Bir Bakış: Kadızâdeliler Hareketi," *Türk Kültürü Araştırmaları* 17–21, nos. 1–2 (1979–83): 208–25; Thomas, *A Study of Naima*, 106–10. For background on the later period (1661–83) of the movement, see Madeline Zilfi, "The Kadızadelis: Discordant Revivalism in Seventeenth-Century Istanbul," *Journal of Near Eastern Studies* 45 (October 1986): 251–69; Zilfi, *The Politics of Piety*, 146–59. See also Gottfried Hagen, "Ottoman Understandings of the World in the Seventeenth Century," in Dankoff, *An Ottoman Mentality*, 244–56. On the link between the Halvetis and the sultans, such as Bayezid II, see *EI²*, s.v. "Khalwatiyya," by F. de Jong.

39. Katip Çelebi, *Fezleke*, 2:396.

40. Karaçelebizade, *Ravzatü'l-ebrâr zeyli*, 31, 52–53, 165–67.

41. Abdi Pasha, *Vekāyi'nāme*, fols. 24a, 140a, 38a. The former sheikhulislam was dismissed from office in 1651, the latter in 1662.

42. Baysun, "Mehmed IV," 550.

43. Zilfi, *The Politics of Piety*, 177.

44. Ibid.

45. Anonymous, *Vekāyi'nāme*, Topkapı Museum Palace Library, MS. Hazine 1468, fols. 25a, 46a.

46. Ibid., fol. 46b.

47. Katip Çelebi, *Fezleke*, 2:383; Naima, *Tarih-i Naima*, 5:268.

48. Katip Çelebi, *Fezleke*, 2:383.

49. Evliya Çelebi, *Seyahatname*, quoted in Dankoff, *An Ottoman Mentality*, 70, 71.

50. Naima, *Tarih-i Naima*, 5:54–59.

51. The original title is *Mizanü'l-hakk*. See *The Balance of Truth*, by Katip Chelebi, translated with an introduction and notes by G. L. Lewis, Ethical and Religious Classics of East and West, no. 19 (London: Allen and Unwin, 1957); M. Tayyib Gökbilgin, "Katip Çelebi, Interprète et rénovateur des traditions religieuses au XVIIe siècle," *Turcica* 3 (1971): 71–79.

52. Solakzade, *Tarih-i Al-i Osman*, fol. 487b.

53. Ibid.; Vecihi Hasan Çelebi, *Tarih-i Vecihi*, fols. 85a–87a; Silahdar, *Tarih-i Silahdar*, 1:59.

54. Solakzade, *Tarih-i Al-i Osman*, fols. 487b, 488a.

55. Ahmed Dede, *Jami' al-Duwal*, fol. 776b.

56. Inalcik, *The Ottoman Empire*, 184–85.

57. Ahmed Yaşar Ocak, "Religion," in İhsanoğlu, *History of the Ottoman State, Society and Civilisation*, 1:177–238, 234–35.

58. Ibid., 1:237.

59. Zilfi, "The Kadızadelis," 267.

60. Metin Kunt, "Ethnic-Regional (*Cins*) Solidarity in the Seventeenth-Century Ottoman Establishment," *International Journal of Middle East Studies* 5 (1974): 233–39.

61. Bektashis participated in the siege of Candia, for which they were rewarded with the building of a dervish lodge. Gülsoy, *Girit'in Fethi*, 258–59.

62. Kürd Hatib, *Risāle*, fol. 8b.

63. For example, Mehmed Halife, *Tarih-i Gilmani*, fol. 68b.

64. Karaçelebizade, *Ravzatü'l-ebrâr zeyli*, 318.

65. Abdi Pasha, *Vekāyi'nāme*, fol. 85b; Silahdar, *Tarih-i Silahdar*, 1:59; Naima, *Tarih-i Naima*, 6:237.

66. Solakzade, *Tarih-i Al-i Osman*, fol. 488a.

67. Naima, *Tarih-i Naima*, 6:223.

68. Gökyay, *Evliya Çelebi Seyahatnâmesi*, 117.

69. Ahmed Dede, *Jami' al-Duwal*, fol. 777b; Silahdar, *Tarih-i Silahdar*, 1:226.

70. Ahmed Dede, *Jami' al-Duwal*, fol. 778b.

71. Mehmed Halife, *Tarih-i Gilmani*, fols. 59b, 37a–b.

72. Ibid., fols. 42a, 43a, 44a.

73. Gökyay, *Evliya Çelebi Seyahatnâmesi*, 117; Nihadi, *Tarih-i Nihadi*, fol. 173b.

74. Kürd Hatib, *Risāle*, fol. 9a.

75. Mantran, *Istanbul*, 254; Vecihi Hasan Çelebi, *Tarih-i Vecihi*, fols. 106a–108a; Silahdar, *Tarih-i Silahdar*, 1:226.

76. Karaçelebizade, *Ravzatü'l-ebrâr zeyli*, 323, 325.

77. Ibid., 326–28, 335.

78. Kürd Hatib, *Risāle*, fols. 9a–b.

79. Anonymous, "Chiosei Basi/Capo del Chiosero Reggie," Staatliche Museen zu Berlin, Preußischer Kulturbesitz, Kunstbibliothek, Lipperheide OZ 52, 66; Anonymous, "Mehter basi/Capo d'instrumenti di Guera," Staatliche Museen zu Berlin, Preußischer Kulturbesitz, Kunstbibliothek, Lipperheide OZ 52, 64.

80. Kürd Hatib, *Risāle*, fols. 9b–10a.

81. Karaçelebizade, *Ravzatü'l-ebrâr zeyli*, 286.

82. Parry, "The Period of Murād IV, 1617–48," 156.

83. İsmail Hakkı Uzunçarşılı's influential 1950s account of Ottoman history, arranged chronologically and divided into sultanic reigns, skipped from a section on Ibrahim and the problems that attended his reign to "The Situation of the State between 1648 and 1656," followed two sections later by "The Period of the Köprülüs." Uzunçarşılı, *Osmanlı Tarihi* 3 (1). This framework is followed in the recent work of Turkish scholars such as Feredun Emecen, who includes the period in "The Solution Sought After for Military Success: The Köprülüs," and in the work of American and western European historians. These include Norman Itzkowitz, who chose "The Köprülü Era"; Hans Kissling, who wrote an article entitled "Die Köprülü Restauration"; Shaw, who labels a section less than ten pages long concerning the entire epoch of Mehmed IV in his Ottoman history as "The Köprülü Years, 1656–83"; and, most recently, Suraiya Faroqhi's "Köprülü Restoration" and Caroline Finkel's "Rule of the Grandees." Feridun Emecen, "From the Founding to Küçük Kaynarca," 3–62, 49–52; Itzkowitz, *Ottoman Empire and Islamic Tradition*, 77–85, 99–100; Hans Kissling, "Die Köprülü Restauration," in *Internationales Kulturhistorisches symposium Mogersdorf 1969* (Eisenstadt, Austria: 1972), 75–84; Shaw, *History of the Ottoman Empire*, 1:207–16; Suraiya Faroqhi, "Crisis and Change, 1590–1699," in Suraiya Faroqhi et al., *An Economic and Social History of the Ottoman Empire*, vol. 2: *1600–1914* (Cambridge: Cambridge University Press, 1994), 419–20; Suraiya Faroqhi, *Geschichte des Osmanischen Reiches* (München: C. H. Beck, 2000), 61–62, "Die Restauration der Köprülüs"; Finkel, *Osman's Dream*, 253–88.

84. Finkel, *Osman's Dream*, 253.

85. Kurat, "The Reign of Mehmed IV, 1648–87," 168; Silahdar, *Tarih-i Silahdar*, 1:226.

86. Carter Vaughn Findley, *The Turks in World History* (New York: Oxford University Press, 2005), 119.

87. Naima, *Tarih-i Naima*, 6:403.

88. Imber, *The Ottoman Empire, 1300–1650*, 324. Imber seconds Marshall Hodgson's emphasis on Shariah as a glue that held Islamic societies together in times of

crisis. Marshall G. S. Hodgson, *Rethinking World History: Essays on Europe, Islam, and World History*, ed. Edmund Burke III (New York: Cambridge University Press, 1993).

89. Halil Inalcik, "The Rise of the Ottoman Empire," in *The Cambridge History of Islam*, ed. P. M. Holt, Ann K. S. Lambton, and Bernard Lewis (New York: Cambridge University Press, 1970), 1:295.

90. Naima, *Tarih-i Naima*, 6:294.

CHAPTER 4

1. Irene Bierman, *Writing Signs: The Fatimid Public Text* (Berkeley: University of California Press, 1998). See especially chap. 1, "Preliminary Considerations."

2. Wolper, *Cities and Saints*, 3.

3. Mehmed Halife, *Tarih-i Gilmani*, fol. 61b.

4. Mustafa Cezar, "Osmanlı Devrinde İstanbul Yapılarında Tahribat Yapan Yangınlar ve Tabii Afetler," *Türk Sanat Tarihi Araştırma ve İncelemeleri* 1 (Istanbul, 1963): 327–414; Mantran, *Istanbul*, 36; *EI²*, s.v. "Istanbul," by Halil Inalcik.

5. Mehmed Halife, *Tarih-i Gilmani*, fols. 60a–61a.

6. Ibid., fol. 61a.

7. Vecihi Hasan Çelebi, *Tarih-i Vecihi*, fol. 144b.

8. Abdi Pasha, *Vekâyi'nâme*, fols. 128b–129b.

9. Mehmed Halife, *Tarih-i Gilmani*, fol. 61b.

10. Vecihi Hasan Çelebi, *Tarih-i Vecihi*, fol. 145a.

11. Mehmed Halife, *Tarih-i Gilmani*, fol. 62a.

12. Nasuh Paşazade Ömer Bey, *Turhan Vâlide Sultan Vakıfnamesi*, Suleimaniye Library, Istanbul, MS. Turhan Vâlide Sultan 150, fol. 17b; Vecihi Hasan Çelebi, *Tarih-i Vecihi*, fol. 145a.

13. Vecihi Hasan Çelebi, *Tarih-i Vecihi*, fols. 145a, 62b.

14. Nihadi, *Tarih-i Nihadi*, fol. 188a.

15. Mehmed Halife, *Tarih-i Gilmani*, fols. 62b, 63a.

16. Ibid., fol. 63b.

17. Vecihi Hasan Çelebi, *Tarih-i Vecihi*, fol. 145b.

18. Anonymous, *Vekâyi'nâme*, fol. 41a.

19. Mehmed Halife, *Tarih-i Gilmani*, fol. 64a.

20. Nihadi, *Tarih-i Nihadi*, fol. 188b.

21. Gökyay, *Evliya Çelebi Seyahatnâmesi*, 124.

22. Kürd Hatib, *Risâle*, fol. 20a. Silahdar adds that it was the advice of the head architect Mustafa Efendi that sealed the case for Eminönü. Silahdar, *Tarih-i Silahdar*, 1:218.

23. Kürd Hatib, *Risâle*, fol. 20a.

24. On rebuilding Catholic churches in Galata, see Louis Mitler, "The Genoese in Galata: 1453–1682," *International Journal of Middle East Studies* 10 (1979): 86–91. But see also Inalcik, "Ottoman Galata." On the dislocation of Jews, see Uriel Heyd, "The Jewish Community of Istanbul in the Seventeenth Century," *Oriens* 6 (1953): 311–13; Avram Galanté, *Histoire des juifs d'Istanbul* (Istanbul: Imprimerie Hüsnutabat, 1941),

15, 53; Yerasimos, "La Communauté juive," 108. On the mosque, see Peirce, *The Imperial Harem*, 206–9; Lucienne Thys-Şenocak, "The Yeni Valide Mosque Complex at Eminönü," *Muqarnas* 15 (1998): 58–70; Ali Saim Ülgen, "Yenicami," *Vakıflar Dergisi* 2 (1942): 387–97; Aslanapa, *Osmanlı Devri Mimarîsi*, 347–55.

25. In the narrative of Kurdish Preacher Mustafa, the imperial council's negligence in constructing an impregnable citadel along the Dardanelles following Venetian occupation of Bozca and Limni Islands infuriated the sultana, which caused "the sea of her ardor" to come "to a boiling point so she had two sound citadels constructed." Kürd Hatib, *Risāle*, fol. 17a. "Praise be to God," Kurdish Preacher Mustafa continues, "because of that valide sultan's exalted endeavor and zeal," infidel captains cannot even consider entering the channel, but Muslim vessels "flow like water," and as they pass they offer praises and thanks to her, which will be to her benefit on the Day of Judgment. Katip Çelebi also credits the valide sultan for constructing the citadels. Katip Çelebi, *Fezleke*, 2:360.

26. Karaçelebizade, *Ravzatü'l-ebrâr zeyli*, 272.

27. Thys-Şenocak, "The Yeni Valide Mosque Complex at Eminönü," 62–63.

28. Ibid., 62–63. See also Ülgen, "Yenicami," 389.

29. Gökyay, *Evliya Çelebi Seyahatnâmesi*, 124.

30. Mottahedeh, *Loyalty and Leadership*, 179.

31. Gökyay, *Evliya Çelebi Seyahatnâmesi*, 124.

32. Silahdar, *Tarih-i Silahdar*, 1:218; Kürd Hatib, *Risāle*, fols. 22a–b. The cost of the mosque complex was either 3,080 purses of gold (Kürd Hatib) or 5,000 purses (Evliya Çelebi). Gökyay, *Evliya Çelebi Seyahatnâmesi*, 124.

33. The fire began on the afternoon of July 24 and ended on the afternoon of July 26; construction began on July 22 the following year. Abdi Pasha, *Vekâyi'nâme*, fol. 128b; Silahdar, *Tarih-i Silahdar*, 1:218.

34. Kürd Hatib, *Risāle*, fols. 2a–b, 18a, 22a.

35. Heyd, "The Jewish Communities," 303; Galanté, *Histoire des juifs d'Istanbul*, 162–73.

36. On Zeitouni/İzdin, see İstanbul Müftülüğü, Şer'iye Sicilleri Arşivi (Office of the Istanbul Mufti, Islamic Law Court Records Archive), Istanbul Şer'iye Sicilleri (hereafter cited as IŞS) 9, fol. 52a, July 8, 1661, and IŞS 10, fol. 82a, June 5, 1662; on German, see IŞS 9, fol. 85a, July 31, 1661, and IŞS 9, fol. 216a, December 18, 1661; on Istanbul, see IŞS 9, fol. 86a, August 13, 1661; on Dimetoka, see IŞS 9, fol. 177b, October 27, 1661; on Aragon, see IŞS 9, fol. 216a, December 18, 1661; on Antalya and Borlu, see IŞS 10, fols. 113b–114a, September 16, 1661; on Borlu, see IŞS 9, fol. 143b, September 29, 1661.

37. Heyd, "The Jewish Communities," 300–305.

38. IŞS 9, fol. 143b, September 29, 1661; IŞS 10, fol. 82a, June 5, 1662.

39. Silahdar, *Tarih-i Silahdar*, 1:218–19.

40. Spanish congregation members: IŞS 9, fol. 110a, August 31, 1661; Yasef son of Yako: IŞS 9, fol. 174a, October 30, 1661; İshak son of Avraham: IŞS 9, fol. 194b, October 26, 1661.

41. Gökyay, *Evliya Çelebi Seyahatnâmesi*, 176.

42. Heyd, "The Jewish Communities," 310–14.

43. Silahdar, *Tarih-i Silahdar*, 1:218.

44. Kürd Hatib, *Risāle*, fols. 19b–20a. The fire actually occurred in 1070.

45. Gökyay, *Evliya Çelebi Seyahatnâmesi*, 124, 176.

46. Nasuh Paşazade Ömer Bey, *Turhan Vâlide Sultan Vakıfnamesi*, fols. 17b–18a.

47. Despite the distinction in Arabic between synagogue (*kanis*) and church (*kanisa*), the single term *kanisa* (*kenise* in Turkish) is used in the Shariah court records to refer to both church and synagogue.

48. Gökyay, *Evliya Çelebi Seyahatnâmesi*, 125.

49. Joseph Pitton de Tournefort, *Voyage d'un Botaniste*, vol. 2: *La Turquie, la Géorgie, l'Arménie*, notes and bibliography by Stéphane Yerasimos (Paris: FM/La Découverte, 1982), 27.

50. Gökyay, *Evliya Çelebi Seyahatnâmesi*, 125. While rebuilding the harem after a fire in 1665, the valide sultan had innovative Iznik tilework depicting Mecca and Medina placed in the eunuch's mosque and her oratory. She also had a tile depicting a tented camp of pilgrims on the hajj installed in the corridor near the prince's quarters. Silahdar, *Tarih-i Silahdar*, 1:384; Godfrey Goodwin, *A History of Ottoman Architecture* (Baltimore: Johns Hopkins University Press, 1971), 355–56.

51. Abdi Pasha, *Vekāyi'nāme*, fol. 193a; Raşid, *Tarih-i Raşid*, 1:106–7; Kürd Hatib, *Risāle*, fols. 22b–24b.

52. Kürd Hatib, *Risāle*, fol. 22b.

53. Silahdar, *Tarih-i Silahdar*, 1:390.

54. Kürd Hatib, *Risāle*, fols. 22b–24b.

55. Gökyay, *Evliya Çelebi Seyahatnâmesi*, 124.

56. Gülrü Necipoğlu-Kafadar, "The Süleymaniye Complex in Istanbul: An Interpretation," *Muqarnas* 3 (1985): 113.

57. Thys-Şenocak, "The Yeni Valide Complex at Eminönü," 61.

58. Gökyay, *Evliya Çelebi Seyahatnâmesi*, 125.

59. Naima, *Tarih-i Naima*, 4:80–81. Before a hunting trip Ibrahim stated, "I am going to hunt and ride about. If the viziers and leading magistrates come as well, the commoners will flock there from every direction and hinder the outing. Let those who have complaints and claims go to the Divan."

60. Paul Monod, review of Brian Weiser, *Charles II and the Politics of Access* (Rochester, NY: Boydell Press, 2003), *American Historical Review* 110 (December 2005): 1592.

61. De Tournefort, *Voyage*, 28.

62. Gökyay, *Evliya Çelebi Seyahatnâmesi*, 124.

63. Thys-Şenocak, "The Yeni Valide Mosque Complex of Eminönü," 74–75.

64. Gökyay, *Evliya Çelebi Seyahatnâmesi*, 125.

65. Thys-Şenocak, "The Yeni Valide Mosque Complex at Eminönü," 67.

66. For comparison, see Necipoğlu-Kafadar, "The Süleymaniye Complex."

67. Wolper, *Cities and Saints*, 3.

68. Yerasimos, "La Communauté juive," 119–20, 124, 130.

69. Mark Epstein, *The Ottoman Jewish Communities and Their Role in the Fifteenth and Sixteenth Centuries*, Islamkundliche Untersuchungen Bd. 56. (Freiburg: K. Schwarz, 1980), 28–30.

70. Anonymous, *Vekāyi'nāme*, fol. 47b.

71. De Tournefort, *Voyage*, 28; Necipoğlu, *The Age of Sinan*, 67.

72. Silahdar, *Tarih-i Silahdar*, 1:352, 354.

73. Gökyay, *Evliya Çelebi Seyahatnâmesi*, 125.

74. IŞS 10, fol. 156b, May 9, 1662. For the purchase of the land, see IŞS 9, fol. 96b, August 17, 1661. Loss of the lands: IŞS 10, fol. 86a, June 3, 1662, and IŞS 10, fols. 82b, 84b–85a, June 2, 1662. Property being awarded in lieu of seized property: entries for the week of June 2–9, 1662, in IŞS 10, fols. 82a–86b, 88a–89b.

75. IŞS 9, fol. 95a, June 22, 1662.

76. IŞS 9, fol. 82b, June 2, 1662.

77. The chronogram for his death was "Köprülü stepped onto the bridge [*köprü*] of the kingdom of non-existence." Nihadi, *Tarih-i Nihadi*, fol. 188b.

78. Rycaut, *The Present State of the Ottoman Empire*, 262. His short-sightedness "caused him to knit his brows and pore very intently when any strange person entered his presence." Anonymous, *Vekāyi'nāme*, fol. 58a; Gökyay, *Evliya Çelebi Seyahatnâmesi*, 117; Hasan Agha, *Cevahir et-Tarih*, Topkapı Palace Museum Library, MS. Revan 1307, fols. 3a–b.

79. Ahmed Dede, *Jami' al-Duwal*, fol. 781a.

80. IŞS 9, fols. 83b–96b, 142a–157a, 247a–253a; IŞS 10, fols. 82a–95a, 156b. For the number of churches, see *EI²*, s.v. "Istanbul," by Halil Inalcik; Eremya Çelebi, *İstanbul Tarihi*; Mantran, *Istanbul*, 51, 54–55.

81. Inalcik, "Ottoman Galata," 275–99, 349–50.

82. See Mantran, *Istanbul*, 561–62; Eremya Çelebi, *İstanbul Tarihi*, 223–26. The five churches are French Capuchin Saint George, which had formerly been Byzantine and then Genoese (IŞS 9, fol. 96b, August 17, 1661); Italian Saint Francis (San Francesco), Saint Anne (Santa Anna), and a bell tower (IŞS 9, fol. 247a, January 3, 1662); San Sebastian (IŞS 9, fol. 96b, August 17, 1661); and originally Genoese Dominican Saints Peter and Paul (Santi Apostoli Pietro e Paolo; IŞS 9, fol. 96a, August 17, 1661), which became a French church at the beginning of the eighteenth century.

83. IŞS 9, fols. 96a–b, August 17, 1661.

84. IŞS 10, fol. 247a, January 3, 1662. Among the men are Giovanni son of Carlo, Nicola son of Franco, Francesco son of Giovanni, and Domenico son of Giovanni.

85. Rycaut, *The Present State of the Ottoman Empire*, 195–96.

86. IŞS 10, fol. 156b, May 9, 1662.

87. Under the guise of repairing the roof of the Church of the Nativity in Bethlehem a decade later, for which they had acquired permission, Orthodox Christians "rebuilt a more splendid prayer hall than had ever existed since the Ottoman conquest." Oded Peri, *Christianity under Islam in Jerusalem: The Question of the Holy Sites in Early Ottoman Times* (Boston: Brill, 2001), 94.

88. Hasan Agha, *Cevahir et-Tarih*, fols. 6a–b, 7a–b, 17b.

89. Silahdar, *Tarih-i Silahdar*, 1:276, 282.

90. Hasan Agha, *Cevahir et-Tarih*, 6b.

91. Minkarizade Yahya b. Ömer, *Fetāvā-i Minkarizade Efendi*, Suleimaniye Library, MS. Hamidiye 610, fols. 37a–b.

92. IŞS 9, 52a, July 8, 1661; IŞS 9, 86a, August 13, 1661.

93. Today Saint George is located within the complex of the Austrian High School.

94. The Armenian churches Surp (Saint) Sarkis and Surp Nigoğos in Kumkapı burned in the fire and were subsequently repaired. On orders of the grand vizier, the latter was razed in 1661 and the former in 1674. See Eremya Çelebi, İstanbul Tarihi, 3 nn. 84–85.

95. She had a reputation for charitable giving, establishing a foundation supporting a hospital and soup kitchen in Mecca. Hathaway, The Politics of Households in Ottoman Egypt, 150.

96. Defterdar Sarı Mehmed, Zübde-i Vekayiât (Ankara: Türk Tarih Kurumu Basımevi, 1995), 606–7.

97. The Garden of the Mosques: Hafız Hüseyin Al-Ayvansarayî's Guide to the Muslim Monuments of Ottoman Istanbul, trans. Howard Crane (Leiden: Brill, 2000), 357–58.

98. The Valide Sultan Mosque in Eminönü is one of the most important mosques and one of the leading tourist attractions in Istanbul today. It is undergoing renovation. The Valide Sultan Mosque in Galata, however, was demolished in 1936 to create the Galata Hardware Market. Semavi Eyice, Galata ve Kulesi (Istanbul: Türkiye Turing ve Otomobil Kurumu, 1969), 16.

99. Katip Çelebi, Fezleke, 2:225, Naima, Tarih-i Naima, 4:18–19.

100. IŞS 9, fol. 244a, January 13, 1662.

101. Başbakanlık Osmanlı Arşivi (hereafter cited as BOA, Prime Ministry's Ottoman Archive), Istanbul, Şikâyet Defteri (Complaint Register): 6, 105, no. 456, December–January 1668.

102. About one hundred Jewish households eventually resettled in Eminönü. But because Jews were accused of engaging in many "abominable acts," they were expelled in 1727 so that only Muslims could reside near the mosque. Ahmed Refik, Onikinci Asr-ı Hicrî'de İstanbul Hayatı (1689–1785) (1930; Istanbul: Enderun Kitabevi, 1988), 88–89. Today a kosher restaurant overlooks the plaza between the mosque and Egyptian Market.

103. IŞS 10, fols. 67b–68a, June 4, 1662.

104. IŞS 10, fol. 110b, July 7, 1662.

105. BOA, Şikâyet Defteri: 8, 481, no. 2338, May 18–27, 1673.

106. İstanbul Müftülüğü, Şer'iye Sicilleri Arşivi, Galata Şer'iye Sicilleri (hereafter cited as GŞS) 110, 126, undated 1671–73.

107. İstanbul Müftülüğü, Şer'iye Sicilleri Arşivi, Yeniköy Şer'iye Sicilleri (hereafter cited as YŞS) 18/54, 168, May 27, 1664; YŞS 164, February 12, 1665.

108. Hayati Develi, "İstanbul'a Dair 'Risâle-i Garîbe," İstanbul Araştırmaları 1 (Bahar 1997), 111 (fols. 63b–64a).

CHAPTER 5

1. Abdi Pasha, Vekāyi'nāme, fol. 3a. Subsequent references to this source are cited parenthetically throughout the text.

2. Denise Spellberg, *Politics, Gender, and the Islamic Past: The Legacy of 'A'isha bint Abi Bakr* (New York: Columbia University Press, 1996).

3. Jacques Derrida, *Of Grammatology*, trans. Gayatri Chakravorty Spivak (Baltimore: Johns Hopkins University Press, 1976), 156.

4. Mehmed Halife, *Tarih-i Gilmani*, fol. 92a.

5. Ibid., fols. 287a–b, 302b–303a, 385b. Beyzavi, or al-Baydawi in Arabic, was a thirteenth-century Shafi'i scholar and chief magistrate in Shiraz, best known for his commentary on the Qur'an, a condensed version of the commentary of well-respected twelfth-century scholar al-Zamakhshari. See *EI²*, s.v. "Al-Baydāwī," by J. Robson, and s.v. "Al-Zamakhsharī," by C. H. M. Versteegh.

6. Mehmed Halife, *Tarih-i Gilmani*, fols. 283b–284a. The year was 1669.

7. Kürd Hatib, *Risāle*, fols. 3b, 27b.

8. Ibid., fols. 28a, 30a–b, 33a. Even writers who wrote treatises extolling the sultan and valide sultan articulated the frustration of loyal, pious servants fruitlessly waiting to receive their just rewards. Kurdish Preacher Mustafa, whose treatise offers lavish praise of the sultan and sultana, includes an implicit critique as well. After serving the sultan as Friday imam and preacher, residing in the palace, and even predicting the birth of the first prince, he still had to spend twelve years constantly petitioning for reward. He appealed to the sultan's "gaze of affection and eye of compassion" for years to no avail. At first he requested promotion to the rank of the magistrate of Bursa and a stipend, but when he was informed that that request was contrary to Shariah and violated secular statute, he requested a pension instead, which he ultimately received. This way Kurdish Preacher Mustafa could both depict the court as following religious and secular law while critiquing it for not seeing the value of a devoted servant (fols. 38a–42a).

9. Jonathan D. Spence, *Emperor of China: Self-Portrait of K'ang-hsi* (New York: Vintage Books, 1988), 44, 58.

10. Kürd Hatib, *Risāle*, fols. 14a–b.

11. Defterdar, *Zübde-i Vekayiât*, 210. Raşid uses the same phrase, Râşid Mehmed Efendi, *Târîh-i Râşid* (Istanbul, 1282/1865), 1:483. On his speaking Kurdish, see Abdi Pasha, *Vekāyi'nāme*, fols. 108b–109b.

12. Kürd Hatib, *Risāle*, fols. 14a–b.

13. Nihadi, *Tarih-i Nihadi*, fol. 191b.

14. Rycaut, *The Present State of the Ottoman Empire*, 124. Here Rycaut refers to the dangers of puritanism.

15. Hasluck, *Christianity and Islam*, 2:423.

16. Nihadi, *Tarih-i Nihadi*, fol. 191b.

17. Ocak, "Religion," 236, claims that Köprülü Mehmed Pasha put a permanent end to the movement in 1656. Goffman repeats this error, arguing, "The organization never fully recovered from this blow." Goffman, *The Ottoman Empire and Early Modern Europe*, 120.

18. The entry is dated January 29, 1666.

19. The entry is dated June 13, 1667.

20. The entry is dated August 1, 1667. Most of his audience consisted of pages from the inner palace.

21. See also *Raşid*, 1:134–35.

22. Baysun, "Mehmed IV," Abdi Pasha, *Vekāyi'nāme*, fol. 364a; BOA, Ali Emiri Tasnifi, Mehmed IV: 1169–72, 1986; Hüseyin Behçeti, *Mirac'üz-zafer*, Süleymaniye Library, Esad Efendi MS. 2368, fols. 52b–53a, 56a.

23. Anonymous, *Vekāyi'nāme*, fol. 47a.

24. Peirce, *Imperial Harem*, 194.

25. Anonymous, *Vekāyi'nāme*, fol. 47b.

26. Hasluck, *Christianity and Islam*, 1:419–23.

27. *Risāla fī hakk al-farż wa al-Sunna wa al-bid'a fī ba'z al-'amal*, Suleimaniye Library, MS. Lala İsmail 685/1; *Risāla fī karāhat al-jahr bi al-zikr*, Suleimaniye Library, MS. Hacı Beşir Ağa 406/3.

28. *Risāla fī karāhat al-jahr bi al-zikr*, fols. 186b–188b; Erdoğan Pazarbaşı, *Vânî Mehmed Efendi ve Araisü'l-Kur'an*, Van Belediyesi Kültür ve Sosyal İşler Müdürlüğü, no. 5 (Ankara: Acar Matbaası, 1997), 179–85.

29. Hagen, "Ottoman Understandings of the World," 246.

30. Pazarbaşı, *Vânî Mehmed Efendi ve Araisü'l-Kur'an*, 183–84, quoting Vani Mehmed Efendi, *Araisu'l-Kur'an*, Kayseri, Raşid Efendi Kütüphanesi 21525, fols. 26a–27b.

31. For the decision to outlaw the public performance of Sufi rituals, see Zilfi, "The Kadızadelis," 263; Baha Doğramacı, *Niyazi–yi Mısrî: Hayatı ve Eserleri* (Ankara: Kadıoğlu Matbaası, 1988), 9.

32. The entry is dated February 24, 1665.

33. Silahdar, *Tarih-i Silahdar*, 1:378; Raşid, *Tarih-i Raşid*, 1:94. See also Ahmed Yaşar Ocak, *Osmanlı Toplumunda Zındıklar ve Mülhidler (15.–17. Yüzyıllar)* (Istanbul: Tarih Vakfı Yurt Yayınları 60, 1998), 245–47; Rycaut, *The Present State of the Ottoman Empire*, 245–46. Rycaut claimed that Lari Mehmed had a peculiar proof that there was no God: "One of this Sect called Mahomet Effendi [sic], a rich man, Educated in the knowledge of the Eastern Learning, I remember, was in my time executed for impudently proclaiming his blasphemies against the being of a Deity; making it in his ordinary discourse, an argument against the being of a God, for that either there was none at all, or else not so wise as the Doctors preached he was, in suffering him to live who was the greatest enemy and scorner of a Divine Essence that ever came into the world." He did not live long after this boastful claim.

34. Ocak, *Zındıklar ve Mülhidler*, 247. Among his confiscated effects were books "written in an infidel script."

35. Raşid, *Tarih-i Raşid*, 1:139–40; Zilfi, "The Kadızadelis," 263.

36. The entry is dated October 3, 1667.

37. Rycaut, *The Present State of the Ottoman Empire*, 269. "I remember at Adrianople to have seen the ruine of one of these Monasteries situated on a pleasant Hill, and in good Air, that oversees the whole City and Plains round about; which upon enquiry I understand was demolished by the famous Vizier Kuperli, because it was discovered to be a Rendezvous of the lewd Women of the Town, and a Stew where the young Gallants debauched the Wives of the richest Turks, to whom their Husbands had given liberty in honour to the Sanctity of the place, to be often present at the devotion of the Sufies; but their way of practice being too publick and scandalous, the Foundation of their House by the order of the Vizier was razed to the ground."

38. *İslâm Ansiklopedisi*, 1960, s.v. "Niyâzî," by Abdülbaki Gölpınarlı. See also Doğramacı, *Niyazi–yi Mısrî*.

39. Balivet, *Byzantins et Ottomans*, 227.

40. Doğramacı, *Niyazi–yi Mısrî*, 11.

41. He died on the island in 1694 following his third pardon and renewed exile.

42. Cahit Kayra and Erol Üyepazarcı, *Mekânlar ve Zamanlar: Kandilli, Vaniköy, Çengelköy*, İstanbul Büyükşehir Belediyesi Kültür İşleri Dairesi Başkanlığı Yayınları, no. 13 (Istanbul, İstanbul Büyükşehir Belediyesi, 1993), 94–95.

43. Abdülbaki Gölpınarlı, *Mevlânâ'dan Sonra Mevlevîlik* (Istanbul: İnkilâp Kitabevi, 1953), 168.

44. Mehmed Halife, *Tarih-i Gilmani*, fol. 92b.

45. Anonymous, "Ciurzi/Sonatrice di Chitara," Staatliche Museen zu Berlin, Preußischer Kulturbesitz, Kunstbibliothek, Lipperheide OZ 52, 80; Anonymous, "Tamburzi/Sonatrice di Cittera," Staatliche Museen zu Berlin, Preußischer Kulturbesitz, Kunstbibliothek, Lipperheide OZ 52, 83.

46. Anonymous, "Asich ve Masuch/Linamorato et linamorata," Staatliche Museen zu Berlin, Preußischer Kulturbesitz, Kunstbibliothek, Lipperheide OZ 52, 76.

47. For a translation of the imperial decree, see Bernard Lewis, *Istanbul and the Civilization of the Ottoman Empire* (Norman: University of Oklahoma Press, 1963), 130–31.

48. For imperial decrees concerning taverns in offensive locations and Muslim consumption of wine in late sixteenth-century Galata and İstinye, see Ahmed Refik, *Onuncu Asr-ı Hicrî'de İstanbul Hayatı (1495–1591)* (1917; Istanbul: Enderun Kitabevi, 1988), 50–51; Ahmed Refik, *Onbirinci Asr-ı Hicrî'de İstanbul Hayatı (1592–1688)* (1931; Istanbul: Enderun Kitabevi, 1988), 14–15.

49. Develi, "İstanbul'a Dair 'Risâle-i Garîbe," 111–12 (fols. 63b, 65b), 118 (fol. 75b).

50. IŞS 13, fol. 29b, February 24, 1664.

51. Dr. John Covel, "Covel's Diary," in *Early Voyages and Travels in the Levant*, ed. J. Theodore Bent (London: Hakluyt Society, 1893), 87:234 and 269, respectively.

52. See also Raşid, *Tarih-i Raşid*, 1:250; 'İsâ-zâde, *'İsâ-zâde Târîhi*, ed. Ziya Yılmazer (Istanbul: Istanbul Fetih Cemiyeti, 1996), 108; Silahdar, *Tarih-i Silahdar*, 1:559.

53. Beşiktaş Şer'iye Sicilleri (hereafter cited as BŞS), 23/78, fol. 135a, September 9, 1670.

54. BŞS, 23/81, fol. 137a, undated 1679–80.

55. BOA, Şikayet Defteri 7, 34 no. 134. The entry is dated August 26–September 4, 1671.

56. BŞS, 23/79, fol. 98a, August 21, 1675.

57. Rycaut, *The Present State of the Ottoman Empire*, 225.

CHAPTER 6

1. Matt Goldish, *The Sabbatean Prophets* (Cambridge, MA: Harvard University Press, 2004).

2. Zilfi, *The Politics of Piety*, 146–57; Jane Hathaway, "The Grand Vizier and the False Messiah: The Sabbatai Sevi Controversy and the Ottoman Reform in

Egypt," *Journal of the American Oriental Society* 117, no. 4 (January–April 1997): 665–71.

3. Mehmed Kamil Pasha, *Tarih-i Siyasi–yi Devlet-i Âliye-yi Osmaniye*, 3 vols. (Istanbul: Matbaa-yi Ahmet İhsan, 1325/1909), 2:104.

4. Gershom Scholem, *Sabbatai Sevi The Mystical Messiah 1626–76*, trans. R. J. Zwi Werblowsky, Bollingen Series, no. 93 (Princeton, NJ: Princeton University Press, 1973), 433.

5. Rycaut, *The Present State of the Ottoman Empire*, 179, 177. See also the comments of the Armenian scholar Eremya Çelebi Kömürciyan, quoted in Avram Galanté, *Nouveaux documents sur Sabbetaï Sevi: Organisation et us et coutumes de ses adeptes* (Istanbul: Société anonyme de papeterie et d'imprimerie [Fratelli Haim], 1935), 92.

6. Scholem, *Sabbatai Sevi*, 435.

7. Galanté, *Nouveaux documents*, 104.

8. Scholem, *Sabbatai Sevi*, 446–47, 444.

9. For an account of Shabbatai Tzevi's life between 1626 and 1664, see Scholem, *Sabbatai Sevi*, 103–98. Concerning Izmir's Jewish community, see Jacob Barnai, "Ha-kehilim be-izmir be-me'ah ha-sheva-esreh," *Pe'amim* 48 (1992): 66–84.

10. Moshe Idel argues contra Scholem that rather than Palestine-based sixteenth-century Lurianic Kabbalah and messianism, Shabbatai Tzevi's messianism followed forms of Kabbalah that developed centuries before Rabbi Isaac Luria's innovations. In fact, Shabbatai Tzevi did not study Lurianic Kabbalah and even opposed some of its doctrine. Idel claims that the rabbi was most influenced by the doctrines of the thirteenth-century Kabbalist Abraham Abulafia. See Moshe Idel, *Kabbalah: New Perspectives* (New Haven, CT: Yale University Press, 1988), 250–71; Moshe Idel, "'One from a Town, Two from a Clan.' The Diffusion of Lurianic Kabbala and Sabbateanism: A Re-Examination," *Jewish History* 7, no. 2 (Fall 1993): 79–104; Moshe Idel, *Messianic Mystics* (New Haven, CT: Yale University Press, 1998), 183–211.

11. Scholem, *Sabbatai Sevi*, 174.

12. For the history of the movement in the Ottoman Empire between 1665 and 1676, see ibid., 199–460, 603–749, 821–929.

13. Gershom Scholem, "Teudah hadashah me-reshit ha-tenua ha-Shabata'ut," in *Mehkarim u-mekorot le-toledot ha-Shabta'ut ve-gilguleha* (Jerusalem: Mosad Bialik, 1982), 218–32, 225; and Scholem, *Sabbatai Sevi*, 212–13.

14. For the reaction of Jews in Hamburg, see *The Memoirs of Glückel of Hameln*, trans. Marvin Lowenthal (New York: Schocken Books, 1977), 45–47.

15. See the following chapter.

16. For more information about the latter, see Geoffrey Lewis and Cecil Roth, "New Light on the Apostasy of Sabbatai Zevi," *Jewish Quarterly Reviw* 53 (1963): 219–25.

17. It is striking how often modern scholars continue to confuse these two figures. Vani Mehmed Efendi was not the sheikhulislam, but scholars today continue to label him as such. For a recent example, see İlber Ortaylı, "Ottoman Modernisation and Sabetaism," in *Alevi Identity: Cultural, Religious, and Social Perspectives*, ed. Tord Olsson, Elisabeth Özdalga, and Catharina Raudvere (Istanbul: Swedish Research Institute in Istanbul, 1999), 97.

18. Minkarizade, *Fetāvā*, fol. 34a.

19. Abdi Pasha, *Vekāyi'nāme*, fols. 224a–b. This is the earliest Ottoman account. The narrative also occurs, with slight variation, in Silahdar, *Tarih-i Silahdar*, 1:431–32. Other than differences in vocabulary, the textual variations between Abdi Pasha and Silahdar are as follows: Abdi Pasha dates the meeting of the council in Edirne October 16, 1666, but Silahdar dates it one month earlier. Instead of the New Pavilion, Silahdar writes that the council was held in the Pavilion of the Privy Chamber. Silahdar adds two other details missed by Abdi Pasha: the sultan watched the council "without being seen," and Shabbatai Tzevi's 150 akçe stipend was per diem. Abdi Pasha's text is trans-literated in İbrahim Alâettin Gövsa, *Sabatay Sevi: İzmirli meşhur sahte Mesih hakkında tarihî ve içtimaî tetkik tecrübesi* (Istanbul: Lûtfi Kitabevi, 1939), 48; and in approximate French translation in Galanté, *Nouveaux documents*, 80–81.

20. Raşid, *Tarih-i Raşid*, 1:133.

21. Reproduced in *Padişahın Portresi: Tesavir-i Âl-i Osman* (Istanbul: Türkiye İş Bankası Kültür Yayınları, 2000), 360.

22. See Joel Kraemer, "Apostates, Rebels, and Brigands," *Israel Oriental Studies* 10 (1980): 34–73.

23. Abdi Pasha, *Vekāyi'nāme*, fols. 231b–232a, 233a–b.

24. Cengiz Şişman, "A Jewish Messiah in the Ottoman Court: Sabbatai Sevi and the Emergence of a Judeo-islamic Community, 1666–1720" (PhD diss., Harvard University, 2004), 172.

25. Antoine Galland, *İstanbul'a Ait Günlük Hâtıralar (1672–1673)*, trans. Nahid Sırrı Örik, 2 vols., 2nd ed. (Ankara: Türk Tarih Kurumu Basımevi, 1987), 1:171, 183; Scholem, *Sabbatai Sevi*, 859.

26. Scholem, *Sabbatai Sevi*, 847, 729.

27. Ibid., 683.

28. Avram Galanté, *Médecins juifs au service de la Turquie* (Istanbul: Imprimerie Babok, 1938); Bernard Lewis, "The Privilege Granted by Mehmed II to His Physician," *Bulletin of the School of Oriental and African Studies* 14 (1952): 550–63; Bernard Lewis, *The Jews of Islam* (Princeton, NJ: Princeton University Press, 1984), 130; Eleazar Birnbaum, "Hekim Yakub, Physician to Sultan Mehemmed the Conquerer," *Harofe Haivri: The Hebrew Medical Journal* 1 (1961): 222–50; Uriel Heyd, "Moses Hamon, Chief Jewish Physician to Sultan Süleyman the Magnificent," *Oriens* 16 (1963): 152–70.

29. Stanford Shaw, *The Jews of the Ottoman Empire and Turkish Republic* (New York: New York University Press, 1991), 86–87, 141. Disregarding seventeenth-century developments and evidence, Shaw writes incorrectly, "There was a whole group of Jewish physicians serving in the Ottoman palace during the seventeenth century, particularly during the reign of Murad IV and Mehmed IV (1648–87) and the reforming Köprülü Grand Vezirs, all making such major contributions to the Ottoman Ruling Class that they were felt to be indispensable. They, along with the Jewish community were awarded handsomely in return" (92).

30. A Jewish poem concerning physician Moshe Benvenest's exile to Rhodes in 1584 is discussed in Meir Benayahu, "Rofeh he-hatzer rav Moshe Benvenest ve-shir al-higliyito le-Rodos me-rav Yehudah Zarko," *Sefunot* 12, Sefer Yavan II (1971–78): 123–44.

The physician was apparently a member of the court faction punished for supporting peace with Spain and not France.

31. İsmail Hakkı Uzunçarşılı, *Osmanlı Devletinin Saray Teşkilatı*, 2nd ed. (Ankara: Türk Tarih Kurumu Basımevi, 1984), 364–65.

32. Ibid.

33. ʿAyn ʿAli Efendi, *Kavânîn-i Âl-i Osman der Hülâsa-i Mezâmin-i Defter-i Dîvân* (Istanbul: Enderun Kitabevi, 1979), 94.

34. *Eyyubî Efendi Kânûnnâmesi, Tahlil ve Metin*, ed. Abdülkadir Özcan (Istanbul: Eren, 1988), 36.

35. BOA, Kâmil Kepeci Tasnifi, Küçük Ruznamçe (KR, Palace Salary Register) 3401, 3411, 3413, 3415, 3427.

36. BOA, KR: 3411, March 3, 1667. See also BOA, KR: 3422.

37. Uzunçarşılı, *Osmanlı Devletinin Saray Teşkilatı*, 364–65; BOA, KR: 3439.

38. BOA, KR: 3401, 3427.

39. İzzet Kumbaracızade, *Hekim-Başı odası, İlk eczane, Baş-Lala kulesi* (Istanbul: Kader Matbaası, 1933), 27; Epstein, *The Ottoman Jewish Communities*, 30.

40. BOA, KR: 3412, 3437.

41. Heyd, "Moses Hamon," 154; Kumbaracızade, *Hekim-Başı odası*, 33; Galanté, *Médecins juifs*, 15; BOA, KR: 3438, 3439.

42. Avigdor Levy, *The Sephardim in the Ottoman Empire* (Princeton, NJ: Darwin Press, 1991), 76.

43. See Galanté, *Médecins juifs*, 13–14. BOA, KR: 3413 is his first listing on the palace payroll. In Abdi Pasha, *Vekâyiʿnâme*, fol. 291a, the author notes that a writ was issued so that Hayatizade could replace the deceased Salih Efendi as head physician on August 31, 1669.

44. For a discussion of the term see Avram Galanté, *Esther Kyra d'après de nouveaux documents* (Constantinople: Fr. Haim, 1926), 3–5.

45. B. Lewis, *The Jews of Islam*, 144; Peirce, *The Imperial Harem*, 225–26; Esther Benbassa and Aron Rodrigue, *Sephardi Jewry: A History of the Judeo-Spanish Community, 14th–20th Centuries* (Berkeley: University of California Press, 2000), 38.

46. Kürd Hatib, *Risâle*, fol. 18b.

47. Jews also remarked on her power. In the responsa of Rabbi Shlomo ben Avraham HaKohen we find, "The frightening and menacing lady, she has the power and the name in kings, courts, and castles, and her small word is enough to cause damage in anything she wishes, to his body or his capital." Quoted in Minna Rozen, *A History of the Jewish Community in Istanbul: The Formative Years, 1453–1566* (Leiden: Brill, 2002), 206 n. 36.

48. Peirce, *Imperial Harem*, 242–43; Rozen, *A History of the Jewish Community in Istanbul*, 206–7.

49. This is corroborated by Silahdar, *Tarih-i Silahdar*, 2:578.

50. Kürd Hatib, *Risâle*, fols. 18b–19b.

51. Zilfi, *The Politics of Piety*, 155, 180 n. 109; Kumbaracızade, *Hekim-Başı odası*, 33. The mansion remained in the family for more than two hundred years. In the nineteenth century, when the family had no more sons, the daughters married into the

Dürrizade family while retaining the seaside mansion. The Dürrizade family boasted many religious scholars. At the beginning of the 1920s Sheikhulislam Abdullah Efendi resided there. He gained fame, or notoriety, as the mufti who issued a fatwa calling for the death of Mustafa Kemal (Atatürk) for rebelling against the sultan. The mansion was later replaced by a corn oil factory, which was then converted into the mansion of the tenth richest family in Turkey. The author of this book was the private tutor of the family's eldest son. See Kayra and Üyepazarcı, *Mekânlar ve Zamanlar*.

52. The effort failed and the Jews were burned at the stake. Rozen, *A History of the Jewish Community in Istanbul*, 36–37.

53. BOA, KR: 3430 is his last listing on the palace payroll. His replacement appears in 1691, KR: 3431.

54. Defterdar, *Zübde-i Vekayiât*, 398.

55. Silahdar, *Tarih-i Silahdar*, 2:578–79.

56. Sultan Ahmed III (1703–30) employed a German Jew and then a Portuguese Jew as his physician, and the latter played a role in Ottoman diplomacy. But these men were rare exceptions to the trend, which led to the disappearance of Jewish palace physicians who both cared for the sultan and represented the empire abroad. Levy, *Sephardim*, 77.

57. Refik, *Onikinci Asr-ı Hicrî'de İstanbul Hayatı (1689–1785)*, 28–30.

58. William McNeill, *Venice, the Hinge of Europe (1081–1797)* (Chicago: University of Chicago Press, 1974), 213–14.

59. Levy, *Sephardim*, 77. The Venetian Israel Conegliano, a Jewish physician who resided in Istanbul serving Grand Vizier Kara Mustafa Pasha, served as secretary to the Venetian representative.

CHAPTER 7

1. Mohammed Arkoun, *Rethinking Islam: Common Questions, Uncommon Answers*, trans. Robert D. Lee (Boulder, CO: Westview Press, 1994), 89.

2. Rambo, *Understanding Religious Conversion*, 70.

3. Vyronis, *The Decline of Medieval Hellenism*; El-Leithy, "Sufis, Copts and the Politics of Piety."

4. On this topic see Wolper, *Cities and Saints*.

5. Piterberg, *An Ottoman Tragedy*, 2, 5–6.

6. Goffman, *The Ottoman Empire and Early Modern Europe*, 123.

7. Ruth Mazo Karras, *From Boys to Men: Formations of Masculinity in Late Medieval Europe* (Philadelphia: University of Pennsylvania Press, 2003), 8; Anthony Fletcher, *Gender, Sex, and Subordination in England, 1500–1800* (New Haven, CT: Yale University Press, 1995), 3–29. See Elizabeth Badinter, *XY: On Masculine Identity*, trans. Lydia Davis (New York: Columbia University Press, 1995), 10–13. Badinter argues that because men define themselves in relation to women, crises are set off when women question the role of men and demand the overturning of gendered norms. Ottoman women may not have demanded their overturning, but actively undermined them as they gained power.

8. Finkel, *Osman's Dream*, 154.

9. Necipoğlu, *Architecture, Ceremonial, and Power*, 30, 102–6.

10. Finkel, *Osman's Dream*, 195.

11. Kafadar, *Between Two Worlds*, 146, 152.

12. According to a Venetian report quoted in Finkel, *Osman's Dream*, 184–85.

13. Peirce, *Imperial Harem*, 91–112.

14. Vatin and Veinstein, *Le Sérail ébranlé*, 266, 185–92.

15. Ibid., 207–8.

16. Necipoğlu, *Architecture, Ceremonial, and Power*, 143–44.

17. Quataert, *The Ottoman Empire, 1700–1922*, 91.

18. Katip Çelebi, *Fezleke*, 2:219, 220. Three horses he had ridden into ghaza, saddled backward, led his funeral procession to Ahmed I's mausoleum on the Hippodrome.

19. Goodwin, *A History of Ottoman Architecture*, 356.

20. Piterberg, *An Ottoman Tragedy*, 17.

21. Imber, *The Ottoman Empire, 1300–1650*, 126–27, 119.

22. Peirce, *The Imperial Harem*, 91–112; Imber, *The Ottoman Empire*, 153; Hathaway, *The Politics of Households in Ottoman Egypt*, 139–40.

23. Shih-shan Henry Tsai, *The Eunuchs in the Ming Dynasty* (Albany: State University of New York Press, 1996).

24. Matthew Sommer, "Dangerous Males, Vulnerable Males, and Polluted Males: The Regulation of Masculinity in Qing Dynasty Law," in *Chinese Femininities/Chinese Masculinities: A Reader*, eds. Susan Brownell and Jeffrey N. Wasserstrom (Berkeley: University of California Press, 2002), 68.

25. Robert Van Gulik, *Sexual Life in Ancient China: A Preliminary Survey of Chinese Sex and Society from ca. 1500 B.C. till 1644 A.D.* (Leiden: Brill, 1961), 296, cited in Brownell and Wasserstrom, "Introduction: Theorizing Feminities and Masculinities," in *Chinese Femininities/Chinese Masculinities*, 19. Whereas the Manchu vision of masculinity was based on martiality, the Han promoted filiality and literacy. See Angela Zito, *Of Body and Brush: Grand Sacrifice as Text/Performance in Eighteenth-Century China* (Chicago: University of Chicago Press, 1997), cited in Brownell and Wasserstrom, "Introduction: Theorizing Feminities and Masculinities," in *Chinese Femininities/Chinese Masculinities*, 19.

26. Meisami, *Persian Historiography*, 291.

27. Fahri Çetin Derin, *Abdurrahman Abdi Paşa Vekâyi'nâme'si: Tahlil ve Metin Tenkîdi, 1058–1093/1648–1682* (Doktora Tezi, İstanbul Üniversitesi, 1993), xxiii.

28. Strohm, *England's Empty Throne*, 196–97.

29. Kafadar, *Between Two Worlds*, 148.

30. Imber, *The Ottoman Empire, 1300–1650*, 145.

31. Rıfat Osman, *Edirne Sarayı*, ed. Süheyl Ünver, 2nd ed. (Ankara: Türk Tarih Kurumu Basımevi, 1989), 31–32.

32. Gökyay, *Evliya Çelebi Seyahatnâmesi*, 114.

33. Derin, *Abdurrahman Abdi Paşa Vekâyi'nâme'si*, xxvii–xlv.

34. Paul Strohm, *Theory and the Premodern Text* (Minneapolis: University of Minnesota Press, 2000), 65, 77.

35. Strohm, *England's Empty Throne*, xii.

36. Strohm, *Theory and the Premodern Text*, 79.

37. Abdi Pasha, *Vekāyi'nāme*, fol. 3a.

38. Mehmed Halife, *Tarih-i Gilmani*, fol. 47b.

39. Mehmed Necati, *Tarih-i Feth-i Yanık*, Topkapı Palace Museum Library, Revan 1308, fols. 50b, 4a, 4a–b, 5b. Mehmed IV took on the Venetians soon after deciding to wage war on the Habsburgs. Subsequent references to this source are cited parenthetically in the immediately following paragraphs.

40. Christine Woodhead, *Ta'lîkî-zâde's şehnâme-i hümâyûn: A History of the Ottoman Campaigns into Hungary, 1593–4* Islamkundliche Untersuchungen. Bd. 82 (Berlin: K. Schwarz, 1983), 27.

41. Mehmed Halife, *Tarih-i Gilmani*, fol. 91b.

42. Abdi Pasha, *Vekāyi'nāme*, fols. 215b–216b.

43. Anonymous, *A Description of Vienna in its Ancient and Present state; With an exact and compleat Account of the SIEGE thereof: Began by the Ottoman Emperour on the 16th of July, 1683, and Continued until the 12th of September following; at which time the Siege was Rais'd, and a Total Defeat given to the Turkish Army, by the Christians* (London: Printed for Randolph Taylor, 1683).

44. Anonymous, "Mahomet Istivs Nominis IIII Tvrcarvm et Totivs Orientis Imperator Infestissimvs Christianæ Religionis Hostis," Österreichische Nationalbibliothek, Vienna, Porträtsammlung, Bildarchiv und Fideikommißbibliothek, Pg 26 25/1, Ptf. 30: (28).

45. Vani Mehmed Efendi, *Münşe'at Vani Efendi*, Suleimaniye Library, MS. Hagia Sophia 4308, fols. 1b–15a. Subsequent references to this source are cited parenthetically in the immediately following paragraphs.

46. The work, *Cevahir et-Tarih*, is also referred to as *The History of the Conquest of the Citadel of Candia (Tarih-i Feth-i Kale-i Kandiye)*.

47. Hasan Agha, *Cevahir et-Tarih*, fols. 1b–2a. Subsequent references to this work are cited parenthetically in the immediately following paragraphs.

48. Ahmed Dede, *Jami' al-Duwal*, fol. 783a.

49. Silahdar, *Tarih-i Silahdar*, 1:393.

50. "Osmanlı Kanûnnâmeleri," 500; *Osmanlılarda Narh Müessesesi*, 360.

51. Vani Mehmed Efendi, *Münşe'at*, fols. 16b–28a. See Molly Greene, *A Shared World: Christians and Muslims in the Early Modern Mediterranean* (Princeton, NJ: Princeton University Press, 2000), 13–44.

52. Vani Mehmed Efendi, *Münşe'at*, fol. 16b.

53. Ibid., fols. 27b–28a, 28b.

54. Ibid., fol. 16b.

55. Hasan Agha, *Cevahir et-Tarih*, fol. 110b.

56. Ibid., fols. 135b–136a.

57. Gökyay, *Evliya Çelebi Seyahatnâmesi*, 124.

58. Hasan Agha, *Cevahir et-Tarih*, fols. 149b–150a.

59. Ibid., fol. 150a.

60. Ibid., fol. 153b.

61. Ibid., fol. 154a.

62. Ibid., fol. 156a.

63. Ibid.

64. Silahdar, *Tarih-i Silahdar*, 1:495.

65. Hasan Agha, *Cevahir et-Tarih*, fols. 158b, 159a.

66. Silahdar, *Tarih-i Silahdar*, 1:506.

67. Hasan Agha, *Cevahir et-Tarih*, fol. 170a.

68. Ibid.; Ahmed Dede, *Jami' al-Duwal*, fol. 784a.

69. Gülsoy, *Girit'in Fethi*, 197–98.

70. Hasan Agha, *Cevahir et-Tarih*, fol. 170b.

71. Ibid., fols. 291a, 178a.

72. Using language similar to Kurdish Preacher Mustafa, Hasan Agha wrote, "This great valide is such a pious and chaste Muslim lady that she has no equal. For ten years she continually fasted and prayed from night until morning." Ibid., fol. 178b.

73. Ibid., fol. 179a. In contrast to narratives written at the time of the siege, critical voices appeared years later. Unlike Hasan Agha, who was writing to honor Fazıl Ahmed Pasha, Silahdar relates accounts of rebellion among the ranks of soldiers besieging Candia. Commanders complained that they spent as much time fighting their troops as the enemy. Silahdar, *Tarih-i Silahdar*, 1:498–501.

74. *EI²*, s.v. "Kandiya," by C. J. Heywood; Rycaut, *The Present State of the Ottoman Empire*, 218.

75. Ahmed Dede, *Jami' al-Duwal*, fol. 783a.

76. Abdi Pasha, *Vekāyi'nāme*, fol. 293a.

77. Ibid., fol. 294a.

78. Rycaut, *The Present State of the Ottoman Empire*, 221–22.

79. Abdi Pasha, *Vekāyi'nāme*, fol. 298a.

80. Silahdar, *Tarih-i Silahdar*, 1:557.

81. Whereas Greene emphasizes the role of religious conversion in changing the demography of the island, arguing that there was rapid and massive conversion to Islam in the wake of the Ottoman conquest, Gülsoy does not mention religious conversion in his study, but instead focuses on the Christians' exodus and the colonization of the island by Muslims. Greene, *A Shared World*, 39–44; Gülsoy, *Girit'in Fethi*, 246–52, 279–82.

82. Silahdar, *Tarih-i Silahdar*, 1:525–26, 544–48.

83. Ibid., 1:525–26; Greene, *A Shared World*, 78–87; Gülsoy, *Girit'in Fethi*, 252–67.

84. Silahdar, *Tarih-i Silahdar*, 1:525–26.

85. Defterdar, *Zübde-i Vekayiat*, 15–16.

86. Hasan Agha, *Cevahir et-Tarih*, fol. 185a.

87. Katip Çelebi, *Fezleke*, 2:259–61; Ahmed Dede, *Jami' al-Duwal*, fol. 771a.

88. Katip Çelebi, *Fezleke*, 2:259–61.

89. Katip Çelebi, *Fezleke*, 2:286–89; Ahmed Dede, *Jami' al-Duwal*, fol. 771a.

90. Dankoff, *An Ottoman Mentality*, 49.

91. Hasan Agha, *Cevahir et-Tarih*, fol. 117b.

92. Greene, *A Shared World*, 84; Gülsoy, *Girit'in Fethi*, 244–45, 263–64. Prior to the beginning of the construction of the mosque in Eminönü in her name, a church in Resmo had been converted into the valide sultan's mosque.

93. Greene, *A Shared World*, 180.

CHAPTER 8

1. Hajji Ali Efendi, *Fethname-i Kamaniça*, Suleimaniye Library, MS. Lala Ismail 308, fols. 2a–b, 2b–3b. According to Silahdar, the sultan intended to launch a naval campaign against Zeydi Shi'is in Yemen who were attacking pilgrim routes. Perhaps because Mehmed IV's court was most concerned with battling what it considered Sunni vice, it was not overly concerned with Shi'is and Shi'ism. Silahdar, *Tarih-i Silahdar*, 1:563–64.

2. Gökyay, *Evliya Çelebi Seyahatnâmesi*, 124.

3. Rycaut, *The Present State of the Ottoman Empire*, 237.

4. Hajji Ali Efendi, *Fethname-i Kamaniça*, fol. 121a. Subsequent references to this source are cited parenthetically in this paragraph and in the immediately following paragraphs.

5. Yusuf Nabi, *Fethname-i Kamaniça*, Topkapı Saray Museum Library, MS. Hazine 1629. Subsequent references to this source are cited parenthetically in this paragraph and in the immediately following paragraphs.

6. Abdi Pasha, *Vekāyi'nāme*, fol. 314b; Yusuf Nabi, *Fethname-i Kamaniça*, fols. 9a, 315a, 316a.

7. Hajji Ali Efendi, *Fethname-i Kamaniça*, fol. 42a.

8. Abdi Pasha, *Vekāyi'nāme*, fol. 316a.

9. Silahdar, *Tarih-i Silahdar*, 1:569.

10. Hajji Ali Efendi, *Fethname-i Kamaniça*, fol. 1b.

11. Nihadi, *Tarih-i Nihadi*, fol. 211b.

12. Yusuf Nabi, *Fethname-i Kamaniça*, fol. 9b.

13. Ibid., fols. 14a–b.

14. Abdi Pasha, *Vekāyi'nāme*, fol. 322b. Subsequent references to this source are cited parenthetically in this paragraph and in the immediately following paragraphs.

15. Hajji Ali Efendi, *Fethname-i Kamaniça*, fols. 42b, 57b, 59b, 130b–134a. Yet he was hindered, as again was his favorite's carriage, by heavy rain and mud. Abdi Pasha, *Vekāyi'nāme*, fols. 355b–356a.

16. Rycaut, *The Present State of the Ottoman Empire*, 240–41. Hajji Ali Efendi claims that those in Kamaniça's citadel and town were allowed to remain where they were. Hajji Ali Efendi, *Fethname-i Kamaniça*, fol. 85b.

17. Yusuf Nabi, *Fethname-i Kamaniça*, fol. 60b.

18. Hajji Ali Efendi, *Fethname-i Kamaniça*, fols. 134b, 136a.

19. Silahdar, *Tarih-i Silahdar*, 1:606.

20. The dismissed sheikhulislam was given a 1,000 akçe per diem, half of which came from the poll tax (*jizya*) of Jews. Abdi Pasha, *Vekāyi'nāme*, fol. 369a.

21. Abdi Pasha, *Vekāyi'nāme*, fols. 377b, 379a, 380a–b, 384a.

22. Silahdar, *Tarih-i Silahdar*, 1:659.

23. Topkapı Palace Museum Archive, IV Mehmed, No. E., Ar. 11679. The document is dated November 3, 1676.

24. Rycaut writes, "Wine, that great abomination to the Turkish law, which four years past was by the Imperial Decree forbidden under pain of Death and a thousand Execrations and Curses, was now the common Drink, the Vizier himself having been excessively intemperate therein, had extinguished the natural heat of his stomach, which could be warmed by no less heat than what proceeds from *Aqua Vitae*; by which debauchery and indisposition all Businesses were slowly and negligently dispatched, and according to his example the Commanders and Ministers acted in their Affairs, which in former times being always dispatched by nine a Clock in the Morning, that became now the time and hour of rising." Rycaut, *The Present State of the Ottoman Empire*, 251. Covel adds that he had found the grand vizier "crop sick" (sick with repletion) several times. Covel, "Covel's Diary," 245.

25. Topkapı Palace Museum Archive, IV Mehmed, No. E., Ar. 11679.

26. Gökyay, *Evliya Çelebi Seyahatnâmesi*, 117.

27. *EI²*, s.v. "Köprülü," by M. Tayyib Gökbilgin and R. C. Repp.

28. Abdi Pasha, *Vekâyi'nâme*, fols. 405a–b.

29. Hüseyin Behçeti, *Mirac'üz-zafer*, fols. 3a–b, 6b.

30. Abdi Pasha, *Vekâyi'nâme*, fols. 412a–b.

31. Hüseyin Behçeti, *Mirac'üz-zafer*, fols. 52b, 53a.

32. Befitting tribal customs of that era, all men were executed in the market at Medina, and the women and children were sold into slavery.

33. This refers to the oasis of Khaybar.

34. Hüseyin Behçeti, *Mirac'üz-zafer*, fol. 56a.

35. The "faithless who will not believe" are the Banu Qurayza.

36. Abdi Pasha, *Vekâyi'nâme*, fols. 340a–b. Nearly three decades later, the returning Poles disinterred the Muslim corpses. Dariusz Kołodziejczyk, *The Ottoman Survey Register of Podolia (ca. 1681), Defter-i Mufassal-i Eyalet-i Kamaniçe*, part 1: Text, Translation, and Commentary, Studies in Ottoman Documents Pertaining to Ukraine and the Black Sea Countries (Cambridge, MA: Harvard University Press, 2004), 3:51.

37. Kołodziejczyk, *The Ottoman Survey Register of Podolia*, 3:51.

38. Naima, *Tarih-i Naima*, 4:150.

39. Kritovoulos, *History of Mehmed the Conqueror*, in *The Islamic World*, ed. William H. McNeill and Marilyn Robinson Waldman (Chicago: University of Chicago Press, 1983), 312–36; 336.

40. Hajji Ali Efendi, *Fethname-i Kamaniça*, fol. 89b.

41. Yusuf Nabi, *Fethname-i Kamaniça*, fol. 45b. Ibn Bibi records similar sentiment in a speech of the twelfth-century Seljuk Sultan Suleimanshah II: "Let me convert their churches and monasteries to masjids and madrasas. Let me make the inhabitants of that land hear the chanting of the verses of the Qur'an in place of the sound of the organ. Let me make them hear the call of the muezzin proclaiming God's unity and Muhammad's prophecy rather than the sound of cymbal and church bell." Ibn Bibi,

El-Evâmiru'l-Alâiye fi Umûri'l-Alâiye, trans. Mürsel Öztürk, 2 vols. (Ankara: Kültür Bakanlığı Yayınları, 1996), 1:90.

42. Yusuf Nabi, *Fethname-i Kamaniça*, fol. 46a.

43. Hajji Ali Efendi, *Fethname-i Kamaniça*, fols. 89b–90a.

44. Ibid.; Abdi Pasha, *Vekâyi'nâme*, fol. 341a.

45. Yusuf Nabi, *Fethname-i Kamaniça*, fol. 47b.

46. Hajji Ali Efendi, *Fethname-i Kamaniça*, fol. 90a.

47. Yusuf Nabi, *Fethname-i Kamaniça*, fols. 48a, 90b.

48. Abdi Pasha, *Vekâyi'nâme*, fol. 340b.

49. Ibid., fol. 343a.

50. Yusuf Nabi, *Fethname-i Kamaniça*, fol. 48b. This is echoed by Defterdar in the eighteenth century, who writes, "The light of Islam diffused light to the great citadel walls." Defterdar, *Zübde-i Vekayiât*, 29.

51. Kürd Hatib, *Risâle*, fol. 10a. This was also echoed by Defterdar, who wrote that Bozca Island "again became illuminated with the radiant signs of Islam" following its reconquest. Defterdar, *Zübde-i Vekayiât*, 4.

52. Vecihi Hasan Çelebi, *Tarih-i Vecihi*, fol. 1b.

53. Mehmed Halife, *Tarih-i Gilmani*, fol. 67a.

54. Pál Fodor, "The View of the Turk in Hungary: The Apocalyptic Tradition and the Red Apple in Ottoman–Hungarian Context," in Fodor, *In Quest of the Golden Apple*, 71–103, 98–99.

55. Mehmed Halife, *Tarih-i Gilmani*, fol. 86a.

56. B. Lewis, *Istanbul and the Civilization of the Ottoman Empire*, 9.

57. Pál Fodor, "Ottoman Policy towards Hungary, 1520–1541," *Acta Orientalia Academiæ Scientiarum Hungaricæ* 45 (1991): 271–345, reprinted in Fodor, *In Quest of the Golden Apple*, 105–169, 107.

58. Gökyay, *Evliya Çelebi Seyahatnâmesi*, 124.

59. Topkapı Palace Museum Archive, Arzlar E. 2445/114.

60. Hasan Agha, *Cevahir et-Tarih*, fol. 31a.

61. Mehmed Halife, *Tarih-i Gilmani*, 89–90; Hasan Agha, *Cevahir et-Tarih*, fols. 79a–b.

62. Sometimes conversion could be a ruse. In 1649 a Venetian admiral feigned conversion following the Battle of Foça. He was given a ship and crew as reward, but then apostasized and returned with the ship to the enemy's harbor. Katip Çelebi, *Fezleke*, 2:344–46. Two years later in Crete another leading defender became Muslim in the presence of the ghazi commander and asked for two thousand ghazis to lead in battle against his former allies. The commander did not believe him. It was indeed a ploy; the next day he and his men fled to the citadel. Naima, *Tarih-i Naima*, 5:214.

63. Hasan Agha, *Cevahir et-Tarih*, fol. 31a. Ottoman forces put most of the enemy they found to the sword. At Ostergon in Hungary, prisoners "became prey to the sword of the ghazis," who loaded the thousands of corpses on the battlefield onto carts, drove them away, "placed them in the pit of Hell," and left. Hasan Agha, *Cevahir et-Tarih*, fol. 18a. Evliya Çelebi describes countless scenes of slaughter, where "battling white-skinned infidels in the snow they ran them through with the teeth of their swords and

made them melt like the snow," and scenes of imprisonment, not conversion. Gökyay, *Evliya Çelebi Seyahatnâmesi*, 120. In one battle en route to Kamaniça in 1672, Ottoman forces killed three thousand enemy troops and took six thousand captive; later all were killed without a chance to convert. Yusuf Nabi, *Fethname-i Kamaniça*, fol. 20b.

CHAPTER 9

1. Michel Foucault, "Governmentality," in *The Foucault Effect: Studies in Governmentality*, ed. Graham Burchell, Colin Gordon, and Peter Miller (Chicago: University of Chicago Press, 1991), 87–103; Michel Foucault, *The History of Sexuality: An Introduction*, trans. Robert Hurley (New York: Random House, 1978), 1:133–57; Michel Foucault, *Discipline and Punish: The Birth of the Prison*, trans. Alan Sheridan (New York: Vintage Books, 1977).

2. Baysun, "Mehmed IV," 549.

3. Mehmed Halife, *Tarih-i Gilmani*, fol. 60a.

4. Abdi Pasha, *Vekāyi'nāme*, fols. 238a–b. Subsequent references to this source are cited parenthetically throughout this chapter.

5. Metin And, *Osmanlı Tasvir Sanatları: 1 Minyatür* (Istanbul: Türkiye İş Bankası, 2002), 190–91, 194–95, 197.

6. Ahmed Dede, *Jami' al-Duwal*, fol. 770b. In the winter of 1558 Suleiman I "moved his court to Adrianople [Edirne], according to his usual custom. His object was to threaten Hungary with invasion, while at the same time he was attracted by the opportunities offered for hawking and for enjoying a climate more bracing than that of Constantinople, both of which he regarded as beneficial to his health. Near Adrianople a large area of flooded country is formed where the rivers converge, abounding in wild ducks, geese, herons, sea eagles, cranes, hawks, and other birds. To capture these, he makes use of the assistance of small eagles." Ogier de Busbecq, *Turkish Letters* (London: Sickle Moon Books, 2001), 61.

7. Anonymous, "Padisach Doganzisi/Falconiero del Rei," Staatliche Museen zu Berlin, Preußischer Kulturbesitz, Kunstbibliothek, Lipperheide OZ 52, 8.

8. Mehmed Halife, *Tarih-i Gilmani*, fol. 91b.

9. Kürd Hatib, *Risāle*, fol. 13a.

10. Gökyay, *Evliya Çelebi Seyahatnâmesi*, 114.

11. Silahdar first mentions hunting in 1660. Silahdar, *Tarih-i Silahdar*, 1:211.

12. Naima, *Tarih-i Naima*, 5:43–44.

13. Orhan Pamuk, *The White Castle*, trans. Victoria Holbrook (New York: Vintage International, 1998), 50–51. In the novel the court astrologer interprets the event as meaning that the sultan will face enemies from unseen quarters but will escape unharmed.

14. See also Silahdar, *Tarih-i Silahdar*, 1:727.

15. See Juvainî, "From the History of the World Conqueror," in *The Islâmic World*, ed. William H. McNeill and Marilyn Robinson Waldman (Chicago: University of Chicago Press, 1983), 253–58.

16. Spence, *Emperor of China*, xi–xxvi, 5.

17. Anonymous, "Awzi/Caciator Reggio," Staatliche Museen zu Berlin, Preußischer Kulturbesitz, Kunstbibliothek, Lipperheide OZ 52, 130.

18. The entry is dated December 11, 1667.

19. Silahdar, *Tarih-i Silahdar*, 1:223.

20. Covel, *Covel's Diary*, 207.

21. Spence, *Emperor of China*, 9.

22. Hajjı Ali Efendi, *Fethname-i Kamaniça*, fols. 134b–135a.

23. The incident occurred March 12, 1665. The story is also related in Raşid, *Tarih-i Raşid*, 1:94–95, without the sultan's speech and the conclusion contained in Abdi Pasha's narrative.

24. See Kürd Hatib, *Risāle*, fol. 29a. In certain circumstances, this sultan used sign language. He could not escape all the customs of his high station. Yet even when using "the language of those who cannot speak," with a harem eunuch at court in the early 1660s, in which the two signed with head and hand and "without sound or letter understood each other's wishes," the sultan quickly broke the silence and turned to palace imam Kurdish Preacher Mustafa, asking him if he knew sign language. When the preacher replied negatively, the sultan taught the fundamental signs and explained the conversation he had had with the harem eunuch. In this situation he dropped the custom of speaking in sign much more quickly.

25. Covel, "Covel's Diary," 209–10. For a description of the festival, see Nutku, *IV. Mehmet'in Edirne Şenliği*. The princes were circumcised on the thirteenth day of festivities. Abdi Efendi's *Surname*, the Ottoman narrative written to commemorate the princes' circumcision, narrates how up to 3,500 sons of the Muslim rich and poor were circumcised by more than three hundred surgeons "deft of hand" gathered from Bursa, Edirne, and Istanbul. Up to sixty boys at a time were circumcised amid musicians and jugglers present to divert their attention. The festivities lasted a week and were accompanied by the performance of archers, musicians, singers, and wrestlers. Abdi Efendi, *Sur-name*, fols. 5a–b. See also Rycaut, *The Present State of the Ottoman Empire*, 253.

26. Daniel J. Vitkus, "Turning Turk in *Othello*: The Conversion and Damnation of the Moor," *Shakespeare Quarterly* 48, no. 2 (Summer 1997): 145–76.

27. "Osmanlı Kanûnnâmeleri," 542.

28. Çetin, *Sicillere Göre Bursa'da İhtida Hareketleri*; Lowry, *Trabzon Şehrinin İslamlaşması*; Minkov, *Conversion to Islam in the Balkans*.

29. Minkov, *Conversion to Islam in the Balkans*, 144. Seventeenth-century petitions have been compared to modern petitions: standard applications for membership in the Communist Party and applications by Turks in Bulgaria to have their names changed. All appear equally unreliable sources for the study of processes termed "voluntary." Maria Todorova, *Balkan Identities, Nation and Memory* (New York: New York University Press, 2004), 145.

30. Minkov, *Conversion to Islam in the Balkans*, 124.

31. The dispersal of clothing to new Muslims recorded in this register first occurred in 1609, when Ahmed I was sultan. BOA, Ali Emiri Tasnifi, Ahmed I: 757, January 3, 1610. Seven documents registered the same day during the religious festival of Id al-Adha record the distribution of muslin cloth wrapped around a cloth cap, which

together comprise a turban and purses of coins to nine new Muslims, five of whom were women. The next recorded example of new Muslims converting at court and receiving new clothing occurs during the reign of Sultan Murad IV (1623–40). BOA, İbnülemin Tasnifi, Hil'at Defteri (Imperial Register of Cloaks): 17, March 3, 1625. Two documents record the bestowal of turbans and coins to four converts. Three documents recorded the same day in 1626 provide the information that fifteen converts received material for turbans and purses of coins. BOA, Ali Emiri Tasnifi, Murad IV: 278, March 24, 1626.

32. BOA, Ali Emiri Tasnifi, Mehmed IV: 9911, April 11, 1667.

33. Hajji Ali Efendi, *Fethname-i Kamaniça*, fol. 135a.

34. Travel estimates are based on ibid., fols. 15a, 16a, 17b, 18a–19b, 132a. These times are the maximum required for the sultan and his retinue to travel between resting stations while on campaign.

35. See also Hajji Ali Efendi, *Fethname-i Kamaniça*, fol. 10b.

36. Goodwin, *A History of Ottoman Architecture*, 350.

37. BOA, Ali Emiri Tasnifi: Mehmed IV: 626.

38. BOA, Ali Emiri Tasnifi, Mehmed IV: 10286.

39. BOA, Ali Emiri Tasnifi, Mehmed IV: 9946.

40. Minkarizade, *Fetāvā*, fols. 34a–b.

41. *Osmanlılarda Narh Müessesesi*, 341–67.

42. On the importance of the body of subject and king alike in early modern France, see Sara Melzer and Kathryn Norberg, introduction to *From the Royal to the Republican Body*, ed. Sara Melzer and Kathryn Norberg (Berkeley: University of California Press, 1998), 1–10.

43. Clifford Geertz, *Negara: The Theater State in Nineteenth-Century Bali* (Princeton, NJ: Princeton University Press, 1980).

44. BOA, Ali Emiri Tasnifi, Mehmed IV: 9852, 9911, 9915, 9928, 9957, 504.

45. Rycaut, *The Present State of the Ottoman Empire*, 65.

46. *Eyyubî Efendi Kānûnnâmesi*, 27–29. As an example of how architecture reflected ceremony, the treasury where the fine cloaks were stored in Topkapı Palace is located next door to the room used for meetings of the imperial divan.

47. BOA, Ali Emiri Tasnifi, IV Mehmed: 9852, 9911, 9915, 9928, 9957.

48. *Sources ottomanes sur les processus d'Islamization aux Balkans*, Traduction des documents A. Velkov et al, Serie sources-2 (Sofia: Éditions de l'Academie bulgare des sciences, 1990), 35–37. The document referred to is Док. 16, л. 3.

49. Ibid., Док. 16, л. 1б–2а, Док. 16, л. 2б.

50. Dursun Ali Tökel, "Şâirin Tarihe Düştüğü Not: Şâir Gözüyle Merzifonlu Kara Mustafa Paşa ve Çehrin Seferi," in *Merzifonlu Kara Mustafa Paşa Uluslararası Sempozyumu* (Ankara: Merzifon Vakfı Yayınları, 2001), 371–82.

51. Abdi Pasha, *Şerh-i Kasîde-i Bürde*, Topkapı Palace Museum Library, MS. H. Hüsnü Paşa 1013/2.

52. Sergio Bertelli, *The King's Body: Sacred Rituals of Power in Medieval and Early Modern Europe*, trans. R. Burr Litchfield (University Park: Pennsylvania State University Press, 2001), 4.

53. Pamuk, "In the Absence of Domestic Currency," 345–66; Bertelli, *The King's Body*, 143.

54. Rycaut, *The Present State of the Ottoman Empire*, 188.

CHAPTER 10

1. Gülrü Necipoğlu, "Süleymân the Magnificent and the Representation of Power in the Context of Ottoman-Habsburg-Papal Rivalry," in *Süleymân the Magnificent and His Time*, ed. Halil İnalcik and Cemal Kafadar (Istanbul: Isis Press, 1993), 163–94.

2. Hajji Ali Efendi, *Fethname-i Kamaniça*, fols. 17b, 130b.

3. Vani Mehmed Efendi, *'Ara'is al-Kur'an wa Nafa'is al-Furkan*, Suleimaniye Library, Yeni Cami 100. Subsequent references to this source are cited parenthetically throughout this section. The commentary is discussed, and several sections are loosely translated into Turkish in Pazarbaşı, *Vânî Mehmed Efendi ve Araisü'l-Kur'an*.

4. In his summary translation of this and other passages, Pazarbaşı, *Vânî Mehmed Efendi ve Araisü'l-Kur'an*, omits any references to Kurds found in the original.

5. See Wolper, *Cities and Saints*, 92–98.

6. Musavvir Hüseyin, *Silsilenâme*, Vakıflar Genel Müdürlüğü (Ankara: Kasa no. 4-181 4, 2000), fol. 40a.

7. Musavvir Hüseyin, *Silsilenâme*, Österreichische Nationalbibliothek, Vienna, Handschriftensammlung A.F. 50; *Rosenkranz der Weltgeschichte/Subat al-Ahbar*, Vollständige Wiedergabe Im Originalformat von Codex Vindobonensis A.F. 50 (Graz: Akademische Druck–u. Verlagsanstalt, 1981), 16a.

8. *Rosenkranz der Weltgeschichte/Subat al-Ahbar*, fol. 16b.

9. V. J. Parry, "The Reign of Sulaimān the Magnificent, 1520–66," in Cook, *A History of the Ottoman Empire to 1730*, 83–84.

10. Gökyay, *Evliya Çelebi Seyahatnâmesi*, 117.

11. Hagen, "Ottoman Understandings of the World," 231–33.

12. Silahdar, *Tarih-i Silahdar*, 1:757–58.

13. Anonymous, *Vekāyi'nāme*, fol. 63b.

14. This official recorded the participants in meetings of the council, the type of cloaks distributed to them, and gifts presented to the sultan. Topkapı Palace Museum Library, MS. Revan 1310. A summary translation of the work was published as *Kara Mustafa vor Wien: Das türkische Tagebuch der Belagerung Wiens 1683, verfasst vom Zeremonienmeister der Hohen Pforte*, Herausgegeben von Richard F. Kreutel (1955; München: Deutscher Taschenbuch Verlag GMBH, 1967); and a Turkish translation of the German appeared as *Devlet-i Aliyye Teşrifatçıbaşısı Ahmed Ağa'nın Viyana Kuşatması Günlüğü*, çeviren, düzenleyen, açıklayan Richard F. Kreutel, Türkçesi Esat Nermi (Istanbul: Milliyet Yayınları, 1970).

15. Silahdar, *Tarih-i Silahdar*, 2:9–10, 13–14.

16. Géza Dávid, "New and Little Known Sources Concerning Merzifonlu Kara Mustafa Pasha and His Time," in *Merzifonlu Kara Mustafa Paşa Uluslararası Sempozyumu*, 75–90, 87.

17. Silahdar, *Tarih-i Silahdar*, 2:14.

18. Kreutel, *Kara Mustafa vor Wien*, 13–14, 16; Nermi, *Viyana Kuşatması Günlüğü*, 29–30, 32.

19. Kreutel, *Kara Mustafa vor Wien*, 15, 16, 17; Nermi, *Viyana Kuşatması Günlüğü*, 31, 33–34, 35.

20. Kreutel, *Kara Mustafa vor Wien*, 24; Nermi, *Viyana Kuşatması Günlüğü*, 47.

21. Dávid, "New and Little Known Sources Concerning Merzifonlu Kara Mustafa Pasha," 81, 89–90.

22. Rycaut, *The Present State of the Ottoman Empire*, 290. Rycaut covered the period up to 1676; events of the following decade appear in a continuation by Sir Roger Manley, Knight. Rycaut translated the text to read as follows: the sultan sent his army to take Vienna "and establish there the Cult of our Divine Religion; 'tis therefore, that before we draw our fatal Cymetars, as our chief End is the Propagation of the Musselman Faith, and that is expressly commanded us by the Laws of Our Holy Prophet, first and before all things, to exhort you to embrace our Holy Religion, we do hereby advertise you, that if you will cause your selves to be instructed in our Mysteries, you will find the Salvation of your Souls therein."

23. Kreutel, *Kara Mustafa vor Wien*, 19, 20; Nermi, *Viyana Kuşatması Günlüğü*, 39, 40.

24. Kreutel, *Kara Mustafa vor Wien*, 20–21, 31–32; Nermi, *Viyana Kuşatması Günlüğü*, 41–45, 57–59, 61, 72, 82. Other terms referring to swine were also used; in Ottoman texts a covered gallery in a fortification is called a "pigsty."

25. Kreutel, *Kara Mustafa vor Wien*, 25; Nermi, *Viyana Kuşatması Günlüğü*, 48.

26. Kreutel, *Kara Mustafa vor Wien*, 27–28, 30; Nermi, *Viyana Kuşatması Günlüğü*, 51, 52–53, 55.

27. Kreutel, *Kara Mustafa vor Wien*, 31–32, 44, 47, 48; Nermi, *Viyana Kuşatması Günlüğü*, 57, 58, 74, 75, 80–81.

28. Kreutel, *Kara Mustafa vor Wien*, 57; Nermi, *Viyana Kuşatması Günlüğü*, 92. She passed away August 4. See Silahdar, *Tarih-i Silahdar*, 2:116.

29. Silahdar, *Tarih-i Silahdar*, 2:117.

30. Kreutel, *Kara Mustafa vor Wien*, 61, 62, 65, 67; Nermin, *Viyana Kuşatması Günlüğü*, 99, 100, 104, 107.

31. Kreutel, *Kara Mustafa vor Wien*, 68, 69–70; Nermin, *Viyana Kuşatması Günlüğü*, 108, 110–11.

32. Kreutel, *Kara Mustafa vor Wien*, 71, 74; Nermin, *Viyana Kuşatması Günlüğü*, 113, 118.

33. Kreutel, *Kara Mustafa vor Wien*, 76; Nermin, *Viyana Kuşatması Günlüğü*, 121.

34. Anonymous, *A Description of Vienna*.

35. Kreutel, *Kara Mustafa vor Wien*, 76; Nermin, *Viyana Kuşatması Günlüğü*, 121.

36. Kreutel, *Kara Mustafa vor Wien*, 77; Nermin, *Viyana Kuşatması Günlüğü*, 122.

37. Nihadi, *Tarih-i Nihadi*, fol. 225b.

38. Kreutel, *Kara Mustafa vor Wien*, 77–78; Nermin, *Viyana Kuşatması Günlüğü*, 123.

39. This makes for a gripping narrative, but in fact, although the symbolic loss would have been immense, it would not have been a complete calamity if that banner

had been captured. The Ottoman dynasty had much earlier divided Muhammad's banner into three pieces, sending one on campaign and keeping two in the treasury.

40. Anonymous, *A Description of Vienna*.

41. Kreutel, *Kara Mustafa vor Wien*, 78, 80; Nermin, *Viyana Kuşatması Günlüğü*, 124, 127.

42. *The Letter of the King of Poland, To His Excellency the Marquess De Grana, From the Turkish Camp in the Viziers Tent at Vienna, the 13th of September 1683* (London: Walker Davis, 1683).

43. Silahdar, *Tarih-i Silahdar*, 2:117.

44. Abdi Pasha, *Vekāyi'nāme*, fol. 2b.

45. Baysun, "Mehmed IV," 552.

46. Kreutel, *Kara Mustafa vor Wien*, 79–80; Nermin, *Viyana Kuşatması Günlüğü*, 125, 126.

47. Kreutel, *Kara Mustafa vor Wien*, 81, 82–86; Nermin, *Viyana Kuşatması Günlüğü*, 129–32.

48. Nihadi, *Tarih-i Nihadi*, fol. 225b.

49. Silahdar, *Tarih-i Silahdar*, 2:91–92.

50. Baysun, "Mehmed IV," 554.

51. Kreutel, *Kara Mustafa vor Wien*, 87, 88; *Viyana Kuşatması Günlüğü*, 135–36, 137, 138.

52. Silahdar, *Tarih-i Silahdar*, 2:118. Subsequent references to this source are cited parenthetically throughout this section.

53. Nihadi, *Tarih-i Nihadi*, fol. 225a.

54. Anonymous, *Vekāyi'nāme*, fol. 48b.

55. The tomb and mosque were destroyed in a nineteenth-century earthquake. Ayvansarâyî Hüseyîn Efendi, *Hadîkatü'l-cevâmi' (Istanbul Câmileri ve Diğer Dînî–Sivil Mi'mârî Yapılar)*, hazırlayan Ahmed Nezih Galitekin (Istanbul: İşaret Yayınları, 2001), 575–76; *The Garden of the Mosques*, 478.

56. BOA, Ali Emiri Tasnifi, Mehmed IV: 10290, August 23, 1686; 10288, August 23, 1686; 10282, September 18, 1686.

57. BOA, Ali Emiri Tasnifi, Mehmed IV: 10292, August 24, 1686; 10293, September 14, 1686.

58. BOA, Ali Emiri Tasnifi, Mehmed IV: 10278, September 18, 1686.

59. BOA, Ali Emiri Tasnifi, Mehmed IV: 10274, August 23, 1686. This town is adjacent to the Rhodope region, which witnessed wide-scale conversion to Islam during this period.

60. BOA, Ali Emiri Tasnifi, Mehmed IV: 10280, September 11, 1686.

CHAPTER II

1. Silahdar, *Tarih-i Silahdar*, 2:241. Subsequent references to this source are cited parenthetically throughout this section.

2. Silahdar had previously modified the term "hunting" with the phrase "according to ancient custom," or "in a legal manner." The first linked the sultan to precedent, the second gave legitimacy to the activity.

3. Topkapı Palace Museum Archive, Arzlar E. 2445/132. The document is dated June 29, 1685.

4. Anonymous, *Vekāyi'nāme*, fol. 67a.

5. Baysun, "Mehmed IV," 555.

6. Baysun, "Mehmed IV," 555.

7. Katip Çelebi, *Fezleke*, 2:330; Naima, *Tarih-i Naima*, 4:333.

8. Anonymous, *Vekāyi'nāme*, fol. 80a.

9. Kafadar, *Between Two Worlds*, 148–50.

10. Gabriel Piterberg, "The Alleged Rebellion of Abaza Mehmed Paşa: Historiography and the Ottoman State in the Seventeenth Century," *International Journal of Turkish Studies* 8, nos. 1–2 (Spring 2002): 14.

11. Piterberg, *An Ottoman Tragedy*, 191–200.

12. Musavvir Hüseyin, *Silsilenâme*, Österreichische Nationalbibliothek, Vienna, Bildarchiv, Handschriftensammlung A.F. 17, fols. 36a, 35b.

13. Baysun, "Mehmed IV," 556.

14. Spence, *Emperor of China*, 8.

15. Anonymous, *Vekāyi'nāme*, fols. 48b–52a. Subsequent references to this source are cited parenthetically throughout this section.

16. Rycaut, *The Present State of the Ottoman Empire*, 114, 132. See also 221, where Rycaut relates that Jews froze to death while forced to act as drovers for the sultan who was wintering outside Salonica in 1669.

17. Ahmed Dede, *Jami' al-Duwal*, fol. 772b. Yusuf Nabi refers to the sultan as "the brocade of the divan of the sultanate." Yusuf Nabi, *Fethname-i Kamaniça*, fol. 3a.

18. Müneccimbaşı Ahmed b. Lutfullah, *Saha'ifu'l-ahbar*, Topkapı Palace Museum Library, MS. Baghdad 244, fol. 175a.

19. Müneccimbaşı Ahmed b. Lutfullah, *Sahaifu'l-ahbar*, 3 vols. (Istanbul: Matbaa-ı Amire, 1285/1868–69).

20. Selim I was not referred to as "the Grim" during his reign; likewise, Suleiman I was not called "the Lawgiver" while he was in power. Kafadar, *"The Myth of the Golden Age,"* 40.

21. Nihadi, *Tarih-i Nihadi*, fols. 1b–2a, 225a.

CONCLUSION

1. Piterberg, *An Ottoman Tragedy*, 164.

2. See Abou-El-Haj, *The 1703 Rebellion and the Structure of Ottoman Politics*.

3. Kafadar, *Between Two Worlds*, 149; also quoted in Piterberg, *An Ottoman Tragedy*, 165.

4. Köprülü Fazıl Mustafa served as the grand vizier of Mehmed IV's successor, Suleiman II, and Köprülü Hüseyin served as grand vizier under Mustafa II. The Kadızadelis may have had lost influence, but the Köprülüs had not.

5. B. Lewis, *The Jews of Islam*, 46–52.

6. Necipoğlu, *Architecture, Ceremonial, and Power*, 255–56.

7. Kathryn Babayan, *Mystics, Monarchs, and Messiahs: Cultural Landscapes of Early Modern Iran* (Cambridge, MA: Harvard University Press, 2002), xv, xxiv–xxxviii.

8. Ibid., xxviii.

9. Vera Basch Moreen, *Iranian Jewry's Hour of Peril and Heroism: A Study of Bābāī Ibn Lutf's Chronicle (1617–1662)* (New York: American Academy for Jewish Research, 1987).

10. Babayan, *Mystics, Monarchs, and Messiahs*, 411, 428–29, 144–45, 3–7, 230–31, 386, 471, 484–85.

11. Eaton, *The Rise of Islam and the Bengal Frontier*.

12. Marshall G. S. Hodgson, *The Venture of Islam: Conscience and History in a World Civilization* (Chicago: University of Chicago Press, 1974), 3:92–98.

13. Ira Lapidus, *A History of Islamic Societies* (New York: Cambridge University Press, 1988), 463.

14. The Russian empire was far more brutal in its treatment of people whose religion differed from that of the ruler. Russian czars perceived converting the population to Christianity to be an imperial raison d'état and a cornerstone of policy toward diverse imperial subjects. The Romanov dynasty conceived of itself as ordained by destiny to bring Christianity to its territories. Russian officials ensured that converts practiced Christianity and chained and jailed those who apostasized until they appeared to be believing Christians. Without a means of imposing orthodoxy, Ottoman authorities were incapable of implementing policies such as these: nothing like Christian inquisitorial tribunals, which identified, prosecuted, and punished heretics, existed in the Islamic empire. See Khodarkovsky, *Russia's Steppe Frontier*, 2, 186, 189, 191, 192.

15. For the reign of Abdülhamid II, see Selim Deringil, *The Well-Protected Domains: Ideology and the Legitimation of Power in the Ottoman Empire, 1876–1909* (London: I. B. Tauris, 1998), 171.

16. Eugene Rogan, *Frontiers of the State in the Ottoman Empire: Transjordan, 1850–1920* (New York: Cambridge University Press, 1999), 197–201; Selim Deringil, "The Struggle against Shi'ism in Hamidian Iraq," *Die Welt des Islams* 30 (1990): 45–62.

17. Lisa Wedeen, *Ambiguities of Domination: Politics, Rhetoric, and Symbols in Contemporary Syria* (Chicago: University of Chicago Press, 1999), 6, 12, 14, 18, 19, 21.

18. This is similar to what was later attempted in revolutionary France. See Mona Ozouf, *Festivals and the French Revolution*, trans. Alan Sheridan (Cambridge, MA: Harvard University Press, 1988).

POSTSCRIPT

1. What was purported to be his skull was paraded around Vienna during the 250th anniversary of the siege of the city in 1933. Kerstin Tomenendal, "Die Vermeintliche Rippe Kara Mustafa Paschas İn Kremsmünster, Oberösterreich," in *Merzifonlu Kara Mustafa Paşa Uluslararası Sempozyumu*, 281–86; N. Berin Taşan, "Merzifonlu Kara Mustafa Paşa'nın Mezarı ve Viyana Müzesindeki Kafatası," in *Merzifonlu Kara Mustafa Paşa Uluslararası Sempozyumu*, 287–98.

2. Kołodziejczyk, *The Ottoman Survey Register of Podolia*, 52.

3. Quataert, *The Ottoman Empire, 1700–1922*, 2.

4. Keane, *Christian Moderns*, 41, 79–80.

5. Galland, *Istanbul*, 1:210–11.

6. Today the town lies in Montenegro. The Kurdish boy redeemer who had also led a threatening religious movement died of plague in the palace in Edirne in 1675. His movement had no lasting significance. Silahdar, *Tarih-i Silahdar*, 1:435.

7. Unfortunately, there is no trace of Shabbatai Tzevi's tomb. Nathan of Gaza's tomb in Skopje, Macedonia, survived until the early twentieth century.

8. Yehuda Liebes, *Studies in Jewish Myth and Jewish Messianism*, trans. Batya Stein (Albany: State University of New York Press, 1993), 100–101.

9. Marc Baer, "The Double Bind of Race and Religion: The Conversion of the Dönme to Turkish Secular Nationalism," *Comparative Studies in Society and History* 46, no. 4 (October 2004): 678–712.

Bibliography

EARLY MODERN SOURCES

Ottoman Literary Sources

MANUSCRIPT COLLECTIONS, ISTANBUL, TURKEY

Topkapı Palace Museum Library

Abdi Efendi. *Sur-name-i Sultan Mehmed ibn Ibrahim Han*. Revan 823.

Abdurrahman Abdi Pasha. *Şerh-i Kasîde-i Bürde*. H. Hüsnü Paşa 1013/2.

Anonymous. *Vekāyi'-i Beç*. Revan 1310.

Anonymous. *Vekāyi'nāme*. Hazine 1468.

Hasan Agha. *Cevahir et-Tarih*. Revan 1307.

Kürd Hatib Mustafa. *Risāle-i Kürd Hatīb*. Eski Hazine 1400.

Mehmed Halife. *Tarih-i Gilmani*. Revan 1306.

Mehmed Hemdani Solakzade. *Tarih-i Al-i Osman*. Ahmed III 3078.

Mehmed Necati. *Tarih-i Feth-i Yanık*. Revan 1308.

Minkârī Ali Halife Efendi. *Şifa' al-Mü'min*. Antalya-Tekelioğlu 397.

Müneccimbaşı Ahmed b. Lutfullah. *Saha'ifu'l-ahbar*. Bağdat 244.

Nihadi. *Tarih-i Nihadi*. Bağdat 219.

Sârī Abdullah Efendi. *Nasīhât al-mülūk targīben li-hüsn al-sülūk*. Esad Efendi 1910.

Vecihi Hasan Çelebi. *Tarih-i Vecihi*. Revan 1153.

Yusuf Nabi. *Fethname-i Kamaniça*. Hazine 1629.

Suleimaniye Library

Ahmed Dede ibn Lutfullah. *Jami' al-Duwal fi al-Tarikh*. Esad Efendi 2101–2103.

Çatalcalı Ali ibn Mehmed Efendi. *Fetāvā-i 'Ali Efendi*. Serrez 1113.

Hajji Ali Efendi. *Fethname-i Kamaniça*. Lala Ismail 308.

Hüseyin Behçeti. *Mirac'üz-zafer*. Esad Efendi 2368.

Minkarizade Yahya b. Ömer. *Fetāvā-i Minkarizade Efendi*. Hamidiye 610.

Nasuh Paşazade Ömer Bey. *Turhan Vâlide Sultan Vakıfnamesi*. Turhan Vâlide Sultan 150.

Vani Mehmed Efendi. *'Ara'is al-Kur'an wa Nafa'is al-Furkan*. Yeni Cami 100.

―――. *Münşe'at Vani Efendi*. Hagia Sophia 4308.

―――. *Risāla fī hakk al-farż wa al-sunna wa al-bid'a fī ba'z al-'amal*. Lala İsmail 685/1.

―――. *Risāla fī karāhat al-jahr bi al-zikr*. Hacı Beşir Ağa 406/3.

Köprülü Library

Abdurrahman Abdi Pasha. *Vekāyi'nāme*. 216.

MANUSCRIPT COLLECTIONS, BERLIN, GERMANY

Staatliche Museen zu Berlin, Kunstbibliothek

Anonymous. *Türkische Trachtenbuch*. Lipperheide OZ 52.

MANUSCRIPT COLLECTIONS, VIENNA, AUSTRIA

Österreichische Nationalbibliothek, Porträtsammlung, Bildarchiv und Fideikom-missbibliothek

Anonymous. "Mahomet Istivs Nominis IIII Tvrcarvm et Totivs Orientis Imperator Infestissimvs Christianæ Religionis Hostis." Pg 26 25/1, Ptf. 30: (28).

Musavvir Hüseyin. *Silsilenâme*. Handschriftensammlung A.F. 17.

―――. *Silsilenâme*. Handschriftensammlung A.F. 50.

PUBLISHED LITERARY SOURCES

Abdurrahman Abdi Pasha. "Osmanlı Kanûnnâmeleri." *Millî Tetebbu'lar Mecmûʿası* 1, no. 2 (Temmuz-Ağustos 1331/1912): 497–544.

'Ayn 'Ali Efendi. *Kavânîn-i Âl-i Osman der Hülâsa-i Mezâmin-i Defter-i Dîvân*. Istanbul: Enderun Kitabevi, 1979.

Ayvansarâyî Hüseyîn Efendi. *Hadîkatü'l-cevâmi.' Istanbul Câmileri ve Diğer Dînî-Sivil Mi'mârî Yapılar*. Hazırlayan Ahmed Nezih Galitekin. Istanbul: İşaret Yayınları, 2001.

Defterdar Sarı Mehmed. *Zübde-i Vekayiât*. Ankara: Türk Tarih Kurumu Basımevi, 1995.

Derin, Fahri Çetin. *Abdurrahman Abdi Paşa Vekâyi'nâme'si: Tahlil ve Metin Tenkîdi, 1058–1093/1648–1682*. Doktora Tezi, İstanbul Üniversitesi, 1993.

Develi, Hayati. "İstanbul'a Dair 'Risâle-i Garîbe." *İstanbul Araştırmaları* 1 (Bahar 1997): 95–190.

Devlet-i Aliyye Teşrifatçıbaşısı Ahmed Ağa'nın Viyana Kuşatması Günlüğü. Çeviren, düzenleyen, açıklayan Richard F. Kreutel. Türkçesi Esat Nermi. Istanbul: Milliyet Yayınları, 1970.

Eremya Çelebi Kömürciyan. *İstanbul Tarihi: XVII Asırda İstanbul*. Trans. Hrand D. Andreasyan. 2nd ed. Istanbul: Eren, 1988.

Eyyubî Efendi Kânûnnâmesi, Tahlil ve Metin. Ed. Abdülkadir Özcan. Istanbul: Eren, 1988.

Gökyay, Orhan Şaik. *Evliya Çelebi Seyahatnâmesi, 1 Kitap: Istanbul*. Topkapı Sarayı Bağdat 304 Yazmasının Transkripsiyonu-Dizini. Istanbul: Yapı Kredi Yayınları, 1996.

Hafız Hüseyin Al-Ayvansarayî. *The Garden of the Mosques: Hafız Hüseyin Al-Ayvansarayî's Guide to the Muslim Monuments of Ottoman Istanbul*. Trans. Howard Crane. Leiden: Brill, 2000.

Ibn Bibi. *El-Evâmiru'l-Alâiye fi Umûri'l-Alâiye*. Trans. Mürsel Öztürk. 2 vols. Ankara: Kültür Bakanlığı Yayınları, 1996.

'Îsâ-zâde. *'Îsâ-zâde Târîhi*. Ed. Ziya Yılmazer. Istanbul: Istanbul Fetih Cemiyeti, 1996.

Kara Mustafa vor Wien: Das türkische Tagebuch der Belagerung Wiens 1683, verfasst vom Zeremonienmeister der Hohen Pforte. Herausgegeben von Richard F. Kreutel. 1955. Munich: Deutscher Taschenbuch Verlag GMBH, 1967.

Karaçelebizade Abdülaziz Efendi. *Ravzatü'l-ebrâr zeyli* (Tahlîl ve Metin). 1732. Ed. Nevzat Kaya. Ankara: Türk Tarihi Kurumu Basımevi, 2003.

Katip Chelebi. *The Balance of Truth, by Katip Chelebi*. Translated with an introduction and notes by G. L. Lewis. Ethical and Religious Classics of East and West, no. 19. London: Allen and Unwin, 1957.

———. *Fezleke*. 2 vols. Istanbul: Ceride-i Havadis Matbaası, 1286/1869.

McNeill, William H., and Marilyn Robinson Waldman, eds. *The Islamic World*. Chicago: University of Chicago Press, 1983.

Mehmed Kamil Pasha. *Tarih-i Siyasi-yi Devlet-i Âliye-yi Osmaniye*. 3 vols. Istanbul: Matbaa-yi Ahmet İhsan, 1325/1909.

Müneccimbaşı Ahmed b. Lutfullah. *Sahaifu'l-ahbar*. 3 vols. Istanbul: Matbaa-ı Amire, 1285/1868–69.

Musavvir Hüseyin. *Silsilenâme*. Ankara: Vakıflar Genel Müdürlüğü, Kasa no. 4-181 4, 2000.

Mustafa Naima, *Tarih-i Naima, Ravzat ül-Hüseyn fi hulasat-i ahbar el-hafikayn*. 6 vols. Istanbul: Matbaa-yi Âmire, 1864.

Râşid Mehmed Efendi. *Târîh-i Râşid*. 2 vols. Istanbul, 1282/1865.

Rosenkranz der Weltgeschichte/Subat al-Ahbar. Vollständige Wiedergabe Im Original format von Codex Vindobonensis A.F. 50. Graz: Akademische Druck-u. Verlagsanstalt, 1981.

Silahdar Fındıklılı Mehmed Ağa. *Silahdar Tarihi*. 2 vols. Istanbul: Devlet Matbaası, 1928.

OTTOMAN ARCHIVAL SOURCES, ISTANBUL, TURKEY

Topkapı Palace Museum Archive

Arzlar (Writs) E. 2445/114, 2445/132, 7002/1-E. 7002/86, 7008/17
IV Mehmed, No. E., Ar. 11679
Tahriratlar (Dispatches) E. 3890, 7645, 10267

Office of the Istanbul Mufti, Islamic Law Court Records Archive

Beşiktaş Şer'iye Sicilleri 23/73, 23/75–23/85
Galata Şer'iye Sicilleri 78, 80, 82, 85, 87, 89, 91–92, 95, 98, 100, 102, 104, 106, 108, 110, 112, 114, 116, 118, 120, 122, 125–26, 128, 131, 134, 137, 141, 143–44, 146
Hasköy Şer'iye Sicilleri 19/8–19/11

Istanbul Şer'iye Sicilleri 8–18
Yeniköy Şer'iye Sicilleri 18/50–18/75

Prime Ministry's Ottoman Archive (BOA)

Ali Emiri Tasnifi, Ahmed I: 671, 757
Ali Emiri Tasnifi, Mehmed IV: 504, 608–9, 626, 1169–72, 1642, 1676, 1710, 1729,
       1732, 1986, 2175, 2187–89, 4454, 4766, 4820, 4823–24, 5145, 7016, 9845, 9853,
       9911, 9915, 9928, 9946, 9957, 10273–95, 10297–98
Ali Emiri Tasnifi, Murad IV: 278
İbnülemin Tasnifi, Hil'at Defteri (Imperial Register of Cloaks): 17
Kâmil Kepeci Tasnifi, Küçük Ruznamçe (Palace Salary Register): 3399–439
Şikâyet Defteri (Complaint Register): 5, 6, 7, 8

Published Archival Sources

Kołodziejczyk, Dariusz. *The Ottoman Survey Register of Podolia (ca. 1681), Defter-i
       Mufassal-i Eyalet-i Kamaniçe,* part 1: Text, Translation, and Commentary. Studies in
       Ottoman Documents Pertaining to Ukraine and the Black Sea Countries. Vol. 3.
       Cambridge, MA: Harvard University Press, 2004.
Refik, Ahmed. *Onbirinci Asr-ı Hicrî'de İstanbul Hayatı (1592–1688).* 1931. Istanbul:
       Enderun Kitabei, 1988.
———. *Onikinci Asr-ı Hicrî'de İstanbul Hayatı (1689–1785).* 1930. Istanbul: Enderun
       Kitabevi, 1988.
———. *Onuncu Asr-ı Hicrî'de İstanbul Hayatı (1495–1591).* 1917. Istanbul: Enderun
       Kitabevi, 1988.
Sources ottomanes sur les processus d'Islamization aux Balkans. Traduction des docu-
       ments A. Velkov et al. Serie sources 2. Sofia: Éditions de l'Academie bulgare des
       sciences, 1990.

CENTRAL AND WESTERN EUROPEAN SOURCES

Anonymous. *The Character of a Coffee-House.* London, 1661.
Anonymous. *A Description of Vienna in its Ancient and Present state; With an exact and
       compleat Account of the SIEGE thereof: Began by the Ottoman Emperour on the 16th
       of July, 1683, and Continued until the 12th of September following; at which time the
       Siege was Rais'd, and a Total Defeat given to the Turkish Army, by the Christians.*
       London: Printed for Randolph Taylor, 1683.
Busbecq, Ogier Ghislain de. *Turkish Letters* [with a new introduction by Philip Mansel].
       London: Sickle Moon Books, 2001.
Covel, John. "Dr. Covel's Diary." In *Early Voyages and Travels in the Levant,* ed. J. Theodore
       Bent. Vol. 87. London: Hakluyt Society, 1893, 99–287.
de Tournefort, Joseph Pitton. *Voyage d'un Botaniste.* 2 vols. Vol. 2: *La Turquie, la
       Géorgie, l'Arménie.* Notes and bibliography by Stéphane Yerasimos. Paris: FM/La
       Découverte, 1982.

Galland, Antoine. *İstanbul'a Ait Günlük Hâtıralar (1672–1673)*. Trans. Nahid Sırrı Örik. 2 vols. 2nd ed. Ankara: Türk Tarih Kurumu Basımevi, 1987.

The Letter of the King of Poland, To His Excellency the Marquess De Grana, From the Turkish Camp in the Viziers Tent at Vienna, the 13th of September 1683. London: Walker Davis, 1683.

The Memoirs of Glückel of Hameln. Trans. Marvin Lowenthal. New York: Schocken Books, 1977.

Rycaut, Paul. *The Present State of the Ottoman Empire*. London: Printed for Tho. Basset, 1687.

REFERENCE WORKS

Dictionaries and Paleographic Guides

Dankoff, Robert. *An Evliya Çelebi Glossary: Unusual, Dialectical and Foreign Words in the Seyahat-name*. Ed. Şinasi Tekin. Sources of Oriental Languages and Literatures 14. Turkish Sources 12. Cambridge, MA: Harvard University, Department of Near Eastern Languages and Civilizations, 1991.

Devellioğlu, Ferit. *Osmanlıca-Türkçe Ansiklopedik Lûgat*. 13th ed. Aydın Kitabevi Yayınları Sözlük Dizisi, no. 1. Ankara: Aydın Kitabevi, 1996.

Günday, Dündar. *Arşiv Belgelerinde Siyakat Yazısı Özellikleri ve Divan Rakamları*. Atatürk Kültür, Dil ve Tarih Yüksek Kurumu Türk Tarih Kurumu Yayınları VII. Dizi—Sa. 57a. Ankara: Türk Tarih Kurumu Basımevi, 1989.

Öztürk, Said. *Osmanlı Arşiv Belgelerinde Siyakat Yazısı ve Tarihî Gelişimi*. Osmanlı Araştırmaları Vakfı Yayınları, no. 12. Istanbul: Cihan Matbaası, 1996.

Pakalın, M. Zeki. *Osmanlı Tarih Deyimleri ve Terimleri Sözlüğü*. 3 vols. Istanbul: Milli Eğitim Basımevi, 1946–54.

Redhouse, James W. *A Turkish and English Lexicon shewing in English the significations of the Turkish terms*. 2nd ed. Çağrı Yayınları Lûgatlar Dizisi, no. 3. Istanbul: Eko Matbaası, 1992.

Reychman, Jan, and Ananiasz Zajaczkowski. *Handbook of Ottoman-Turkish Diplomatics*. Trans. Andrew S. Ehrenkreutz. Ed. Tibor Halasi-Kun. Publications in Near and Middle Eastern Studies, Columbia University, no. 7. The Hague: Mouton, 1968.

Steingass, F. *A Comprehensive Persian-English Dictionary including the Arabic Words and Phrases to Be Met with in Persian Literature*. 2nd ed. London: Kegan Paul, Trench, Trubner, 1930.

Tarama Sözlüğü. 8 vols. 3rd ed. Atatürk Kültür, Dil ve Tarih Yüksek Kurumu Türk Dil Kurumu Yayınları, no. 212. Ankara: Ankara Üniversitesi Basımevi, 1995.

Bibliographies, Encyclopedias, Catalogs, and Other Aids

Akgündüz, Ahmed. *Şer'iye Sicilleri: Mahiyeti, Toplu Kataloğu ve Seçme Hükümler*. Vol. 1. Istanbul: Türk Dünyası Araştırmaları Vakfı, 1988.

Babinger, Franz. *Die Geschichtsschreiber der Osmanen und ihre Werke*. Leipzig: Otto Harrassowitz, 1927.

Başbakanlık Osmanlı Arşivi Katalogları Rehberi. Ankara: T.C. Başbakanlık Devlet
 Arşivleri Genel Müdürlüğü Osmanlı Arşivi Daire Başkanlığı, 1995.

Danişmend, İsmail Hâmi. *İzahlı Osmanlı Tarihi Kronolojisi.* 5 vols. Istanbul: Türkiye
 Yayınevi, 1971–72.

Dankoff, Robert, and Klaus Kreiser. *Materialien zu Evliya Çelebi II. A Guide to the
 Seyāhat-nāme of Evliya Çelebi.* Bibliographie raisonnée, Beihefte zum Tübinger
 Atlas des Vorderen Orients, Reihe B (Geisteswissenschaften), no. 90/2. Wies-
 baden: Ludwig Reichart, 1992.

Encyclopaedia Iranica. 13 vols. 1983–present. London: Routledge and Kegan Paul.

Encyclopaedia of Islam. New ed. 11 vols. 1960–present. Leiden: Brill.

Encyclopaedia Judaica. 17 vols. 1972. New York: Macmillan.

An Historical Atlas of Islam. Ed. William C. Brice. Leiden: Brill, 1981.

İlmiye Sâlnâmesi. Istanbul: Matbaa-i Âmire, 1334.

İslam Ansiklopedisi. 13 vols. 1940–86. Istanbul: Maarif Basımevi.

Karatay, Fehmi Edhem, ed. *Topkapı Sarayı Müzesi Kütüphanesi, Türkçe Yazmalar
 Kataloğu.* 2 vols. Topkapı Sarayı Müzesi Yayınları, no. 11. Istanbul: Topkapı Sarayı
 Müzesi, 1961.

Kassis, Hanna. *A Concordance of the Qur'an.* Foreword by Fazlur Rahman. Berkeley:
 University of California Press, 1983.

Konularına Göre Kur'an (Sistematik Kur'an Fihristi). Ed. Ömer Özsoy and İlhami Güler.
 Fecr Yayınevi, no. 44. Ankara: Fecr Yayınevi, 1997.

The Koran. Trans. N. J. Dawood. 4th rev. ed. New York: Penguin Books, 1985.

Kur'ân-ı Kerim ve Yüce Meâli. Ed. Ayntabî Mehmed Efendi. Istanbul: Huzur Yayın, n.d.

Mostras, C. *Dictionnaire géographique de l'Empire ottoman.* 1873. Istanbul: Pera Turizm
 ve Ticaret Limited Şirketi, 1995.

Pitcher, Donald Edgar. *An Historical Geography of the Ottoman Empire.* Leiden: Brill,
 1972.

Süreyya, Mehmed. *Sicill-i Osmanî.* Eski Yazıdan Aktaran Seyit Ali Kahraman. 6 vols.
 Tarih Vakfı Yurt Yayınları 30. 1890–99. Istanbul: Numune Matbaacılık, 1996.

Türkiye Diyanet Vakfı İslam Ansiklopedisi. 30 vols. 1988–present. Istanbul: Türkiye
 Diyanet Vakfı.

Unat, Faik Reşit. *Hicrî Tarihleri Milâdî Tarihe Çevirme Kılavuzu.* 7th ed. Ankara: Türk
 Tarih Kurumu Basımevi, 1994.

MODERN WORKS CITED IN THE TEXT

Abou-El-Haj, Rifa'at Ali. *The 1703 Rebellion and the Structure of Ottoman Politics.* Leiden:
 Nederlands Instituut voor het Nabije Oosten, 1984.

Akdağ, Mustafa. *Celâlî İsyanları, 1550–1603.* Ankara: Ankara Üniversitesi Basımevi, 1963.

Alderson, A. D. *The Structure of the Ottoman Dynasty.* 1956. Westport, CT: Greenwood
 Press, 1982.

And, Metin. *Osmanlı Tasvir Sanatları: 1 Minyatür.* Istanbul: Türkiye İş Bankası, 2002.

Arkoun, Mohammed. *Rethinking Islam: Common Questions, Uncommon Answers.* Trans.
 Robert D. Lee. Boulder, CO: Westview Press, 1994.

Aslanapa, Oktay. *Osmanlı Devri Mimarîsi: Orhan Gaziden başlıyarak sonuna kadar Padişahlara göre gelişmesi*. İstanbul: İnkılâp Kitabevi, 1986.

Babayan, Kathryn. *Mystics, Monarchs, and Messiahs: Cultural Landscapes of Early Modern Iran*. Cambridge, MA: Harvard University Press, 2002.

Badinter, Elizabeth. *XY: On Masculine Identity*. Trans. Lydia Davis. New York: Columbia University Press, 1995.

Baer, Marc. "The Double Bind of Race and Religion: The Conversion of the Dönme to Turkish Secular Nationalism." *Comparative Studies in Society and History* 46, no. 4 (October 2004): 678–712.

———. "Islamic Conversion Narratives of Women: Social Change and Gendered Religious Hierarchy in Early Modern Ottoman Istanbul." *Gender and History* 16, no. 2 (August 2004): 425–58.

Balivet, Michel. *Byzantins et Ottomans: Relations, interaction, succession*. Analecta Isisiana 35. Istanbul: Les Éditions Isis, 1999.

Barkan, Ömer Lütfi. "Osmanlı İmparatorluğunda Bir İskan ve Kolonizasyon Metodu Olarak Vakıflar ve Temlikler I: İstila Devirlerinin Kolonizatör Türk Dervişleri ve Zaviyeler." *Vakıflar Dergisi* 2 (1942): 279–386.

Barnai, Jacob. "Ha-kehilim be-Izmir be-me'ah ha-sheva-esreh." *Pe'amim* 48 (1992): 66–84.

Bayly, C. A. *Imperial Meridian: The British Empire and the World, 1780–1830*. London: Longman, 1989.

Benayahu, Meir. "Rofeh he-hatzer rav Moshe Benvenest ve-shir al-higliyito le-Rodos me-rav Yehudah Zarko." *Sefunot* 12, Sefer Yavan II (1971–78): 123–44.

Benbassa, Esther, and Aron Rodrigue. *Sephardi Jewry: A History of the Judeo-Spanish Community, 14th–20th Centuries*. Berkeley: University of California Press, 2000.

Bertelli, Sergio. *The King's Body: Sacred Rituals of Power in Medieval and Early Modern Europe*. Trans. R. Burr Litchfield. University Park: Pennsylvania State University Press, 2001.

Bierman, Irene. *Writing Signs: The Fatimid Public Text*. Berkeley: University of California Press, 1998.

Birge, John Kingsley. *The Bektashi Order of Dervishes*. London: Luzac, 1937.

Birnbaum, Eleazar. "Hekim Yakub, Physician to Sultan Mehemmed the Conquerer." *Harofe Haivri: The Hebrew Medical Journal* 1 (1961): 222–50.

Brownell, Susan, and Jeffrey N. Wasserstrom. "Introduction: Theorizing Femininities and Masculinities." In *Chinese Femininities/Chinese Masculinities: A Reader*, ed. Susan Brownell and Jeffrey N. Wasserstrom. Berkeley: University of California Press, 2002, 1–41.

Çetin, Osman. *Sicillere Göre Bursa'da İhtida Hareketleri ve Sosyal Sonuçları (1472–1909)*. Ankara: Türk Tarih Kurumu Basımevi, 1994.

Cezar, Mustafa. "Osmanlı Devrinde İstanbul Yapılarında Tahribat Yapan Yangınlar ve Tabii Afetler." *Türk Sanat Tarihi Araştırma ve İncelemeleri* 1 (Istanbul, 1963): 327–414.

Choksy, Jamsheed. *Conflict and Cooperation: Zoroastrian Subalterns and Muslim Elites in Medieval Iranian Society*. New York: Columbia University Press, 1997.

Clark, Christopher. *The Politics of Conversion: Missionary Protestantism and the Jews in Prussia 1728–1941*. Oxford: Clarendon Press, 1995.

Clayer, Nathalie. *Mystiques, état et société: Les Halvetis dans l'aire balkanique de la fin du Xve siècle à nos jours*. Islamic History and Civilization, Studies and Texts 9. New York: Brill, 1994.

Comaroff, Jean, and John Comaroff. "Christianity and Colonialism in South Africa." *American Ethnologist* 13 (1986): 1–22.

Cook, Michael. *Commanding Right and Forbidding Wrong in Islamic Thought*. New York: Cambridge University Press, 2000.

Dankoff, Robert. *The Intimate Life of an Ottoman Statesman: Melek Ahmed Paşa (1588–1662) as Portrayed in Evliya Çelebi's Book of Travels (Seyahat-name)*. Translation and commentary by Robert Dankoff, with a historical introduction by Rhoads Murphey. Albany: State University of New York Press, 1991.

———. *An Ottoman Mentality: The World of Evliya Çelebi*. Afterword by Gottfried Hagen. Leiden: Brill, 2004.

Dávid, Géza. "New and Little Known Sources Concerning Merzifonlu Kara Mustafa Pasha and His Time." In *Merzifonlu Kara Mustafa Paşa Uluslararası Sempozyumu*. Ankara: Merzifon Vakfı Yayınları, 2001, 75–90.

Dawson, Lorne. "Who Joins New Religious Movements and Why: Twenty Years of Research and What Have We Learned?" In *Cults and New Religious Movements: A Reader*, ed. Lorne Dawson. Malden, MA: Blackwell, 2003, 116–30.

Deringil, Selim. "The Struggle against Shi'ism in Hamidian Iraq." *Die Welt des Islams* 30 (1990): 45–62.

———. *The Well-Protected Domains: Ideology and the Legitimation of Power in the Ottoman Empire, 1876–1909*. London: I. B. Tauris, 1998.

Derrida, Jacques. *Of Grammatology*. Trans. Gayatri Chakravorty Spivak. Baltimore: Johns Hopkins University Press, 1976.

DeWeese, Devin. *Islamization and Native Religion in the Golden Horde: Baba Tükles and Conversion to Islam in Historical and Epic Tradition*. University Park: Pennsylvania State University Press, 1994.

Doğramacı, Baha. *Niyazi-yi Mısrî: Hayatı ve Eserleri*. Ankara: Kadıoğlu Matbaası, 1988.

Eaton, Richard. *The Rise of Islam and the Bengal Frontier, 1204–1760*. Berkeley: University of California Press, 1993.

Edgerton, Samuel Y. *Theaters of Conversion: Religious Architecture and Indian Artisans in Colonial Mexico*. Albuquerque: University of New Mexico Press, 2001.

El-Leithy, Tamer. "Sufis, Copts and the Politics of Piety: Moral Regulation in Fourteenth-Century Upper Egypt." In *Le développement du soufisme en Égypte à l'époque mamelouke*, ed. Richard McGregor. Cahier des Annales islamologiques 27. Cairo: Institut français d'archéologie orientale, 2006, 75–119.

Emecen, Feridun. "From the Founding to Küçük Kaynarca." In *History of the Ottoman State, Society and Civilisation*, ed. Ekmeleddin İhsanoğlu. 2 vols. Istanbul: Research Centre for Islamic History, Art and Culture, 2001, 1:3–62.

Epstein, Mark. *The Ottoman Jewish Communities and Their Role in the Fifteenth and Sixteenth Centuries*. Islamkundliche Untersuchungen Bd. 56. Freiburg: K. Schwarz, 1980.

Erünsal, İsmail. "II. Bâyezid Devrine Ait Bir İn´âmât Defteri." *Tarih Enstitüsu Dergisi* 12 (1981–82): 303–42.

Eyice, Semavi. *Galata ve Kulesi.* Istanbul: Türkiye Turing ve Otomobil Kurumu, 1969.

Faroqhi, Suraiya. "Crisis and Change, 1590–1699." In Suraiya Faroqhi et al., *An Economic and Social History of the Ottoman Empire,* vol. 2: *1600–1914.* Cambridge: Cambridge University Press, 1994, 411–623.

———. *Geschichte des Osmanischen Reiches.* Munich: C. H. Beck, 2000.

Findley, Carter Vaughn. *The Turks in World History.* New York: Oxford University Press, 2005.

Finkel, Caroline. *Osman's Dream: The Story of the Ottoman Empire, 1300–1923.* New York: Basic Books, 2005.

Fleischer, Cornell. *Bureaucrat and Intellectual in the Ottoman Empire: The Historian Mustafa Âli (1541–1600).* Princeton, NJ: Princeton University Press, 1986.

———. "From Şehzade Korkud to Mustafa Âli: Cultural Origins of the Ottoman Nasihatname." In *Proceedings.* 3rd Congress on the Social and Economic History of Turkey, Princeton University, August 24–26, 1983. Ed. Heath Lowry and Ralph S. Hattox. Istanbul: Isis Press, 1989, 67–77.

Fletcher, Anthony. *Gender, Sex, and Subordination in England, 1500–1800.* New Haven, CT: Yale University Press, 1995.

Fletcher, Richard. *The Barbarian Conversion: From Paganism to Christianity.* Berkeley: University of California Press, 1999.

Fodor, Pál. "Ahmedī's Dāsitān as a Source of Early Ottoman History." In *In Quest of the Golden Apple: Imperial Ideology, Politics, and Military Administration in the Ottoman Empire.* Analecta Isisiana 45. Istanbul: Isis Press, 2000, 9–22.

———. "Ottoman Policy towards Hungary, 1520–1541." *Acta Orientalia Academiæ Scientiarum Hungaricæ* 45 (1991): 271–345. Reprinted in *In Quest of the Golden Apple: Imperial Ideology, Politics, and Military Administration in the Ottoman Empire.* Analecta Isisiana 45. Istanbul: Isis Press, 2000, 105–169.

———. "State and Society, Crisis and Reform, in 15th–17th Century Ottoman Mirror for Princes." In *In Quest of the Golden Apple: Imperial Ideology, Politics, and Military Administration in the Ottoman Empire.* Analecta Isisiana 45. Istanbul: Isis Press, 2000, 23–44.

———. "Ungarn und Wien in der osmanischen Eroberungsideologie (im Spiegel der *Târîh-i Beç krâlı,* 17. Jahrhundert)." In *In Quest of the Golden Apple: Imperial Ideology, Politics, and Military Administration in the Ottoman Empire.* Analecta Isisiana 45. Istanbul: Isis Press, 2000, 45–69.

———. "The View of the Turk in Hungary: The Apocalyptic Tradition and the Red Apple in Ottoman-Hungarian Context." In *In Quest of the Golden Apple: Imperial Ideology, Politics, and Military Administration in the Ottoman Empire.* Analecta Isisiana 45. Istanbul: Isis Press, 2000, 71–103.

Foucault, Michel. *Discipline and Punish: The Birth of the Prison.* Trans. Alan Sheridan. New York: Vintage Books, 1977.

———. "Governmentality." In *The Foucault Effect: Studies in Governmentality,* ed. Graham Burchell, Colin Gordon, and Peter Miller. Chicago: University of Chicago Press, 1991, 87–103.

———. *The History of Sexuality: An Introduction*. Vol. 1. Trans. Robert Hurley. New York: Random House, 1978.

Galanté, Avram. *Esther Kyra d'après de nouveaux documents*. Constantinople: Fratelli Haim, 1926.

———. *Histoire des juifs d'Istanbul*. Istanbul: Imprimerie Hüsnutabat, 1941.

———. *Médecins juifs au service de la Turquie*. Istanbul: Imprimerie Babok, 1938.

———. *Nouveaux documents sur Sabbetaï Sevi: Organisation et us et coutumes de ses adeptes*. Istanbul: Société anonyme de papeterie et d'imprimerie (Fratelli Haim), 1935.

Gallagher, Eugene. *Expectation and Experience: Explaining Religious Conversion*. Atlanta, GA: Scholars Press, 1990.

Geertz, Clifford. *Negara: The Theater State in Nineteenth-Century Bali*. Princeton, NJ: Princeton University Press, 1980.

Goffman, Daniel. "Izmir: From Village to Colonial Port City." In *The Ottoman City between East and West: Aleppo, Izmir, and Istanbul*, ed. Edhem Eldem, Daniel Goffman, and Bruce Masters. Cambridge: Cambridge University Press, 1999, 79–134.

———. *The Ottoman Empire and Early Modern Europe*. New York: Cambridge University Press, 2002.

Gökbilgin, M.Tayyib. "Katip Çelebi, Interprète et rénovateur des traditions religieuses au XVIIe siècle." *Turcica* 3 (1971): 71–79.

Goldish, Matt. *The Sabbatean Prophets*. Cambridge, MA: Harvard University Press, 2004.

Gölpınarlı, Abdülbaki. *Mevlânâ'dan Sonra Mevlevîlik*. Istanbul: İnkilâp Kitabevi, 1953.

Goodwin, Godfrey. *A History of Ottoman Architecture*. Baltimore: Johns Hopkins University Press, 1971.

Gordon, Stewart. "A World of Investiture." In *Robes and Honor: The Medieval World of Investiture*, ed. Stewart Gordon. New York: Palgrave, 2001, 1–19.

Gövsa, İbrahim Alâettin. *Sabatay Sevi: İzmirli meşhur sahte Mesih hakkında tarihî ve içtimaî tetkik tecrübesi*. Istanbul: Lûtfi Kitabevi, 1939.

Greene, Molly. *A Shared World: Christians and Muslims in the Early Modern Mediterranean*. Princeton, NJ: Princeton University Press, 2000.

Griswold, William. *The Great Anatolian Rebellion, 1000–1020/1591–1611*. Islamkundliche Untersuchungen Bd. 83. Freiburg: K. Schwarz Verlag, 1983.

Gülsoy, Ersin. *Girit'in Fethi ve Osmanlı İdaresinin Kurulması, 1645–1670*. Istanbul: Tarih ve Tabiat Vakfı, 2004.

Hagen, Gottfried. "Ottoman Understandings of the World in the Seventeenth Century." In Robert Dankoff, *An Ottoman Mentality: The World of Evliya Çelebi*. Leiden: Brill, 2004, 215–56.

Hardy, Peter. "Modern European and Muslim Explanations of Conversion to Islam in South Asia: A Preliminary Survey of the Literature." In *Conversion to Islam*, ed. Nehemia Levtzion. New York: Holmes and Meier, 1979, 68–99.

Hasluck, F. W. *Christianity and Islam under the Sultans*. Ed. Margaret Hasluck. 2 vols. 1929. New York: Octagon Books, 1973.

Hathaway, Jane. "The Grand Vizier and the False Messiah: The Sabbatai Sevi Controversy and the Ottoman Reform in Egypt." *Journal of the American Oriental Society*
117, no. 4 (January–April 1997): 665–71.

———. *The Politics of Households in Ottoman Egypt: The Rise of the Qazdağlıs.* New
York: Cambridge University Press, 1997.

Hefner, Robert. "Introduction: World Building and the Rationality of Conversion."
In *Conversion to Christianity: Historical and Anthropological Perspectives on a Great
Transformation*, ed. Robert Hefner. Berkeley: University of California Press, 1993,
3–44.

Heyd, Uriel. "The Jewish Community of Istanbul in the Seventeenth Century." *Oriens*
6 (1953): 299–314.

———. "Moses Hamon, Chief Jewish Physician to Sultan Süleyman the Magnificent."
Oriens 16 (1963): 152–70.

Hodgson, Marshall G. S. *Rethinking World History: Essays on Europe, Islam, and World
History.* Ed. Edmund Burke III. New York: Cambridge University Press, 1993.

———. *The Venture of Islam: Conscience and History in a World Civilization.* 3 vols.
Vol. 3. Chicago: University of Chicago Press, 1974.

Howe, John. "The Conversion of the Physical World: The Creation of a Christian Landscape." In *Varieties of Religious Conversion in the Middle Ages*, ed. James Muldoon.
Gainesville: University Press of Florida, 1997, 63–78.

Hurvitz, Nimrod. "From Scholarly Circles to Mass Movements: The Formation of
Legal Communities in Islamic Societies." *American Historical Review* 108, no. 4
(October 2003): 985–1008.

Idel, Moshe. *Kabbalah: New Perspectives.* New Haven, CT: Yale University Press, 1988.

———. *Messianic Mystics.* New Haven, CT: Yale University Press, 1998.

———. "'One from a Town, Two from a Clan.' The Diffusion of Lurianic Kabbala and
Sabbateanism: A Re-Examination." *Jewish History* 7, no. 2 (Fall 1993): 79–104.

Imber, Colin. *The Ottoman Empire, 1300–1650: The Structure of Power.* Hampshire, UK:
Palgrave Macmillan, 2002.

———. "What Does *Ghazi* Actually Mean?" In *The Balance of Truth: Essays in Honour
of Professor Geoffrey Lewis*, ed. Çiğdem Balım-Harding and Colin Imber. Istanbul:
Isis Press, 2000, 165–78.

Inalcik, Halil. "The Emergence of the Ottomans." In *The Cambridge History of Islam*,
ed. P. M. Holt, Ann K. S. Lambton, and Bernard Lewis. New York: Cambridge
University Press, 1970, 1:263–91.

———. "Military and Fiscal Transformation in the Ottoman Empire, 1600–1700."
Archivum Ottomanicum 6 (1980): 283–337.

———. *The Ottoman Empire: The Classical Age, 1300–1600.* Trans. Norman Itzkowitz
and Colin Imber. New York: Praeger, 1973.

———. "Ottoman Galata, 1453–1553." In *Essays in Ottoman History.* Istanbul: Eren,
1998, 275–376.

———. "The Rise of the Ottoman Empire." In *The Cambridge History of Islam*, ed.
P. M. Holt, Ann K. S. Lambton, and Bernard Lewis. New York: Cambridge University Press, 1970, 1:295–321.

İstanbul Kanatlarımın Altında. Dir. Mustafa Altıoklar. Film. Umut Sanat Filmcilik ve Sinemacılık, 1996.

Itzkowitz, Norman. *Ottoman Empire and Islamic Tradition.* Chicago: University of Chicago Press, 1972.

James, William. *The Varieties of Religious Experience: A Study in Human Nature.* 1902. Cambridge, MA: Harvard University Press, 1985.

Kafadar, Cemal. *Between Two Worlds: The Construction of the Ottoman State.* Berkeley: University of California Press, 1995.

——. "The Myth of the Golden Age: Ottoman Historical Consciousness in the Post Süleymânic Era." In *Süleymân the Second and His Time,* ed. Halil İnalcik and Cemal Kafadar. Istanbul: Isis Press, 1993, 37–48.

Kafesçioğlu, Çigdem. "The Ottoman Capital in the Making: The Reconstruction of Constantinople in the Fifteenth Century." PhD diss., Harvard University, 1996.

Karras, Ruth Mazo. *From Boys to Men: Formations of Masculinity in Late Medieval Europe.* Philadelphia: University of Pennsylvania Press, 2003.

Kayra, Cahit, and Erol Üyepazarcı. *Mekânlar ve Zamanlar: Kandilli, Vaniköy, Çengelköy.* İstanbul Büyükşehir Belediyesi Kültür İşleri Dairesi Başkanlığı Yayınları, no. 13. Istanbul: İstanbul Büyükşehir Belediyesi, 1993.

Keane, Webb. *Christian Moderns: Freedom and Fetish in the Mission Encounter.* Berkeley: University of California Press, 2007.

Kent, Eliza. *Converting Women: Gender and Protestant Christianity in Colonial South India.* New York: Oxford University Press, 2004.

Khodarkovsky, Michael. *Russia's Steppe Frontier: The Making of a Colonial Empire, 1500–1800.* Bloomington: Indiana University Press, 2002.

Kissling, Hans. "Die Köprülü Restauration." In *Internationales Kulturhistorisches symposium Mogersdorf 1969.* Eisenstadt, Austria: 1972, 75–84.

Koçu, Reşad Ekrem. *Osmanlı Padişahları.* 1960. Istanbul: Doğan Kitap, 2002.

Kraemer, Joel. "Apostates, Rebels, and Brigands." *Israel Oriental Studies* 10 (1980): 34–73.

Kumbaracızade, İzzet. *Hekim-Başı odası, İlk eczane, Baş-Lala kulesi.* Istanbul: Kader Matbaası, 1933.

Kunt, Metin. "Ethnic-Regional (*Cins*) Solidarity in the Seventeenth-Century Ottoman Establishment." *International Journal of Middle East Studies* 5 (1974): 233–39.

Kurat, A. N. "The Reign of Mehmed IV, 1648–87." In *A History of the Ottoman Empire to 1730: Chapters from* The Cambridge History of Islam *and* The New Cambridge Modern History, by V. J. Parry, H. Inalcik, A. N. Kurat, and J. S. Bromley, ed. M. A. Cook. New York: Cambridge University Press, 1976, 157–77.

Kütükoğlu, Mübahat S., ed. *Osmanlılarda Narh Müessesesi ve 1640 Tarihli Narh Defteri.* Enderun Yayınları 13. Istanbul: Ünal Matbaası, 1983.

Lapidus, Ira. *A History of Islamic Societies.* New York: Cambridge University Press, 1988.

Levtzion, Nehemia. "Toward a Comparative Study of Islamization." In *Conversion to Islam,* ed. Nehemia Levtzion. New York: Holmes and Meier, 1979, 1–23.

Levy, Avigdor. *The Sephardim in the Ottoman Empire.* Princeton, NJ: Darwin Press, 1991.

Lewis, Bernard. *Istanbul and the Civilization of the Ottoman Empire*. Norman: University of Oklahoma Press, 1963.

———. *The Jews of Islam*. Princeton, NJ: Princeton University Press, 1984.

———. "Ottoman Observers of Ottoman Decline." *Islamic Studies* 1, no. 1 (1962): 71–87.

———. "The Privilege Granted by Mehmed II to His Physician." *Bulletin of the School of Oriental and African Studies* 14 (1952): 550–63.

Lewis, Geoffrey, and Cecil Roth. "New Light on the Apostasy of Sabbatai Zevi." *Jewish Quarterly Review* 53 (1963): 219–25.

Liebes, Yehuda. *Studies in Jewish Myth and Jewish Messianism*. Trans. Batya Stein. New York Albany: State University of New York Press, 1993.

Lofland, John, and Norman Skonovd. "Conversion Motifs." *Journal for the Scientific Study of Religion* 20 (1981): 373–85.

Lowenthal, David. *The Past Is a Foreign Country*. New York: Cambridge University Press, 1985.

Lowry, Heath. *The Nature of the Early Ottoman State*. Albany: State University of New York Press, 2003.

———. *Trabzon Şehrinin İslamlaşması ve Türkleşmesi 1461–1583*. Trans. Demet Lowry and Heath Lowry. 2nd ed. Istanbul: Boğaziçi Üniversitesi Yayınevi, 1998.

MacCormack, Sabine. *Religion in the Andes: Vision and Imagination in Early Colonial Peru*. Princeton, NJ: Princeton University Press, 1991.

Mantran, Robert. "Un document sur la cizye a Istanbul a la fin du XVIIe siècle." *Journal of Turkish Studies* 11 (1987): 11–15.

———. *Istanbul dans la seconde moitié du XVIIe siècle: Essai d'histoire institutionnelle, économique et sociale*. Bibliothèque Archéologique et Historique de L'Institut Français D'Archéologique D'Istanbul, no. 12. Paris: Librairie Adrien Maisonneuve, 1962.

McNeill, William. *Venice, the Hinge of Europe (1081–1797)*. Chicago: University of Chicago Press, 1974.

Meisami, Julie Scott. *Persian Historiography: To the End of the Twelfth Century*. Edinburgh: Edinburgh University Press, 1999.

Mélikoff, Irène. *Hadji Bektach: Un mythe et ses avatars. Genèse et évolution du soufisme populaire en Turquie*. Leiden: Brill, 1998.

Melzer, Sara, and Kathryn Norberg. Introduction to *From the Royal to the Republican Body*, ed. Sara Melzer and Kathryn Norberg. Berkeley: University of California Press, 1998, 1–10.

Ménage, V. L. "The Islamization of Anatolia." In *Conversion to Islam*, ed. Nehemia Levtzion. New York: Holmes and Meier, 1979, 52–67.

Minkov, Anton. *Conversion to Islam in the Balkans: Kisve Bahası Petitions and Ottoman Social Life, 1670–1730*. Leiden: Brill, 2004.

Mitchell, W. J. T. "Space, Place, and Landscape." In *Landscape and Power*, ed. W. J. T. Mitchell. 2nd ed. Chicago: University of Chicago Press, 2002, vii–xii.

Mitler, Louis. "The Genoese in Galata: 1453–1682." *International Journal of Middle East Studies* 10 (1979): 71–91.

Monod, Paul. Review of Brian Weiser, *Charles II and the Politics of Access* (Rochester, NY: Boydell Press, 2003). *American Historical Review* 110, no. 5 (December 2005): 1592.

Moreen, Vera Basch. *Iranian Jewry's Hour of Peril and Heroism: A Study of Bābāī Ibn Lutf's Chronicle (1617–1662)*. New York: American Academy for Jewish Research, 1987.

Mottahedeh, Roy P. *Loyalty and Leadership in an Early Islamic Society*. Princeton, NJ: Princeton University Press, 1980.

Muldoon, James. "Introduction: The Conversion of Europe." In *Varieties of Religious Conversion in the Middle Ages*, ed. James Muldoon. Gainesville: University Press of Florida, 1997, 1–10.

Necipoğlu, Gülru. *The Age of Sinan: Architectural Culture in the Ottoman Empire*. London: Reaktion Books, 2005.

———. *Architecture, Ceremonial, and Power: The Topkapı Palace in the Fifteenth and Sixteenth Centuries*. Cambridge, MA: MIT Press, 1991.

———. "Süleymân the Magnificent and the Representation of Power in the Context of Ottoman-Habsburg-Papal Rivalry." In *Süleymân the Magnificent and His Time*, ed. Halil İnalcik and Cemal Kafadar. Istanbul: Isis Press, 1993, 163–94.

———. "The Süleymaniye Complex in Istanbul: An Interpretation." *Muqarnas* 3 (1985): 92–117.

Nock, A. D. *Conversion: The Old and the New in Religion from Alexander the Great to Augustine of Hippo*. 1933. Baltimore: Johns Hopkins University Press, 1998.

Nutku, Özdemir. *IV. Mehmet'in Edirne Şenliği, 1675*. 2nd ed. Ankara: Türk Tarih Kurumu Basımevi, 1987.

Ocak, Ahmed Yaşar. *Osmanlı Toplumunda Zındıklar ve Mülhidler (15.–17. Yüzyıllar)*. Istanbul: Tarih Vakfı Yurt Yayınları 60, 1998.

———. "Religion." In *History of the Ottoman State, Society and Civilisation*, ed. Ekmeleddin İhsanoğlu. 2 vols. Istanbul: Research Centre for Islamic History, Art and Culture, 1994–98, 1:177–238.

———. "XVII Yüzyılda Osmanlı İmparatorluğunda Dinde Tasfiye (Püritanizm) Teşebbüslerine Bir Bakış: Kadızâdeliler Hareketi." *Türk Kültürü Araştırmaları* 17–21, nos. 1–2 (1979–83): 208–25.

Ortaylı, İlber. "Ottoman Modernisation and Sabetaism." In *Alevi Identity: Cultural, Religious, and Social Perspectives*, ed. Tord Olsson, Elisabeth Özdalga, and Catharina Raudvere. Istanbul: Swedish Research Institute in Istanbul, 1999, 97–104.

Osman, Rıfat. *Edirne Sarayı*. Ed. Süheyl Ünver. 2nd ed. Ankara: Türk Tarih Kurumu Basımevi, 1989.

Özel, Oktay. "Population Changes in Ottoman Anatolia during the 16th and 17th Centuries: The 'Demographic Crisis' Reconsidered." *International Journal of Middle East Studies* 36 (2004): 183–205.

Padişahın Portresi: Tesavir-i Âl-i Osman. Istanbul: Türkiye İş Bankası Kültür Yayınları, 2000.

Pamuk, Orhan. *The White Castle*. Trans. Victoria Holbrook. New York: Vintage International, 1998.

Pamuk, Şevket. "The Disintegration of the Ottoman Monetary System during the Seventeenth Century." *Princeton Papers in Near Eastern Studies* 2 (1993): 67–81.

———. "In the Absence of Domestic Currency: Debased European Coinage in the Seventeenth-Century Ottoman Empire." *Journal of Economic History* 57, no. 2 (June 1997): 345–66.

Parry, V. J. "The Period of Murād IV, 1617–48." In *A History of the Ottoman Empire to 1730: Chapters from* The Cambridge History of Islam *and* The New Cambridge Modern History, by V. J. Parry, H. Inalcik, A. N. Kurat, and J. S. Bromley, ed. M. A. Cook. New York: Cambridge University Press, 1976, 133–57.

———. "The Reign of Sulaimān the Magnificent, 1520–66." In *A History of the Ottoman Empire to 1730: Chapters from* The Cambridge History of Islam *and* The New Cambridge Modern History, by V. J. Parry, H. Inalcik, A. N. Kurat, and J. S. Bromley, ed. M. A. Cook. New York: Cambridge University Press, 1976, 79–102.

Pazarbaşı, Erdoğan. *Vânî Mehmed Efendi ve Araisü'l-Kur'an*. Van Belediyesi Kültür ve Sosyal İşler Müdürlüğü, no. 5. Ankara: Acar Matbaası, 1997.

Peirce, Leslie. *The Imperial Harem: Women and Sovereignty in the Ottoman Empire*. New York: Oxford University Press, 1993.

Peri, Oded. *Christianity under Islam in Jerusalem: The Question of the Holy Sites in Early Ottoman Times*. Boston: Brill, 2001.

Petry, Carl. "Robing Ceremonials in Late Mamluk Egypt: Hallowed Traditions, Shifting Protocols." In *Robes and Honor: The Medieval World of Investiture*, ed. Gordon Stewart. New York: Palgrave, 2001, 353–77.

Pincus, Steven. "Coffee Politicians Does Create: Coffee Houses and Restoration Political Culture." *Journal of Modern History* 67 (1995): 807–34.

Piterberg, Gabriel. "The Alleged Rebellion of Abaza Mehmed Paşa: Historiography and the Ottoman State in the Seventeenth Century." *International Journal of Turkish Studies* 8, nos. 1–2 (Spring 2002): 13–24.

———. *An Ottoman Tragedy: History and Historiography at Play*. Berkeley: University of California Press, 2003.

Quataert, Donald. *The Ottoman Empire, 1700–1922*. New York: Cambridge University Press, 2000.

Rafael, Vicente. *Contracting Colonialism: Translation and Christian Conversion in Tagalog Society under Early Spanish Rule*. Durham, NC: Duke University Press, 1993.

Rambo, Lewis. *Understanding Religious Conversion*. New Haven, CT: Yale University Press, 1993.

Rogan, Eugene. *Frontiers of the State in the Ottoman Empire: Transjordan, 1850–1920*. New York: Cambridge University Press, 1999.

Rozen, Minna. *A History of the Jewish Community in Istanbul: The Formative Years, 1453–1566*. Leiden: Brill, 2002.

Sanders, Paula. *Ritual, Politics, and the City in Fatimid Cairo*. Albany: State University of New York Press, 1994.

———. "Robes of Honor in Fatimid Egypt." In *Robes and Honor: The Medieval World of Investiture*, ed. Gordon Stewart. New York: Palgrave, 2001, 225–39.

Sandos, James. *Converting California: Indians and Franciscans in the Missions*. New Haven, CT: Yale University Press, 2004.

Scholem, Gershom. *Sabbatai Sevi: The Mystical Messiah 1626–76*. Trans. R. J. Zwi Werblowsky. Bollingen Series, no. 93. Princeton, NJ: Princeton University Press, 1973.

———. "Teudah hadashah me-reshit ha-tenua ha-Shabata'ut." In *Mehkarim u-mekorot le-toledot ha-Shabta'ut ve-gilguleha*. Jerusalem: Mosad Bialik, 1982, 218–32.

Sells, Michael. *Approaching the Qur'an: The Early Revelations*. Ashland, OR: White Cloud Press, 1999.

Shaw, Stanford J. *History of the Ottoman Empire and Modern Turkey*. 2 vols. Vol. 1: *Empire of the Gazis: The Rise and Decline of the Ottoman Empire, 1280–1808*. New York: Cambridge University Press, 1976.

———. *The Jews of the Ottoman Empire and Turkish Republic*. New York: New York University Press, 1991.

Şişman, Cengiz. "A Jewish Messiah in the Ottoman Court: Sabbatai Sevi and the Emergence of a Judeo-Islamic Community, 1666–1720." PhD diss., Harvard University, 2004.

Sommer, Matthew. "Dangerous Males, Vulnerable Males, and Polluted Males: The Regulation of Masculinity in Qing Dynasty Law." In *Chinese Femininities/Chinese Masculinities: A Reader*, ed. Susan Brownell and Jeffrey N. Wasserstrom. Berkeley: University of California Press, 2002, 67–88.

Spellberg, Denise. *Politics, Gender, and the Islamic Past: The Legacy of 'A'isha bint Abi Bakr*. New York: New York University Press, 1996.

Spence, Jonathan D. *Emperor of China: Self-Portrait of K'ang-hsi*. New York: Vintage Books, 1988.

Spiegel, Gabrielle M. *The Past as Text: The Theory and Practice of Medieval Historiography*. Baltimore: Johns Hopkins University Press, 1997.

Stowasser, Karl. "Manners and Customs at the Mamluk Court." *Muqarnas* 2 (1984): 13–20.

Strohm, Paul. *England's Empty Throne, Usurpation and the Language of Legitimation, 1399–1422*. New Haven, CT: Yale University Press, 1998.

———. *Theory and the Premodern Text*. Minneapolis: University of Minnesota Press, 2000.

Taşan, N. Berin. "Merzifonlu Kara Mustafa Paşa'nın Mezarı ve Viyana Müzesindeki Kafatası." In *Merzifonlu Kara Mustafa Paşa Uluslararası Sempozyumu*. Ankara: Merzifon Vakfı Yayınları, 2001, 287–98.

Taylor, William B. "Two Shrines of the Cristo Renovado: Religion and Peasant Politics in Late Colonial Mexico." *American Historical Review* 110 (October 2005): 945–74.

Tekin, Şinasi. "XIV. Yüzyılda Yazılmış Gazilik Tarikası 'Gâziliğin Yolları' Adlı Bir Eski Anadolu Türkçesi Metni ve Gazâ Cihâd Kavramları Hakkında." *Journal of Turkish Studies* 13 (1989): 139–63.

Thomas, Lewis. *A Study of Naima*. Ed. Norman Itzkowitz. New York: New York University Press, 1972.

Thys-Şenocak, Lucienne. "The Yeni Valide Mosque Complex at Eminönü." *Muqarnas* 15 (1998): 58–70.

————. "The Yeni Valide Mosque Complex of Eminönü, Istanbul (1597–1665): Gender and Vision in Ottoman Architecture." In *Women, Patronage, and Self-Representation in Islamic Societies*, ed. D. Fairchild Ruggles. Albany: State University of New York Press, 2000, 69–89.

Todorova, Maria. *Balkan Identities, Nation and Memory*. New York: New York University Press, 2004.

Tökel, Dursun Ali. "Şâirin Tarihe Düştüğü Not: Şâir Gözüyle Merzifonlu Kara Mustafa Paşa ve Çehrin Seferi." In *Merzifonlu Kara Mustafa Paşa Uluslararası Sempozyumu*. Ankara: Merzifon Vakfı Yayınları, 2001, 371–82.

Tomenendal, Kerstin. "Die Vermeintliche Rippe Kara Mustafa Paschas İn Kremsmünster, Oberösterreich." In *Merzifonlu Kara Mustafa Paşa Uluslararası Sempozyumu*. Ankara: Merzifon Vakfı Yayınları, 2001, 281–86.

Tsai, Shih-shan Henry. *The Eunuchs in the Ming Dynasty*. Albany: State University of New York Press, 1996.

Ülgen, Ali Saim. "Yenicami." *Vakıflar Dergisi* 2 (1942): 387–97.

Uzunçarşılı, İsmail Hakkı. *Osmanlı Devletinin Saray Teşkilatı*. 2nd ed. Ankara: Türk Tarih Kurumu Basımevi, 1984.

————. *Osmanlı Tarihi*, 3 (1). 3rd ed. Ankara: Türk Tarih Kurumu Basımevi, 1983.

Van Gulik, Robert. *Sexual Life in Ancient China: A Preliminary Survey of Chinese Sex and Society from ca. 1500 B.C. till 1644 A.D.* Leiden: Brill, 1961.

Vatin, Nicholas, and Gilles Veinstein. *Le Sérail ébranlé: Essai sur les morts, depositions et avènements des sultans ottomans (XIVe–XIXe siècle)*. Paris: Fayard, 2003.

Viswanathan, Gauri. *Outside the Fold: Conversion, Modernity, and Belief*. Princeton, NJ: Princeton University Press, 1998.

Vitkus, Daniel J. "Turning Turk in *Othello*: The Conversion and Damnation of the Moor." *Shakespeare Quarterly* 48, no. 2 (Summer 1997): 145–76.

Vyronis, Spyros, Jr. *The Decline of Medieval Hellenism in Asia Minor and the Process of Islamization from the Eleventh through the Fifteenth Century*. Berkeley: University of California Press, 1971.

————. "Religious Change and Continuity in the Balkans and Anatolia from the Fourteenth through the Sixteenth Century." In *Studies on Byzantium, Seljuks, and Ottomans: Reprinted Studies*. Malibu, CA: Undena, 1981, 127–40.

Weber, Max. *The Sociology of Religion*. 1963. Boston: Beacon Press, 1993.

Wedeen, Lisa. *Ambiguities of Domination: Politics, Rhetoric, and Symbols in Contemporary Syria*. Chicago: University of Chicago Press, 1999.

Wittek, Paul. *The Rise of the Ottoman Empire*. London: Royal Asiatic Society, 1938.

Wolper, Ethel Sara. *Cities and Saints: Sufism and the Transformation of Urban Space in Medieval Anatolia*. University Park: Pennsylvania State University Press, 2003.

Woodhead, Christine. *Ta'lîkî-zâde's şehnâme-i hümâyûn: A History of the Ottoman Campaigns into Hungary, 1593–4*. Islamkundliche Untersuchungen. Bd. 82. Berlin: K. Schwarz, 1983.

Yerasimos, Stéphane. "La Communauté juive d'Istanbul a la fin du XVIe siècle." *Turcica* 27 (1995): 101–30.

Zilfi, Madeline. "The Kadızadelis: Discordant Revivalism in Seventeenth-Century Istanbul." *Journal of Near Eastern Studies* 45 (October 1986): 251–69.

——. *The Politics of Piety: The Ottoman Ulema in the Postclassical Age.* Minneapolis: Bibliotheca Islamica, 1988.

Zito, Angela. *Of Body and Brush: Grand Sacrifice as Text/Performance in Eighteenth-Century China.* Chicago: University of Chicago Press, 1997.

Index

Necati, Mehmed, 147
Nedim, Ahmed, 243
Nihadi
  Parthenios III and, 59–60
  view of Mehmed IV by, 244

Ocak, Ahmed Yaşar, 74
Ortaköy, 32
Osman II, 238
Ottoman Empire
  author's unique perspective on, 12–13
  as bureaucratic and sedentary, 141
  conversion debate and, 21–23,
    263n66, 263n69
  co-option of rebels in, 130
  Crete siege by, 53–55, 56, 154–59
  decline of, 255
  duty of, 209
  Europe and, 23, 210
  expansion of, 10
  financial challenges of, 48–53
  ghaza/jihad debate and, 20–21, 261n52,
    262n55
  grand viziers and royal women in, 45–48
  historians, 139
  Mecca and, 163
  mercenary units and upstart military
    and, 43
  Mughal empire and, 248, 249
  Nebi rebellion in, 58–59
  political economy changes in, 43–44
  Safavid empire and, 247–49
  Shariah court and, 3, 4–5
  1656 revolt in, 56–57
  sultanate and, 78–80
  Venetian navy defeat and, 77–78
  Venetian shipping lane blockade and,
    57–58

palace treasurer, 199–200
Pamuk, Orhan, 163, 182
Parthenios III, 59–60, 269n119
physician(s), palace
  cleansing of, 137
  conversions of, 9–10, 121–22, 132–38
  decline of Jewish, 137–38, 285n56
  Fevzi as, 134, 284n43
  history regarding, 132–33, 283nn29–30
  numbers of, 133–34
  rise of Christian, 138

salaries of, 133
piety
  Chronicle and, 107–8
  conversion link with, 6
  Mehmed IV's newfound, 9–11
  resistance of, 67–68
Piterberg, Gabriel, 141
Polish campaign, first
  background on, 163–64
  outset of, 167
  sacred space conversion in, 169
  surrender terms in, 168–69
  victory in, 168
  weather challenges of, 167–68
Polish campaign, second, 163–64
politics
  Christian space and, 99
  conversion and, 7
  economy and, 43–44
  Kösem Sultan and, 35, 36
  palace factional, 46
  religious conversion and, 18
  theory, religious conversion, and, 18,
    260n39
  Vienna sieges and, 221–27
prohibition, 118–19
property reclamation, 97–99
purse of coins, 202

Qur'anic commentary (of Mehmed, Vani)
  Constantinople and, 207
  conversion and conquest link in, 206
  duty and, 209
  incitement to conquest conversion in,
    206–10
  Isaac/Turk link in, 207–8
  Manzikert battle in, 208–9
  Turks and Arabs and, 206–7
  Turks history in, 208
  Vienna siege regarding, 209–10

rebellion
  financial challenges leading to, 52–53
  general, 59
  Nebi's, 58–59
  Parthenios III and, 59–60, 269n119
religious geography
  Crete and, 160–61, 288n81
  Islamizing Istanbul and, 81–82
  Istanbul's, 87–88

DATE DUE

DEMCO, INC. 38-2931